HISTORICISM AND FASCISM IN MODERN ITALY

During the early decades of the twentieth century, Italy produced distinctive innovations in both the intellectual and political realms. On the one hand, Benedetto Croce (1866–1952) and Giovanni Gentile (1875–1944) spearheaded a radical rethinking of historicism and philosophical idealism that significantly reoriented Italian culture. On the other hand, the period witnessed the first rumblings of fascism. Assuming opposite sides, Gentile became the semi-official philosopher of fascism while Croce argued for a renewed liberalism based on 'absolute' historicism.

In *Historicism and Fascism in Modern Italy*, David D. Roberts uses the ideological conflict between Croce and Gentile as a basis for a wider discussion of the interplay between politics and ideas in Italy in the twentieth century. Roberts examines the connection between fascism and the modern Italian intellectual tradition, arguing that the relationship not only deepens our understanding of generic fascism and liberalism but also illuminates ongoing dangers and possibilities in the wider Western world. This set of twelve essays by one of the leading scholars in the field represents an authoritative view of the modern Italian intellectual tradition, its relationship with fascism, and its enduring implications for history, politics, and culture in Italy and beyond.

(Toronto Italian Studies)

DAVID D. ROBERTS is Albert Berry Saye Professor of History at the University of Georgia.

Historicism and Fascism in Modern Italy

David D. Roberts

UNIVERSITY OF TORONTO PRESS
Toronto Buffalo London

Toronto Buffalo London

ISBN 978-0-8020-9308-0 (cloth)
ISBN 978-0-8020-9494-0 (paper)

Library and Archives Canada Cataloguing in Publication Data

Roberts, David D. (David Dion), 1943–
Historicism and fascism in Modern Italy / David D. Roberts.

(Toronto Italian Studies)
Includes bibliographical references and index.
ISBN 978-0-8020-9308-0 (bound) ISBN 978-0-8020-9494-0 (pbk.)

1. Fascism – Italy – History – 20th century. 2. Italy – Intellectual life – 20th century. 3. Croce, Benedetto, 1866–1952. 4. Gentile, Giovanni, 1875–1944. 5. Historicism. 6. Italy – History – 20th century. I. Title. II. Series.

DG571.R63 2007 945.09 C2007-901489-5

Cover image: Mario Sironi (Sassari, 1885 – Milano, 1961), *Study for Italy among the Arts and Sciences*, oil on paper with canvas backing. Collection of Banca CIS Spa, Cagliari.

The University of Toronto Press acknowledges the financial assistance to its publishing program of the Canada Council for the Arts and the Ontario Arts Council.

University of Toronto Press acknowledges the financial support for its publishing activities of the Government of Canada through the Book Publishing Industry Development Program (BPIDP).

Contents

HISTORICISM AND FASCISM IN MODERN ITALY

Introduction: Historicism, Fascism, and the Wider Significance of the Modern Italian Experience

Seeking Connections

I am grateful to those colleagues on both sides of the Atlantic who have suggested that I publish a selection of my essays on modern Italian topics. Doing so enables me to bring together a set of pieces, most previously published, but several as yet unpublished, that explore interlocking themes from a variety of angles. I thought it might be useful to make even those already published more readily available, especially because their publication has been in disparate venues, some hard to find in North America or the anglophone world. A few have been published only in Italian. But I also believed the combination, in the same volume, of this particular set of essays to be potentially illuminating, as the intersections among my areas of interest may not be apparent at first glance. So I welcome this chance to connect my somewhat disparate angles and to reflect a bit upon their intersection.

Broadly speaking, I have been concerned with two different topics as I have explored, on the one hand, fascism and totalitarianism and, on the other, historicism and issues in contemporary historical culture. What has most obviously bridged the two areas has been my longstanding interest in the modern Italian intellectual tradition centring upon Benedetto Croce and Giovanni Gentile. Together, these two thinkers wrought something approaching a cultural revolution in Italy as they came to exercise a leading position in Italian intellectual life during the first decades of the twentieth century. Although it was fundamentally anti-positivist, the distinctive tradition to which they were central has always been hard to characterize: idealist? neo-Hegelian? historicist? or perhaps historicist-idealist, whatever that might mean? That even such first-level characterization proves so problematic turns out to be part of the ongoing interest – and wider significance – of that tradition.

Whatever the characterizations, I have found that some know one 'half' of my work and some, the other half. Indeed, some are surprised to learn that there *is* another half. But the two sides have been mutually reinforcing, and I believe an underlying set of concerns connects them – concerns that might usefully be drawn out explicitly. The opportunity to bring together the present collection challenges me to articulate these unifying themes as I have not done before.

Although I have worked in both directions from a distinctively Italian angle, I have always been concerned with the wider relevance of idiosyncratic Italian concerns and innovations. More precisely, I have felt that, paradoxical though it might seem, it was precisely such idiosyncrasies that made aspects of the modern Italian experience more widely relevant or symptomatic. Thus I have sought to show how attention to that experience might deepen our understanding of, on the one hand, generic fascism and/or totalitarianism and, on the other, wider issues of contemporary culture and the place of historical understanding within it. In other words, addressing the specifically Italian problems surrounding fascism and the Croce-Gentile intellectual tradition seemed to enable me to develop a particular angle on those wider issues.

So underlying all these essays are questions about what we might still have to learn from fascism, the modern Italian intellectual tradition, and whatever connection there might have been between them. Part of my task has been to seek to persuade others, outside the Italian field, of the value of encompassing these aspects of the modern Italian experience within the wider reaches of humanistic discussion. But I also had to engage Italianists, both Italian and non-Italian, about what, in the Italian phenomena at issue, was most of wider relevance and about how best to mediate whatever it was to the wider discussion in both domains.

Addressing such questions has obviously required attention to how these matters have so far been treated, both in Italy and abroad. My sense that those connections had not adequately been made raised higher-order, 'meta' questions about patterns of influence, misrepresentation, and neglect. Indeed, a tendency to marginalize the Italian case in the wider, extra-Italian discussions of both overall topics was readily discernible. As I reached into both areas, I sometimes found myself trying *not* to tip my Italian hand for fear that doing so would invite precisely such marginalization.

I found it depressingly symptomatic that my 1987 book, *Benedetto Croce and the Uses of Historicism*, was reviewed by the *American Historical Review* in the Italian section, whereas, at almost exactly the same time, the review of a comparable book on the German thinker Ernst Cassirer was placed in the opening 'general,' historiographical section.[1] And this, despite the fact that Cassirer, whatever his overall merits, had surely not been as influential as Croce in historiography and the philosophy of history. The editors seemed to have assumed that, despite his undoubted earlier prominence, Croce had somehow become a provincial figure of interest only to Italianists.

Although there were major exceptions like Ernst Nolte, Italian fascism was long portrayed – and in wider cultural circles is still often viewed – as a semi-comic charade, a merely authoritarian dictatorship, or a distinctly minor version of German Nazism. So although the term *fascism* and, more surprisingly, even the term *totalitarianism* stemmed from the Italian experience, the Italian fascist regime, with all its totalitarian pretensions, seemed of interest primarily to Italianists. Still in some ways archetypal is the treatment by Hannah Arendt in her famous study of totalitarianism. She judged fascist Italy, at least until its last phase, to have been merely authoritarian – and thus distinctly peripheral to the overall consideration of totalitarianism.[2] Most importantly, fascist Italy lacked the terror apparatus and camp system of the Nazi and Stalinist regimes, but Arendt also cited fascism's apparent statism, which seemingly contrasted with the movement-party dynamism of the other two. From a perspective like Arendt's, it was certainly not to be claimed that an Italian angle might offer special insight into the wider totalitarian temptation of the era, *even though* totalitarianism was not only an Italian term but also became central to the fascist self-understanding.

Whatever the diffidence or prejudice in wider circles, I also sensed that Italian scholars, fundamentally indebted though I was to many of them, had not always addressed the relevant issues in a way that encouraged the wider mediation I found desirable. The fate of the Crocean legacy in Italy, explored especially in chapter 2 here, seemed the most symptomatic example. Partly at issue were sensitive matters of provincialism and even reverse provincialism that, I eventually concluded, needed to probed explicitly, and from several angles.

Especially in light of such concerns about the contingencies of influence and marginalization, I came ever more to believe that under present circumstances non-Italian scholars, with an indirect angle, might be especially well positioned to provide the necessary mediation between Italy and the wider culture. As I sought to play such a role, I sometimes found it appropriate to articulate explicitly some of its complexities, in interface with the Italians, on the one hand, and with the non-Italian scholarly world, on the other. In the first essay here, I ponder, in an informal, occasionally jocular way, some of the vicissitudes of my effort. But quite apart from the limitations I have encountered and whatever successes I have enjoyed, the wider questions about influence, misrepresentation, and neglect provide one unifying theme for this set of essays.

Historicism and Fascism?

Even my combination of historicism and fascism in the title of the present collection is problematic. Yet the questions about connections that it raises suggest another unifying theme. Although the term has become notorious for varied usage, *historicism* is widely viewed as having emerged in nineteenth-century Germany, finding various iterations from Herder to Ranke to Dilthey, then reaching a 'crisis' in thinkers like Ernst Troeltsch and Friedrich Meinecke by the first third of the twentieth century.[3] But Croce was often critical of the German historicist tradition, so the specifically Italian brand of historicism that he developed, based partly on his reading of his Neapolitan predecessor Giambattista Vico (1668–1744), stands in uncertain relationship with historicism as usually understood. Thus any connection between historicism and fascism might involve generic historicism and/or the more specifically Italian version. And thus Crocean historicism might be more, or less, linked to fascism than historicism understood more generically.

In questioning the connection between historicism and fascism, we might first recall Karl Popper, whose way of linking 'historicism,' tendencies toward a 'closed society,' and modern totalitarianism remains influential in some circles. Although Popper's use of *historicism* has long been viewed as idiosyncratic or wayward among specialists, his understanding of the notion, especially in its interface with totalitarianism, is surely worth revisiting in light of recent changes in the intellectual landscape. I myself hope to contribute to such an effort in a future study. But Popper's conception of historicism does not remotely encompass the distinctive Italian brand associated especially with Croce.

The question becomes more pressing when we note that some who have focused on Croce specifically have insisted that Crocean historicism, precisely in its distinctiveness, prepared the way for fascism.

Writing in 1950, the American historian Chester McArthur Destler found Croce the outstanding exponent of a dangerous new philosophy that stressed relativism in values, subjective activism for the individual, violence as a mode of social action, and success as the supreme value in public affairs. Croce, according to Destler, had thereby 'helped lay the intellectual foundations of Italian fascism.'[4] Influential exiled scholars like Giuseppe Antonio Borgese and Gaetano Salvemini, each of whom ended up teaching at major universities in the United States, levelled comparable charges during and immediately after the fascist period. Referring dismissively to 'the philosophy of history taught by a few self-satisfied professors, that whatever has happened in history was good and rational,' Borgese found a justification of fascism implicit in Croce's thought: 'The success of Mussolini, success being the only test that validates political happenings, was tantamount to a kingly anointment performed by the Goddess History through her idealistic high-priests.' Indeed, continued Borgese, 'all the books and essays of Croce had played into the hand of Mussolini.'[5]

In light of such views, which, though less prominent than they once were, have yet to disappear, I emphasize that the present essays do not suggest any such direct relationship between Crocean historicism and fascism. Not only did Croce, after some initial hesitation, pursue activities on a variety of levels that made him perhaps the world's most notable anti-fascist, but he worked out his mature intellectual position, combining a recast liberalism with what he came to term *absolute historicism,* precisely in response to the fascist (and wider totalitarian) challenge.[6]

Still, deeper questions about connections suggest themselves, especially because both Crocean historicism and the first fascism emerged, each as specifically Italian, from within a culture that the historian E.J. Hobsbawm once aptly characterized as 'both extremely sophisticated and relatively provincial.'[7] In other words, although that culture was idiosyncratic vis-à-vis the Western mainstream, it was not to be dismissed as merely backward, trying to catch up. So, disparate though they may have been on one level, innovations emerging from within that 'extremely sophisticated and relatively provincial' culture might well have been related in some deeper way. And, although the suggestion seems paradoxical at first glance, grasping the complex, ragged connection between Italian historicism and Italian fascism proves one key to grasping the wider relevance of both, despite the lack of the sort of direct link that those like Borgese and Destler insisted upon.

Even as Croce turned to an anti-fascist neo-liberalism, his long-time collaborator Gentile became the fascist regime's single most important ideologue, providing, for example, much of the substance of the theoretical portion of Mussolini's well-known 'Doctrine of Fascism,' published in the new *Enciclopedia italiana* (Italian Encyclopedia) in 1932. Before the advent of fascism, however, Croce had been considerably more important than Gentile in fostering the notion that liberal democracy, as usually understood, was incongruent with the new Italian philosophy. Thus Gentile and other fascists claimed that Croce was one of them, 'a fascist without the black shirt.'[8] Even in the face of Croce's long opposition to fascism, the noted historian Carlo Ginzburg, writing decades later, still found Croce the vehicle of Gentile's baneful 'fascist' influence on Hayden White, a confluence explored in chapter 11.

Once we have Gentile on the table together with Croce, a deeper and more instructive set of questions about historicism and fascism begins to open. In a sense Gentile stands in the middle, between Crocean historicism and the fascist impulse, so his place with respect to each proves crucial. Yet even the nature of the intellectual relationship between Croce and Gentile is hard to pin down. And this difficulty is not surprising because, quite apart from their political split, which has of course added fuel to the fire, the intellectual centre of gravity of each has been subject to dispute. But thus we have not fully understood the nature and extent of the undoubted overlap between the two; nor have we adequately considered the interface between their intellectual relationship and their political divergence. In principle, grasping whatever deeper basis there was for that divergence, as it emerged from within this 'extremely sophisticated and relatively provincial' culture, might uniquely illuminate aspects of the ongoing modern political experiment.

Gentile was more determinedly a philosophical idealist than Croce was, and thus questions arise about the extent to which he was part of the 'historicist' side of the modern Italian intellectual tradition. As I seek to explain especially in chapter 5, but also in chapters 6 and 11, I have come to believe that Gentile is usefully paired with Croce as 'historicist' in a certain sense, and that the two diverged from within a common historicist framework, the terms of which still require clarification. But even if we manage to reconstruct the concerns underlying Gentile's philosophical abstractions, we wonder what relevance his ideas could have for understanding the emergence of fascism, which is often seen as activist and anti-intellectual, and which produced a regime that proved haphazard in many respects.

The Relationship between Croce and Gentile

Croce and Gentile both addressed philosophical matters, and we might be tempted to start with their formal philosophies, each of which was developed from within the tradition of philosophical idealism. The two thinkers took it for granted that the idealist orientation, as developed by Kant, Fichte, Schelling, and Hegel, was an essential starting point in any quest for an alternative to the reigning positivism. Idealism posited the active – even creative – role of mind in constructing the specifically human world that we inhabit.

But the two Italians were also fundamentally concerned with *meta*-philosophical questions about the cultural place of philosophy, especially at that historically specific conjuncture, in light of the wider cultural challenges emerging. So their aim from the start was not simply to renew or contribute to philosophical discussion from within the idealist tradition. Rather, they sought broader cultural leadership and civic renewal in response to the perceived inadequacies of an array of mainstream cultural strands. As they saw it, the Italian situation afforded a special challenge, but Italy was not merely idiosyncratically pre-modern, trying to catch up. Somehow the idiosyncratic Italian situation seemed to have brought the terms of a wider developing modern crisis especially close to the surface in Italy. Rather than proponents of an ongoing philosophical tradition, Croce and Gentile saw themselves as pioneers in a wider process of cultural adjustment.

The first terms of the overall challenge are familiar. Put schematically, the modern waning of transcendence – with Nietzsche's proclamation of the death of God but one, over-dramatic manifestation – threatened overreaction into self-indulgence, irrationalism, or nihilism. The key, as the two Italians saw it, was to adjust to a purely secular world of radical immanence and to find the basis for proceeding in a measured, responsible way within it. Among other things, that seemed to require making new sense, from within a modern secular framework, of certain enduring insights of the Western religious traditions. Christianity was not merely illusion, reducible to wishful thinking, let alone superstition, fostered by priests for their own ends. Croce remarked explicitly that the task of his generation had been to recast the terms of the old religion, with its mythological underpinnings, for the modern world.[9] For both Croce and Gentile, that meant positing human being as 'spiritual,' defined partly by a sense of ethical capacity, of responsibility and care.

The two thinkers each recognized that Hegel and Marx had been onto something – and it may surprise that each started with Marx before tackling Hegel systematically. Yet even as brought down to earth with Marxism, the whole Hegelian approach betrayed too much of an a priori framework, reflecting a residual belief in transcendence. Although it had sought to take history more seriously than ever before, that tradition had not been radical and thoroughgoing enough in confronting the historicity of the world – or in conceiving how history is bound up with ongoing human activity.

In reacting against positivism, Croce and Gentile were seeking to undermine the contemporary vogue of science – and especially the notion that we can orient ourselves by applying the methods of the natural sciences to the human, historical, social world. Croce insisted explicitly that science, though essential in its sphere, merely offers rough-and-ready generalizations in light of particular, historically specific instances, and in response to the particular questions human beings have decided to ask. It does not afford some key to the way things really are, apart from human being.

At the same time, the two thinkers found untenable the reigning justifications for liberal democracy. Insofar as it rested on a claim to individual rights, liberalism, like Marxism, was too dependent on a residual transcendence to be convincing. Insofar as it invited the pursuance of individual interests, liberalism did not adequately embrace the human ethical capacity, the potential human sense of responsibility for the world.

The orientation necessary to move beyond this array of cultural claimants required specifying the place of human being, understood as 'spiritual,' free, creative, and responsible, in a world that ceaselessly comes to be in history, with no a priori frame or telos. From this perspective, we give up any belief in supra-historical values that we can simply pluck from some transcendent sphere; we turn even from any belief in some stable 'nature' existing apart from us, the knowledge of which might afford the modern, secular orientation we need. We are radically on our own, but once we better understand what we are, and how we are caught up in history, we realize that we have what we need to proceed.

In one sense central, then, was the overall relationship between philosophical idealism and historicism – a relationship that, it seems to me, has yet to be understood in all its ramifications. As usually (but not always) conceived in light of German traditions, the two have often seemed antithetical, although each has periodically been linked to totalitarianism in some sense. Certainly the historicist concern with, and valorization of, historically specific individualities emerged to some extent in reaction against the totalizing and teleological tendencies in the Hegelian tradition. But Croce was not that sort of historicist, and Gentile was not that sort of idealist. If anything, in fact, we can call Croce a totalizing historicist and Gentile a historicizing idealist. So whereas the two Italians, in insisting on the fundamental historicity of the world, can be considered 'historicist' in one sense, their historicism was not of the individualizing versus totalizing variety. From their perspective, in fact, that was a false dichotomy breeding cultural confusion.

We begin better to see how our tendency to pigeonhole the Croce-Gentile tradition in terms of such ready labels as *historicism* and *idealism* throws us off. A certain understanding of those two categories has been central to our intellectual history, and thus to our own self-understanding, but insofar as we take their German usages as archetypal or definitive, we may not grasp what these Italians were saying, even as they used some of the same terminology. Thus we may marginalize them prematurely, and, conversely, restrict our sense of the possible meanings and implications of the ideas that fed these traditions. We thereby delimit our own intellectual historical self-understanding.

To grasp the Italian direction, we must first recall the key points at issue. By bringing the idealist insight together with history, Hegel had thought it possible to overcome the problems left over from earlier efforts to conceive the relationship between mind and reality in idealist terms; history is the overcoming of the apparent separation as spirit becomes conscious of its own freedom. But Hegel's putative solution required positing a master thread and telos given a priori by what spirit *is* on some level. To critics, this teleological framework was merely arbitrary and did not do justice to the individuality and variety of history – or even to the human capacity for free creativity and the world's capacity for novelty. Thus in part the critical accents of the German historicists. But in rejecting Hegel's teleological framework, they were also precluding Hegel's way of transcending the finitude that seemed the problematic reverse side of their own accent on historical individuality and particularity. Their alternative to Hegel seemed to confine human beings to a world of finite, historically specific situations, with no direct access to a supra-historical realm of value, meaning, or truth.

From the perspective of Croce and Gentile, the idealist and historicist traditions afforded some essential building blocks – in a way that positivism, for example, did not. But it was essential to transcend the dichotomy of idealism and historicism if the contemporary cultural challenge was to be confronted. This required encompassing three insights simultaneously: (a) the idealist sense in which the world as we know it is a creation of mind; (b) the Hegelian way of understanding reality as history and history as a totality; and (c) the historicist accent on ongoing variety and novelty. On that basis it would be possible to eschew Hegel's teleological framework while also showing that a purely historical world of finite particulars is adequate in light of what we are and need.

From the Italian perspective, the interplay of finite, individuated human beings with the provisional, historically specific world is in a sense all there is. At every moment the world is some particular way – has *become* some particular way – as the resultant of all of history so far. The responses of individuals to that world endlessly coalesce to produce some new totality, some new finite, particular world, which then elicits a new round of human response. In that sense the world is continuously coming to be in history through history-making human response. Thus we at once belong to history and make history; thus the need to conceive human activity and history as two sides of the same coin.

But though we are necessarily historically specific, we need not feel ourselves confined, limited. We are not cut off from something; we are not missing some world 'outside' or 'above' that we, as merely human or merely historical, can never apprehend fully. The point is not, as for later German historicists from Dilthey to Troeltsch and Meinecke, to determine how we might glimpse something supra-historical from our finite, historically specific vantage point. We at last quit longing for some external world, some higher realm of value, truth, and meaning, and turn in the other direction, fully adjusting to our place in a concrete, human, historical world. Value, truth, and meaning do not drop out, but we understand them in terms of radical immanence, in terms of ongoing human response. We realize that we collectively are making the world as we act, with action understood broadly, to encompass not only responding morally in the particular way we do, but also thinking in the particular way we do, using language in the particular way we do, knowing the world in the particular way we do. In our finite, particular individual responses, we mesh with a totality that is itself finite, particular, historically specific – and provisional.

In seeking the basis for the essential modern orientation, Gentile was more insistent than Croce on the value of reconnecting with Italian intellectual traditions. Although his thinking was just as distinctively Italian, Croce worried that to dwell on Italian distinctiveness would invite chauvinism and provincial myth-making, a concern I discuss especially in essay 6. So even as he recognized a major debt to such earlier Italian thinkers as Vico and Francesco De Sanctis, he played up his wider European heritage – and he would prove one of the century's most cosmopolitan intellectuals. But it was especially by reconnecting with the Italian humanistic tradition, as channelled through Vico, that both Croce and Gentile could claim to have conceived the world, more consistently than had ever been done before, in terms of radical immanence, as a total history, forever coming to be some particular way through free, creative human response. Still, Croce's circumspection meant that it was Gentile who sought to specify – sometimes, indeed, in exaggerated, chauvinistic terms – what especially equipped contemporary Italians to assume a leading role on the European level.

In preparing his college graduation thesis during the 1890s, Gentile became interested in the nineteenth-century Neapolitan reading of Hegel and, more particularly, in the neo-Hegelian Bertrando Spaventa's notion of the circulation of Italian ideas within European philosophy.[10] Gentile immediately fastened upon Vico, but by 1905 he was looking even further back, to Renaissance humanism. As he saw it, the humanistic tradition that those like Marsilio Ficino and Giordano Bruno had initiated, in reaction against medieval assumptions about transcendence, remained at the origins of the modern world.[11] But the modern mainstream, developing from Descartes through the Enlightenment to contemporary positivism, had grown from that foundation in such a way as to privilege the natural sciences. Aspects of the original Italian insight had been marginalized, persisting only as a kind of counter-tradition.

Whereas that mainstream tradition started with the natural world, as described ultimately in mathematics, the Italian tradition started with human being, understood as self-creating through history. Gentile insisted in 1912 that we find first in Bruno 'the truly modern notion of the seriousness and importance of history, as the actuality of the spirit in its development.' Even knowing must be understood as constructive activity. And as Bruno had been the first to discern, not only knowledge but the mind itself grows and develops and thereby makes itself over time, in history. What happens is not, as we assume from a dualistic perspective, mind developing through stimulus from without 'but ... autoformation of mind itself, which makes of each step reached the basis for further steps that would not otherwise have been possible.'[12]

On the basis of this insight, Gentile went on, it would eventually become possible to see beyond the dualism of mind and reality, for we do not simply accumulate ever more knowledge of an external, independent reality.[13] Mind is necessarily more active, even creative, than that – not simply in providing categories of understanding that afford an a priori structure to sense data, but in responding to what mind has made of the world so far. So the world, or anything we might mean with our term *reality*, is more radically a happening in history, and its development is more radically a function of the creative response of human mind, than the eventual mainstream would be able to grasp. Rather than apprehend a stable, external world, we respond in ever-new ways to the ever-new world that we have made.

As Gentile saw it, the dualistic, anti-historical conception had clearly triumphed by the eighteenth century, though Vico, marginal to the mainstream, managed to give Bruno's insight more systematic elaboration. Hegel would then encompass some of the Italian insight, but his way of bringing together spirit, nature, becoming, and the dialectic ultimately failed to convince. Yet the Italian humanistic tradition continued in Italy as well, in Vincenzo Cuoco early in the nineteenth century, then in the Neapolitan Hegelians of the 1860s and 1870s. And it was from within that ongoing Italian tradition that Gentile found the bases for moving beyond Hegel. Bertrando Spaventa, the most innovative of the Neapolitan Hegelians, had accented thought in action, or thought as activity, in a way that suggested how to conceive historical becoming more radically than Hegel had. By developing certain of Spaventa's insights, Gentile thought it possible to dissolve the problems left over from German idealism and to offer a consistent philosophy of immanence, avoiding any problematic subject-object dualism, and positing spirit, or human being, as self-creating in history.[14]

Croce came to much the same conception of human being and history from a slightly different angle. In marked contrast with Gentile, he found Spaventa's speculations arid, even 'theological,' and, embracing one side of Vico, he placed greater emphasis than Gentile did on the inherent creativity of our uses of language. Indeed, the book that brought Croce to international attention, his *Aesthetic* of 1902, was less a contribution to aesthetics, understood as a delimited sphere in philosophy, than an effort to specify the creativity of language and, on that basis, to begin outlining what proved a proto-historicist conception of the world. Thus the book's full title, *Aesthetic as the Science of Expression and of the Linguistic in General.*[15]

As I discuss in chapter 4, the unusual juxtaposition of themes in this book, in which Croce was just beginning to fit together his central ideas, helped launch a tradition of misrepresentation and misunderstanding. He certainly had points to make about art in its usual sense, but his insistence on the autonomy of art invited the mistaken assumption, on the part of critics and proponents alike, that his aim was to defend 'art for art's sake.' His wider point was that 'art' is a moment in human activity, a moment that cannot be reduced to cognitive, moral, or utilitarian response. In responding to any present moment, we stretch our language to encompass what the world has newly become, and in the process we begin producing further novelty. In that sense 'art,' as the moment of initiating novelty by creatively projecting beyond the present, is *not* a thing apart but is contiguous with all human activity.

Whatever their initial differences in accent, Croce and Gentile were clearly peas in a pod in their effort to show how creative human being meshes with history in a world of radical immanence. Together they came to believe by the eve of the First World War that in engaging the leading ideas of their own time, especially those coming from Germany, they themselves had moved to the forefront of contemporary thought. It was partly this sense of occupying the cutting edge that made them exciting to many educated young Italians.

Yet some of their accents and concerns had differed from the start, and the two thinkers began to split publicly over philosophical matters in 1913. Then the challenge of addressing the cultural implications of the Italian war effort, in light of the country's voluntary intervention on the Entente side in 1915, led to further divergence, as I explored when I first tackled the two thinkers in tandem in an essay published in 1981.[16] Whereas Croce remained cautionary and 'agnostic,' warning against the chauvinism that seemed likely to follow from any effort to cast the war in cultural terms, Gentile gradually began to suggest that Italy, thanks to its wartime experience, was becoming sufficiently mature to play a more distinctive role vis-à-vis *both* France and Germany. The intellectual renewal that he and Croce had spearheaded might even begin to take political form.

At this point, however, we encounter the other set of questions that arises once we place Gentile 'in the middle,' for it is not only his 'historicism' or his intellectual relationship with Croce that remains problematic. The question of what we might learn from Gentile's commitment to fascism is trickier still. At issue is not only Gentile's place in fascism but the more general question of the possible significance of that place, in light of the nature and outcome of the fascist regime. These are matters explored especially in chapters 5, 6, and 7.

The most fundamental question has been raised forcefully by Gennaro Sasso, a major Italian expert on the Croce-Gentile tradition: Did Gentile's embrace of fascism in fact stem from his philosophy? Sasso's answer is decidedly negative. Whereas Gentile's turn to fascism was not merely anomalous or self-serving, neither was it the logical outcome of his philosophy, despite Gentile's pretensions to the contrary. Rather, it was a political decision reflecting the wishful thinking that Sasso found bound up with Gentile's wilful, tendentious reading of Italian history since the Renaissance. That reading betrayed his a priori determination to construct a distinctively Italian tradition with special contemporary relevance.

In chapter 6, I offer a counter-argument, claiming that something like the fascist departure had been adumbrated in Gentile's thought almost from the beginning, around the turn of the century. Conversely, it was partly Gentile's contribution, stemming precisely from his wider thinking, that made fascism at once distinctively Italian and more widely symptomatic. That contribution reflected some of the new sense of the human relationship with history that Gentile shared with Croce, but we can see in retrospect that the philosophical differences that became public in 1913 foreshadowed the later political split.

At issue was how to conceive the modes of collective world-making once we grasp the human place in what had come to seem a purely historical world, a world of radical immanence. How does the world go on being made, or how could and should it get made? As Croce and Gentile diverged in 1913, Croce found 'mysticism' in Gentile's way of unifying thinking, willing, and acting, whereas Gentile called Croce's attention to 'that sense of profound melancholy that pervades your whole contemplation of the world.'[17] Without a unified culture – without, Gentile would soon insist, a totalitarian ethical state that nurtures, focuses, and enables us collectively to exercise our distinctively human ethical capacities – we are likely to lapse into mere self-indulgence or into cynical indifference in the modern secular world. Croce, in turn, sought to show how we might proceed in a more humble, pluralistic way, even in light of the finitude, futility, and loneliness we may feel in a world that simply does not allow for the sort of unified culture, or for the more grandiose, unified sort of collective world-making, that Gentile envisioned.

We can best hold for below further consideration of what we might learn from Gentile's overtly totalitarian fascism, in light of the wider problems of interpretation that European fascism and totalitarianism present. For now let us simply note that from within the wider Crocean-Gentilian frame, we find, first, the emergence of one kind of totalitarian ideal, but it would almost immediately prompt Croce to recast liberal democracy in historicist terms. In doing so, he was seeking both to show that totalitarianism is not the logical political corollary of Italian-style historicism and to specify a more convincing liberalism, not relying on natural law or rights. The Croce-Gentile divergence thus illuminates the wider totalitarian moment, as secular and historically specific, but it also suggests how we might conceive the lessons of the totalitarian overreach and thereby move beyond it from within the same secular framework.

Crucially for Croce that framework was *not* one of mere absurdity, inviting a premium on existentialist gesture, as it was for so many Europeans in the wake of the disasters of the era. Rather, he continued to accent the scope for proceeding in a sober, moderate, even rational way, as I seek to show especially in chapters 6 and 9. It is no surprise that he was often at odds with Italian existentialists during the political-cultural transition surrounding the defeat of fascism. As Croce saw it, the Italian historicist framework, now understood in neo-liberal terms, was more important for Western culture than ever.

Accounting for Fascism as Italian

Despite my more recent concerns, I must admit that my initial interest in Italian fascism had nothing to do with the Croce-Gentile tradition. Indeed, I was somewhat intimidated by that tradition's reputation for difficulty when preparing my first book, *The Syndicalist Tradition and Italian Fascism*, published in 1979. Thus I found reason to keep Gentile, especially, at a distance as I considered syndicalism in tandem with the Nationalism of Enrico Corradini, Alfredo Rocco, et al. Still, in seeking to show that the Italian syndicalist evolution from Marxism to fascism was more plausible, that syndicalist ideas had greater force, and that the syndicalist component was of more enduring significance to fascism – especially in steering the regime toward corporativism – than had been recognized to that point, I to some extent had Gentile in mind as a foil.

I was saying that insofar as we needed to come to terms with 'fascist ideology,' or, more to the point, with antecedent ideas that affected practice, we needed to focus on something besides the quasi-official philosophy of Gentile, which students of fascism had often trotted out, if only to dismiss it as window-dressing.

But soon after publishing my book on the syndicalist-fascist connection I came better to grasp the deeper symptomatic importance of Gentile's fascism as well. It was necessary to account for, to find a place for, both the syndicalist and the Gentilian currents among the others in the fascist mix. More specifically, it was important to probe both the tensions and the areas of overlap in these two especially significant fascist strands.

As I was becoming interested in Gentile, the import of the Italian syndicalist tradition became more widely recognized, thanks in part to the writings of Zeev Sternhell. But though he was widely reputed an authority on 'fascist ideology,' Sternhell's work raised all sorts of questions about the content and significance of the syndicalist contribution to fascism. Indeed, it also raised questions about the place of Gentile and, more generally, about the overall role of 'ideology,' or antecedent ideas, in Italian fascism. My study of the syndicalists well predated Sternhell's and, like his, focused on the place of syndicalism within the wider revision of Marxism, on the interface between French and Italian ideas, and on the relationship between Italian syndicalism and the form of nationalism preached by the Italian Nationalist Association. But my accents proved different from his in all three areas.

In considering the terms of the wider revision of Marxism, I found that the syndicalist link between wider European developments and the emergence of Italian fascism was first to be found not, as essentially for Sternhell, in some irrationalist revolt against the Enlightenment but in the tensions and uncertainties within the European radical tradition itself. And whereas it is surely true, as Sternhell emphasized, that syndicalism emerged first in France, the major syndicalist theorist, Georges Sorel, had been caught up in a supranational discussion involving a number of Italians, including Croce, with whom, in fact, Sorel maintained a correspondence until Sorel's death in 1922. In his determination to make Sorel central to a French-based anti-Enlightenment revolt, Sternhell offered a one-sided reading of Sorel that missed some of what was distinctive, and innovative, in his thinking. But more importantly, Sternhell overlooked the distinctive accents that became evident as Italians began creating their own recognizably syndicalist current within

Italian socialism around 1902. And whereas it is true and important that, in light of their evolution beyond the Marxian framework for radical change, the syndicalists ended up converging sufficiently with the Nationalists to work with them within the fascist regime, I found that even as fascists, the syndicalists and the one-time Nationalists remained antithetical in deeply symptomatic ways. Sternhell, in contrast, had the two currents merging essentially seamlessly.

Because of Italy's idiosyncrasies, Italians were participating in the wider revision of Marxism from a particular angle, asking their own innovative questions. They were thus able to question the dominant radical framework in a way that proved fruitful, in the immediate sense, for other Italians seeking a radical alternative to the liberal mainstream; that rethinking helped galvanize a distinctive new movement – fascism – that not only achieved power but steered Italy in a post-liberal direction. The notion that to understand the emergence of fascism required coming to terms with a kind of 'post-Marxist' and 'populist' radical substance, which could not be understood in the then-standard reductionist terms, was central to my first article, 'Petty-bourgeois Fascism in Italy: Form and Content,' completed in 1975.[18]

Especially because it stemmed in important measure from this wider rethinking of the whole radical tradition, which had come to be wound around Marxism, the new Italian direction proved to have wider implications. It is partly for this reason that Italian fascism can still help us better conceive the wider eruption of post-democratic politics, the changing sense of radical possibilities, and the content of the alternatives that emerged at that point. But none of this is to deny that while such rethinking was fruitful in the immediate political sense, the outcome proved disastrous. Probing the rethinking at issue illuminates the force and the appeal of the novel fascist constellation, but it also illuminates the limits and blind spots that led to such a disastrous outcome.

It was especially the distinctively Italian angle that Sternhell seemed singularly ill-prepared to grasp. Before turning systematically to Italy in *The Birth of Fascist Ideology*, he had published *Neither Right nor Left*, a well-known study of putatively proto-fascist ideas in France.[19] In focusing on Italy thereafter, he seems simply to have assumed that the relevant Italian ideas were adaptations of what French thinkers like Georges Sorel and Charles Maurras had already elaborated. And other authorities were remarkably quick to accept Sternhell's overall argument. Stanley Payne, while accenting the near-absence of fascism on the political level in France, remarked that 'Zeev Sternhell has conclusively demonstrated that nearly all the ideas found in fascism first appeared in France.'[20]

But when deciding that fascism had been born in France, Sternhell had not fully encountered the Italian evidence that he analyzed later. Indeed, he obviously approached the Italian evidence with a certain conceptual framework, derived from France, already in place. In fact the genesis of the Italian ideas in question can be grasped only in terms of a deeper understanding of the Italian context. In analyzing them from within his French-based framework, Sternhell was almost bound to find what he expected to find. But thus he could not really be sure what the ideas meant, what the relevant categories were, how they meshed, and in what proportions. His approach left no scope for challenge by ideas that, precisely as Italian, might have been (and prove in fact to have been) less familiar and harder to read than we tend to assume. In fact it was easy to show that this led him seriously to misread the resonance of a number of Italian fascist themes. What he derived from his study of France proved mostly a set of blinders.

Even though, when he turned to Italy, Sternhell was concerned especially with syndicalism and Nationalism, the two traditions I had studied years earlier, he seemed particularly loath to deal seriously with my account, apparently because it defied the framework to which he was by then wedded. At the same time, his framework was singularly inadequate for making sense of Gentile's ideas and their appeal in Italy. To top it off, Sternhell's understanding of the options and dilemmas in the interwar period was so simplistic that he included Croce prominently among those he criticized for insufficient vigilance on the side of the wholesome Enlightenment tradition. In short, I had many beefs with Sternhell, and, in chapter 7, I seek to show the limits of his reading of 'fascist ideology.'

From the Problem of Fascism to Wider Historiographical Questions

In my earlier work on fascism I encountered what seemed to me problematic assumptions and tensions that led to wider historiographical questions about presentism and reductionism, about modes of reflexivity and the scope for learning from difference, and about the varieties of historical inquiry and the uses of historical understanding. In light of my Italian interests, these led me eventually to Croce, who, I quickly concluded, still had something to offer contemporary historiographical discussion, although he was increasingly marginalized both in Italy and abroad.

In his intellectual-political contest with Gentile, Croce had came out on top, but it was a pyrrhic victory, for he was soon declared passé (*superato*) even in Italy, especially in light of the strong attraction of Antonio Gramsci's posthumous legacy among Italian intellectuals. But Croce's further relevance was questioned even by some, like Guido De Ruggiero, who had been generally within his orbit. Croce himself did not always address such questions effectively, and many found something prejudicially conservative in the political stance he adopted as head of the revived Liberal party by the mid-1940s. I treat the strange vicissitudes of Croce's intellectual-political role during the 1940s in essay 3, one of my earliest pieces on Crocean themes.

Especially widely heard was the claim that Croce's thinking warranted a vacuously passive acceptance of whatever has resulted from history. As I noted earlier, such notions informed the charge that Crocean historicism had helped pave the way for fascism. But whatever Croce's limits on the immediate political level in the mid-1940s, to charge passivity was fundamentally to misconstrue his thinking, which was an invitation to endless history-making action informed by historical understanding.

My sense that Croce was being widely misrepresented, when he was not neglected altogether, led me to conclude that a reassessment of his whole intellectual enterprise was required if we were to take advantage of his historiographical insights. At issue was the very centre of gravity of his thought, wound around what he himself came to term 'absolute historicism,' explicitly in opposition to philosophical idealism or neo-Hegelianism. I sought to offer such a reassessment in my *Benedetto Croce and the Uses of Historicism* (1987). Partly on the basis of the perspective I developed there, I then expanded my inquiry in *Nothing but History* (1995), where I placed Croce alongside Nietzsche and Heidegger, seeking to show how his overall cultural strategy occupies a kind of moderate position in fruitful tension with the contrasting extremes that Nietzsche and Heidegger blocked out.

All three thinkers, I suggested, were responding to a new sense of the human relationship with history emerging by the end of the nineteenth century. The set of issues that they were the first to address then found further exploration from within the new cultural terrain that opened in light of that change in historical consciousness. So in *Nothing but History* I worked from Nietzsche, Croce, and Heidegger through Hans-Georg Gadamer, Michel Foucault, Jacques Derrida, and Richard Rorty and on to several key figures in contemporary historiographical discussion, including, among others, Hayden White, Joan Scott, and Carlo Ginzburg. Considering Croce in such company showed up some of his weaknesses and blind spots, but it also suggested the enduring value of certain of his insights and prescriptions.

Although I sought to eschew the problematic term *postmodernism* to the extent possible, I was concerned essentially with cultural possibilities and priorities in light of what by now we have come to call, *faute de mieux*, the postmodern turn. Necessary and potentially fruitful though I found it, that turn seemed to have invited confusion and overreaction, but I felt that Croce's historicist thinking could help us better understand the terms of the postmodern challenge – and the range of possibilities that opened in its wake. In light of the dominant cultural tendencies at work, his sober, moderate orientation, though it had been offered partly in response to the disasters of his own time, was arguably as relevant as ever. It was important to show that an alternative to positions based on transcendence, foundationalism, or teleology did not have to posit absurdity or mere flux, or end up accenting personal edification.

In using the shorthand phrase 'history as thought and action' to characterize his cultural program, Croce was suggesting, first, that historical understanding uniquely affords orientation for action, and, second, that everything we do has a history-making dimension, helping to shape what the world becomes at the next moment. Insofar as we grasp, and genuinely experience, how we are bound up with history in a world without transcendence, we come to understand that the need to act, stemming in part from our sense of responsibility for what the world is next to become, opens us to the true understanding that orients us for such action.

As I seek to show especially in chapters 9, 10, and 11, the Crocean legacy, wound around that program, is usefully contrasted with a variety of contemporary cultural tendencies. It stands up, for example, to the almost wilful misrepresentations by Hayden White, on the one hand, and Carlo Ginzburg, on the other, both of whom used Croce as a foil as they sought to justify their own more extreme positions. But seeking to restore Croce to contemporary humanistic discussion has proven an uphill battle, and I offer these essays as part of my continuing effort in that direction.

One dimension of that effort has been to suggest to specialists, starting with those in Italy, that Croce is best understood not as a parochially

Italian possession but precisely as a player on this wider stage. Though I remain fundamentally indebted to the long tradition of Italian scholarship on Croce, I came to believe that critical exegesis from within the Italian philosophical tradition could not afford the essential connection to the wider culture. In making this argument, I was departing from many distinguished scholars, from Gennaro Sasso to Michele Maggi, who, in their different ways, seemed to me to have delimited the focus excessively.

But merely to develop a supranational focus is not in itself sufficient, of course. One major strand of Italian scholarship, associated with such distinguished scholars as Pietro Rossi and Fulvio Tessitore, places Croce in a wider European context – but only to conclude that he suffers in comparison with German historicism and especially with Max Weber's synthesis of historicism and social science. I have long found their criteria misplaced, for reasons I seek to explain especially in essay 2. In any case, their reading was obviously not likely to restore Croce to currency in the circles I thought appropriate.

In presenting Croce from the angle I did, I certainly was not claiming privilege, although I knew I was parting company not only with Rossi, Tessitore, and their allies, but also with a wider range of distinguished Croce scholars, some of them Croce partisans. And though I surely did not set out to antagonize anyone, I knew I was not following certain Italian expectations of deference in engaging the Italians as I did. I sought at once to offer a challenge and to invite dialogue, but with a certain urgency, since I felt that the longer the wider cultural discussion proceeded without Croce, the more difficult it would be to restore him to it.[21]

Fortunately, my effort attracted the attention of the noted philosopher and historian of philosophy Mario Corsi, who invited me to present three lectures at the Scuola Superiore Sant'Anna in Pisa in 1992. These enabled me to seek to show what might be gained by considering Croce together with, for example, Nietzsche, Gadamer, and Rorty.[22] Thanks to an invitation from Mario Agrimi, I was able further to develop my ideas in this direction before a different Italian audience in two lectures at the Istituto italiano per gli studi filosofici in Naples in 1997.[23]

The notion that Croce needs to be considered in such wider company – and that he illuminates such company – has remained central to my enterprise. I had occasion to develop the argument further in a paper presented at a conference in Brescia in 2004.[24] Yet I had to note that in seeking, for example, to place Croce alongside Nietzsche, I was departing even from so distinguished a Crocean as Girolamo Cotroneo, who, in an earlier essay, had concluded that serious intellectual encounter between Croce and Nietzsche was, and by implication remains, impossible – or, worse still, useless, for as Cotroneo saw it, the worlds of the two thinkers were simply incommensurable.[25] Although Croce did not simply condemn Nietzsche, as some might assume, he did not find Nietzsche worth seriously engaging either, especially because, as Cotroneo saw it, he found Nietzsche lacking in philosophical rigour. In contrast, I had sought to elucidate a deeper kinship – an example of what seemed to me the need to stretch to show the wider relevance of Crocean historicism, its connection with cultural preoccupations and directions that might indeed seem disparate at first glance.[26]

Learning from Fascism and Totalitarianism from an Italian Angle

Not surprisingly, I make no claim for the enduring relevance of Gentile in a comparably direct sense. But it has still seemed worth pondering Gentile's place, as well as the higher-level questions about the place of ideas like his, if we are to overcome longstanding obstacles to understanding the emergence of the first fascism, with its overtly totalitarian pretensions, from within the particular Italian context.

Even in the face of longstanding assumptions about fascist activism and anti-intellectualism, it is not hard to show that attention to Gentile can illuminate the dynamics of the fascist regime. For all his determination to distinguish Gentile the fascist from Gentile the philosopher, Gennaro Sasso would not deny that Gentile's myriad activities as a cultural organizer were central to one significant chapter in the regime's history, concerned with the much-contested effort to produce a distinctively fascist culture. Even the rationale for a further step is not hard to grasp. Giuseppe Calandra is typical of those who recognize the importance not simply of Gentile's activity but of his ideas, with their particular content. For Calandra, the regime embraced Gentile's philosophy because, in light of the varied, even contradictory, quality of fascist elements, it needed an overarching ideological principle of unification. Gentile's abstract philosophy filled the bill, lending Mussolini's hodgepodge regime a facade of coherence.[27]

This sort of reductionist put-down was long the favoured tack for those who found it worthwhile to consider Gentile's role in fascism. It is striking, however, that during the fascist era a number of major foreign observers took it for granted that Gentile was central in revealing, or even establishing, something closer to the very core of the fascist self-understanding. Yet they associated his thinking with everything from an irrational worship of 'activity for its own sake' to a conservative, statist Hegelianism.[28] Recent years have seen a renewed attempt to take Gentile's fascism seriously, but even those who find his vision central have often found it difficult to characterize its substance. Emilio Gentile (no relation), the leading contemporary Italian historian of fascism, has characterized Gentile as 'the chief theologian' of fascist Italy's sacralization of politics, but this characterization meshes uneasily with the new-culturalist and party-centred accents of his overall account.[29] Because of such difficulties, we have not fully grasped the seductiveness of Gentile's ideas, nor have we pinpointed the basis of their undoubted waywardness.

Ultimately at issue is what Gentile might tell us not merely about the internal dynamics of Italian fascism but about the wider eruption and meaning of totalitarianism in the era of the two world wars. In his penetrating survey of the idea of totalitarianism, the Soviet specialist Abbott Gleason was much struck with the strength of Gentile's thinking. Deeming Gentile's conception of the totalitarian state 'extraordinary' and 'prophetic,' Gleason concluded that 'Gentile deserves to be called the first philosopher of totalitarianism.'[30] This was to suggest that there was potentially much to be learned if we could get a better handle on Gentile's totalitarian vision, understanding its rationale and wider symptomatic importance.

On the specifically Italian level, Gentile helps us grasp the initial sense of openness and possibility, of the scope for moving beyond both liberalism and Marxism, that fed fascism in the first place. Even his abstract philosophical categories, as post-positivist and post-liberal, helped shape the sense of the political-cultural opportunity that had opened for Italy – and that seemed to give fascism world-historical significance. In other words, Gentile enables us better to grasp the confident self-assertion, the sense of leapfrogging the mature democracies, that helped fuel the fascist departure. At the same time, his ideas underpinned the commitments of more down-to-earth fascists like Giuseppe Bottai and Camillo Pellizzi, even as his ideas also stand in illuminating contrast with those of, say, Alfredo Rocco, with whom he is often lumped. That contrast makes it clear that even fascist totalitarianism was not monolithic; even its overtly totalitarian strands stemmed from different aspirations and had different implications for practice. Most basically, Gentile helps us understand the stakes of the notion, so central to the fascist self-understanding, that fascism – precisely as totalitarian – was 'spiritual' or cultural, as opposed to materialistic (like Communism) or naturalistic (like Nazism).

Once we understand Gentile's ideas within the Italian fascist mix, we begin to see how they can deepen our understanding of the sources, the range, the content, the force, *and* the disastrous outcomes of the antiliberal, often overtly totalitarian aspirations of the era. His totalitarian ideal defies one widespread view, famously elaborated by Hannah Arendt, that takes totalitarianism to have been an effort to snuff out free human creativity and thereby to produce predictable automatons. For Arendt, the point was not simply to enhance power for its own sake but somehow to do the work of history, and she was surely on the right track in linking totalitarian mobilization to a new sense of scope, even the responsibility, for history-making. But Gentile helps us to see how totalitarianism could seem not antithetical to human ethical capacities but essential to nurture them – and why such totalitarian mobilization could have seemed the key to the essential new form of collective, history-making action. At the same time, however, precisely because his vision may initially seem more seductive, it is arguably still more dangerous than what Arendt had in mind, as I discuss in chapters 1, 5, and 6. None of this is to suggest that Gentile offers some golden key to understanding, but any attempt to account for the troubling novelty of the period that neglects his thinking is likely to be one-sided and incomplete.[31]

As I pondered our ongoing effort to learn the lessons of fascism and totalitarianism, two wider sets of questions suggested themselves – questions that, it seemed to me, might also fruitfully be addressed in light of the Italian tradition. Yet these possibilities, too, seemed to have been neglected, even by those interested in Croce. I had occasion to address those questions late in the fall of 2002, in papers at two conferences marking the fiftieth anniversary of Croce's death.

The first of these efforts, included as essay 8 here, sought to bring Croce's program to bear on the enduring attempt to understand fascism historically. After all, Croce had claimed that we orient ourselves for action through historical understanding and that 'all history is contemporary,' stemming from some present concern. Problems bound up with the earlier fascist or totalitarian moment had continued to vex both contemporary Italy and the wider West in ways that were sometimes obvious but sometimes more subtle, and thus not generally recognized. On both levels, orientation for ongoing action was arguably difficult because we had not yet accounted for fascism and totalitarianism historically, at least not as effectively as we might have. Such questioning and learning, in light of our contemporary need to act, seemed to constitute a major cultural priority from a Crocean perspective. Yet even as he stressed the scope for writing the history of one's own time, Croce himself had pulled back, admitting that he could not write the essential history of fascism.

In one sense, Croce's reticence was not surprising, and he sought explicitly to explain it. He hated fascism too much, he said, and, in any case, it had fallen to him actively to combat fascism, as opposed to writing its history. But while his reasons and distinctions were plausible up to a point, Croce was sidestepping certain questions. When *would* we be able to write the history of fascism? Only after all the partisan concerns had died down? If so, was not the essential connection between historical understanding and contemporary action being severed? What sort of orientation was necessary to question fascism historically and genuinely to learn from its historically specific eruption and disastrous trajectory? And what would it take to write its history in such a way as to serve our orientation for response to our present world? Here was the test, I thought, of the connection between two of my abiding concerns – the wider relevance of Crocean historicism and the problem of fascism/totalitarianism.

In his most lucid moments, Croce understood that the obstacle was not simply that he hated fascism too much, or that his task had been one of practical opposition. Rather, he sensed that he did not yet have the categories necessary to understand fascism historically. He famously worried, and tinkered, in an effort to adjust his understanding of 'utility,' or the non-ethical, 'economic' side of human action, as he sought to make sense of all that, in his own time, had so unexpectedly become part of our world. So how *do* we rethink our categories and thereby elaborate those we need in order to come to terms with phenomena that were not merely unprecedented – those were to be expected, from a historicist point of view – but that seemingly constituted a qualitative and tragic departure, beyond any such expectation?

There is plenty of evidence of Croce's anguish by the mid-1940s, and it seems to have stemmed from some undecidable combination of such intellectual uncertainty and disillusionment with many of the directions he saw around him, even after the fall of fascism. Not only was the totalitarian temptation ongoing, as he saw it, in the renewed vogue of communism, but some embraced a misguided existentialism, others sought a return to transcendence – whether in religious or natural law forms – and still others, like his sometime disciple Guido Calogero, confused practical priorities by misconstruing the relationship between freedom and justice. But however we account for its sources, the anguish seems hard to square with what seems Croce's ongoing confidence in the framework he had established. Indeed, as we noted, he was being accused, at precisely this time, of a blandly optimistic acceptance of whatever history metes out. Not surprisingly, there has long been controversy over the extent to which Croce was changing his mind, even undergoing a full-blown intellectual crisis, in his later years.

Versus those who discern an intellectual crisis in the late Croce, Michele Maggi accented Croce's overall serenity in a book published in 1998. As I suggest in essay 6, Maggi's account offers a valuable corrective up to a point, but ultimately I found it necessary to transcend the dualistic opposition of anguish-serenity as it is usually expressed. And in that spirit, I sought to think a little more radically, even adventurously, about Croce's place in his own time and to specify how the wider insights of Crocean historicism might inform an inquiry into fascism/totalitarianism.

Even as Croce recognized that, on some level, he himself was not intellectually ready to explain fascism historically, his hope and faith were surely that those coming later would manage to do so, partly on the basis of the philosophical or meta-historical clarifications that he himself had provided throughout his career. He never departed from the spirit he expressed in 1909 in his once-famous conclusion to *The Philosophy of the Practical*:

> Every philosopher, upon completing some piece of research, discerns the first uncertain lines of another, that he himself, or someone who comes after him, will undertake. And with this modesty, which stems from the nature of things and not simply from my own personal sentiment – with this modesty, which is also faith in not having laboured in vain – I end my work, offering it to the well disposed as an instrument of labour.[32]

In the case at hand, this sense of things surely meant that the challenge for those coming later was, first, to draw out Croce's indications of how fascism and totalitarianism might be treated historically, but also, second, to pinpoint blind spots or limitations in his thinking so that we might hope to work beyond them, drawing, when helpful, on additional intellectual sources.

Whatever his own immediate hesitations, Croce's conception of the human place in history suggests ways of probing the historically specific sources of the totalitarian impulse, in its irreducible ethical-political dimension, so that we might get beyond the too-facile combination of ahistorical psychological propensities and delimited national idiosyncrasies that is so often invoked in the quest for understanding. But on that basis we also better grasp where and how the totalitarians went wrong, from within the historically specific modern conjuncture that continues to play out in and through us. From a Crocean perspective, then, we might learn precisely from these troubling dimensions of our own history how more effectively to proceed in the aftermath, putting the era of fascism and totalitarianism more firmly behind us. In essay 8, based on my paper at the 2002 commemorative conference in Naples, I seek to suggest how fascism and totalitarianism might be questioned in a Crocean mode.[33]

As presented at the conference, my paper elicited fewer comments than many of the others. When, after the conference had moved to Messina, I finally worked up the courage to ask Italian friends why this had been, they told me the paper had not been understood. I did not press them further. But a lack of comprehension was perhaps not surprising, for there seemed little interest in the interface between philosophy and historiography at the conference – a fact that was symptomatic in itself. To be sure, a prominent participant in the concluding roundtable discussion in Naples was the noted historian Giuseppe Galasso, who has contributed, among many historical works, a major intellectual biography of Croce, contextualizing Croce's thought in its own time. Partly in light of his engagement with Croce, he has also contributed to wider ongoing discussions in historiography.[34] But whereas the roundtable and some of the papers treated historical topics on Croce – Croce's criticism of his own time, for example – there was no discussion of historiographical priorities or the cultural uses of historical understanding in light of the perspectives Croce opened up. Practising historians were little in evidence. Apart from Galasso, I was perhaps the only one of the participants – and there were close to a hundred – who would have described himself as a historian first and foremost.

The title for this, the major Italian conference commemorating the fiftieth anniversary of Croce's death, was '*Croce filosofo,*' yet even to characterize him as 'philosopher' was surely one-sided on several levels. Questions about the relationship between philosophy and historiography were central to Croce's thought virtually from the start. He had only a modicum of training in philosophy, and it was a set of very concrete problems in historiography that led him to ask philosophical questions in the first place. He came to argue that the point of philosophy is not to provide some system, or the answers to some enduring set of problems, but simply to furnish the clarification we need to question history effectively. It is surely symptomatic that, as his institutional legacy, Croce founded the Istituto italiano per gli studi storici – an institute for *historical*, not philosophical, studies – in Naples in 1947. But what he clearly envisioned, ultimately, was the sort of dialogue between philosophers and historians that would help produce historically informed philosophers and philosophically informed historians. In what I hope to be that spirit, I have trumpeted the need for such dialogue whenever possible in my interaction with Italian colleagues.

Bound up with the problem of understanding fascism and totalitarianism historically are questions about what lessons are to be learned, beyond mere triumphalism, and about how we are to proceed in the aftermath. No one treated the matter more explicitly than Croce, and some of his diagnoses and prescriptions were taken quite seriously in his own lifetime. But his contribution fell from view even as something like an ongoing tradition of 'post-totalitarian thought' gradually emerged. That tradition encompasses, most obviously, the contributions of Hannah Arendt, starting with her famed study of totalitarianism and her encounter with Adolf Eichmann, which raised still controversial questions about categories of understanding. But her wider political thought is also at issue, for it stemmed, virtually explicitly, from her deep engagement with totalitarianism, which she understood as an ongoing modern possibility. In chapter 2, I consider Arendt's neglect of Croce, Gentile, and Italian tradition in light of the vicissitudes our intellectual history. I hope at some point to consider the stakes of this missed encounter more systematically in an essay to be entitled 'If Hannah Arendt Had Read the Italians.'

The tradition of post-totalitarian thought also came to encompass the 'post-totalitarianism' that emerged in response to the decaying communism in east-central Europe by the 1970s and 1980s. Although thinkers like Adam Michnik and George Konrád could also be considered, Milan Kundera and Václav Havel were especially central, despite the illuminating tensions between them. Such a subsequent writer as Jeffrey Goldfarb was eager to suggest that wider insights into the dangers and possibilities of modern politics could be derived from some combination of Arendt and the later post-totalitarian thinkers of east-central Europe.[35]

Croce has been entirely absent from this discussion, as has the wider, very rich debate about modern political possibilities and priorities that accompanied the collapse of fascism in Italy. In light of some of the accents of the ongoing tradition of post-totalitarian thought, I felt that, despite certain blind spots, Croce's ideas could still fruitfully contribute. Thus my effort in chapter 9 to show what that contribution might entail.

Back to the Question of Wider Cultural Priorities

Just as even philosophers interested in Croce showed little engagement with contemporary historiographical issues, historians, in Italy as elsewhere, evidenced little if any interest in Croce. Although his was still a name that anglophone historians recognized in the later 1960s, he largely fell from view thereafter. Thus, for example, Peter Novick, in his widely read history of the 'objectivity' question that has periodically bedevilled historians in the United States, treated Charles Beard and Carl Becker as archetypal yet barely mentioned Croce, who was crucial to both Beard and Becker, as I discuss in chapter 4.[36]

Yet even as he was neglected for the most part, Croce served notably as a foil for two of the most influential figures in Western historiography over the last thirty-five years or so, Carlo Ginzburg and Hayden White. Though educated in Italy, Ginzburg became widely known, even revered, in the anglophone world as the leading pioneer of 'microhistory,' exemplified most famously in *The Cheese and the Worms: The Cosmos of a Sixteenth-Century Miller.* I considered the stakes of his way of reacting against Croce in a lecture in Naples in 1998, the basis for chapter 10 here. Although Ginzburg's microhistory, focusing on 'what is really dead' in the past, certainly has its uses, Ginzburg was misconstruing the basis for Croce's alternative accent on 'what is living' – on what, in any past moment, led on to the next, and on to the present. To clarify the role for both approaches, and the relationship between them, seemed to me to point the way beyond certain ongoing confusions in historiography. The scope for such a pluralistic understanding of the uses of historical writing is among the themes in chapter 12, which concludes the present volume.

Ginzburg's reading of Croce – indeed, of the whole Croce-Gentile tradition – was also central to his noted attack on Hayden White for propounding a relativistic orientation that, as Ginzburg saw it, invited a quasi-fascist emphasis on 'might makes right' in historiography. And the source of this dangerous heresy Ginzburg found in none other than

Gentile, though the mediation to White had been mostly indirect, via Gentile's often unrecognized influence on Croce, whom White had initially embraced, even as he soon went on to reject him. In all the discussion that followed from Ginzburg's assault on White, it went unnoticed that the Croce-Gentile tradition had been systematically misrepresented on both sides. As I seek to show in chapter 11, already mentioned, such misrepresentation not only further marginalized the Italian tradition prejudicially but also delimited the discussion of historiographical possibilities and priorities.

That discussion seemed for a while to be stimulated by the postmodern turn, which seemed to threaten the self-understanding of mainstream historians in certain ways, yet which also seemed to invite deeper and expanded cultural roles for historical thinking and writing. In *Nothing but History* I had already discussed why encounter with Croce might help practising historians better to grasp the sense in which postmodernism constituted not a threat but an opportunity. Conversely, it seemed to me that the changing intellectual framework might at last have made it possible for contemporaries to encompass Croce in a way that, for example, American historical thinkers from Beard and Becker to Maurice Mandelbaum and Peter Novick had not been prepared to do.

Yet Croce and the Italians remained neglected even as a spate of books and articles in the anglophone world claimed to address 'postmodernism and history.' By the early years of the new century, some were proclaiming that the encounter between postmodernists and historians had run its course – a notion prompting a combination of incredulity, frustration, and bemusement on my part. The encounter had often been manifestly superficial, as postmodernists and defensive mainstream historians had each tended to caricature the other – and to proceed with smug self-satisfaction in the aftermath. A multitude of questions about the place of historical inquiry and understanding, in light of wider cultural changes, had yet to be adequately addressed. If the encounter was indeed over, a significant cultural opportunity had surely been lost.

I noted the need to prolong the discussion in a review essay starting with Ernst Breisach's *On the Future of History* in 2005, and I have sought to contribute further in a recently completed introduction to a reprint edition of *Nothing but History*.[37] But especially in the present chapter 12, completed early in 2006, I seek to specify the sense in which the agenda remains unfinished. Partly because this piece was invited for an Italian publication, I treat Croce only in passing, but I note that a lack of intellectual historical depth has delimited the discussion, and Croce is prominent among those missing. Yet again, my counter-argument seeks to show how, from a perspective derived partly, though certainly not exclusively, through encounter with Croce, we historians might better address challenges, clear up confusions, and seize opportunities in light of our changing cultural framework. In insisting, if only implicitly, on the continued potential relevance of the marginalized Italian tradition, this essay seemed to me to provide an appropriate conclusion to the present volume.

A Balance Sheet

Although Italian fascism has attracted renewed interest in recent years, a panel on the place of Italian historiography at the annual meeting of the American Historical Association in January 2006 suggested that, whereas the Italian experience remained central to study of the medieval and early modern periods of European history, the situation of the modern period was more problematic.[38] The paper by Marla S. Stone, who had conceived and organized the conference, was entitled 'Moving Twentieth-Century Italy from the Periphery to the Center of European History,' a title that well expressed a sense of fruitful possibility, but also a certain frustration over the ongoing tendency to marginalize modern Italy. And by implication the aim, again, was not some sort of fairness to Italy or Italians but the wider illumination that could be gained if twentieth-century Italy were to be taken not as a case apart but as central, even in its undoubted idiosyncrasy, to the wider European and even modern experience.

The essays in the present collection reflect much the same combination of frustration and confidence that Stone expressed. We can deepen our cultural and political self-understanding if we more fully draw aspects of the modern Italian experience into our wider discussion. And whereas my particular interests in historicism and fascism certainly do not exhaust the possibilities, these remain particular interests because I believe the Italian experience with both is particularly illuminating, though the effort to learn from each encounters special obstacles. These two areas especially suggest that if the modern Italian experience is to challenge and expand our wider self-understanding, that experience must be taken on its own terms, not merely subsumed within a framework based on categories derived from more familiar experiences elsewhere. My hope is that these essays will contribute to the essential mediation, showing how we might make wider connections precisely on the basis of what is distinctive to the modern Italian experience.

In preparing this volume, I have encountered three problems that surely confront the author of any such collection to some extent. First, these are *selected* essays, and of course the actual selection has not been easy. In light of the underlying concerns expressed in this introduction, I have chosen those that most explicitly address the combination of distinctively Italian themes and wider connections. This has meant omitting most of those, in the areas of both fascism/totalitarianism and historicism/historiography, in which my Italian angle was understated or only implicit.[39]

Quite apart from such substantive criteria, I have been concerned to minimize areas of overlap, although I recognize that a measure of overlap and repetition remains. This stems from the second problem, or dilemma: whether to revise these essays or to publish them as originally published or presented. Rather than revise them, partly to minimize repetition, I thought it best to offer them in their original form, apart from a very occasional update (as indicated in brackets) in the endnotes. So I can only beg the reader's indulgence as, for example, I repair more than once to the passage from Hobsbawm already quoted in this introduction. At the same time, substantive material from certain of the endnotes appears in more than one chapter. I thought it best to leave this material in place, despite the repetition, so that each essay can be read on its own, as originally presented. The strategy I have chosen preserves the 'occasional' quality of these pieces, each of which was conceived and written at a particular time for a particular purpose. In separate introductions, I seek to explain the circumstances of each essay as appropriate. To have sought to revise and better integrate this material would have been to produce a quite different book.

The third problem concerns background. As I have noted in the present introduction, I have published several books that address some of the issues in these essays. And obviously these books treat those issues more systematically and in greater depth. But it is surely not necessary to have read the books to penetrate the present essays. Conversely, these essays contain a number of ideas that are not to be found in the books – and that, of course, is the major reason for offering the present volume.

chapter 1

An Indirect Italian Angle on a Few Big Historical Questions

This is my inaugural lecture as Albert Berry Saye Professor of History at the University of Georgia. I presented it on 18 March 2004, after it had to be postponed from the originally scheduled date, 26 February, because a rare Athens snowfall forced the university to close that day. I've left the lecture as written, though I began informally by thanking Ed Larson, then department chair, for his introduction and (in absentia) Dr Bibb Saye, of Baton Rouge, Louisiana, who had played a major role in establishing this professorship. It honours his uncle, Albert Berry Saye, who taught political science and history at the University of Georgia for many years, beginning in 1939.

In my halting attempts to warm up the audience in the first paragraph, I refer to a then-recent but still notorious incident during a Super Bowl halftime show. The Lamborghini I mention a bit later is (alas) fictional.

The notes, of course, were not part of the lecture, but in preparing it I inserted a few that I thought might be helpful, should I seek to publish the lecture down the road. I have not heretofore sought to do so, thinking that it might serve as an appropriate introduction for such a collection as this.

We've not had a tradition of such inaugural lectures in our department, and I'm honoured that Ed has asked me to start one. In the European tradition, such lectures were often noble exercises in civic education. And I'd love to pronounce upon the state of the republic in light of Iraq, or perhaps the state of American popular culture in light of Super Bowl halftime shows and wardrobe failures. But I have no special expertise in American foreign policy, and though I am indeed male, I have to admit that, despite appearances, I'm not actually part of the vaunted nineteen- to thirty-four-year-old cohort, so my views on popular culture would be of no interest. Still, I like to think that in developing the angles I have, I might be contributing in some small way to the wider cultural framework from within which we interact, disagree, and come to our collective decisions in response to such contemporary challenges. At the risk of self-indulgence, I thought I'd use this occasion to reflect on those wider angles, letting certain seams and tensions show as I do so.

Having focused largely on supranational issues, from totalitarianism to the wider reaches of Western intellectual history, I'm not really an Italian-area specialist. But I've always found myself drawn back to Italy, and I've developed something of an Italian angle on the issues I confront. My angle is 'indirect,' of course, because I'm not actually Italian, nor do I have, as far as I know, any Italian ethnic ancestry – whatever difference that might make. So the 'Italian angle' I've developed is at another remove.

Still, such indirectness might have advantages of its own, depending on what the angle itself might entail. Surely any such outside angle can mean, and has meant in my case, a certain tension, or set of sparks, with the scholarly mainstream in the country at issue. That can be productive, if also, on occasion, frustrating. To put my own case simply, I can say things that the Italians can't, or won't, or don't, and I find that having done so prompts – no surprise – a varied and not always predictable range of reactions on their part. I've encountered the gamut from extravagant public praise to contemptuous dismissal.

Almost immediately after I joined the University of Georgia faculty fifteen years ago, my history colleague Kirk Willis started urging me to write something on 'why Italy matters,' the implication being that attention to modern Italy was, if anything, actually declining, thanks to the short-sighted presumption, more prevalent in America than elsewhere, that immediate military and diplomatic clout somehow indicates the significance of a national experience. Kirk's premise was not that modern Italy didn't matter, but that it did, yet that many seemed ever less able to grasp *why* it did. Moreover, he was suggesting, the point was not merely to give Italy its due, as a matter of fairness; rather, by marginalizing Italy we could be missing something that the Italian experience might reveal about the wider European, Western, or modern human experience.

We don't want to go overboard in accepting the premise of marginalization. It's well known that in the postwar period alone, Italy has developed one of the most important film traditions and a number of noted writers, and led the design of everything from furniture to men's fashions. Come to think of it, my Lamborghini is parked right outside. But there *is* an issue here; the very fact that Kirk raised the question is symptomatic.

We may be increasingly able to appreciate the stakes in light of the cultural turn that we have come to call 'postmodernism.' By now this unfortunate term connotes all sorts of unnecessary excess, but it needn't scare us. We have become postmodern insofar as, most basically, we have pulled back from the master narrative of modernization, with its dichotomies of modernity and backwardness, normality and waywardness. Instead of a master narrative, we have diverse angles revealing different aspects of the wider modern experience. We've come to recognize, moreover, that 'margins,' or whatever is outside the perceived mainstream, may be of special interest, whether by disrupting restrictive master narratives or by opening new angles and unexpected possibilities.

In retreating from master narratives, we also become more sensitive to historical contingency, including the contingencies of encounter and influence. Even the reasons why paths did not in fact cross, why one thinker was neglected by another, may be worth probing. That effort requires historical questions about patterns of access, influence, misunderstanding, and neglect across national cultures – then and now. Such questioning might even lead to fruitful reconnection with what had been neglected or marginalized. I suggest that our relationship with modern Italian history presents us with a textbook case of margins and contingencies.

Writing in 1974, the noted British historian E.J. Hobsbawm observed that the Italian culture from which the influential Marxist thinker Antonio Gramsci had emerged, around the time of the First World War, was 'both extremely sophisticated and relatively provincial.' This was to suggest that the Italian tradition at issue might have been a bit more different, and thus harder to penetrate, than those abroad, *especially* those in the perceived mainstream, would have recognized. By implication, that tradition might usefully be studied in precisely the provincial sophistication that made it a bit different.

Let us back up for a moment. Recalling Metternich's famous put-down from the early nineteenth century, Italy was at that point a mere 'geographical expression.' But it had a long history and a distinguished cultural tradition, though one that had gradually been marginalized, on the European level, by the early nineteenth century. The traditions stemming from Renaissance humanism had not died out, but the scientific revolution and its Enlightenment aftermath had established a new mainstream, and by that point Italy was scrambling to catch up.

And after unification in 1861, the young country certainly had lots of catching up to do. However, Italy was not *only* playing catch-up but in certain respects quickly became a full participant in the modern European political and cultural mainstream. It experienced decades of parliamentary government, and Italian intellectuals interacted, and contributed, on the European level. Still, partly because it was not easy to make this fragile new country work, Italians had to confront issues that were not found in the same way elsewhere, but that were not merely local or idiosyncratic either. And some of them seemed to require not just catch-up but innovation.

By the early twentieth century we find lots of insights and innovations that could only have come from Italy – sometimes with ambiguous or unhappy results. We think of the pioneering critiques of democratic institutions and myths by Gaetano Mosca and Vilfredo Pareto, two of the notable innovators in the history of socio-political analysis. We think of the futurist movement in the arts, which has been increasingly appreciated for a generation and more, though it was extreme, with its overtly provocative relationship with the audience, its contention that war is the only hygiene of the world, and its subsequent meshing with fascism.

And fascism may well come first to mind if we think of Italian innovation that proved negative. It wasn't uniquely Italian, of course, but it was certainly an Italian invention. The word itself was Italian, coined in 1919, as was, perhaps more surprisingly, the term *totalitarianism*, which proved central to the fascists' self-understanding.

Insofar as such innovative departures led, like fascism, to disaster, it was especially hard for subsequent Italians to mediate their experience to the rest of us, to show how it might relate to wider ongoing concerns. Indeed, the whole question about why modern Italy's somewhat marginalized experience might matter leads to sensitive issues of originality and idiosyncrasy; sophistication, provincialism, and reverse provincialism; and the bases of influence, rejection, and neglect. I suggest that the whole package invites the outsider's angle.

Our present self-understanding derives partly from the overall twentieth-century political experience, including its unforeseen anti-democratic extremes, with all their disastrous outcomes. Yet a certain triumphalism, and perhaps a certain nervous reticence, has delimited our engagement with that earlier experience, aspects of which were quickly marginalized, with ideas neglected and aspirations explained away. So a better sense of what fed the anti-democratic experiments might deepen our understanding of the possibilities and limitations of modern politics. But even insofar as we have managed to confront these big questions, we have tended, for reasons that prove dubious, to marginalize Italian fascism – to miss what it might tell us.

In my first book I focused on a major source of fascism, revolutionary syndicalism, which had emerged first in France, partly from the impasse and revision of classical Marxism around the turn of the century. It had been well known that much of the Italian syndicalist current – which had been independent of Mussolini – had flowed into fascism, but what to make of the fact was little understood. The syndicalists were dismissed as rootless adventurers, opportunists. So when I began reading them systematically, I was surprised at the intellectual force of what I found, which seemed to defy the mainstream account of fascism's origins. I argued that the syndicalists' evolution from Marxism to fascism stemmed from an innovative, step-by-step replacement of Marxian categories. It reflected their reading of the Italian situation, in light of the penetrating critiques of parliamentary democracy that the unusual Italian experience had engendered.

The result was a kind of proto-corporativism, a vision of a new, more intense form of politics based on the workplace, on economic roles. The syndicalist current proved the single most important source of the corporativist direction central to the subsequent fascist regime. Syndicalist debates with leading liberals over contemporary political priorities illuminate both the ambiguity in liberal thinking by the early 1920s and the appeal of the fascist alternative. The sense of building an innovative corporativist state was crucial to the fascists' energizing sense that they had moved to the modern forefront, responding to the inadequacies of parliamentary democracy in a way that Marxism, reflecting nineteenth-century experience, could not. And the corporativist transformation of the Italian state was much discussed abroad, especially as the Depression set in and the Soviet experiment turned toward Stalinism by the early 1930s.[1]

Corporativism was intended at once to involve people more constantly and directly in public life and to expand the sovereignty of the state, most basically by encompassing the economy within the political realm. From both directions, this was to move toward totalitarianism, but we cannot understand the impulse at work in terms of power and domination, escape from freedom, or counter-revolutionary regimentation.

I was challenging the master narrative in arguing that, though pre-fascist economic elites surely sought to exploit fascism, the initial fascist aspiration could not be understood in reductionist terms. And perhaps it was a kind of proto-postmodern perspective, an insistence that Italy was not merely backward, that led me to see something different than Zeev Sternhell and A. James Gregor, two other non-Italians who also went beyond much of the Italian mainstream. From my perspective, each was too quick to fold the corporativist impulse within safe, familiar categories reflecting the master narrative of modernization, rather than face up to the challenge of an unfamiliar but innovative direction.

But of course innovation does not mean desirability, let alone success. Ambiguities in the corporativist conception, tensions with other fascist strands, and the regime's compromises with pre-fascist elites led to poor performance. And though corporativist innovation continued, frustration among committed fascists bred much criticism and debilitating infighting. In light of the inflated expectations and claims at the outset, frustration also bred a tendency toward myth-making and ever more grandiose rhetoric as style and spectacle, soon linked to military adventure, gradually replaced the originating substance.

In light of this outcome, the corporativist vision sometimes gets only cursory treatment, if that, in otherwise innovative scholarship today. Yet marginalizing it means we cannot understand the original Italian self-assertion, the sense of offering a superior modernity, that fuelled the first overtly totalitarian departure.

Intersecting with the problem of fascism and totalitarianism, though from an especially uncertain angle, is the distinctive modern Italian intellectual tradition that Benedetto Croce and Giovanni Gentile initiated around the turn of the century. Based on a recasting of historicism and philosophical idealism, that tradition was surely central to all that Hobsbawm had in mind. Although they made lots of enemies along the way, the two thinkers dominated Italian intellectual life for close to fifty years.

During his lifetime, Croce was one of the world's best-known intellectuals.[2] His bimonthly review *La critica,* which appeared for more than four decades, was among the most respected journals of its kind ever published and is now to be found in virtually every major research library – including, of course, our own. The same is true of the Italian encyclopedia of 1929–36, for which Gentile served as a very hands-on editor-in-chief, and which is right there with the other major encyclopedias on the first floor of our library. Among those passing through the Croce-Gentile orbit were a number of others, from Guido De Ruggiero to Galvano della Volpe, who were at one time or another fairly widely known outside Italy. It is not too much to say that in its range and impact, this particular Italian intellectual tradition remains unique in modern European history.

Although they learned from the idealist tradition in philosophy, Croce and Gentile were responding to a broader challenge, not confined to Italy, bound up with modernity and especially secularization. Partly by recasting marginalized Italian traditions, especially the surely provincial, periodically influential, and recently almost fashionable Neapolitan Giambattista Vico, who died in 1744, they claimed to offer a uniquely relevant cultural orientation, best understood as a radical and thoroughgoing historicism. This was not only to supplant the reigning positivism, based on French influence, but also to transcend the best current German thinking, reflecting both the Hegelian legacy and the countervailing German historicist strand running from Herder to Ranke to Dilthey to Meinecke. Contrasting though they were, these two German traditions had both rested, as positivism did not, on a sense of the centrality of the human relationship with history. The challenge, as the two Italians saw it, was to come to terms with that relationship more consistently and radically than ever before.

Denying any a priori direction in history, Croce and Gentile insisted that what the world becomes depends on our collective response at every moment. The perpetual incompleteness of the world is a measure of our own freedom, creativity – and responsibility, for we come to grasp as never before that what becomes of the present is up to us. A broad cultural program seemed to follow. For both thinkers, the point was not merely to understand the world, but to go on responding to it, changing it, experiencing the history-making implications as we do so. And though our responses stem from our care for the world, we can orient ourselves for action by learning how the present world came to be through history.

Having taken the measure of what seemed the best ideas from abroad, Croce and Gentile came to believe, by the eve of the First World War, that they constituted the cutting edge of modern thought in the West. This was not to make a cult of idiosyncratic Italianness; the implicit claim was simply that Italians were now reassuming the leadership from within the common European culture. Still, the notion could obviously lead to provincial excess. But to gauge the extent to which the claim was merely self-serving or myth-making requires assessing it on its merits.

Though they continued to share a common framework, Croce and Gentile eventually became bitter rivals. Gentile established his philosophical distance from his older partner in 1913 and over the next few years outlined his own distinctive position. By the early 1920s, he had become not only Italy's leading philosopher but an especially influential civic educator. He joined with fascism in 1923, becoming Mussolini's minister of education, and quickly established himself as the fascist regime's most important cultural power broker and ideologue, offering ideas central to its totalitarian self-understanding. Indeed, Gentile was surely the most significant intellectual to play so pivotal a role in European fascism. Although his direct influence declined during the 1930s, his categories remained central, and he himself hung on to the bitter end, even embracing Mussolini's late Repubblica di Salò before being assassinated by a partisan in 1944.

Croce, in contrast, became perhaps the world's best-known anti-fascist and, in the process, a bitter critic of his erstwhile partner Gentile. But the two thinkers remained innovative, partly because each continued to play off the other. From the start, *neither* had had any use for the conventional justifications for liberal democracy. But rather than simply turn back to the Enlightenment tradition, saying he must earlier have been mistaken, Croce tried to push on to a modern recasting of liberalism in response to the wider totalitarian challenge. He concluded that his own radical historicism, not conventional notions of utility, 'negative' freedom, or individual rights, afforded the only convincing framework for a modern liberal politics. On that basis, he specified a humble, pluralistic mode of collective world-making that he deemed truer to the human condition than Gentile's grandiose totalitarian alternative. At the same time, Croce thought his conception sufficient to head off the other extreme, the overreaction into self-indulgence or nihilism that threatened with the seeming loss of transcendent guideposts in the modern world.

Whether or not we find Croce convincing, the Croce-Gentile opposition might seem especially illuminating as we seek to understand the origins and lessons of totalitarianism. Indeed, it might well have broader implications for our cultural self-understanding. Yet as the contingencies of our intellectual history would have it, each of the two thinkers was marginalized, and re-engagement has proven difficult.

Although R.G. Collingwood in England owed a major debt to the two Italians, Croce and Gentile did not have much enduring impact abroad. Even foreigners who claimed to embrace Croce's thinking, like the noted historians Carl Becker and Charles Beard in the United States, had difficulty putting his ideas in perspective. And he was widely misrepresented. In 1950 the American historian Chester McArthur Destler charged in the *American Historical Review* that Croce's thinking had fostered the relativism, and the worship of success, that had undermined democracy and fed fascism and totalitarianism.[3] A few understood that something anomalous was at work. Writing in the influential *Journal of Aesthetics and Art Criticism* in 1952, the year of Croce's death, Frederic Simoni noted, without exaggeration, that 'reference to Croce in current literature constitutes a comedy of errors.'[4]

During the interwar period, Gentile's thinking had been widely viewed abroad, at least among non-Marxists, as revealing the underlying sources and purposes of Italian fascism. German observers, Nazi and anti-Nazi alike, took Gentile's centrality as a given, but the contingencies of the Nazi challenge made them especially prone to misread him, contributing to his eventual marginalization. He was generally associated, as for Franz Neumann, with a conservative brand of statist Hegelianism, but he was also portrayed as warranting blind activism and a veneration of success. This latter was the view of Herbert Marcuse, who offered a critique of Gentile in 1941 as he sought to rescue Hegel from discredit through association with fascism.[5] Neither Neumann nor Marcuse found in Gentile some novel modern challenge, some ongoing totalitarian temptation. From their perspective, in fact, the putative Hegelian statism of Gentile and fascism simply reflected Italy's relative backwardness; having failed to develop the strong state traditions that had been established in Germany, the Italians had fastened onto Hegel in an effort to catch up.[6] So for those reared from within German traditions, any effort to think beyond totalitarianism, understood as troublingly modern, could proceed without engaging Gentile.

Even in Italy, Croce and Gentile both suffered a precipitous decline in influence with the end of the fascist era. Gentile, of course, had been discredited with the outcome of fascism, but certainly engagement with his thinking might seem to have been essential to any Italian effort to come to terms with the fascist past. Croce, in contrast, had been central to Italy's rich debate about post-fascist political possibilities, but even he gradually fell from view. Many among the intellectuals who had earlier embraced Croce and/or Gentile turned to the Marxist Antonio Gramsci, whose debt to the Croce-Gentile tradition was considerable, but who offered a pointed critique of Croce in his now-famous *Prison Notebooks*, published posthumously during the late forties. Even before his death in 1952, at the age of eighty-six, Croce was being widely deemed *superato*, passé.

The flight from Croce stemmed especially from a determination to break from what now seemed to have been an embarrassingly provincial embrace of the Italian tradition. The 'schools' that had formed around Croce and Gentile had indeed betrayed a measure of provincial smugness that led to neglect of concurrent ideas from abroad. So it seemed by the later 1940s that Italians needed to catch up at last to all that had emerged elsewhere.

Thus, to mention just two currently prominent Italian intellectuals, Carlo Ginzburg developed his internationally influential 'micro' approach to history partly as he explicitly rejected Croce in favour of the French approaches that grew from the by-then fashionable *Annales* school. Gianni Vattimo ignored the earlier Italian tradition as he turned especially to Nietzsche and Heidegger, then, during the 1980s, attracted an international audience through *pensiero debole*, or 'weak thought,' his innovative contribution to postmodernism. By 1978 Raffaello Franchini, the most distinguished of the last cohort of Croce's followers, was lamenting that Croce had become taboo in the dominant circles of Italian culture.[7] As for Gentile, Norberto Bobbio commented in 1974 that Gentile's philosophy seemed not only dead, but literally incomprehensible.[8]

Among those rejecting Croce by the early fifties were not only Marxists, Catholics, and existentialists but also a number who claimed to be historicists. But they sought to reconnect with the German historicist tradition and dismissed Croce as a mere throwback to Hegel. Assuming that the Croce-Gentile hegemony had indeed held Italy back, Pietro Rossi embraced Max Weber, who had synthesized social science and German historicism. Rossi's work of the 1950s was a major source of the late H. Stuart Hughes's *Consciousness and Society*, published in 1958, and for several decades the most influential work of modern European intellectual history in English.[9] Another noted scholar, Fulvio Tessitore, similarly found German historicism the key to any contemporary humanism and dismissed Crocean historicism as the blandly optimistic culmination of abstract Enlightenment thinking.[10]

The tradition around Rossi and Tessitore is still much in evidence in Italy, but from my perspective, these are not the scholars to mediate the

Crocean legacy to wider humanistic discussion. Indeed, precisely the opposite; they continue to get in the way. And this current is, shall we say, not friendly to me. Not only have I, as an outsider, dared to claim to reinterpret Croce, but I've attacked Rossi and Tessitore by name for what I take to be their misrepresentations.

While I've gotten a cold shoulder from some, I've been embraced by the heirs of Raffaello Franchini, who, while criticizing Rossi, especially, had shown during the 1950s and early 1960s why any such conflation with Hegel was wayward and why Croce's thinking provided a possibly more convincing, and certainly more radical, solution than Weber's to the much-discussed 'crisis' of German-style historicism. In more accurately disentangling the German and Italian traditions, Franchini was highlighting – subtly, only implicitly, but unmistakably – the sense in which the earlier Italians may indeed have been in the forefront.[11] It was that sense that many Italians coming of age during the fifties and sixties proved unwilling or unable to contemplate.

Perhaps this tendency to denigrate Italian traditions reflected a kind of reverse provincialism, as the noted historian Rosario Romeo suggested in 1985, lamenting the mediocrity that had resulted from what he called the de-nationalization of culture in postwar Italy. In the same vein Michele Ciliberto, writing in 1993, took it for granted that earlier, during the reign of Croce and Gentile, Italians had indeed been too quick to assume the universal import of the Italian tradition. But by now, he said, the commonplace charge of provincialism was itself prejudicial – the mirror image of the earlier provincialism. It was time for a reassessment.

And reassessment has been proceeding in Italy over the last fifteen or twenty years. The question is on what basis, on what level, the Croce-Gentile tradition might fruitfully be reconnected with the mainstream intellectual history of the West.

One possibility, prominent in the recent Italian effort, is to start by revisiting the formal philosophies of the two thinkers, based on the premise that the philosophical dimension constitutes the rigorous core of any body of thought. The tension in my own role enters especially here, because I'm not a philosopher but claim a wider perspective as an intellectual historian. Yet in Italy the Crocean tradition remains almost exclusively the province of philosophers and literary scholars. Fifteen months ago I was one of sixteen featured speakers at a major conference in Naples commemorating the fiftieth anniversary of Croce's death. Five of us were foreigners, but I believe I was the only one of the sixteen trained as a historian and claiming to practise history. I contend that I'm actually truer to the Croce-Gentile tradition in denying any privilege to formal philosophy. From my perspective, in fact, the commemorative Naples conference of 2002, which carried the title *Croce filosofo* (Croce the philosopher), was fundamentally mistaken in conception.

The place of philosophy has been central to the reassessment of cultural proportions that has marked Western intellectual history for over a century – and especially since about 1960, with the cultural turn that has brought us to postmodernism. We hear of 'the end of philosophy,' or at least the end of metaphysics and any foundational role for philosophy. In light of that wider framework, I've suggested that for all their idealist language Croce and Gentile were more radical in their understanding of the role of philosophy, and thus harder to place, than the dominant understanding has recognized.

Croce specified explicitly that even his most seemingly formal philosophical categories grew from his encounter with the concrete problems of life, in its historical specificity. We must constantly re-elaborate such categories in order to come to terms with historical novelty. But this is to enable us to understand our present world in its historical genesis so that we can better respond to it in action. To seek to do philosophy in the abstract, and especially to re-elaborate or re-explain Croce's own categories, is thus not true to Croce's basic insight. And it's surely the overall Crocean cultural program that can most fruitfully contribute to the wider ongoing discussion in the humanities.

Yet when I lectured on Carlo Ginzburg's misreading of Croce at the University of Naples a few years ago, even some of my closest Italian friends concluded simply that Ginzburg didn't understand Croce's philosophical concept of the historical judgment. Because Ginzburg was philosophically naive, we didn't have to worry about him. Yet he was quite influential beyond Italy, fostering the utterly anti-Crocean notion that historiography is to focus on what is dead in the past, as opposed to what lived on, producing the next moment. Croce certainly doesn't merit the last word on this, but if, as my friends were implying, Ginzburg didn't understand the basis for Croce's position, it would seem essential to address him and his influence on that wider level, concerning the cultural uses of historical understanding. Ginzburg's failure to grasp the basis for what he was rejecting may have led him to overreact, misconstruing the possibilities.

In the same vein, consider the recent treatment of Gentile's fascism by Gennaro Sasso, no doubt the leading Italian authority on this whole tradition. For Sasso, Gentile was fundamentally a philosopher, and his political choice for fascism was utterly unrelated to his philosophical thinking. But I've argued that this approach is at once to sanitize the philosophy and to keep us from learning from all aspects of Gentile's thought as we seek to understand the sources of totalitarianism.

Croce and Gentile were also eclipsed abroad, though it was occasionally noted that something anomalous had been at work and that reconnection might be worthwhile. Writing in the early 1990s, the distinguished historian of criticism René Wellek found it odd that in movements influential since Croce's death – from Russian formalism and structuralism to hermeneutics and deconstruction – Croce was ignored, though he had discussed many of the same problems and offered similar solutions. This was so strange for Wellek because, in his judgment, Croce had been arguably the most erudite and wide-ranging figure in the history of criticism.

A bit later the Soviet specialist Abbott Gleason, in his study of the uses and misuses of the 'totalitarianism' category, found Gentile's conception of the totalitarian state 'extraordinary' and 'prophetic.' Although he was quick to conflate Gentile's thinking with both 'conservative Hegelianism' and, as he put it, 'George Orwell's demonic visions,' Gleason did not claim a serious grasp of Gentile, and his overall argument invited a deeper reading.

From my indirect outsider's angle, I've had a number of occasions to seek to show what might be gained by adding these marginalized voices to the wider discussion of political and cultural possibilities. I have time for just a few indications, but I hope to give you a sense of the kinds of issues I have in mind.

Neglect of Gentile has reflected wider confusion about the role of ideology and/or ideas in fascism, especially the commonplace but ill-informed notion that fascism had no ideology or that, if it did, ideas don't matter to regimes run by power-hungry dictators. This wider dimension is too complex to consider today, but let me try to suggest one relatively accessible way that engagement with Gentile can deepen our understanding of the wider totalitarian departure. I must note first that in light of our present assumptions, Gentile's categories might seem easily ridiculed, but the point of opening to margins, remember, is to let ourselves be challenged by listening to unfamiliar voices.

As Croce and Gentile diverged in 1913, Croce found 'mysticism' in Gentile's way of unifying thinking, willing, and acting, whereas Gentile called Croce's attention to 'that sense of profound melancholy that pervades your whole contemplation of the world.' Although Croce claimed to offer an orientation sufficient to invite individual responsibility, Gentile sensed that a mass secular age is likely to fall into irony, cynicism, indifference, perhaps mere consumerism or some mindless popular culture – anything but the sense of collective history-making that breeds responsibility for the whole and for the future. As an antidote, Gentile thought it possible for the human ethical capacity to be marshalled and focused first through education, then through mobilization for more constant and direct participation in public life. Everyone could come to share in that sense of total ongoing responsibility.

So in response to the question of how the world could and should get made, Gentile specified a new mode of collective action through what he termed explicitly a totalitarian ethical state. Put simply, as our sense of responsibility grows in the modern, secular world, we need to expand our capacity to act, to shape what the world becomes. To concentrate and expand power through the state expands our collective freedom to act. Indeed, freedom requires that the state's reach be potentially limitless, totalitarian. Not that the totalitarian state is ever fully realized in some tangible, empirical institution; rather, it's constantly under construction, ceaselessly being recreated, as the ethical capacity of individuals is called forth, and as history generates new challenges. In that sense, the totalitarian state values individuation and presupposes anything but a lifeless uniformity. Still, all are to be involved, all the time.

Note that there's nothing here about exclusion, whether based on race, class, or some other principle. Gentile, and the Italian fascists more generally, found Nazi and Soviet accents crudely naturalistic and deterministic. The necessary virtues were a matter of 'education,' then consciousness, free human choice, so participation was open to all who wanted to belong, regardless of class or ethnic background.

Insofar as our account of totalitarianism starts with the German and Soviet cases, we tend to accent the moment of exclusion, based on putative race or class. And we know how tragic that exclusionary effort became in both cases. But if, by looking at the whole combination from an indirect Italian angle, we put that exclusionary effort in wider perspective, we get to the deeper totalitarian aspiration at work in all three of these troubling experiments. Ultimately, it dealt not with exclusion but with forging the capacity to act collectively in the new 'total' ways that had come to seem necessary and possible. At issue was who could be part of a community capable of acting as one, exercising collective human responsibility. Whereas the Soviets and the Nazis started with an a priori exclusionary principle, Gentile started with openness to all, based on human freedom and ethical potential.

Insofar as we understand the underlying totalitarian aspiration in this 'positive' way, we better grasp the problem. Whereas Gentile may seem more attractive in accenting inclusion, it was *mandatory* inclusion, as our sense of responsibility inflates. We are all to live lives of total public commitment, total responsibility. There's no place for contemplative withdrawal, or self-cultivation, or mere alienation – let alone for some challenge to the overall vision. And if we start with human freedom and the assumption of inclusion, the totalitarian enterprise carries the potential for more manipulative education, more constant mobilization, more intrusive vigilance than it does if we start with a priori exclusion based on the putative limitations of race or class.

In giving the wider aspiration its most idealistic expression, Gentile defies the familiar categories that enable us to dismiss totalitarianism in terms of hate, or some 'assault on humanity,' or some quest for total domination as an end in itself. We thereby better grasp its appeal to those at the time who were not merely brainwashed or coerced or escaping from freedom. We also better grasp that totalitarian excess might come not just from those who hate, or seek power – from those Others, oh so different from us – but from within us, even as we follow our most noble ideals.

Croce's legacy could surely have seemed more accessible and relevant in light of the renewed humanistic discussion, centring upon the place of science, social science, and the alternatives, that brought such thinkers as Hans-Georg Gadamer, Thomas Kuhn, Jacques Derrida, and Hayden White to the fore during the 1960s. Yet he seemed increasingly a provincial figure from the past. But thus to the reader of Croce, Gadamer, for example, seems sometimes to have been reinventing the wheel, as when he offered a way beyond relativism in 1971 that echoed Croce's of 1915 – over a half century earlier.[12]

Not, of course, that Croce merits the last word; any such suggestion would be utterly un-Crocean. The point, again, is simply to show what his voice could contribute to the mix. In my book *Nothing but History* I tried, among other things, to position Croce vis-à-vis Nietzsche and Heidegger, who strongly influenced the cultural turn that began in the sixties, and who, in the process, fostered certain extreme cultural tendencies. I concluded that the sober, constructive, moderate orientation that Croce derived from within the same radically modern or, if you prefer, postmodern framework usefully plays against both sets of extremes.

But let us back up to consider a particularly striking example of the neglect of the whole Italian tradition. On the face of it, the interplay between Croce and Gentile might particularly have interested Hannah Arendt, in light of her effort to renew the broadly liberal tradition, and even to rethink the nature of politics, in light of what she deemed the ongoing modern danger of totalitarianism.[13] That she neglected the Italian tradition instead raises wider questions about German-Italian cultural relations, even though she herself settled in the United States in 1941.

Many of Arendt's framing insights that her admirers in the English-speaking world continue to take as noble and original had been commonplaces of the Italian tradition for decades. But, more importantly, there seems something prejudicial and limiting about Arendt's positive prescriptions. We must create and preserve a free political space, but not so much to enable us to go on responding collectively to historically specific problems as to enable individuals to differentiate themselves and assert their individuality. The political sphere affords the basis for leaving behind an everlasting name, for passing on the memory of one's deeds, in the face of the oblivion that lurks in light of the tragedy of the human situation.

Although her accent on the scope for novelty was to take history seriously up to a point, Arendt conflated history-making action with efforts to shape the world through arbitrary, deterministic rational blueprints and, ultimately, violence. Cognitive activity had its place, to be sure, but she was prone to privilege philosophy without pondering its relationship with the kind of thinking that enables us to understand the actual historical world.[14]

Croce specified precisely what Arendt tended to preclude, a mode of action that lies between the totalist imposition she feared and the individual gestures of authenticity she ended up inviting. We experience what we do as history-making not in a grandiose, totalitarian mode – that was Gentile – but in a weak, even tragic mode. Still, that mode is sufficient. In acting, we seek to shape the future through the effects of what we do, not merely to leave an immortal name. Such action is responsible, and not a mere personal gesture, insofar as it is disciplined by historical understanding.

Even in this delimited encounter, the point is not to give Croce the last word. The culture can encompass Crocean accents in tension with those more attuned to futility and self-assertion, as I once sought to show in bringing Croce together with Albert Camus.[15] The problem is that whereas Arendt is routinely compared with Camus, she is rarely paired with Croce – and in the English-speaking world, virtually never.[16]

Since her death in 1975, Arendt has remained central to what has proven an ongoing tradition of post-totalitarian thought. Two notable recent contributors have been the sometimes warring Czechs, Milan Kundera and Václav Havel, each of whom was concerned with a cluster of intersecting themes, including memory and forgetting, innocence and responsibility, in light of their experience of decaying communism.[17] But crucially for both, that experience simply manifested, in garish form, certain deeper tendencies of the modern world. Havel noted that people are manipulated in infinitely more subtle ways in the West.

This phase of post-totalitarian thought obviously reflects experience beyond Arendt's – and might seem to indicate how irrelevant Croce's program has become. Kundera seems to be mocking the Crocean accent on the immortality of the act when he observes in *The Book of Laughter and Forgetting* that 'our only immortality is in the police files.'[18] We now recognize that the historical understanding that, for Croce, is to orient us for action is constructed partly from evidence that, in Kundera's universe, seems fatally compromised. Tomas, recognizing that the place might be bugged, fears that the police will twist his words, quoting him out of context. And thus he notes that he has no ambition to be quoted by future historians.[19] For Kundera, whatever sense we have of being caught up in history is anything but the source of the weight we seek.

Though I lack the time for a convincing argument today, I've sought to show elsewhere that a Crocean orientation stands up even to those like Kundera and Havel, many of whose dicta have come to seem self-recommending in our cynical age. Though Havel had greater confidence in the political sphere, he and Kundera both fed the wider premium on ongoing disruption, personal gesture, or mere withdrawal that has marked the culture in the wake of our disillusioning political experiences. From a Crocean perspective, it's possible to pinpoint the excesses in those responses and to show why, even in the face of the modern tendencies that troubled Kundera and Havel, we may seek to construct as opposed to disrupt, and to orient ourselves though historical inquiry as we do so.

The Italian tradition was not lost entirely outside Italy. Indeed, it was central to a much-discussed recent encounter in the United States, though its place was curious indeed. The encounter, or semi-encounter, involved the noted historian Carlo Ginzburg, whom we have already met, and the theorist Hayden White. Though easily the most influential theorist of historical study over the past forty years, White has seemed to many practising historians to invite a dangerous, 'anything goes' relativism. And he had begun as a self-proclaimed Crocean, though he found reason to reject Croce by the later 1960s.

Troubled by Holocaust denial and its implications for historiography, Ginzburg sought to pinpoint the sources of White's apparent relativism during a symposium on representing the Holocaust in 1991. Indeed, Ginzburg went so far as to find fascist implications – essentially 'might makes right' – in White's influential position. And for Ginzburg the source of White's waywardness was none other than the fascist Gentile, though as filtered through Croce, whose thinking allegedly embodied certain undigested Gentilian elements. Ginzburg's charge gained plausibility from the fact that White himself, in an influential 1982 essay, recognized that the 'sublime' historical consciousness he advocated might plausibly be associated with fascism. He even mentioned Gentile by name, together with Nietzsche and Heidegger. Still, White also claimed to foster pluralism and tolerance as he invited a more active, culturally relevant role for historians.

So Ginzburg's critique of White rested on Ginzburg's own reading of Croce, on Croce's relationship with Gentile, and on White's relationship with the whole Italian tradition. Although White did not respond directly, Ginzburg's assault elicited a significant discussion, involving – obviously – some of the most sensitive matters of contemporary historical culture. Yet though the place of the earlier Italian tradition was centrally at issue, the ways in which both White and Ginzburg had used it drew no sustained analysis. I've recently sought to show that a bizarre multiple misreading of that tradition was at work, with important costs for our understanding of contemporary cultural alternatives.

Indispensable though their contributions have been, White and Ginzburg each fed a wider cultural tendency toward overreaction precisely as each, for reasons of his own, eschewed deeper engagement with Croce. In characterizing Croce as the sterile culmination of nineteenth-century traditions in his pivotal book *Metahistory* of 1973, White seems deliberately to have ignored Croce's sustained premium on ongoing action, his sustained accent on human creativity and the scope for novelty. What was most deeply at issue between Croce and White was not action or passivity but the *mode* of action, *how* action is bound up with both the human ethical capacity and the scope for truth. Although others had reason to assume that White knew his Croce, at a particular moment in American intellectual history – the mid 1960s – White took on an agenda that led him manifestly to misrepresent Croce, rather than face up to the challenge the Crocean legacy offered, and would continue to offer, to the more extreme position that White had come to prefer.

At the same time, Ginzburg missed the sense in which Croce's mode of presentism, in contrast to White's, might actually serve the worthy effort to box out relativism. Conversely, a premium, like Ginzburg's, on getting at the dead past may warrant not disciplined detachment, as might first seem the case, but a blurring with fiction, insofar as the aim is not to orient for present action but to engender, as explicitly for Ginzburg, a certain quasi-religious sensibility.

So, an indirect angle on marginalized Italian traditions leads the outsider to some odd, occasionally painful, contortions and to some complex axes of contest. But if this angle is frustrating in certain respects, it at least opens the possibility of a reconnection that, in light of the contingencies, seems less likely from any more direct angle. My thanks again to Bibb Saye and all those who have made possible the Albert Berry Saye Professorship in History. It will greatly assist my continuing efforts from the unusual, but I hope fruitful, indirect Italian angle I have developed.

chapter 2

Franchini's Disillusionment: Rereading the *Intervista su Croce* from Abroad

This is a slightly modified and augmented version of a paper I presented at a conference at the University of Naples (Frederick II), 'Il diritto alla filosofia: Seminario di Studi su Raffaello Franchini' in December 2000. I presented the paper in Italian under the title 'Il disinganno di Franchini: Rileggere l'*Intervista su Croce* dall'estero,' on 5 December. It was published under that title in the acts of the conference: Giuseppe Cantillo and Renata Viti Cavaliere, eds., *Il diritto alla filosofia: Atti del seminario di studi su Raffaello Franchini* (Soveria Manelli: Rubbettino, 2002), 213–32. With the permission of the editors, it is published in English here for the first time.

The conference was organized to commemorate the tenth anniversary of the death of Raffaello Franchini (1920–90), arguably the most distinguished – and certainly the most important to me – of the last generation of Croce's immediate followers. From his position in philosophy at the University of Naples, Franchini trained a number of the leading scholars of the next generation – scholars who have not only contributed to the study of Croce's corpus but who have tackled a wide range of philosophical and cultural issues from a perspective informed by their study of Croce. Among them are Girolamo Cotroneo, Giuseppe Gembillo, Ernesto Paolozzi, Raffaele Prodomo, and Renata Viti Cavaliere.

My essay starts from the disillusionment Franchini expressed, in an interview published in 1978, over the fate of the Crocean legacy in Italy to that point.

1: Sophistication and Provincialism

It is a particular pleasure for me to return to this distinguished university to honour the memory of Raffaello Franchini, whom I never met personally, but whose works were fundamental to me as I wrote my book of 1987 on Croce and the contemporary relevance of his absolute historicism. I am most grateful to Professors Cantillo and Viti Cavaliere for their invitation to participate. As an American intellectual historian, I thought I could best contribute to our common enterprise of renewing Franchini's legacy if I returned to his *Intervista su Croce* (Interview on Croce) of 1978, which expressed his disillusionment over Croce's fate by that point. Franchini himself had done his best to mediate the Crocean legacy, and it seems to me that, with all due respect to Carlo Antoni, Alfredo Parente, and the other later Croceans, no one had done it better. Yet somehow it had not worked; by the time of the interview, Croce had become, as Franchini put it, taboo in his own country.[1]

For obvious reasons, Franchini was concerned most immediately with the situation in Italy, but there was also a supranational dimension to his disillusionment by 1978. Croce had been widely translated and was long discussed in some circles outside Italy. Writing in 1937, a long-time antagonist, the émigré scholar Giuseppe Antonio Borgese, found him 'the most famed Italian abroad, at least in the scholarly world, since the days perhaps of Galileo.'[2] But Croce's thought had continued to develop during his lifetime, and foreigners had difficulty putting his ideas in perspective. Failure to understand his intellectual centre of gravity led to widespread misrepresentation, dismissal – and eventually neglect.[3] Even though Croce's legacy, by the time of Franchini's interview in 1978, might have seemed more relevant and accessible in light of the growing doubts about social science and the vogue of thinkers like Hans-Georg Gadamer, Thomas Kuhn, and Hayden White, he was by then in almost total eclipse abroad.[4]

The fact that Croce had been marginalized in Italy obviously did not help, but the international dimension is inherently more complex. Insofar as, in our postmodern mood, we retreat from master narratives, we have become more sensitive to the contingencies of encounter and influence. The American neo-pragmatist Richard Rorty speaks of 'haphazard matings,' from 'who happened to bump into whom.'[5] An effective metaphor – but it is not necessarily mere chance when such bumping does *not* occur, and the reasons why paths did not in fact cross, why one thinker was neglected by another, may be worth probing. Such probing requires historical questions about the actual patterns of access, encounter, influence, misunderstanding, and neglect across national cultures – then and now. The answers might reopen other questions, even make possible the recovery of lost possibility. But any such reassessment leads us into sensitive matters of provincialism, innovation, and the distinctiveness of national traditions.

Franchini charged that the Italian academic world of his own time either had not studied Croce's *Logica* – for Franchini, one of the key works of the century – or had studied it badly, almost wilfully to misunderstand it. That was due in part to the legacy of Gramsci and the Marxist cultural hegemony, which, we can now see, was close to its peak at precisely the time of Franchini's *Intervista.*[6] But a wider tendency was obviously at work as well. Response to Croce by this point reflected the concern about cultural provincialism that had led many Italians to embrace ideas from abroad after the pervasive influence of both Croce and Gentile during the first half of the century. Though Franchini found 1966, the centennial of Croce's birth, to be the turning point for Croce's legacy in Italy, the process began even before Croce's death, during the later 1940s, when many Italians began declaring him *superato* – passé – as they eagerly embraced ideas from abroad.[7]

But that preoccupation could produce a kind of reverse provincialism, as another Crocean, the noted historian Rosario Romeo, lamented in 1985 in deploring the de-nationalization of culture in postwar Italy. Openness to all others had gone hand-in-hand with a kind of cultural self-denigration, and cultural mediocrity was the result.[8] The contemporary tendency to undervalue anything that had been specifically Italian included, most prominently, the whole anti-positivist culture that Croce and Gentile had spearheaded earlier in the century. And whereas echoes of the longstanding dispute between Croce and Gentile were still audible in Franchini's *Intervista,* we have since come to recognize that for certain key questions we need to start with a common Italian tradition, encompassing both Croce and Gentile, and then to probe the basis for their crucial divergence from within it.[9]

Writing in 1974, a famed non-Italian historian, E.J. Hobsbawm, had that same tradition in mind when he noted that the Italian culture from which Gramsci had emerged, around the time of the First World War, was 'both extremely sophisticated and relatively provincial.'[10] This suggests that the Italian tradition might be a bit more different, and harder to penetrate, than those abroad would immediately have recognized – and that it might usefully be studied in precisely the provincial sophistication that made it a bit different. Indeed, the current vogue of 'margins,' of whatever is outside the mainstream, would seem to invite those abroad to a renewed and continuing interaction with a tradition that surely *was* outside the international mainstream, yet 'extremely sophisticated.'

Or has the 'relatively provincial' side of Hobsbawm's characterization proven the more important, so that among non-Italians that idiosyncratically Italian tradition merits the attention only of those with a special interest in Italy? Although it was hard to charge that Croce himself had been provincial – in one sense, he was arguably the most cosmopolitan intellectual of his time – he conveyed a supreme confidence, even a kind of omniscience, that put some people off. And the 'schools' that formed around Croce and Gentile during the heyday of the Italian tradition did invite a measure of provincial exaggeration, or smugness, that led to neglect of concurrent ideas from abroad. Thus, again, the sense among later Italians that it was necessary to turn away from that overall Italian tradition if they were to de-provincialize, to expand their horizons, by the second half of the century.

In fact, of course, we can find provincialism on all sides on the international level during the period when the Croce-Gentile tradition was prominent. Massimo Mastrogregori noted the lack of interchange between Crocean historiography and the French *Annales* School; though each could have learned from the other, each went its own provincial way. Still, the *Annales* eventually triumphed, becoming 'universal,' so it was Crocean ethical-political history that was left looking provincial, time-bound, *superato.*[11]

Responding in the *Intervista* to the standard provincialism charges, Franchini similarly noted that there had been neglect on both sides, but he added a dimension in observing that scholars ask why Croce never studied Carl Gustav Jung, for example, but not why Jung never read Croce.[12] This was to suggest not simply parallel provincialisms but that Croce was by now the victim of a double standard. Whereas *he* was accused of provincialism, those who neglected or misrepresented his thinking – whether in Italy or abroad – were not. Franchini's way of posing the question was to protest this double standard, which clearly *was* at work in Italy – and perhaps more widely, as the notion that the earlier Italian tradition had been especially provincial spilled over to non-Italians.

Writing in 1993, Michele Ciliberto took it for granted that earlier, during the reign of Croce and Gentile, Italians had indeed been too quick to assume the universalism of the Italian tradition. But by now, he said, the commonplace charge of provincialism had itself become an ideological prejudice – the mirror image of the earlier provincialism. It was time for a reassessment, which Ciliberto sought to promote in his aptly titled collaborative volume *Croce e Gentile fra tradizione nazionale e filosofia europea.*[13]

In short, provincialism is surely at issue, but there remain questions about where it lay – and lies – and about what difference it made – and makes. We must examine the reasons for confidence and neglect on all sides; we must consider who was – and is – misreading or neglecting whom and on what basis.

2: Representing and Misrepresenting Croce's Legacy

In the *Intervista*, Franchini pinpointed what he took to be the keys in Croce's legacy that were being missed or misrepresented. Croce was not a philosophical system-builder but the philosopher of the end of rules, of openness, and thus of spontaneity, of daily practice, of individual ethical judgment. But Franchini found it equally important to accent the other side of the coin, showing why Croce does not leave us with 'anarchy,' with mere individual caprice or gesture.[14] At the same time, Franchini accented concreteness: 'spirit' is not ethereal or abstract but simply human activity, even including economic or utilitarian activity.[15] However, he placed particular emphasis on the ethical and on Croce's way of conceiving politics as the instrument of ethical response. And this pointed to the core of Croce's thought, 'history as thought and action,' which Franchini insisted was no mere formula but an overall cultural orientation that followed from Croce's innovative, radically historicist conception of the relationship between humanity and history.[16]

Franchini also emphasized Croce's links with Vico and, as the other side of the coin, de-emphasized his debt to Hegel.[17] To be sure, Croce wrestled with the Hegelian legacy throughout his career, but he proved one of the notable anti-Hegelian thinkers precisely because he was operating on the same level as Hegel in important respects. Denying the element of transcendence in Hegel, Croce insisted that what the world becomes depends on our response at every moment; there is no a priori providence, or telos, at work in history. On first encounter, of course, Croce seems bland and disappointing compared to the grandiose Hegel – as Croce himself recognized again and again. But there is only so much that can be said in advance; the key is our ongoing response and the resulting growth of the world. Our challenge is to adjust to that radical immanence without overreacting into irrational self-indulgence or nihilistic despair.

It is striking that what Franchini chose to accent continues to be missed or misrepresented by several of the most influential among those few in the English-speaking world who have recently dealt with

Croce. And, to be honest, my first impulse was to focus on an interesting set of four of them in my presentation today.[18] But I decided that it would be more illuminating to bring Franchini's accents to bear on an earlier instance of neglect from within a national tradition, Germany's, that was seemingly far more congruent than Britain or America with the Croce-Gentile current. I have in mind, of course, the partly overlapping legacies of philosophical idealism and historicism, which were long central in Germany and Italy as they had never been in France, Britain, or the United States.

3: Italians and Germans

Franchini mentioned Jung, but if we want to consider why a particular connection was not made, and the difference it makes even now, the case of Hannah Arendt is particularly instructive. She ended up in the United States, of course, and those of my generation grew up with her, far more than with Croce and Franchini. But she spent her formative years in Germany, studying with Heidegger, among others, and her failure to engage the Italian tradition reflects her German roots.

Following the lead of such scholars as Nicola Matteucci and Girolamo Cotroneo, scholars within the Franchini tradition have devoted considerable attention to Arendt in recent years. I note especially the probing and sympathetic exegesis by Professor Viti Cavaliere that appeared just months ago.[19] And Arendt certainly offers a plausible line of inquiry for those in the Croce-Franchini lineage, most obviously because she too sought to renew the broadly liberal tradition after totalitarianism. Indeed, she has remained central to post-totalitarian political thought in a way that Croce has not.[20] Whatever the degree of kinship, there would at least seem the basis for fruitful comparison between the two thinkers.

At first glance we might have expected Arendt to have been eager to read Croce – and Gentile as well – in light of her effort to rethink politics in response to the recent experience of totalitarianism, which she deemed an ongoing modern danger.[21] To be sure, the reasons she found Italian fascism in practice merely authoritarian, and not genuinely totalitarian, are well-known. But in light of her accent on 'ideologies of motion,' she might usefully have tackled the seductive and overtly totalitarian Gentile in tandem with Marxism and Darwinism, Hitler and Stalin, and those who ran the various camps, where, in her view, totalitarianism came closest to realization.[22]

At the same time, Arendt's effort to suggest a neo-liberal orientation in light of the totalitarian challenge exactly paralleled one of Croce's major concerns since the 1920s. To be sure, Croce's immediate diagnoses of fascism and totalitarianism, relying on categories like 'moral depression,' '*antistoricismo*,' and 'parenthesis,' were not very helpful.[23] But the advent of totalitarianism led him to begin drawing out the political implications of his earlier thinking. And though he was reluctant to admit it, he was at least implicitly responding to Gentile as he sought to make new sense of the political – its interface with individual ethical response, on the one hand, and history, on the other – for a world that had known totalitarianism. This entailed reviewing the basis of his philosophical divergence from Gentile, which had become public in 1913, prompting Gentile's observation that a 'sense of profound melancholy' pervaded Croce's 'whole contemplation of the world.'[24]

On the face of it, the interplay between Croce and Gentile might particularly have interested Arendt, coming of age as she did at the pivotal moment, in the late thirties and early forties, when the crisis of fascism prompted much discussion of the terms of liberal rebirth. But she neglected the Italian tradition altogether. Her neglect leads to wider questions about German–Italian cultural relations, about what Germans were prepared to hear from Italy, and about what difference it made – and makes – that they heard what they did.

First, we must note that on this level, too, there was an element of provincialism on both sides during the 1930s. Gennaro Sasso, exploring Gentile's relations (or non-relations) with Heidegger, especially in the context of Heidegger's 1936 visit to Rome to lecture on Hölderlin at the German Academy, accented the mutual indifference of the two thinkers, despite the efforts of Ernesto Grassi and Armando Carlini to establish bridges between them. Sasso found Heidegger's attitude symptomatic of German cultural arrogance in general and anti-Italian prejudice in particular. But Gentile, for his part, showed no more interest in the possible encounter than Heidegger did.[25]

As for Heidegger and Croce, I have suggested elsewhere that the mature Heidegger could usefully have confronted Croce directly in light of the contemporary tendencies that Heidegger sought to resist or overcome, whereas Croce, for his part, was too quick to preclude the sensibility and mode of experience that Heidegger at least glimpsed – a kind of post-historicist religiosity.[26] In this instance, too, we find sophistication but also a measure of provincialism on both sides. But the situation is quite different when we come to students of Heidegger who eschewed Heideggerian disengagement and turned back toward the public, political world. At this point we have not merely a parallel provincialism but an asymmetry, for the sophisticated but provincial Italians, especially through their engagement with Vico, had carried historicism and philosophical idealism in directions not seen in Germany.[27] Indeed, the Germans, assuming a kind of proprietary grasp of those traditions, were especially unprepared to explore or even recognize the distinctive departures of the Italian tradition, in both its Crocean and Gentilian currents.

Though it was widely characterized at the time as neo-Hegelian or neo-idealist, the Italian tradition entailed a major departure from Hegel, just as Franchini emphasized in the case of Croce. But the Germans were especially prone to miss or play down that fact during the fascist period, when there was much comparative discussion of Italian fascism and German Nazism on the part of Nazis and non-Nazis alike. Virtually from the start, German observers took Gentile's centrality to fascism as a given, but the contingencies of the Nazi challenge made them especially prone to misread him, contributing to a certain delimited way of connecting his thinking with the Hegelian tradition. Gentile was generally associated, as by Franz Neumann, with a conservative brand of Hegelianism, linked to statism, but he was also portrayed as warranting blind activism and a veneration of success. This latter was the view especially of Herbert Marcuse, who offered a critique of Gentile in 1941 as he sought to rescue the Hegelian legacy from any association with fascism.[28] From the perspective of neither Neumann nor Marcuse did Gentile manifest some novel modern challenge, some ongoing totalitarian temptation. If anything, in fact, the Hegelian statism of Gentile and fascism simply reflected Italy's relative backwardness; having so far failed to develop the strong state traditions that had been established in Germany, the Italians fastened onto Hegel in an effort to catch up.[29] So it was easy for a German to assume that an effort to think beyond totalitarianism, as troublingly modern, to a new liberalism could proceed without considering Gentile. Indeed, the contemporary German reading of Gentile was congruent with Arendt's reasons for marginalizing Italian fascism altogether – as merely conservative statism.

But what about Croce? His place on the immediate political spectrum was obvious, but not how his neo-liberalism related to the idealist and historicist traditions that Italy shared with Germany. Insofar as the political divergence of Croce and Gentile stemmed from something deeper than a contingent assessment of contemporary political possibilities, what were its sources and implications? The point was surely not that Croce was somehow truer to Hegel, for not only did Croce remain in ongoing critical dialogue with Hegel, but he would soon suggest that *idealism* was a term to be abandoned altogether.[30]

By the time he did so, in 1945, Croce had concluded that the cultural orientation he outlined was better understood as a form of historicism. This only raised further questions, however, for not only did the term call to mind another German tradition, but it was a tradition that had emerged in opposition to Hegelianism and that, in Germany at least, seemed by now to be in crisis.[31] Croce avoided the historicist label for years precisely to resist conflation with this German tradition, variously associated with Ranke, Dilthey, and Meinecke.[32] And in finally embracing the term in 1939, he took pains to adopt *absolute* historicism to specify that his position was quite different from, and more radical than, the German variety. Even before addressing the question of terminology, he had claimed explicitly to point beyond the German tradition and the reasons for its perceived crisis. In *La storia come pensiero e come azione*, published in 1938, Croce noted that Ernst Troeltsch was concerned to overcome historicism to reclaim the rights of the moral *coscienza* – but there was no need, he insisted, because the moral *coscienza* is at the base of historicism.[33]

But it proved difficult even for many Italians to grasp how Croce's position, however characterized, related to the Scylla of Hegelianism and the Charybdis of German-style historicism. Thus Franchini found it imperative in his *Esperienza dello storicismo* of 1953 to compare Italian and German historicist strands, then, a few years later, to offer a pointed critique of the influential work of his contemporary Pietro Rossi.[34] Assuming that the Crocean-Gentilian hegemony had held Italy back, Rossi accented the superiority of the German historicist tradition, with its emphasis on individualities, and portrayed Max Weber, with his synthesis of historicism and social science, as the progressive next step.[35]

The noted scholar Fulvio Tessitore was prominent in developing this line of thinking. Whereas he found German historicism the key to any contemporary humanism, he portrayed Crocean historicism as simply the culmination of the abstract reason of the Enlightenment; history is the history of reason, with everything explained and the irrational excluded.[36] For the Rossi-Tessitore tradition, Croce's departure from German historicism was but a retreat back to the totalizing of Hegel. In associating Crocean historicism with passive acquiescence in whatever happens, they were lumping Croce with a decidedly conservative brand of Hegelianism, just as the earlier German observers had done with Gentile, though now it was a different conservative strand.

But Franchini's writings of the 1950s had shown why any such conflation with Hegel was wayward and why Croce's thinking provided the solution to the much-discussed 'crisis of historicism.' First, Crocean historicism had showed the way beyond the concerns with relativism and objectivity, the concern to glimpse something supra-historical, that still lurked in German historicism, occasioning the sense of impasse and crisis. And, second, Croce's thinking did not entail idealism, Hegelianism, or passive acceptance, but ongoing critical response to the present, as the provisional outcome of history so far. Franchini had offered a more convincing and fruitful way of disentangling the German and Italian traditions. And in doing so, he had highlighted – subtly, but unmistakably – the sense in which the Italian tradition had been in the forefront.[37] It was that sense that many of those coming of age during the 1950s and 1960s proved especially unwilling or unable to recognize.

Meanwhile, back in Germany, it was crucial to Heidegger's self-understanding that he believed himself to be thinking beyond the German historicist tradition that had culminated in Dilthey – and that portended a wider crisis of Western culture. And though Hans-Georg Gadamer's cultural strategy proved very different, he, too, took it for granted that the first step was to think beyond historicism. Heidegger had surely opened some fruitful directions, but there was something facile and prejudicially limiting about his way of bequeathing historicism as a category to the next generation in Germany.[38] Still, in light of what historicism had come to mean, those coming from within Heidegger's orbit would not be likely to contemplate the possibility that any self-proclaimed historicism, even an *absolute* historicism, might afford an alternative solution to the crisis of German historicism – or even a direction that might fruitfully be engaged. And any such engagement became ever less likely as bright young Italians began insisting that what remained living in the Italian tradition could best be found in German historicism, that Weber had showed the next step, that the *absolute* in Croce's historicism was not an innovative departure but a throwback to Hegel.

In fact, however, the more radically historicist Italian tradition had thought beyond the earlier understanding of both Hegelianism and historicism even before the First World War – and in ways the Germans, assuming a privileged mastery of those traditions, yet hung up on delimited understandings of both, did not quite grasp. Indeed, though the Germans were in one sense the best positioned to engage the sophisticated side of the Italian tradition, the particular, historically specific circumstances of the era made it especially difficult for them to approach the new Italian thinking on its own terms and to mediate it to the mainstream discussion.

Whatever we make of Heidegger's mature direction, those like Gadamer and Arendt who sought a renewed engagement with the concrete political and historical world might seem to have been especially well positioned to profit from dialogue with the provincial yet sophisticated Italians. That there was a lack of encounter instead had particular consequences for those coming out of the German tradition. As I have sought to show elsewhere, Gadamer surely offered ideas that Croce did not, but he also missed a good deal, and he was sometimes reinventing the wheel, as when he offered a way beyond relativism in 1971 that echoed Croce's of 1915 – over a half century earlier.[39] But Arendt's thinking was more explicitly political than Gadamer's, and her way of turning from Heideggerian disengagement back to the world of action led still more obviously into terrain that Croce and his followers had already begun exploring.

4: If Arendt Had Read Croce

Many of Arendt's framing insights that her admirers in the English-speaking world take as notably noble and original had been commonplaces of the Italian tradition for decades. As we retreat from foundational philosophy, we come to recognize that it is up to us to construct the moral and political order. We must judge and act without rules given from outside, with no guarantee we get things right.[40] For Arendt, exactly as for the Italians, the task is bound up with human freedom, which entails a capacity to initiate the new and unpredictable. This capacity is the other side of the world's capacity for novelty, its endless provisionality and incompleteness. And for both Arendt and the Italians, there follows a shared, collective human responsibility for what the world becomes.[41] The question is how we exercise that responsibility, how our collective activity is bound up with the endless coming to be of the particular world in history. And that is what led to the highly symptomatic divergence of Croce and Gentile.

In seeking an explicitly post-totalitarian politics within this framework of openness and responsibility, Arendt and Croce each accented limits, humility, even a tragic sense. But there was something prejudicial and limiting about Arendt's way of conceiving human being in interface with history. What she failed to engage was precisely the basis for the set of priorities, summed up as history as thought and action, that Franchini pinpointed as the core of Croce.

Although her accent on the scope for novelty was to take history seriously up to a point, Arendt worried that to understand action as history-making was bound to invite hubris, to conflate with 'humanism' understood as some inherently violent effort to shape the world. Though her assumptions no doubt stemmed partly from Heidegger's way of lumping humanism, historicism, and technology together, they also reflected the totalitarian trauma, as was especially explicit in her treatment of Marx.[42] In the same vein, Arendt was quick to conflate rationality with deterministic historical blueprints that demand or justify violence. Cognitive activity or thinking had its place, to be sure, but she was prone to privilege philosophy without pondering its relationship with the mode of thinking that enables us to understand the actual historical world.[43]

Horror of coercive political blueprints led Arendt to play down the scope for collective action intended to produce an effect. Although it was crucial that we create and preserve a free political space, that space proved less the sphere of ongoing collective response to historically specific problems than the arena for differentiated individuals to act in ways that establish their individuality. Such individuality requires the interaction and recognition that the public political space makes possible. The political sphere also affords the basis for leaving behind an everlasting name in the face of the oblivion that lurks in light of the tragedy of the human situation. Indeed, a whole way of conceiving the relationship between individuality and history is bound up with Arendt's premium on passing on the memory of one's deeds, which stands opposed to any premium on the ongoing reconstruction of the world.[44]

Although fruitful up to a point, Arendt's accents entail an element of overreaction that reflects her delimited understanding of the interface of history, politics, and individual experience. Engagement with Croce's moderate alternative to Gentile's genuinely coercive politics would have broadened her sense of the possibilities.

Whereas Arendt conflated reason with violence and thinking with philosophy, Croce accented 'history as thought' to suggest the scope for thinking about the actual through historical questioning, which yields the understanding that affords a measure of rational preparation for political action. Conversely, such action is responsible, and transcends the idiosyncrasy of personal moral response, precisely insofar as it disciplined by historical understanding. Croce was showing the scope for a mode of action that lies between the a priori rational blueprint that Arendt feared and the memorable individual gesture of authenticity that her thinking tended to foster.

Whereas Arendt conflated any accent on action as history-making with rational blueprints and totalitarian violence, Croce's theme of 'history as action' showed the scope for experiencing what we do as history-making in a weak, even tragic mode – and the cultural difference it makes to do so. And Croce's accent on the immortality of the act stands diametrically opposed to Arendt's premium on the quest for future recognition in the face of oblivion. In acting, we seek not to leave an immortal name but to shape the future through the effects of what we do. We take up and transform the world that our predecessors have bequeathed to us, and we know that what we do will endure, helping to shape what the world will be at all subsequent moments.[45] Of course action entails risk, as Croce well understood, for we never know what will become of what we do.[46] But we minimize the risk insofar as our action is informed by historical understanding.

Even as he anticipated the basis for Arendt's later accents on humility, pluralism, risk, and tragedy, Croce outlined a post-totalitarian politics that is arguably more responsible and constructive than hers. Had Arendt engaged the Italian tradition and its Crocean outcome, our discussion of the interplay of politics, history, and individual experience would be richer today.

But this is not to give Croce the last word. The culture can encompass Crocean accents in tension with those more attuned to futility and gesture, as I sought to show in bringing Croce together with Albert Camus in my 1987 book.[47] The problem is that whereas Arendt is routinely compared with Camus, she is rarely paired with Croce – and in the English-speaking world, virtually never.[48] Yet she remains central to post-totalitarian political thought, though her understanding of our possibilities and priorities seems one-sided from a Crocean perspective. But of course the outcome so far is only provisional, and as we engage her thinking as part of our response to that present outcome, we may still bring the distinctively Italian viewpoint to bear.

5: Croce, Franchini, and the Open Future

It seems fair to say, in conclusion, that Franchini sought to mediate to the future a distinctive Italian tradition that was never fully understood abroad, precisely because it was more innovative than even the Germans were prepared to understand. We can see in retrospect that this lack of encounter mattered especially during the pivotal moment of postwar cultural reassessment that prompted such works as Franchini's *Esperienza dello storicismo* and *Metafisica e storia* during the 1950s. But having been bound up with a deeply problematic period in Italian history, that tradition became taboo in Italy and largely forgotten abroad. Thus Franchini's disillusionment by 1978. Despite a measure of renewed interest in Italy in recent years, the Italian tradition still has not been as fruitfully brought into wider international discussion as it might be.

In *Metafisica e storia*, Franchini stressed that Croce's thinking was only a moment in the history of historicism, not a definitive point of arrival.[49] And despite the disillusionment evident in the *Intervista su Croce*, and in the face of all the opposing cultural tendencies, Franchini, perhaps more than anyone else of his generation, helped reanimate the Crocean legacy for the next generation, including many of us. And it has fallen to us, of course, to mediate that legacy to the future as we respond to a cultural situation by now quite different from his.

In the same passage, Franchini also stressed that the ongoing development of that tradition required the encounter of historians and philosophers. As we seek to renew Franchini's legacy, it seems to me worth re-emphasizing and expanding that point. There is room for still more openness, dialogue, and mutual respect between philosophers and historians. There can be fruitful differences of perspective among those equally concerned with this distinctively Italian tradition. And there is room for still more dialogue between Italians and non-Italians. By expanding that dialogue, we can hope to enhance the wider international discussion, which still has much to learn from the tradition of Croce and Franchini.

chapter 3

The Revolt against Croce in Post–Second World War Italian Culture

In 1981, not long after becoming interested in Croce, I was invited to participate in a symposium honouring A. William Salomone upon his retirement as Wilson Professor of History at the University of Rochester. Professor Salomone had numbered Croce among his many interests, so I planned to present something on the late Croce, in light of an article I had just completed on Croce's intellectual and political role during Italy's transition from fascism to democracy (see note 4 here). But Perez Zagorin, one of the conference's organizers, took me aside to note his longstanding puzzlement over Croce's seemingly precipitous decline in influence, even in Italy, by the mid-1940s. In light of Professor Zagorin's suggestion, the topic quickly came into focus, and I presented this paper, as the last of six, at the Salomone Symposium at the University of Rochester on 24 October 1981. The other presenters were Robert Wohl, MacGregor Knox, Raymond Grew, Georg G. Iggers, and Ronald Cunsolo.

It was above all the gratifying response to this paper that stimulated me to push on to a full-scale book on Croce; the result was my *Benedetto Croce and the Uses of Historicism*, published in 1987. I continue to appreciate the kind words of Robert Wohl, Donald Kelley, Bonnie Smith, and, above all, the late Professor Salomone himself. Having determined, in light of such encouragement, to attempt a full-length book, I never sought to publish this essay. But though the book of course incorporates much of what I said in this piece, I have concluded, upon rereading it twenty-five years later, that it might still be of interest in light of its sustained focus on what, in retrospect, seem Croce's most obvious blind spots during the pivotal 1940s. This essay complements the immediately preceding one, on the decline of Croce's influence, but it also anticipates some of the themes in chapters 6 and 8.

By now, of course, much has appeared that any new work on this topic would have to encompass. Limiting myself here to a couple of works in English, I note first the relentlessly negative account by David Ward, *Antifascisms, Cultural Politics in Italy: Benedetto Croce and the Liberals, Carlo Levi and the 'Actionists'* (Madison, NJ: Fairleigh Dickinson University Press, 1996), which provides a good sense of the wider contests of the period even as it parrots certain time-worn, prejudicially anti-Crocean charges on occasion. As counterpoint, I note Fabio Fernando Rizi's far more sympathetic *Benedetto Croce and Italian Fascism* (Toronto: University of Toronto Press, 2003), which, though focused primarily on Croce's anti-fascist activities, includes much sensitive and well-documented discussion of the post-fascist period.

It's well known that Benedetto Croce's influence in Italian intellectual life declined sharply after the collapse of fascism in the early 1940s. There is something puzzling about this, and we'll get to that shortly. First, though, we need to remind ourselves that this wasn't the first revolt against Croce, who had had his ups and downs since his heyday during the first decade of the twentieth century. Moreover, some of the reasons for his eclipse during the 1940s are fairly obvious. We needn't posit some archetypal revolt against the great-grandfather to explain why someone who seemed fresh and exciting in 1903 no longer did so, at the age of eighty, in 1946. Italians, especially young Italians, were bound to shop around when the culture opened up after fascism; not only did Croce no longer carry the excitement of forbidden fruit, but he inevitably seemed a bit provincial as well – despite all he had done to 'de-provincialize' Italian culture earlier in the century. Croce, of course, was heir to the great Italian humanist tradition, but that tradition seemed out of phase with the modern scientific temper, and it seemed to many that Italy had better develop precisely that temper if it was to join the mainstream of the Western world after fascism. Intellectuals determined to cease wandering between two worlds, to overcome the ambivalence that Robert Wohl has identified in the previous generation, could easily see Croce as a symbol of all that must be left behind.[1]

These points are easy to grasp – and must be kept in mind if we are to place Croce's decline in clear perspective. But a more complex mechanism was also at work. Even mature intellectuals like Guido De Ruggiero and Luigi Russo, who had long been associated with Croce, felt that something was missing in Croce's approach to things – and that the subjects Croce did not address, and perhaps could not address, were precisely the ones that most needed to be addressed, given the challenges that Italy faced after fascism. With this void at its centre, Croce's conception seemed at best a quaint and irrelevant relic, at worst a pernicious obstacle to viable renewal. The art historian Ranuccio Bianchi Bandinelli, who edited the influential review *Società* after the war, recorded his growing doubts about Croce in diary entries of the late thirties and early forties. Croce seemed to constitute a limit, a barrier, though Bianchi Bandinelli admitted that it was hard to explain why. By 1947, he was arguing that Croce was a closed door, with Antonio Gramsci the key to proceeding beyond.[2] Most of Croce's critics were willing to recognize the value of his opposition to fascism, but De Ruggiero, for example, noted that young people seeking a positive alternative to fascist irrationalism had quickly encountered the limits of Crocean historicism.[3]

Part of this disaffection reflected the immediate political situation in Italy after fascism. For a variety of reasons, Croce had refused to support the new Action party, which included De Ruggiero and the bulk of non-Marxist anti-fascist intellectuals, and had opted instead for the Liberal party, which played a conservative role that Croce seemed wilfully to misrepresent. I've sought to explain elsewhere the dynamic that Croce's immediate political position set in motion, so I won't go through all of that here.[4] In any case, Croce's curious political stance only exacerbated something deeper – a tendency toward misunderstanding and misrepresentation on the intellectual level – and it's this that we must try to understand

It is easy to go through postwar periodicals like *Belfagor*, *Politecnico*, and *Società* to discover what intellectuals said they didn't like about Croce and to see what they wanted instead. And if Croce was simply saying what these critics seemed to assume he was, then their revolt is largely self-explanatory. But what's striking is the widespread misunderstanding or misrepresentation of Croce's position – and of the potential that his historicism afforded for new questions, even new forms of political action. However, Croce himself did not do well at showing how his position was relevant to areas of vital contemporary concern. On the contrary, he seemed rigid – yet slippery and evasive as well. Thus he invited misunderstanding, overreaction – and blanket rejection. To understand Croce's decline, then, it's imperative to have a hard look at what Croce himself said, didn't say, might have said, about matters of crucial concern at the time. I'll focus on three examples – three related areas where Croce was well equipped to force fruitful discussion, but where his input tended to wither instead: first, the meaning of political disagreement; second, the relationship between individual subjectivity and faith in history; and third, the historical interpretation of fascism. I'll have to be sketchy, but we'll get a sense of the areas at issue and the dynamics at work.

The general case against Crocean historicism is relatively familiar. Croce's has seemed an otherworldly, speculative doctrine breeding passivity or quiescence, since whatever happens has its reasons, and since the historical process necessarily brings about the optimal result. Elio Vittorini, launching his review *Politecnico* in 1945, spoke of 'a culture that consoles us in our suffering.' Nicola Chiaromonte referred to Croce as 'Pangloss reborn' in a polemic of 1944. And Guido De Ruggiero worried that Crocean historicism undercuts any impetus for action.[5]

But this is all a little strange, since Croce ridiculed ivory tower intellectuals and sought, again and again, to deny that his historicism justified passivity.[6] Croce claimed, correctly enough, that he offered a way of understanding the meaning of the countless human actions that create reality and generate the historical process. His was a doctrine of action, of the concrete individual reactions to specific situations that continually recreate our world, the only world there is. The mechanism, in Croce's thinking, is free, creative individual decision, because reality is open-ended and can't be pinned down in the sorts of theories or ideologies that might guide us when it's time for action. Reality is a perpetual challenge to each of us – to judge, to respond, to act. As we respond to the present situation, we *interact*, each on the basis of our particular experience so far; the result of the interaction is the next moment of reality. The outcome of the process at each moment is the measure or test of what has gone before – including the commitments of each individual – so there's no warrant for passivity: if you pull back, simply because history will in a sense justify whatever happens, then surely your opponents will prevail. It's up to you. And certainly the judgment of history is never definitive at any particular moment. People continue to react, and the process continues.

Naturally, Italians wondered about the political implications of this line of thinking in the period of reconstruction after fascism. Croce's emphasis on freedom and openness had served as a source of inspiration against fascism, but what did his historicism mean now, in a context of great hopes for renewal, but also dark fears of renewed reaction? Croce had been seeking since the 1920s to show that liberal political forms, and an attitude of humility and tolerance, follow from his basic historicist conception. He wanted, among other things, to undercut the Marxist claim to privilege. From his perspective, there was room for a radical critique of capitalism, as the particular present economic form, but not for an overarching theory, or speculative philosophy of history, affording privileged insight into the way history must move, and ultimately justifying some form of coercion. Anti-capitalists and pro-capitalists interact politically, and the process determines the economic form appropriate to that moment of reality. So even though Croce himself, in his personal political practice, opted for a relatively conservative position, there was no reason why a Crocean historicist could not study the real terrain of Italian society and conclude that radical socio-economic change was required. In the aftermath of fascism, there were obviously important questions about the scope of change necessary, but there were deeper questions about the political process itself, about the implications of the fact that not all agreed about the scope of change necessary. The situation invited some serious discussion about the basis of our interaction with our political opponents – and how we are to understand our disagreement with them. Is one set of political commitments as good as another, as Croce seemed to imply? Do we simply agree to disagree and let the process decide?

Croce refused to be pinned down about the source of our differing political commitments. He was typically vague when he argued, in 1923, that we all respond to a given situation differently, according to our temperament, our hopes and fears, the vocation we feel within us, the commitments to which we feel tied, the faith we have in certain people and certain things.[7] Ultimately, this indeterminacy of motives means that everybody counts; everybody's experience sums up one chunk of reality. But almost in spite of himself, Croce stuck in qualifiers that suggested the possibility of qualitative differentiation: *if* you act with purity and humility of heart, he said; *if* you are honest; *if* you act with a pure mind, in obedience to an inner command.[8] There seems to be just enough of an opening here for – to take the most obvious example – the Marxist concept of ideology, as one account of the impurity in certain political commitments. But the possibility of seeing through the commitments of political opponents raises questions about what it means to take those opponents seriously. In rethinking the bases of liberalism, Croce had shown that we can act with a measure of humility, even though we are convinced of the rightness of our particular cause, as long as each of us recognizes that our experience is partial, that we are only part of the whole. But this line of argument seemed to be evading part of the question, particularly in light of the touchy situation after fascism. After all, what happens to that humility once you have come to believe you can see a systematic source of impurity in the commitments of your opponents?

In the climate of recrimination in Italy after fascism, it was certainly tempting to use variations on Marxist categories to dismiss the opposition, and this, of course, helped to produce intolerance and extremism in political interaction. Despite his 'pure heart' qualifier, Croce was in a position to propose an important limit, but its nature could emerge, and its value could be debated, only if he was willing to open up a little on the question of political commitments and disagreements, approaching with greater imagination the Marxist concept of ideology.[9] The key was to show that exposure of the systematic impurity in the commitments of others could be done – had to be done – within the framework of historicist humility.

Croce could have begun by admitting that the ideology concept, for example, can have a legitimate part in political debate, as I try to show that my opponents' position reflects a systematic misreading of the present situation. But he could then have gone on to argue that my charge, even if it ultimately proves to have been correct, is but an aspect of the process of political interaction. The fact that I can see through the commitments of some others doesn't mean that I have a privileged grasp of the process as a whole, for my commitments, too, are partial and limited, and they too may be impure in some way. If my commitments do indeed reflect a superior reading of present possibilities, this will come to light in the outcome of our interaction, at the next stage of the process. In other words, part of what we do, in the political interaction that the liberal framework makes possible, is to try to identify and explain the elements of impurity in the commitments of our opponents. But since this clash of ideas is simply part of the process, it need not involve a claim to privilege that justifies dismissing or coercing others. So while Croce's 'pure heart' qualifier interjects the possibility of qualitative differentiation among political commitments, he could still have argued that only the process decides, only the outcome of our present interaction provides the measure of our competing attempts to deconstruct the positions of our opponents.

Since he failed to consider more explicitly the question of qualitative differentiation among political commitments, and since he refused to deal convincingly with the ideology category, Croce's concept of political motivation, his emphasis on our equality in freedom, seemed hopelessly abstract. And his critique of Marxism, charging the Marxists with utopianism, with an almost infantile inability to accept the permanence of conflict and struggle, seemed disappointingly crude – mere propaganda, in fact. Croce was in a position to have forced debate on a crucial set of questions about political interaction, but the tendency to reduce and devalue others was so pronounced in Italian politics that he remained quite rigid, refusing to open up at all on these questions about ideology, impurity, and disagreement. As a result, it was easy to conclude that Croce had nothing to say about this set of issues, and thus the limits he could have proposed, from his historicist position, did not have to be considered.

Croce's repeated insistence, in response to the arguments of critics like De Ruggiero, that there's no transcendent searchlight to guide us, that commitment and action is up to the free individual, suggests the possibility of a dialogue with existentialism, one of the relatively new sets of ideas competing for the attention of Italian intellectuals during the 1940s. Croce's emphasis on the pure heart of individual commitment recalls the Sartrean imperative of authenticity, and of course both Crocean historicism and existentialism were aspects of the contemporary reaction against traditional philosophy in the name of action and concreteness. But despite the attempt of Enzo Paci from the existentialist side, the dialogue was minimal.[10] Croce ridiculed existentialism again and again, while leading existentialists like Nicola Abbagnano often portrayed their doctrine as fundamentally a reaction against Croce's position. Abbagnano complained that Croce's faith in the overarching rationality of history meant a neglect of individual subjectivity, of the phenomenology of personal choice in the human situation of risk, of 'thrownness.' Indeed, the Crocean individual, in Abbagnano's interpretation, was but a manifestation or instrument of some higher spiritual force.[11] More generally, Italian existentialism gave expression to a fairly widespread dissatisfaction with the apparent optimism of Croce's historicism, its faith in the positive nature of history.[12]

Croce complained that the existentialists were misrepresenting him, failing to distinguish his absolute historicism from the old Hegelian variety, with its overarching telos.[13] And certainly Croce had a point; as the years had worn on, he had become ever more insistent on precisely the distinction that Abbagnano refused to make. For Croce, the individual isn't the instrument of anything higher; rather, one is part of something larger – our fundamentally historical human reality. There is only this collection of individual particles, which develop reality – and generate the historical process – through their free creative responses to each present situation. Certainly there is tragedy – especially because individuals are often submerged by processes they don't understand – and thus Croce always emphasized courage. But his position did invite misunderstanding, largely because of his emphasis on faith in history – even in the 'providential' nature of history. After fascism, genocide, and total war, and with the advent of the atomic age, this Crocean theme seemed quaint, to put it charitably. To respond more effectively to the existentialists, Croce needed to explain more fully the relationship between free, creative individual choice and the 'rationality' of the historical process. Did faith in history somehow make it unnecessary, or illegitimate, to say more about personal subjectivity?

Croce was rigid here partly because of a certain puritanical streak, which produced a stern moral disapproval of existentialist emphases. His conception surely had a vital place for personal subjectivity: of course there was risk and anxiety and finitude; of course there was loneliness in individual responsibility and decision. But it was unseemly, even adolescent, to dwell on this aspect of reality, to beat one's breast and wring one's hands with angst. Croce valued the courage of individuals who do what they take to be their duty without making a spectacle of themselves in this way. The disciplined serenity in action that Croce emphasized made it seem as if he had less room than he did for the dimension of personal subjectivity, made it seem as if he was submerging the individual into some overarching process.

But Croce's personal disapproval of existentialism reflected a deeper difference in perceptions. From Croce's perspective, the existentialist preoccupation with individual subjectivity portended nihilism and irrationalism. If we move inward, focusing on the finite individual personality, we encounter the certainty of the death of the subjective particle. Things seem disconnected, absurd: there's no reason for anything; nothing lasts; nothing matters. Thus Croce found preoccupation with death and nothingness to be the core of existentialism and stressed the sterility of its implications.[14] The antidote was what Croce had advocated for decades – to move in the opposite direction, away from the very mortal person and outward, to the immortality of one's actions, which necessarily find their way into history, the only reality there is. History 'overarches' the individual only in the completely neutral sense that each individual is part of a process that will continue after death, and that will in some sense embody his or her actions. History is rational only in a comparably general sense: reality is such that what we do makes a difference, that stronger and more realistic commitments are likely to have a greater impact than weaker and less realistic ones, and that the outcome at the next moment in the process is ultimately, on some level, a fair judgment of what we have done. This very general faith in history affords the courage to act, in the face of our finitude and mortality as individuals, but it does not in any way absolve us of individual responsibility for decision and action, or diminish the drama of every personal commitment, since there's no overarching direction or goal. Croce seems to have felt that to dwell on the dimension of personal subjectivity would undermine this courage, and lead, if not to nihilism, to a premium on the irrational gesture, as opposed to the disciplined action that contributes to the development of reality.

So there remained a gulf between Croce and the existentialists, while there could have been a fruitful dialogue. Croce's unwillingness to 'give' more in the area of personal subjectivity meant that he could easily be misunderstood – and misrepresented – as if he were saying that the benign historical process takes care of everything, a notion that seemed almost gratuitously absurd at a time when much of Europe stood in ruins. Of course, that's not what he meant to say; a dialogue with the existentialists would have forced him to clarify, and perhaps refine, his conception of the crucial relationship between historical consciousness and individual experience. And then, to reverse the coin, the contribution he could have made to clarifying the limits of some basic existentialist insights might have been more effectively considered as well.

Croce's historicism, of course, affords not only the courage to act; it also specifies, in historical understanding, a mode of knowledge that prepares action. Our reaction against some present situation is more that a self-indulgent gesture insofar as we understand that situation in terms of its historical development.[15] Thinking Italians who were trying to get their bearings in light of fascism, war, and defeat were bound to ask what Croce was prepared to deliver in terms of historical understanding, but, here again, Croce proved disappointing.

In devising his conception of ethical-political history in the early 1920s, Croce had abandoned a more flexible earlier conception, which had had room, for example, for historical materialism as one canon of interpretation.[16] For the later Croce, history was to study the leading ideals of a period, and these were necessarily associated with some sort of moral elite. Croce was reacting against several historiographical traditions that he felt had too little room for the free creativity of individual action, but his single-minded emphasis on the thread of freedom meant a neglect of the structuring aspect of the historical process – and thus a neglect of the problems to which the free human spirit responds. Italians hoping for orientation through history after fascism were bound to be a bit puzzled: if liberty is the true and only subject of any history, as Croce liked to proclaim, if history traces the free, creative thread, then how can historical inquiry illuminate present problems, thereby preparing present action?[17] A Crocean history might provide inspiration, or demonstrate the excesses in various deterministic interpretations, but this was hardly to live up to the promise of providing a modicum of usable knowledge. As everyone quickly came to recognize, Croce's famous histories of Italy and Europe were not open-ended inquiries intended to illuminate present problems and possibilities – useful though they may have been in the struggle against fascism.[18]

To show how to write usable history from the perspective of absolute historicism, Croce needed, first, to consider more fully the degrees and varieties of the 'political' passion inevitable in any true work of history. This required that he say more about the difference between history as 'oratory' intended to *inspire* action, and history as a relatively open-ended inquiry intended to provide the understanding necessary for action to be effective.[19] And second, he needed more room for analysis of the structured problems that result from past actions, and that give rise to new creative responses. Given the claims being made for social science, on the one hand, and Marxism, on the other, Croce had always sought to protect the autonomy of history, which, in his account, studies the unique, particular, open-ended process, generated by the free, creative human spirit. But it is not a violation of the basic historicist conception, or a lapse into the sociological heresy, to recognize that the unique process generates structured obstacles, including mentalities, which must be destructured if they are to be confronted effectively. Had Croce maintained his earlier dialogue with Marxism, and particularly had he considered more explicitly the concept of ideology, he would surely have worked toward a more convincing and illuminating conception.

The test came with the historical interpretation of fascism, for to come to terms with fascism was surely essential if Italy was to proceed with maximum effectiveness after the Second World War. And Croce, with his restricted arsenal of interpretive weapons, didn't have much to offer. In a well-known lecture of 1950, he admitted that he hated fascism too much to write its history.[20] One could sympathize, though Croce's reluctance called into question the basic premise of historicist historiography. But of course he had by now already said a great deal about fascism, and he had inevitably offered a historical interpretation, relying primarily on his well-known 'parenthesis' thesis. Fascism, he suggested, was a disease stemming from a germ that was by no means specifically Italian, one that had been nurtured by the war experience, especially, in the otherwise healthy adolescent body of the Italian nation.[21] No one would accept this view as it stands, but Croce had a point here that would have been helpful had it been interjected in a more convincing way into the inevitable debate about fascism. He was seeking, above all, to deflate fascism, against the persistent tendency to portray it as an indictment of *everything* that had gone before – of the whole experience of liberal Italy, as for Ferruccio Parri, even of the whole of previously existing culture, as for Elio Vittorini.[22] Croce wanted to surround fascism, to get its dimensions straight, to get the proportions of the problem right. Even the fact that fascism had lasted for two decades did not indicate, for example, that Italy required radical socio-economic change if it was to return to liberal democracy.

But Croce seemed to be sidestepping the major questions. To make a more convincing case along these lines, he needed more room for the fortuitous in history, in order that he could show that the fascist regime had fed on itself – that it is fallacious to assume, with Alberto Asor Rosa, for example, that all of fascism must have had its source in, must somehow have been contained within, liberal Italy.[23] But for Croce to have emphasized the fortuitous, in light of his overall emphasis on the rationality of history, would have required some clarification of the interaction of the various levels in his historicist conception. In fact, Croce surely could have found room for this sort of fortuitousness, but since he didn't offer the necessary clarification, his conception of fascism seemed almost trivial, and his attempt to deflate the phenomenon seemed merely a conservative political ploy.

But, of course, even if it might be possible to restrict the dimensions of the problem of fascism, some core of fascist aspirations would remain to be explained. Croce insisted that they could not be explained in terms of socio-economic class, but he could usefully have gone a step further, in light of his ethical-political conception, to probe for the element of rationality in fascist aspirations.[24] Croce would have been truer to his historicist orientation, and thus more convincing overall, had he admitted that fascism resulted, in some measure, from a creative attempt to respond to perceived inadequacies in the established political traditions, as crystallized in the period immediately after the First World War. Those fascist aspirations were obviously flawed in a number of ways, but Croce need not have denied them a place in the ongoing attempt, in modern Western culture, to find the political forms most congruent with our present possibilities as human beings. In implying that we had in some sense found the political answers, Croce violated the most fundamental historicist tenet – that the human spirit is never satisfied, that we constantly struggle for something new in reaction to the inadequacies in what we have created so far. Croce's overarching historicism should have equipped him especially well to place fascism in this kind of perspective, particularly since he opposed the widespread tendency to rely on vaguely Marxist socio-economic class categories in the interpretation of fascism. But merely to talk of a civil depression, or a lowering of the consciousness of liberty, as Croce did in fact, hardly offered a convincing alternative to these generally Marxist categories. Ultimately, Croce's interpretation of fascism seemed hopelessly vacuous and was washed away, but the potentially fruitful contribution that he could have made to the debate on fascism was lost as well.

Intellectuals revolted against Croce, then, not merely because he was old-hat, but because he didn't seem to have anything convincing to say on a number of matters of immediate concern, including the three we have just considered. At a moment of dramatic collective decision for his culture, Croce seemed to offer a sterile conception of liberty, an empty faith in history, and an evasive, politically expedient interpretation of fascism. His inadequacies in these specific areas led people to infer that Croce's whole historicist conception was vacuous and irrelevant. And not only was there apparently a hole, or hollowness, in Croce, but he seemed to want to preclude asking certain questions that clearly needed to be asked. I have suggested that Croce had more to contribute to the discussion of these issues than was generally recognized at the time, but that he had to say more if the ongoing value of his conception as a framework for understanding and action was to be clear. And from within the framework of his absolute historicism, there was more he could have said about such matters as political interaction and disagreement, the relationship between individual subjectivity and historical consciousness, and the historical meaning of fascism. But to have made the contribution he might have made, Croce had to be more flexible, more willing to reach out and invite dialogue, more willing to admit that these were open questions.

Croce remained inflexible partly, no doubt, because he feared that, given the sometimes extreme claims of his opponents, what he offered would be contaminated or lost if he gave any ground at all. But, in addition, the mode of argument, and the rhetorical devices, that had served him so well in times past now contributed to his decline. The serene confidence and sense of direction that made him exciting for a few years after 1902, then reassuring under fascism, didn't equip him very well for the dialogue that new challenges demanded. That confidence made him appear almost ridiculous once it became clear that he wasn't prepared to treat the questions we have discussed as open questions, but as questions to which he had the answers, answers that should be obvious to any sensible person. Those who could see that the answers weren't at all obvious were quick to dismiss him, not fully realizing what was being lost to Italian culture as a result. The most sensitive, like Luigi Russo, recognized that Croce had always been especially fruitful as the basis for confrontation with an opposing position.[25] And I have suggested that Croce, in confrontation with the vaguely Marxist devaluation of political opponents, with the existentialist emphasis on individual subjectivity, and the general tendency to inflate fascism, offered a set of limits that could usefully have been debated. But by the end of the 1940s, Russo, too, had grown exasperated, finally dismissing Croce as a bitter and withered old man.[26]

chapter 4

Croce in America: Influence, Misunderstanding, and Neglect

(with a supplement on the fortunes of Giovanni Gentile in the United States and Canada)

This piece has a somewhat complicated publication history, and some of the particulars are found in the author's note below, which originally appeared to introduce the version reproduced here. I began the project when Claudio Cesa of the philosophy faculty at the Scuola Normale Superiore in Pisa invited me to contribute an article on the reception Croce and Gentile in the United States for a special issue of *Giornale critico della filosofia italiana* to commemorate the centennial of the initial collaboration between the two thinkers in 1896. In light of the importance, especially to Gentile studies, of the noted British-born philosopher and historian of philosophy H.S. Harris, who worked primarily in Canada, it seemed essential to cast a glance – a less-than-systematic glance, to be sure – at Canada as well. Once I had submitted the piece to *Giornale critico,* but before it had appeared in print, I adapted it, at the invitation of Professor Cesa, for a lecture at the Scuola Normale Superiore in Pisa, presented 14 April 1994.

After the essay had appeared in *Giornale critico,* Claes Ryn invited me to adapt the Croce portion (which had ended up constituting the great majority) of the original article for publication in *Humanitas.* I reproduce here the piece as it appeared in *Humanitas* 8, no. 2 (1995): 3–34. For this version I slightly expanded and revised the Croce portions of the *Giornale critico* article and dropped the section on Gentile. I also adjusted the original introduction and conclusion to reflect the changed focus. To make available here the original material on Gentile, I include as a supplement sections 1, 5, and 6 of the English version of the original article. The core is section 5, but I thought it best also to include the original introduction and conclusion to indicate my way of presenting together the fortunes of the two thinkers in North America.

I regret that in preparing my article, I did not know of Lienhard Bergel, 'Croce in America' (1953), now in his *L'estetica del nichilismo e altri saggi* (Naples: Bibliopolis, 1980), 31–4. I am grateful to Emanuele Cutinelli-Rèndina for indicating this reference to me. I have found Bergel's accents to be fully congruent with the findings of the present study. Assessing the situation at about the time of Croce's death, which occasioned some new American discussion of the Crocean legacy, Bergel lamented that whereas the Americans could have learned much from Croce, he had been poorly understood in the United States. To be sure, Croce had been central to the annual conferences on Italian culture sponsored by the Casa Italiana at Columbia University, but that discussion did not reach beyond the restricted circle of Italian-speaking specialists to affect the wider mainstream of American culture.

Bergel pinpointed three factors that continued to inhibit a deeper encounter: the particular hegemony of the natural sciences in America, which had of course affected the priorities of philosophy as well as cultural discussion more generally; the American way of distinguishing theory and practice, which had kept Americans from grasping the import of Croce's way of relating them; and the lack of acquaintance with Vico, which had facilitated the widespread but erroneous assumption that Croce's thought was basically an offshoot of Hegelianism. Vico was known especially in connection with James Joyce's *Finnegan's Wake* – not, Bergel noted coyly, the optimum vehicle. In connection with Vico, Bergel cited one article that I knew and should have mentioned, A. William Salomone's 'The "New Sciences" of History in Italian Thought: Machiavelli, Vico, and Croce,' which was originally presented at a conference at Columbia University in April 1951 on the Italian contribution to Western culture, then published in the proceedings of the conference, *Italian Culture and the Western Tradition* (New York: Vanni [Ragusa], 1951), 8–20. Salomone illuminated Croce's itinerary by indicating briefly both what Croce took from Vico and what he rejected in the Vichian legacy. The volume itself, however, was hardly imposing in physical terms and could have done little to raise Croce's profile in the United States.

Bergel concluded that America was simply not yet ready for Croce. For the present, then, the task could only be patient criticism and clarification. To which one might be tempted to add, over half a century later, *plus ça change* ...

I also did not know, when preparing the present essay, that my friend and fellow Croce scholar M.E. Moss was doing a similar piece, though she treated the reception of Croce in the United States only to 1950. Presented originally as a conference paper in Naples, her article was then published as 'Benedetto Croce negli Stati Uniti,' in *I progressi della filosofia nell'Italia del Novecento* (Naples: Morano, 1992). She and I have since exchanged our two pieces and have noted the substantial areas of agreement in our assessments.

Additional relevant work has of course appeared since the present essay was published. Although I will not attempt to survey it systematically here, several items should be mentioned. Emanuele Cutinelli-Rèndina has prepared an exemplary edition of Croce's correspondence with Joel Spingarn, who figures prominently in the present essay as the first to champion Croce's work in the United States. See Emanuele Cutinelli-Rèndina, ed., *Carteggio Croce-Spingarn* (Bologna: Il Mulino [for the Istituto italiano per gli studi storici], 2001). On Gentile, we now have brief books by A. James Gregor, *Giovanni Gentile: Philosopher of Fascism* (New Brunswick, NJ: Transaction Publishers, 2001); and M.E. Moss, *Mussolini's Fascist Philosopher: Giovanni Gentile Reconsidered* (New York: Lang, 2004). Gregor has also made available, in superior English translations, several of Gentile's most important works on fascism; see Giovanni Gentile, *Origins and Doctrine of Fascism, with Selections from Other Works,* trans., ed., and annot. A. James Gregor (New Brunswick, NJ: Transaction Publishers, 2002). Gregor's account in these recent works does not add substantially to the interpretation he had advanced in works cited in the supplement to the present essay.

Whereas it would be too strong to suggest a new wave of interest in Gentile has developed over the past decade, it is significant that the *Journal of Modern History,* the most important U.S. journal devoted to modern European history, published a good introduction to recent Gentile scholarship by Gentile's leading Italian biographer; see Gabriele Turi, 'Giovanni Gentile: Oblivion, Remembrance, and Criticism,' trans. Lydia G. Cochrane, *Journal of Modern History* 70, no. 4 (December 1998): 913–33. Mention should also be made of Abbott Gleason's use of Gentile in his *Totalitarianism: The Inner History of the Cold War* (New York: Oxford University Press, 1995); I discuss this item in a bit more detail in the introduction to the present collection (see p. 25). I might also note that the overall argument of my book *The Totalitarian Experiment in Twentieth-Century Europe: Understanding the Poverty of Great Politics* (London: Routledge, 2006) reflects my engagement with Gentile and offers sustained discussion of Gentile at several points. (See note 31 in the introduction to the present volume.)

In light of the importance of H.S. Harris's engagement with Gentile, mention should also be made of the special issue of *Clio: A Journal of Literature, History and the Philosophy of History* (27, no. 4 [Summer 1998]) devoted to Harris's life and work. This issue carries the overall title 'H.S. Harris and the Vocation of a Scholar.' See especially Harris's memoir, 'Philosophy and Life' (pp. 485–500), and Rik Peters, 'Talking to Ourselves or Talking to Others: H.S. Harris on Gentile's Transcendental Dialogue' (pp. 501–14).

Author's Note: This article has been adapted from my 'La fortuna di Croce e Gentile negli Stati Uniti,' which was invited for inclusion in 'Croce e Gentile un secolo dopo,' special issue, *Giornale critico della filosofia italiana* 73, nos. 2–3

(May–December 1994): 253–81. The editors of that journal asked me to treat both Benedetto Croce and Giovanni Gentile and to give the article a strong bibliographical dimension. At the suggestion of Claes G. Ryn, the editor of *Humanitas,* I have dropped the section on Gentile and expanded the sections on Croce in preparing the present version. Although this essay retains the bibliographical dimension of the original, I have sought here to probe the substantive issues more deeply. The present article is published with the permission of the editors of *Giornale critico della filosofia italiana.*

1: Introduction

Benedetto Croce (1866–1952) was the leading Italian intellectual of the first half of the twentieth century and one of Europe's best-known public figures by the 1940s. The pioneering review he launched in 1903, *La critica,* is to be found in virtually every American research library, as are many of his more than eighty books. First in aesthetics and literary criticism, beginning in about 1910, and then in historiography, beginning in about 1920, Croce's ideas were prominent in American discussion – and remained so into the 1960s. For much of that time, his status as one of the notable European thinkers of the century was taken for granted. Moreover, he was long respected as a champion of 'the religion of liberty' in opposition to fascism. An influential Italian-American scholar, writing in 1937, found him 'the most famed Italian abroad, at least in the scholarly world, since the days perhaps of Galileo.'[1] But Croce did not attract major disciples in the United States or become involved in sustained exchange with American thinkers. Indeed, his ideas were frequently misrepresented, and since the early 1970s he has been virtually forgotten.[2]

The prestige of historical figures rises and falls, and the tendency for the biggest to fall hardest may be especially prevalent in intellectual history. But there seems something anomalous about Croce's case, as René Wellek, the distinguished historian of criticism, has recently emphasized. He noted that in movements influential at various points since Croce's death – from Russian formalism and structuralism to hermeneutics and deconstruction – Croce 'is not referred to or quoted, even when he discusses the same problems and gives similar solutions.' Yet Croce, for Wellek, was arguably the most erudite and wide-ranging figure in the history of criticism.[3]

Croce's fate seems to constitute a potentially significant chapter in the ongoing intellectual history of the West. As Wellek implies, the major questions at issue cannot be confined to a national level – and they admit of no easy answers. Even in Italy, there remains disagreement about the centre of gravity and the enduring import of Croce's intellectual legacy. And because there is no settled criterion, the basis of any misunderstanding is hard to assess. Still, it is worth proceeding country by country in asking the central questions about Croce's fate, not least because, in each case, the answers may reveal idiosyncratic blind spots and significant contingencies in the intellectual histories of the countries at issue. What, then, is the place of the United States in the larger story of Croce's fate? What was noted and what was missed when the Americans encountered Croce?

When Croce first became known in this country, around the turn of the century, he had only recently come to prominence in Italy – in the debate over the scientific status of historical knowledge. His idiosyncratic contribution led him to an aestheticist theory of knowing, based partly on Giambattista Vico, that he outlined in his *Aesthetic* of 1902, the book that brought him to international prominence. With the young philosopher Giovanni Gentile (1875–1944) as his junior partner, Croce launched *La critica* the next year. Now attracting an array of followers, he quickly became a focal point for young Italians of the emerging modernist avant-garde.

In Italy and abroad, Croce and Gentile were promptly lumped together and identified as neo-idealists or neo-Hegelians. But while those labels were used in the United States as well, Americans almost never considered the two thinkers in tandem.[4] Whereas Croce's work in aesthetics drew interest immediately, Gentile began to attract attention only after the First World War, first as a philosopher of education and educational reformer. Although Croce wrote a laudatory introduction to Gentile's *The Reform of Education*, published in the United States in 1922, he and Gentile had begun to fall out over strictly philosophical matters in 1913, when it became clear that Gentile was far more committed to a rigorous idealism, and to philosophical system-building, than was Croce. After the two diverged politically in 1925, in response to the challenge of fascism, Croce levelled some of his most bitter polemics against Gentile and his effort at a systematic recasting of the idealist tradition.

Nevertheless, Croce was quickly typed as a 'neo-idealist' or 'neo-Hegelian' by American critics, and this made it difficult for his ideas seriously to penetrate American culture. There had been an idealist moment in the United States, but idealism was receding by the first years of the century, when Croce and Gentile were establishing themselves as major figures in Italy. So to characterize the Italians as neo-idealists seemed to warrant boxing them out, without seriously confronting what was innovative in their thinking. Whereas in England such philosophers as Bernard Bosanquet, J.A. Smith, Herbert Wildon Carr, and R.G. Collingwood seriously confronted the thought of both Croce and Gentile, neither of the two Italians had any such resonance among major philosophers in the United States.[5]

As Croce's thought developed, it became ever clearer that the neo-idealist characterization simply did not fit him, though it was indeed appropriate to Gentile. Even in essays translated into English, Croce protested against the label 'Italian neo-idealism' and the persistent tendency to identify him with Hegel.[6] For Croce, philosophical system-building was beside the point, and he eventually concluded that the very term *idealism* ought to be abandoned altogether.[7] Writing in the influential *Journal of Aesthetics and Art Criticism* in 1952, Frederic Simoni showed that the idealist stereotype had nurtured a whole tradition of misunderstanding around Croce in America. Simoni concluded, without exaggeration, that 'reference to Croce in current literature constitutes a comedy of errors.'[8]

Even apart from Croce's association with an unfashionable idealism, American ways of viewing the Italian thinker tended to discourage sustained engagement. Croce was variously typed as a romantic, an expressionist, a primitivist, and a partisan of irresponsible private imagination. Such characterizations meshed uneasily with the charge of hyper-rationalism or hypertrophy of philosophy that was implicit in the attribution of neo-Hegelianism – an indication of the difficulty Americans had in grasping the centre of gravity of Croce's thought. In fact, Croce's novelty lay partly in his way of reconceiving the relationship between imagination and intellect.

Even those relatively sympathetic to Croce and his collaborators sometimes viewed him as central to an interesting but provincially Italian culture, not quite part of the European mainstream. John Crowe Ransom, who helped spearhead 'the new criticism' in American literary studies, took inspiration from Croce and recent Italian thinkers – but on the basis of a curious sense of what those thinkers had achieved. Writing to Allen Tate in 1927, Ransom expressed the hope that he and Tate might revive 'southernism' in the United States just as Croce and one or two others seemed to have spearheaded a revival of Italianism among the younger generation of Italians.[9] There is some justification for this perspective in the case of Gentile, who became preoccupied with the Italian tradition, but Croce was arguably the most cosmopolitan European intellectual of his time. Ransom's characterization did not remotely represent Croce's cultural aspiration or achievement.

Over the years, to be sure, a handful of significant American intellectuals, from Joel Spingarn and Carl Becker to René Wellek and Hayden White, sought seriously to engage Croce's thought. But there would seem to have been room for a more fruitful interchange between Croce and the Americans.[10] It did not help, to be sure, that Douglas Ainslie, whom Croce authorized to translate his central philosophical works, most notably *Aesthetic*, *Logic*, and *The Philosophy of the Practical*, was not quite up to the task. His translations were often clumsily literal, and, as Gian N.G. Orsini has emphasized, they conveyed a misleading sense of crucial Crocean terms like *intuizione* and *fantasia*. But such mistranslations were not decisive. Some of Croce's leading American detractors read him in Italian; other English translations of his works were highly competent, even superb.[11] So we must look deeper to make sense of Croce's fortunes within the culture of the United States.

2: The Implications of Croce's Aesthetics

Even before Croce published his *Aesthetic* in 1902, the influential review *The Nation* had begun following his ideas, thanks especially to Joel Spingarn, a young literary scholar who would become Croce's first influential American partisan. Having just discovered Croce's work, Spingarn began corresponding with the Italian thinker in 1899.[12] In brief, unsigned notes in *The Nation* thereafter, Spingarn discussed first Croce's preliminary 'Tesi fondamentali di un'estetica' in 1900, then his full-scale *Aesthetic* in 1902.[13] Moreover, Spingarn helped spearhead the new *Journal of Comparative Literature*, which offered in 1903 what proved an especially influential review of Croce's book.

The reviewer was the philosopher George Santayana, who found Croce's conception abstract, artificial, barren – as was only to be expected, said Santayana, from a 'strictly transcendental philosophy' like Croce's.[14] To be sure, Croce's seminal work of 1902 was not quite what it first seemed. It became ever clearer that in dealing with imagination, intuition, and expression as he did, Croce was not offering what Santayana was expecting, a contribution to the delimited philosophy of art and criticism; rather, Croce was sketching the contours of a radically historicist view of the world. But Santayana was particularly ill-disposed toward Croce's enterprise, and he remained a prominent antagonist, later associating Croce with an aestheticist espousal of 'art for art's sake,' the antithesis of what Croce's 'aestheticism' in fact involved.[15]

Croce's early advocate, Spingarn, was better able to grasp the wider implications of Croce's evolving aesthetics, though even his reading was simplified and selective. Newly appointed professor of comparative literature at Columbia University, Spingarn explicitly proclaimed himself a Crocean in a widely discussed lecture entitled 'The New Criticism' in 1910.[16] Croce had showed, above all, that art was genuine creation, as opposed to mimesis – the expression or representation of something already in existence. And on that basis Spingarn made the soon-to-be-familiar Crocean arguments against moral judgments in art, against fixed genres, rhetorical figures, and rules of decorum, and against reductionist explanations in terms of race, the environment, or 'the times.'[17]

By the second decade of the century, Croce's aesthetics had made his a fashionable name among intellectuals. Thus he was one of twelve scholars from around the world to be invited to present lectures marking the inauguration of the Rice Institute in Houston in 1912. While declining to attend personally, Croce submitted one of his best-known essays, 'Breviario di estetica,' translated by Douglas Ainslie and published immediately as part of the Rice proceedings.[18]

Meanwhile, Joel Spingarn was forced to leave Columbia in a dispute over academic freedom in 1911. But he continued to develop his ideas, always with an eye to Croce, while also becoming active in other pursuits, most notably as a leader in the National Association for the Advancement of Colored People. He also helped establish, in 1919, the important publishing house Harcourt, Brace and Company, which would play an active role in disseminating the work of Croce, Gentile, and other leading contemporary European intellectuals in the United States.

That publisher brought out in 1922 the first full-length study of Croce in this country – by Raffaello Piccoli, an Italian who had found his way to America after studying philosophy in England. In his preface, Piccoli noted that as a student in Italy he had been 'a fervid and enthusiastic follower' of Croce, who had seemed to offer 'the only safe path between the two precipices of a pseudo-scientific materialism on the one hand, and of a mysticism on the other.' But study in England, Piccoli continued, had then exposed him to a very different philosophical tradition – weaning him from his earlier idealism and dogmatism.[19] The implication that Croce's thinking was a dogmatic idealism thus cast a shadow over Piccoli's book. And though Piccoli offered a solid introduction to the basics of Croce's formal philosophy, his conclusion that Croce's greatest achievement was likely to prove his elevation of the economic principle could only have thrown American readers off track.[20] Although Croce's economic category did afford an opening for the questions Piccoli had in mind about nature, the body, and the passions, Americans who found these the key questions were bound to find Croce thin fare when compared with Freud, or with those philosophers who continued to afford cultural privilege to the scientific quest to understand the natural world.

Joel Spingarn sought to head off the misconceptions that were coming to surround Croce's work in the United States, especially the assumption that Croce stood for romantic indulgence and 'art for art's sake.' In 'The Growth of a Literary Myth' (1923), Spingarn responded to H.L. Mencken, the noted iconoclastic essayist, who had criticized the 'Croce-Spingarn-Carlyle-Goethe theory' in response to Spingarn's essays.[21] Spingarn admitted that he had been trying to adapt Croce for an American audience, but he hoped he had not been responsible for the worst of the current misconceptions – the notion that Croce stood for emotional debauch, when in fact Croce had been seeking to transcend the romantic-classic antithesis altogether.

Aesthetics was also the focus of Croce's best known exchange with an American thinker, the noted pragmatist John Dewey.[22] Croce and Dewey had played comparable roles in their respective cultures, and despite substantial differences, there was scope for a significant dialogue between them. The two thinkers respected each other, even as they recognized their difference over philosophical postulates that were fundamental in one sense, secondary in another. Croce explicitly noted that despite those differences, he and Dewey were both seeking to account for the world in terms of human freedom, and he sent heartfelt greetings on the occasion of Dewey's ninetieth birthday in 1949.[23] But when, late in the lives of both, the two finally confronted each other, their intellectual encounter did not live up to its potential.[24]

Although Croce had long given pragmatism credit for accenting the creative or constructive role of the knower, he believed the pragmatists had not been thoroughgoing enough in eschewing the old empiricism. Thus they had remained caught up in the dualism of mind and nature.[25] Dewey, for his part, had treated Croce dismissively in his key work on aesthetics, *Art as Experience*, published in 1934. As Dewey had it, Croce's way of emphasizing intuition and expression stemmed from his deeper idealism, taking only mind as real, and indicated 'the extreme to which philosophy may go in superimposing a preconceived theory upon aesthetic experience, resulting in arbitrary distortion.'[26] Croce took considerable offence at Dewey's charges.[27]

In an excellent summary of this encounter, George Douglas emphasized that not only was Croce never a Hegelian, but his philosophy of experience was not so different from Dewey's, as outlined in *Experience and Nature.*[28] On the other hand, Croce was not convincing in charging that Dewey, to have gotten so much right, must have been borrowing from the Italians without admitting his debt. Croce was too quick to assume that only his own radically anti-empiricist starting point could lead to an orientation to the world as attuned to human freedom and creativity as Dewey's. Though their terminology differed, Croce and Dewey had more in common than either recognized, especially in their common accent on the continuity of art with ordinary experience. So there was scope for a considerably more fruitful encounter than in fact developed.

Interest in Dewey's work has recently revived in the United States, thanks especially to the influential neo-pragmatism of Richard Rorty. But this revival has brought little attention to the possibility of confronting Dewey with Croce. Among recent students of Dewey, Thomas Alexander has offered the most discerning assessment of Dewey's aesthetics, including Dewey's exchange with Croce and the charge of Croce and others that Dewey's aesthetics betrays unacknowledged elements of idealism.[29] But in other reassessments and reappropriations of Dewey, Croce comes up only in passing, if at all.[30]

In his standard biography of Croce, Italo De Feo suggested that the 'immaturity' of Anglo-Saxon culture, with its materialist, positivist, and pragmatist lags, helps explain the lack of appreciation of Croce in the United States.[31] But De Feo, like Croce himself, was surely too dismissive of pragmatism. Fruitful encounter required greater flexibility on both sides, but Croce was at least flexible enough to jettison idealism as he played up absolute historicism, a move that could have opened the way, at least, to a more fruitful discussion.

Croce's aesthetics continued to attract attention after his death in 1952, but his American commentators generally focused on delimited problems of art and criticism rather than push on to his larger, radically historicist conception of the world. Still, those concentrating on aesthetics produced some of the best work on Croce in English, though they argued among themselves about Croce's centre of gravity. The most important contribution was Gian N.G. Orsini's *Benedetto Croce: Philosopher of Art and Literary Critic*, which pointed out flaws in earlier accounts, and which remains one of the best studies of Croce's aesthetics in any language. But Patrick Romanell, Merle Brown, and Giovanni Gullace also contributed significant works.[32] Whereas Orsini found discrete phases in Croce's aesthetic thought, Romanell, for example, highlighted Croce's ongoing insistence on the cognitive significance of art to emphasize the continuity of Croce's thinking.

For about fifteen years after his death in 1952, Croce's thought continued to find a prominent place in major studies of the theory and history of literary criticism. Most important was the chapter entitled 'Expressionism: Benedetto Croce' in the ambitious historical survey published in 1957 by William K. Wimsatt Jr. and Cleanth Brooks, two of the most prominent American literary scholars of the period. In light of all that expressionism had come to mean, however, the title of the chapter was misleading, as was the authors' suggestion that Croce offered 'a master theory of art for art's sake.'[33] Still, Wimsatt and Brooks gave a balanced account of Croce's contributions to criticism and stressed the enduring value of his assault on fixed genres, classical figures of speech, and rules of propriety. And they played up Croce's important, if diffuse, impact: 'The influence of Croce has been like that of Kant in the era 1800 to 1840 in France, of a pervasive and atmospheric kind, blending with a generally favorable climate of opinion so as not always to be clearly distinguishable.'[34]

Croce also drew the continuing interest of René Wellek, perhaps the most distinguished historian of criticism to write in English in the twentieth century. Wellek offered a discerning chapter on Croce in volume 8 (1992) of his monumental *History of Modern Criticism*, but he also considered Croce's influence in the United States in volume 6 (1986) and in essays over several decades.[35]

At the same time, Croce continued to serve as a basis for comparison in works on literary contemporaries who might usefully have engaged his work more systematically. John Paul Russo, author of a monumental intellectual biography of I.A. Richards, offered a penetrating comparison of Croce and Richards in 1991.[36] But his way of using the notorious term historicism interjected a note of ambiguity into his account. As Russo emphasized, Croce's early aesthetics was *anti*-historicist in its reaction against the widespread effort to explain the work of art in terms of historical context or a chain of historical antecedents. But by specifying the scope for creativity and novelty, this reaction served Croce's more radically historicist conception of the world, a conception that was more fundamental than a particular approach to *either* art or history. The notion that Croce was opposing historical approaches, while true in a limited sense, made it difficult for American thinkers to penetrate to the core of his thinking.

Although much of the discussion of Croce before 1930 focused on aesthetics and literary criticism, some major American thinkers understood that Croce's aesthetics pointed to a deeper set of questions about cultural priorities. Among the most important were Irving Babbitt and Paul Elmer More, leaders of 'The New Humanism' that emerged before the First World War, then achieved its greatest influence around 1930. But though Babbitt and More understood the high cultural stakes of Croce's enterprise, neither was able to develop a serious dialogue with Croce's work. Discussing Croce in 1925, Babbitt concluded 'that he combines numerous peripheral merits with a central wrongness and at times with something that seems uncomfortably like a central void.' Babbitt was nervous about the radically historicist tendency of Croce's thought, which seemed to dissolve what Babbitt found essential – eternal standards and values.[37]

According to Babbitt, Croce offered a romantic 'cult of intuition in the sense of pure spontaneity and untrammeled expression' and reduced 'art to a sort of lyrical outflow that is not disciplined to any permanent center of judgment.' Croce's failure to impose standards on the flux, Babbitt charged, entailed a kind of acquiescence in history, because everything is a matter of process and a thing is revealed by what it becomes.[38] Croce resembled Henri Bergson in embracing psychic restlessness and change for its own sake. Indeed, in Babbitt's view, Croce, more than anyone, had given philosophical expression to the modern cult of the speed and power of the outer world.[39]

Babbitt did not do justice to Croce's way of meshing human ethical capacity with the growth of the world in history, but in this he was no different from many of Croce's critics on both sides of the Atlantic. Still, Babbitt's association of Croce with a quasi-futurist cult of speed betrayed a fundamental misunderstanding of Croce's thought. Yet Babbitt was arguably one of the finest American thinkers of his generation.

Paul Elmer More did no better as he criticized Croce's *Nuovi saggi di estetica* of 1920.[40] Not only was Croce a Hegelian in More's reading, but Croce's accent on the autonomy of art manifested the romantic cult of genius; Croce's message to creative writers was that they were not bound by the dictates of morality or truth. More found Croce comparable to the surrealists – or even to James Joyce, with his emphasis on a stream of consciousness not subject to purpose or choice. Croce, in short, was central to the disturbing modern tendency to dissolve the humanistic conception of man as a responsible creature with free will. In fact, Croce's central purpose was to make new sense of precisely that humanistic conception, in light of the eclipse of transcendence and the break into a radically historicist culture. More's was surely one of the most bizarre misreadings of Croce ever written.

Croce, for his part, evinced some interest in Babbitt at first, but he simply ignored Babbitt and More after their ill-informed critiques of the 1920s.[41] Joel Spingarn had long criticized Babbitt's misinterpretations, pinpointing much that they had missed.[42] But Spingarn's concern was primarily with aesthetics and criticism, so whereas he usefully clarified, for example, the distinction between specifying what is art and judging artistic quality, he could not address the deeper questions about Croce's radical historicism that were implicit in the critiques of Babbitt and More. The misreadings of the New Humanists thus ended up impeding fruitful encounter with Croce's work, despite Spingarn's effort at damage control.

The relationship between Croce and Babbitt has been at issue in a potentially more useful way in the efforts of the Swedish-born American political theorist Claes G. Ryn to restore Babbitt's thinking to currency. Although he considered Babbitt the most important source for contemporary cultural renewal, Ryn found Croce essential as a complement. In *Will, Imagination and Reason*, published in 1986, Ryn sharply criticized both Babbitt and More for failing to devote more serious study to Croce, especially to Croce's *Filosofia della Pratica*, which developed a conception of the ethical that could usefully have complemented theirs.[43] Although Ryn, in the final analysis, overvalued Croce's formal philosophy and made Croce too much a philosopher of 'eternal values,' he placed Croce in an appropriate framework for comparison.[44] What was at issue, he understood, was not simply aesthetics or even systematic philosophy, but a more general conception of life and culture.

Despite Babbitt's misreadings of Croce, he and the Italian thinker were both seeking a new cultural balance in light of the tendencies toward self-indulgence and romantic excess that the modern cultural situation seemed to invite. But from a Crocean, radically historicist perspective, Babbitt was still assuming a transcendent framework, still operating under the shadow of the old metaphysics. In attacking the views he imputed to Croce and Spingarn in 1918, Babbitt insisted that 'in creation of the first order ... the imagination does not wander aimlessly, but is at work in the service of a supersensuous truth that is not given to man to seize directly ... Creation of this order ... is something more than the intense expression of some expansive ego, whether individual or national.' In art and life, Babbitt went on, 'our whole modern experiment ... is threatened with breakdown, because of our failure to work out new standards with this type of imagination.'[45] Though he shared precisely Babbitt's diagnosis, Croce posited a more novel solution, based on a particular understanding of historical knowing and history-making action, as he sought to show the way to a post-metaphysical moderation.

Whatever the questions that might be raised about Ryn's use of Croce, Ryn has shown the scope for a fruitful comparison between Croce and Babbitt, and his work is essential to any consideration of the relationship between Croce and the Americans. Moreover, his effort is still very much in progress. But though he is a highly independent thinker, Ryn is generally associated with the culture of the American Right. Thus, if successful, his synthesis of Croce and Babbitt would tend to place the Crocean legacy within the conservative intellectual tradition. From the perspective of the present author, Croce is not appropriately viewed as a conservative, and a conservative appropriation is likely to impede the renewed interest that his legacy merits.[46]

3: Historiography and Politics

With the publication of his *History: Its Theory and Practice* in 1921, Croce was thrust into the centre of a lively discussion that had been gathering force in American historiography for over a decade, thanks to pragmatism and the challenge of 'the new history,' proclaimed by James Harvey Robinson in 1912.[47] Whereas pragmatism raised a now-familiar family of questions about the truth-value of historical writing, the new history sought to give historiography greater contemporary import, especially by fostering ties to the new social science. So some of the most innovative American historians were already debating questions about science and objectivity, about the role of the historical inquirer and the uses of historical understanding, when Croce's book appeared.

Croce immediately attracted a number of these historians because he seemed, as the pragmatists did not, to confront the relevant questions, showing how historians might escape the shadow of science to make new sense of what they do. With his insistence that some contemporary concern energizes any genuinely historical inquiry, Croce seemed to offer the necessary alternative to positivist notions that the historian apprehends some past 'thing-in-itself,' as it actually happened. But Croce's were radical ideas, and they repelled some, even as they attracted others. At issue was the problem of relativism, which had become central to Western culture and which Croce claimed to have dissolved.

The most prominent of those to embrace Croce were Charles Beard and Carl Becker, who remain two of the best-known American historians of the century. Although Croce was not the source of their preoccupations, he significantly affected their understanding of the issues and the direction of their responses.[48] Yet so radical did Croce seem that even Becker and Beard approached him with caution.

Becker reviewed works by Croce and James Harvey Robinson in *The New Republic* in 1922. Although he offered a reasonably discerning account of Croce, even explaining Croce's departure from Hegel, Becker gave Robinson the last word on the scope for accelerating the endless process of reconstructing mind.[49] In fact, Croce had room for precisely the reform effort that Becker envisioned; the difference concerned terminology and the levels of action at issue.

In 'Every Man His Own Historian,' his still-famous presidential address to the American Historical Association in 1931, Becker developed Crocean themes further, invoking Croce explicitly on the contemporaneity of historical inquiry and understanding.[50] Although his conception of truth and fancy, fact and interpretation, was ultimately not Crocean, Becker followed Croce in arguing that all knowing is fundamentally historical and bound up with projection into the future. Our accounts are always imaginative constructions; our ways of colouring the past vary with the present needs that lead us to ask historical questions in the first place.[51] Yet Becker also followed Croce in insisting on the other side of the coin: the fact that historical understanding is always contemporary and provisional does not undermine its value; rather, historical understanding is precisely congruent with what we are and what we need. Still, Becker ultimately insisted on an idea of progress that was foreign to Croce. And because he assumed that historical inquiry serves progress, he paid little attention to all that might compromise the truth-value of historical writing.[52]

Charles Beard's encounter with Croce was ultimately less discerning than Becker's, but he too found Croce a welcome ally. As president of the American Historical Association, Beard even invited Croce to come to the United States to address the association's annual meeting in 1933. Croce declined to appear personally, though he accepted Beard's invitation to convey, by letter, his sense of the present state of historiography. Beard included Croce's letter as part of his noted presidential address, 'Written History as an Act of Faith.' And much like Becker two years earlier, Beard invoked by-then familiar Crocean categories to show that the historian does not apprehend the past as it actually happened but selects and orders on the basis of some contemporary concern.[53]

But Beard believed that Croce, with his apparently idealist presuppositions, was going too far in denying any independent reality, any past actuality. As he pondered what the world must be like, Beard found the later Alfred North Whitehead more convincing than Croce, so it is not surprising that many of Beard's accents ultimately diverged from Croce's.[54] From a Crocean perspective, Beard was too quick to settle for a dichotomy of science and faith, without sufficient attention to the sense in which historical inquiry remains rational, and central to a rational response to the world. Beard suggested, for example, that it is only through an act of faith that we understand the historical world in terms of chaos, cycle, or progress. Beard was more concerned than Becker to counter the hegemony of science, yet he was at once troubled and fascinated by the apparently relativistic implications of doing so. As a result, he did not do justice to Croce's way of positing the connection between historical knowing and practical life.[55] More generally, he did not do as well as Becker at conveying Croce's understanding of the place of history in the present cultural economy – and in the ongoing growth of the world.[56]

Whatever its limits, the vogue of Croce among theoretically adventuresome historians like Becker and Beard provoked the worried opposition of others. Attacking the presentist ideas then in the air, Robert Livingston Schuyler made the obvious points in 1932: 'If we study the past not for its own sake, but for the light that it may throw on the present, our attitude toward history is technological and utilitarian, not scientific and disinterested.'[57] Indeed, we would be better able to get at the past as it actually was if we did *not* know subsequent events, or our own contemporary situation. Elsewhere, Schuyler linked Croce's philosophy of absolute immanence to the new relativist physics and denounced both as guides for historians.[58]

The discussion reached a deeper level in 1938 when a promising young philosopher, Maurice Mandelbaum, confronted Croce, Wilhelm

Dilthey, and Karl Mannheim – taken to be the central modern relativists – in *The Problem of Historical Knowledge: An Answer to Relativism.*[59] In a critical review, Croce responded cryptically though effectively, based on his longstanding way of sidestepping the presuppositions that had led us to believe relativism was a problem.[60] But no American, not even Mandelbaum, fully grasped that position during the relativist debates of the interwar period, when Croce's influence on American historiography was at its height.

A few of the later efforts to reconstruct the debates centring upon Becker and Beard have better conveyed Croce's place in American historiographical discussion. Cushing Strout's *The Pragmatist Revolt in American History* pinpointed some essential differences between Croce and both Becker and Beard, showing, for example, that Beard's eagerness to use Croce against the pretence of scientific history led him to miss the essential subtleties in Croce's way of relating theory and practice, knowing and doing.[61] Too often, however, even such later studies did not grasp the larger contours of Croce's radical historicism and thus simply repeated longstanding misconceptions. While generally doing justice to Croce's emphasis on the involvement of the present inquirer, they failed to show how that involvement can serve truth in Croce's conception and why, in the final analysis, relativism is simply not the issue.[62]

Croce came up as a matter of course in American debates over cognitive issues in historiography until well into the 1960s, although by then he was getting a deeper hearing from philosophers of history than from practising historians. Most significant was Jack W. Meiland's *Skepticism and Historical Knowledge* (1965), which, even without probing Croce's overall framework, proved better able than Mandelbaum to grasp Croce's generally constructivist orientation and the basis of his claim to have sidestepped historiographical relativism.[63] Still, as the analytical approach came to dominate, the philosophy of history focused on precisely the problems that Croce believed he had dissolved, especially causation and explanation, examined from a perspective that assumed the scientific approach to be paradigmatic. Those interested in historiography increasingly lumped Croce with Collingwood, who seemed to occupy a common ground in opposition to that scientific or analytical approach. Because Collingwood was more accessible, he was taken to offer the definitive statement of their position. Croce increasingly became a name, a footnote; there seemed no need to confront him directly.

But the agenda of historiographical discussion changed radically in

1973 with the publication of Hayden White's path-breaking *Metahistory*, which remains central to historiographical discussion in the English-speaking world even today. And Croce figured prominently in White's book; indeed, White was no doubt the most influential American thinker to have confronted Croce during the past half century. Moreover, White was well equipped to understand what Croce was up to. In 1959 he had translated a central work by Carlo Antoni, one of Croce's major disciples, as *From History to Sociology*, and then, in an article published in 1963, proclaimed 'the abiding relevance of Croce's idea of history.'[64] Nothing in English had better showed why history for Croce transcends naturalism to become the story of liberty, or why Croce's historicism entails broadly liberal implications.

But by the time he published *Metahistory* ten years later, White found Croce the ironically sterile culmination of nineteenth-century historiographical traditions.[65] Indeed, wrote White, 'it is difficult not to think of Croce's "revolution" in historical sensibility as a retrogression, since its effect was to sever historiography from any participation in the effort – just beginning to make some headway as sociology at the time – to construct a general science of society.'[66] Croce was indeed hostile to sociology, but White's criteria of 'progression' are dubious at best. And whatever we make of our cultural prospects at present, there is no question that White failed to do justice to Croce's quest for a cultural alternative to social science.

As White saw it, Croce was seeking to eviscerate historical knowledge for conservative purposes. By severing it from the search for usable general knowledge, Croce denied history any present political import and confined it to the haven of art. Like innumerable Italian critics before him, White accused Croce of de-emphasizing action in favour of a passive acceptance based on retrospective understanding. White's own aim was to free us from the concerns about representation in language that had apparently contributed to this ironic disjunction between understanding and action.[67] But his account fundamentally misrepresented Croce's way of relating present concern, historical inquiry, moral response, and history-making action. In fact, Croce was seeking a more central cultural role for historiography, just as White was. But Croce did not settle into the relatively aestheticist position that White's *Metahistory* seems to invite, even though, at first, he seemed headed in precisely that direction. Typically, Croce attempted to posit a middle way, between non-rational creativity and rational discipline, between the ideal of getting the story straight and the giddy sense that the past is open to the historian's creative will. As a result, Croce ended up showing, as no one else has, why historical understanding is the measure – the *only* measure – of rational response.

As a leader in the wider humanistic discussion in the United States, White continued to refine his ideas after publishing *Metahistory*, but he no longer bothered with Croce as he did so. The fact that White, the most influential English-speaking intellectual to have confronted Croce's thought in recent years, ended up criticizing and then neglecting Croce in this way has been central to the fate of Croce's legacy so far.

But whatever the basis of White's intellectual evolution, the direction of historiography since Croce's death made Croce seem ever less relevant to mainstream historians. Croce's own histories, accenting the scope for free human response, were admired during the fascist era and were sufficiently innovative to elicit several solid studies.[68] As recently as 1970, his *Storia del Regno di Napoli* was published in English translation by the University of Chicago Press as part of a series devoted to 'Classic European Historians.' But Croce's focus on a privileged ethical-political strand was utterly at odds with the new social history that developed from the *Annales* school to dominate American historiography by about 1980. Thus Crocean historiography increasingly seemed old-fashioned and irrelevant. His best-known historical work in English, *History of Europe in the Nineteenth Century* (English translation 1932), was long admired as an instrument in the struggle against fascism, but it came to seem fantastically abstract as a history of nineteenth-century Europe.

Still, Croce's role as the upholder of liberty against fascism brought him considerable credit in the United States, even after his death. For example, a special section on contemporary Italy in *The Atlantic* in 1958 included an appreciation by the important Italian intellectual Guido Calogero that played up Croce's role as spiritual leader of the resistance to fascism.[69] During the 1940s, others invoked Croce's authority against Marxism or looked to him for insight into 'the German problem' in light of the Nazi experience.[70]

But few among Croce's American admirers confronted the basis of his recasting of the liberal tradition in response to what he called the 'anti-historicism' of his own time. Indeed, it was not obvious to Americans that the liberal tradition *needed* the sort of recasting Croce was attempting. In his thinking about politics, Croce had not started with the individual rights central to Anglo-American liberalism; indeed, he had had only contempt for the conventional justifications for liberal democracy. Thus it was hard for Americans to find common ground with him. Croce could be admired from a distance, but there seemed no call for Americans to confront systematically the ways in which his commitment to liberalism differed from their own.[71]

Some even charged that, whatever the value of Croce's political stance in response to Mussolini's dictatorship, his thinking had fostered the relativism that had undermined democracy and fed fascism and totalitarianism. Most notoriously, the historian Chester McArthur Destler found Croce not only the major source of a deplorable new presentism in historiography, but also the outstanding exponent of a dangerous new philosophy that stressed relativism in values, impressionism in the arts, subjective activism for the individual, violence as a mode of social action, and success as the supreme value in public affairs. Croce, according to Destler, had thereby 'helped lay the intellectual foundations of Italian fascism.'[72]

The notion that Croce's thought was somehow implicated in the triumph of fascism found apparently more authoritative support from the assaults levelled against Croce by certain Italian émigrés in the United States.[73] Although such attacks had begun during the fascist period, they especially marked the pivotal 1940s, as Italy sought to find its way beyond fascism. The most significant came from two of the most influential Italian intellectuals in this country, Giuseppe Antonio Borgese and Gaetano Salvemini, each of whom had long been critical of Croce, though for somewhat different reasons.

In his arresting *Goliath: The March of Fascism* (1937), Borgese granted Croce's significance as an anti-fascist beacon but still portrayed him as doddering and ineffectual – the result of his neo-Hegelian philosophy. After referring dismissively to 'the philosophy of history taught by a few self-satisfied professors, that whatever has happened in history was good and rational,' Borgese found a justification of fascism implicit in Croce's thought: 'the success of Mussolini, success being the only test that validates political happenings, was tantamount to a kingly anointment performed by the Goddess History through her idealistic high-priests.' Indeed, continued Borgese, 'all the books and essays of Croce had played into the hand of Mussolini.'[74]

Equally central was the anti-Croce posture of Gaetano Salvemini, an admirable humanitarian in many respects and a respected teacher at Harvard. Though he admitted in his more candid moments that he lacked the aptitude and temperament to penetrate Croce's ideas, Salvemini's Harvard post gave him a certain authority in the United

States. And he seized every opportunity to heap scorn on Croce's thought and, after the fall of fascism, his immediate political posture as well.[75] Introducing the first edition of A. William Salomone's pioneering study of Giolittian Italy in May 1945, Salvemini referred disparagingly to the 'pitfalls of "idealistic" historiography, according to which (with Dr Pangloss) everything which is real is rational and everything which is rational is good.'[76]

Borgese and Salvemini were among the contributors to a pamphlet published in Boston in 1946 that bitterly criticized Croce's brand of liberalism and historicism and his role in the political debates that surrounded the end of the war. Though written in Italian, this tract provides vivid testimony that it had become open season on Croce among Italians with American connections.[77] To be sure, Croce also found defenders among knowledgeable Italians and Americans during the years surrounding the end of the war.[78] But the fact that, by the mid-forties, he had gotten caught up in seemingly parochial Italian polemics was bound to compromise his stature among the Americans, who had not been sure what to make of him in the first place.

Despite the limits of his impact and the vicissitudes of his reputation, even in the United States Croce was one of the best-known European intellectuals during the last several decades of his life. And he remained taken for granted as a major figure for roughly two decades after his death in 1952. In his influential *Consciousness and Society* (1958), H. Stuart Hughes included Croce with Freud and Weber as the central figures in the extraordinarily innovative generation of intellectuals that came of age around 1890. Hughes was himself attracted to Croce; as he had written the book, he noted, 'the tranquil persuasiveness of Croce has been ever with me.' But even Hughes proved unable to do justice to the essentials of Croce's thought – for example, the radical immanence of the spirit in Croce's conception.[79]

Writing with the promise of social science at its peak, Hughes linked the development of usable methods in the social sciences to the preservation of the rational Enlightenment tradition, which he found still the best bulwark against the damaging irrationalism that had led to fascism. Hughes's readers could only have come away with an uncertain sense of Croce's enterprise, for Croce, despite his anti-fascism, had remained a persistent critic of the Enlightenment tradition. Thus his efforts to delimit the cultural role of science and to deflate the pretensions of the new social sciences. Croce had apparently been outside the mainstream, and by the 1950s his humanistic historicism could easily seem anachronistic. Destler noted that Croce was 'abysmally and contemptuously ignorant of modern science,' and even Patrick Romanell, sometimes a more sympathetic commentator, charged that Croce, in restricting science, was inflating philosophy in order to establish a Hegelian certainty.[80] Such characterizations did not begin to make sense of Croce's way of placing science, philosophy, and historical understanding within the overall cultural economy.

In 1972, the thought of Croce, twenty years after his death, still attracted the attention of such important intellectuals as Monroe Beardsley, Max Fisch, and Louis Mink, each of whom participated in a major symposium on the Crocean legacy at the University of Delaware that year. This event, however, hardly lived up to its promise. The proceedings were published by a little known German-American publisher in a typescript format that, to the reader who chanced upon the book, could only have suggested that Croce was an obscure, minor figure.[81] In the two decades that followed, no comparable scholarly meeting was devoted to his intellectual legacy.

4: In the Shadows of Vico and Gramsci

Beginning in the 1960s, Croce was relegated to the shadows as Giambattista Vico and Antonio Gramsci became enormously influential in American intellectual life. Interest in Vico developed partly through the laudable and tireless efforts of Giorgio Tagliacozzo, founding director of the Institute for Vico Studies, to show the wide relevance of Vico's work to the contemporary humanities. But as Vico came to prominence, it became *de rigueur*, as in major works by Donald Verene and Michael Mooney, to deplore Croce's alleged idealist deformation of Vico, based especially on the assumption that Croce, as a Hegelian, had afforded privilege to conceptual thought.[82]

In fact, however, Croce took over wholesale Vico's notion of the autonomy of the creative imagination. Thus he could agree with Verene's crucial point that the imagination does not provide images *of* something – something already here.[83] That was precisely the insight that attracted those like Joel Spingarn to Croce in the first place. To be sure, Croce insisted on an ongoing role for the rational concept as well, but he related imagination and cognition in a circle to emphasize that neither is higher or final. 'Poetry' wells up continually, and thus the endless openness and creativity of the world. There is no scope for Hegel's definitive overcoming or telos. Knowing Croce only from a distance, recent American Vichians have failed to grasp that Croce offered not a Hegelian deformation of Vico, but a Vichian recasting of Hegel.

As Vico was gaining currency, a considerable vogue of Gramsci was also developing among historians and critics.[84] 'Hegemony' was everywhere. Even if only by implication, studies of Gramsci fostered the notion that insofar as there had been an especially innovative moment in Italian intellectual life, centring on Croce and Gentile, earlier in the century, it had found its most notable fruit in Gramsci's work. From this perspective, Croce had been a major source of Gramsci's innovative, culturally sensitive brand of Marxism. But Croce had then succumbed to Gramsci's withering critique in his *Prison Notebooks*, published posthumously in the late 1940s. Some American students of Gramsci shaded Gramsci's charges of conservatism against Croce in the most negative way, suggesting at least indirect links between Croce and fascism.[85]

In *Italian Marxism* (1983), Paul Piccone, editor of the influential radical journal *Telos*, marginalized Croce from a different angle as he sought to pit a more genuinely radical Gramsci against the 'official' reading by Palmiro Togliatti and the Italian Communist party. Piccone sought to show how Gramsci's thinking had developed from within a distinctively Italian radical tradition, based on a particular way of appropriating Hegel. Gramsci was connected to Hegel not through Croce and Gentile, but through Antonio Labriola and especially Bertrando Spaventa.[86] Labriola's importance had long been recognized, but Piccone's way of restoring Spaventa was intended to make it clearer that Croce, from within a generally liberal framework, had de-radicalized Labriola's Italian Marxism.

As interest in Gramsci grew, Croce found few who were prepared to take him on his own terms. Ernesto Caserta explored Croce's relationship with Marxism from a generally Crocean point of view, but he settled for publishing his major work on the subject in Italy.[87] Still, Croce was central to three full-length scholarly studies published in the United States during the 1980s. They were disparate in approach, however, and they did not herald a Croce revival.

Edmund Jacobitti's *Revolutionary Humanism and Historicism in Modern Italy* (1981), though useful on the Neapolitan tradition from which Croce emerged, seriously misrepresented Croce's conception of practical life, ethical response, and the relationship of human being to the growth of the world in history.[88] Suggesting that Crocean historicism had proven a dead end by 1915, Jacobitti's critical account simply buttressed longstanding charges of conservatism and passivity. This was hardly an interpretation to invite renewed attention to Croce.

The other two works were more appreciative. In *Benedetto Croce Reconsidered* (1987), M.E. Moss offered a clear, straightforward account of the fundamentals of Croce's philosophy, a useful beginning for those to whom Croce had become just a name. Seeking to place Croce in a wider European perspective, my own *Benedetto Croce and the Uses of Historicism* (1987) played down Croce's formal philosophy and emphasized the import of Croce's absolute historicism to the ongoing humanistic discussion that accompanied the eclipse of foundational philosophy.[89] It is striking that though all three books of the 1980s accented Croce's historicism and historiography, none was selected for review by *History and Theory*, the leading English-language journal on historiography and the philosophy of history.

5: Missed Connections and Ongoing Possibilities

Although Croce had some impact among American intellectuals, especially between the wars, the story of his legacy in the United States is largely one of misunderstanding, misrepresentation, and neglect. He has proven less influential among Americans than Dilthey, Weber, or Cassirer, than Heidegger or Gadamer, than Ortega y Gasset or Collingwood, than Lukács or the Frankfurt School. Among Italian thinkers, both Vico and Gramsci have had considerably greater impact. Yet there surely was scope for Croce's thinking to have played a more fruitful role.

To some extent, Croce's fate rested on mere contingencies, from poor translations to idiosyncrasies in the intellectual agendas of some of those best equipped to appreciate his work. Such, as Richard Rorty reminds us, are the ways of our intellectual history, which often boils down to who happened to bump into whom. Potentially significant encounters – with Babbitt, with Becker, with Dewey, with White – got started but were somehow arrested.

In another sense, however, it is not surprising that Americans have misunderstood or sidestepped Croce – and not only because he wrote in Italian, and in an unfamiliar, seemingly Hegelian idiom. It was very hard to grasp the overall shape of his intellectual enterprise as it unfolded during his long life. He could appear a systematic philosopher, an aesthetician, a literary critic, a historian, a liberal anti-fascist. He was all of them, yet none of those labels adequately represented his enterprise. Indeed, American efforts to characterize Croce during his lifetime bring to mind the blind men confronting the elephant.

Historical outcomes are always provisional, however, and there may still be scope for a more fruitful encounter, even a place for Croce within contemporary humanistic discussion in the United States as elsewhere. Certainly we are better able now, in light of the changes in the intellectual landscape over the last thirty years, to grasp the thrust of his absolute historicism, to appreciate its import, and to respond fruitfully to it. Although we are still wrestling with terms like *historicism, aestheticism,* and *activism,* as well as with dichotomies like experimental and speculative, or even thought and action, we are far better attuned to Croce's concerns than were his American contemporaries, with their confidence in, for example, the social sciences, or the Lockean understanding of liberalism.

In recent years, historians in the United States have gotten caught up again in the issues surrounding presentism and relativism that were associated with Becker and Beard sixty years ago. Central to that discussion has been Peter Novick's eloquent *That Noble Dream,* which, typically, mentions Croce only in passing.[90] Yet the discussion surrounding Novick's work cried out for a Crocean dimension. In the same way, many of the issues involved in the recent revival of pragmatism suggest that the dialogue between Crocean historicism and the Deweyan tradition, apparently aborted forty years ago, might fruitfully be revived today. Rorty neo-liberalism recalls Croce's. And it is striking that Rorty, for all his debt to Dewey, pulled back from Dewey's accent on the cultural centrality of science to emphasize, in ways congruent with Croce's, the creativity of language and the historicity of the world.[91]

More generally, Croce was not so much anachronistic as prescient in his effort to delimit social science and to specify a radically historicist alternative. In developing his absolute historicism, in fact, Croce ended up addressing, in a now-unfamiliar idiom, a number of the problems at issue in the humanistic discussion centring on neo-pragmatism, hermeneutics, and deconstruction – movements that have come to the fore as confidence in social science has waned. He was seeking a kind of post-metaphysical moderation, eschewing appeals to a transcendent or foundational sphere while heading off the tendency toward extremes that the post-metaphysical situation seemed to nurture. In recent years, a number of scholars in this country, from Rorty to David Kolb to Brook Thomas, have pursued similar aims, often mentioning historicism, yet virtually never considering Croce. Though he hardly merits the last word, Croce could fruitfully be placed in that discussion.[92]

Supplement on the fortunes of Giovanni Gentile in the United States and Canada

[Sections 1, 5, and 6 of the version that appeared in Italian as 'La fortuna di Croce e Gentile negli Stati Uniti,' in 'Croce e Gentile un secolo dopo,' special issue, *Giornale critico della filosofia italiana* 73, nos. 2–3 (May–December): 253–81.]

1: Introduction

Croce's *La critica* is to be found in virtually every North American research library, as is Gentile's Treccani *Enciclopedia italiana* of 1929–36. Scholars from the United States and Canada have contributed several of the best works on Croce and Gentile in any language. Yet the story of the two noted Italian thinkers in the United States is essentially one of misunderstanding and neglect.[93]

Although Croce long came up as a matter of course in discussions of aesthetics or historiography, and Gentile drew some attention first as an educational reformer, then as the 'philosopher of fascism,' neither attracted major disciples or sustained exchange with American thinkers. Today, Gentile is largely unknown, and even Croce is increasingly forgotten.

Americans encountered Croce through his work in aesthetics during the first decade of the century; they discovered Gentile only after World War I. Thus Croce and Gentile were generally not treated in tandem, but came up in quite different intellectual contexts.[94] But because each was quickly typed as 'neo-idealist' or 'neo-Hegelian,' it proved difficult for either thinker seriously to penetrate American culture. In the United States, there had been an idealist moment, but idealism was receding by the first years of the century, when Croce and Gentile were establishing themselves as major figures in Italy. So to characterize the two Italians as neo-idealists seemed to warrant boxing them out, without seriously confronting what was innovative in their thinking. Whereas in England such philosophers as Bernard Bosanquet, J.A. Smith, and R.G. Collingwood seriously confronted the thought of Croce and Gentile, neither of the two Italians had any such resonance among major philosophers in the United States.

As Croce's thought developed, it became ever clearer that the neo-idealist characterization was misleading at best.[95] Writing in the influential *Journal of Aesthetics and Art Criticism* in 1952, Frederic Simoni showed that the idealist stereotype had nurtured a whole tradition of misunderstanding that had grown up around Croce. Simoni concluded, without exaggeration, that 'reference to Croce in current literature constitutes a comedy of errors.'[96]

Gentile, in contrast, was indeed a philosophical idealist – one of the most insistent and extreme the Western tradition has known. Still, fruitful encounter with his educational and socio-political thought did not require adherence to his idealistic principles. But because his idealism made his thinking seem particularly abstract on first encounter, Gentile encountered even greater obstacles than Croce in penetrating the American cultural landscape.

Even apart from this association with an unfashionable idealism, American ways of viewing Croce and Gentile tended to discourage sustained engagement. Croce was variously typed as a romantic, an expressionist, a partisan of irresponsible private imagination. Gentile seemed to invite mysticism, or activism, or solipsism, or authoritarian elitism.

Even those relatively sympathetic to Croce and Gentile sometimes viewed the two thinkers as central to an interesting but provincially Italian culture, not quite part of the European mainstream. John Crowe Ransom, who helped spearhead 'the new criticism' in American literary studies, took inspiration from Croce and recent Italian thinkers – but on the basis of a curious sense of what those thinkers had achieved. Writing to Allen Tate in 1927, Ransom expressed the hope that he and Tate might revive 'southernism' in the United States just as Croce and one or two others seemed to have spearheaded a revival of Italianism among the younger generation of Italians.[97] There is some justification for this perspective in the case of Gentile, who became preoccupied with the Italian tradition, but Croce was arguably the most cosmopolitan European intellectual of his time. Ransom's characterization did not remotely represent Croce's cultural aspiration or achievement.

Still, there would seem to have been room for a more fruitful interchange between Croce and Gentile, on the one hand, and the Americans, on the other.[98] And a handful of significant American intellectuals, from Joel Spingarn and Carl Becker to A. James Gregor and Hayden White, did engage the Italians – or sought seriously to do so. So it is illuminating, as a chapter in Western cultural history, to ask what happened when the Americans encountered Croce and Gentile. What was noted and what was missed? At the same time, however, the basis of any misunderstanding is hard to assess, in light of the ongoing disagreement even in Italy about the import of the two thinkers.

...

5: Gentile

With his extreme brand of philosophical idealism, Gentile was never remotely as well known as Croce in the United States. Even in Italy, however, the question of what to make of Gentile hardly admits of easy answers, so it is perhaps not surprising that Americans have generally steered clear of him.[99] Writing in 1960, Gentile's most authoritative expositor in English, the Canadian philosopher H.S. Harris, noted that 'the possibility of Gentile having any influence in America perished when [Josiah] Royce died at the age of sixty-one in 1916.'[100] During his last years, even after most American philosophers had abandoned idealism for a radical empiricism and naturalism, Royce had sought to work from the pragmatism of C.S. Peirce to a kind of idealist historicism. So his death removed the most likely avenue for Gentile to affect philosophical thinking in the United States.

It did not help that Gentile seemed more provincial and idiosyncratically Italian than Croce. Having embarked with a *tesi di laurea* on Rosmini and Gioberti, Gentile became interested in Bertrando Spaventa's notion of the circulation of Italian ideas within European philosophy, and he focused especially on the Italian tradition throughout his career. Thus, as Harris noted, 'the peculiarly "national," and at times almost chauvinistic, character of [Gentile's] culture and ... genius is one of the factors that has impeded the understanding of his work in foreign countries.'[101] This element of cultural nationalism seemed bound up with Gentile's adherence to fascism, which tended to discredit his whole intellectual enterprise for most Americans.

Still, Gentile had some resonance in the United States as a philosopher of education and educational reformer between the wars. Moreover, two philosophers well-versed in the idealist tradition – Roger Holmes and Harris himself – produced major studies on aspects of Gentile's philosophy, and Gentile figured prominently in A. James Gregor's controversial revisionist interpretation of Italian fascism.

Gentile first became known in the United States not through his association with Croce during the early years of *La critica* but only after World War I, when his efforts at educational reform began to attract attention. Again Joel Spingarn was central. He included a translation of Gentile's *La riforma dell'educazione: Discorsi ai maestri di Trieste* (1920) in the 'Library of European Culture' that he was developing for Harcourt, Brace and Company. Gentile reworked the first chapter, and Croce provided a laudatory introduction to what was then published as *The Reform of Education* in 1922.[102] And Gentile's educational philosophy continued sporadically to attract interest throughout the interwar period, partly through the effort of the Casa Italiana at Columbia University, which proved a major centre for the study of Gentile in the United States.[103] To most, however, the philosophy of education seemed a secondary field, and Dewey and his school, experimentalists who considered themselves emancipated from the idealist tradition, dominated what discussion there was. Thus Harris notes that Gentile's book of 1922 'passed unnoticed in philosophical and educational journals.'[104]

Still, even within the school of Dewey, Gentile's actual idealism attracted some attention by the later 1920s. Charles Morris, an influential student of George Herbert Mead, treated Gentile with discernment in a study of approaches to the problem of mind.[105] Portraying Gentile as the extreme form of activism within recent idealism, Morris outlined with particular clarity Gentile's way of positing the act of thought thinking as ultimately real. But though he stressed the value of Gentile's accent on activity as an antidote to notions of mind as a passive receptacle and, more generally, to any dualism of mind and nature, Morris concluded that a naturalistic substratum still lurked in Gentile's conception, which also betrayed the problems long associated with the 'mentalism' side of idealism.

Taking Gentile still more seriously was Roger Holmes in *The Idealism of Giovanni Gentile* (1937), still one of the most important works on Gentile in English.[106] But though he was sympathetic to Gentile's humanistic, non-naturalistic approach, Holmes concluded that Gentile's statement of actual idealism in the *Sistema di logica* of 1922–3 was not sufficiently complete to avoid the contrasting pitfalls of metaphysics and scepticism. Still, Holmes also asked a deeper set of questions – about the purpose, and the cultural stakes, of Gentile's quest for universal and necessary knowledge. Holmes was willing to grant that up to a point Gentile had succeeded – but by assuming what, Holmes asked, and to what end, and at what cost? In some respects, Holmes was suggesting, Gentile's enterprise was narrow, trivial, merely a kind of game.

Especially in addressing these meta-philosophical issues, Holmes raised questions that American philosophers could usefully have taken up. But though Holmes's book was reviewed in major philosophical journals, Gentile's idiom, even as mediated by Holmes, was simply too abstract and foreign to invite serious engagement by Americans.[107] Insofar as Gentile's effort at a rigorous actual idealism was at issue, he could pass virtually without notice. But this was not all Gentile offered, nor was it necessarily what mattered most in his thinking.

Gentile's fascism made him interesting to some for a while, but anathema to others. In the United States, as elsewhere, many found the fascist experiment in Italy worthy of attention, especially before it was overshadowed by Nazism by the mid-1930s. The influential journal *Foreign Affairs* published a translation of Gentile's 'L'essenza del fascismo' as 'The Philosophic Basis of Fascism' in 1928.[108] Although close observers of fascism understood that the fascist educational reform had quickly escaped Gentile's grasp and, more generally, that Gentile's relationship with the Fascist party had grown increasingly problematic, several Americans, from H.W. Schneider to Howard Marraro to Herbert Matthews, brought out the significance of Gentile's role, as the most powerful Italian philosopher, within the ongoing fascist experiment.[109]

At the same time, however, opposition to fascism coloured evaluations even of Gentile's formal philosophy during the fascist period. Reviewing several of Gentile's works in 1926, the influential historian of ideas George Boas endorsed Croce's charge that Gentile's extreme demand for unity had led merely to mysticism and abstraction. And Boas found nothing surprising about Gentile's association with fascism. Gentile's philosophy meant worship of activity for its own sake and ultimately the absorption of individuals in a fascist state that recognized no standard outside itself.[110] By moving from formal philosophy to confront Gentile's fascism, Boas asked potentially more fruitful questions than Morris and Holmes, but he could barely scratch the surface in a brief critical review written as early as 1926.

However, after Gentile's death and fascism's bitter end, it proved even more difficult to make sense of the relationship between Gentile's thought and fascism. Most students of Gentile sought to isolate specific contributions, showing that they merited discussion on their own, apart from Gentile's unfortunate and embarrassing association with Mussolini's regime. Merle Brown and Giovanni Gullace contributed able studies of Gentile's aesthetics, although their efforts failed to draw much attention to this aspect of Gentile's work.[111]

The most significant study of Gentile in English, H.S. Harris's *The Social Philosophy of Giovanni Gentile* (1960), similarly avoided sustained encounter with Gentile's fascism. Harris probed Gentile's socio-political thought as it culminated in *Genesi e struttura della società* (1946), which Harris translated separately with a valuable introduction and a bibliography of works on Gentile in English.[112] Thoroughly grounded in the idealist tradition, Harris was able to engage Gentile on a sophisticated level, and his reach was broad enough to show how fruitful encounter between Gentile and Americans like George Herbert Mead could have developed. But because he sought to separate the valuable core of Gentile's social thought from what seemed Gentile's merely contingent association with fascism, Harris's work proved relatively abstract.

Harris's work on Gentile remains a major contribution to scholarship and the essential starting point for anyone interested in Gentile in the English-speaking world. But its impact was limited, just as Harris anticipated when, introducing his translation, he noted 'what an obscure footnote to the history of Anglo-Saxon philosophy the present essay is likely to be.'[113] Although he contributed occasional articles on both Gentile and Croce, Harris concentrated thereafter on a multi-volume study of Hegel.

On the other hand, Gentile continued to figure in specialized studies of fascism by American scholars. Tracy Koon, for example, offered a balanced consideration of Gentile's educational reform and its fate within fascism in her *Believe, Obey, Fight* (1985).[114] Taking Gentile's role most seriously was the political theorist A. James Gregor, especially in *The Ideology of Fascism* (1969). Gregor provided a good sense of Gentile's intellectual enterprise, showing how Gentile's thought developed partly through encounter with Marx, and how it came to encompass some of the most innovative European thinking about political action. For Gregor, Italian fascism was not only genuinely radical, but also paradigmatic of twentieth-century developmental dictatorships based on national mobilization. And Gentile had provided the capstone of the coherent national developmentalist ideology that Gregor attributed to fascism.[115]

Gregor's books offered a valuable corrective to what had gradually become the prevailing view in the United States – that Italian fascism was an opportunistic, semi-comic charade, a pale shadow of diabolical Nazism. But he was surely making fascism too coherent, and in linking fascism to third-world developmental dictatorships he was not doing justice to what remained most challenging in Gentile's thought. Although published by major houses, Gregor's books were widely viewed as idiosyncratic, even apologetic, so they ultimately did not prove an effective vehicle for restoring interest in Gentile.

Harris, Gullace, Brown, Gregor, and others offered a significant North American contribution to the monumental anthology *Il pensiero di Giovanni Gentile* (1977), but it was published in Italy, and these contributions were testimony more to the idiosyncratic interests of a handful of disparate American scholars than to any sustained Gentilian influence in the United States.[116] Though this was a distinguished group of scholars, had they sought to collect their essays on Gentile into one volume in the United States, they might well have had difficulty finding a major publisher.

6: Missed Connections and Ongoing Possibilities

Neither Croce nor Gentile has had significant resonance in the United States – in comparison with Dilthey, Weber, or Cassirer, with Heidegger or Gadamer, with Ortega y Gasset or Collingwood, with Lukács or the Frankfurt School. Among Italian thinkers, Vico and Gramsci each has had a far more significant impact. But there remains scope for a more fruitful American encounter with both Croce and Gentile.

In recent years, historians in the United States have gotten caught up again in the issues surrounding presentism and relativism that were associated with Becker and Beard sixty years ago. Central to that discussion has been Peter Novick's eloquent *That Noble Dream*, which, typically, mentions Croce only in passing. Yet the discussion surrounding Novick's work cried out for a Crocean dimension. In the same way, many of the issues involved in the recent revival of pragmatism suggest that the dialogue between Crocean historicism and the Deweyan tradition, apparently aborted forty years ago, might fruitfully be revived today.

Gentile's case is more problematic, both because he remains associated with fascism and because his idealism seems abstract and irrelevant. Still, changes in the intellectual landscape, in the United States as elsewhere, suggest that he, too, might draw renewed attention among Americans. The ongoing assault on foundationalist philosophy enables us to reconsider the purposes underlying Gentile's actualism, which responded not simply to the philosophical problem of dualism but to ongoing uncertainties about liberal individualism and democratic politics. Our recent political experience in the West, including the crisis of the traditional Left, has prompted a fresh look at neglected dimensions of our earlier political experience. Gentile's political compromises and the disastrous outcome of fascism are not in dispute, but there is much we might learn by re-examining the political odyssey of him and his circle. In the United States, as in Germany, the Nazi jurist Carl Schmitt has recently attracted renewed interest, and a fresh look at Gentile could be at least as fruitful.

Although there have been significant exceptions, American confrontations with Croce and Gentile have often been misguided, and potentially significant encounters have failed to develop. But despite this legacy of misunderstanding and neglect, there remains scope, even today, for interjecting Croce and Gentile into debates of considerable moment in the United States.

chapter 5

Historicism, Liberalism, Fascism: Rethinking the Croce-Gentile Schism

This is a paper I prepared for a session at the annual meeting of the American Political Science Association, Washington, DC, 28–31 August 1997. Full papers were available throughout the conference; sessions revolved around informal presentations based on the already available papers. I have not sought to publish this essay, which overlaps in part with the second of two lectures I presented in Italian at the Istituto italiano per gli studi filosofici in Naples in April 1997. Some of the thinking on Gentile in the present essay found its way into my book *The Totalitarian Experiment in Twentieth-Century Europe: Understanding the Poverty of Great Politics* (London: Routledge, 2006), but this essay is more obviously focused on what we might learn from the Croce-Gentile schism.

1: An Italian Angle on the Modern Political Experiment

Recent changes in our historical self-understanding invite – or demand – a renewed effort to learn from the twentieth-century political experience, marked by the unforeseen eruption of totalitarian extremes and by the apparent reconfirmation of liberal democracy in the aftermath. The totalitarian variants played off what their advocates claimed were the inadequacies of the liberal mainstream, and, conversely, the confident self-understanding of liberal democracy by the late twentieth century derives partly from the disastrous outcomes of those totalitarian alternatives. The whole experience has led to certain ways of framing the binary dualisms that structure our understanding of the political world.

However, there is more we might learn, from the tragedies of our recent past, about the possibilities and limitations of modern politics.

And to make sense of where we are, we need more creatively to refine the essential categories of our political understanding in light of the political experience we have now had. Yet a certain triumphalism, and a certain nervous reticence, have kept us from the necessary engagement with that earlier experience, much of which was quickly marginalized, with ideas neglected and aspirations explained away.[1]

Writing on postmodernism and historiography in 1989, the historian Jane Caplan found it anomalous that in the ongoing debate about the fascist sympathies of Martin Heidegger and Paul de Man, there was, as she put it, 'a virtually complete silence on both sides about the actual premises and texts of fascist or Nazi ideology: as if this were coherent, already known, yet somehow insignificant.'[2] She went on to propose that the insights of deconstruction might open the way to a riskier, but deeper, more illuminating approach to European fascism. This would entail, she suggested, letting the binary oppositions at work in the discussion of fascism – rational/irrational, for example – themselves be at issue, so that we might open the standard dichotomies, questioning their positive terms.

In light of our deepening sense of the possibilities, I suggest that we might have much to learn from a fresh look at the interlocking political itineraries of the Italian thinkers Benedetto Croce (1866–1952) and Giovanni Gentile (1875–1944), who began, around the turn of the century, as allies in a once noted intellectual revolution, but who then split, first over seemingly rarefied philosophical issues, then over the cultural significance of the First World War, and finally, in 1925, over fascism.

Gentile was the most distinguished European intellectual to identify wholeheartedly with any form of fascism. In recent years, to be sure, much obsessive interest has surrounded Heidegger's Nazi affiliations, but he was merely on the fringes, arbitrarily identifying his ideas with Hitler's regime, whereas Gentile crucially influenced the self-understanding and direction of Italian fascism. An explicit advocate of totalitarianism, he became the fascist regime's quasi-official philosopher, writing the major theoretical portion of Mussolini's 'Dottrina del fascismo,' published in 1932 and widely reproduced in translation. In embracing fascism, Gentile carried many educated young Italians with him. To be sure, the relevance of Gentile's experience and testimony is not obvious, but it is surely anomalous that so many students of the modern political experience blithely ignore Gentile as they proclaim that Italian fascism had no intellectual pedigree or ideology, that it can be understood – or dismissed – in terms of activism, opportunism, and power.

Meanwhile, Croce departed dramatically from his erstwhile collaborator to become perhaps the world's best-known anti-fascist, widely admired as the apostle of 'the religion of liberty.' And, crucially, he proved a *neo*-liberal, because he found it necessary to recast the liberal democratic tradition in light of fascism and the overall totalitarian experience – including all that he found misguided in Gentile's ideas. To return to liberal culture and institutions was not simply a matter of catching up with Britain and the United States. Italy's experience first with liberal democracy, then with fascism, entailed deeper lessons that those countries had not had to learn directly, but that were nevertheless relevant for Western culture as a whole.

The intellectual revolution wrought by Croce and Gentile entailed new and radical forms of historicism and philosophical idealism, articulated first in the assault on positivism at the start of the century. These Italians came to their position partly through encounter with German ideas, and the prominence of idealism and historicism in both countries has long seemed implicated – though in a vague, uncertain way – in the fascist divergence from mainstream liberalism, as institutionalized in Britain, France, and the United States. So a fresh look at the Croce-Gentile split might seem particularly promising on the face of it.

In fact, however, this episode is little known in the English-speaking world and does not figure in international discussion of fascism and totalitarianism.[3] Croce, having come out on the 'right' side, was read for a while, but he was not considered in tandem with Gentile. And by now Gentile, having linked his ideas to fascism, initially appears foolish, or worse. Moreover, from the outset his brand of philosophical idealism was distinctly out of phase with philosophy in most of Western Europe and the United States. Yet even Croce's efforts at a neo-liberalism stand in sharper relief if we grasp what Gentile was up to. In what follows, then, I will focus especially on Gentile, but always keeping in mind his relationship with Croce.

Italian scholars have suggested periodically that confrontation with Gentile's ideas might deepen our approach to the overall problem of fascism.[4] By the early 1980s historians had begun probing the effort, in which Gentile was central, to establish a specifically fascist culture. Their efforts indicated that a new intellectual consensus was developing by the later 1920s, based on the premise that fascism was translating the best of modern thought, as pioneered in Italy, into post-liberal political forms – ultimately, a new, totalitarian kind of state. For Emilio Gentile (no relation), the leading current Italian authority on fascism, Gentile was 'the chief theologian' as fascist Italy pursued a radically new 'sacralization of politics.'[5] But even in the best of such studies, the sources, implications, and significance of Gentile's political-intellectual role remain obscure.[6]

Indeed, there remains much point to Norberto Bobbio's comment of 1974 that even in Italy, Gentile's philosophy seems not only dead, but literally incomprehensible.[7] What concerns could have been at work as Gentile came to posit the world as 'a continuous act of thought thinking'? To carry the point a step further, Gentile's high-blown talk about taking life seriously, or about the spiritual conception of reality, may seem simply vacuous on first encounter. Knowing how the fascist regime turned out, we tend to dismiss his fascist ideas as mere froth, as the window dressing that lent a hodgepodge regime the trappings of respectability and a facade of coherence.[8] Yet Bobbio also noted that not so long before, intelligent, idealistic young Italians had found Gentile's thinking exciting and inspiring.

In response to the inadequacies of modern liberalism and, more fundamentally, to the erosion of the religious foundations of our culture, Gentile drew on both idealism and historicism to recast the earlier 'ethical state' ideal. It is arguable that in doing so he gave the totalitarian impulse of the era its purest expression, yet he reconceived the relationships among power, freedom, responsibility, and participation in a more challenging way than our conventional understanding of 'totalitarianism' would lead us to expect. Gentile offered this conception in explicit opposition to Croce, on the basis of a philosophical dispute that became public in 1913.[9] Although highly abstract in one sense, that dispute brought to the surface underlying conceptions of human possibility with broadly political implications. Gentile was troubled by what he found to be a 'sense of profound melancholy' pervading Croce's 'whole contemplation of the world.'[10]

At that point, Croce was by no means identified with liberal democracy; indeed, he delighted in flaying the liberal ideas of 1789, which he found flaccid and sentimental. But, as Gentile sensed, the radically historicist conception Croce had developed by 1913 was deeper in political implication. In fact it pointed the way to a new kind of liberalism – a liberalism by default – yet Croce still found that austere historicist liberalism adequate, and congruent with the best of our humanity. It was here that Gentile parted company with him.

Precisely because he seemed to offer a more hopeful, affirmative response than Croce, Gentile excited young Italians who were seeking to respond to the unsettled Italian political situation just after the First World War. By that point, in fact, Gentile had elaborated a grandiose, philosophically grounded vision of renewal, a vision that led him and many of his followers to fascism. It was largely the disturbing appeal of Gentile's post-liberal politics – and its catastrophic failure – that led Croce to deepen his understanding of liberalism.

The ideas of Croce and Gentile were deeply woven into the rich Italian political experience of the first half of the century. Confronting the two thinkers in tandem suggests that many of the categories essential to our political self-understanding – liberalism and totalitarianism, rationalism and irrationalism, freedom and power, individualism, participation, activism, fanaticism, and nihilism – are more problematic than we tend to assume. Croce and Gentile force us to rethink these categories and thus to refine our understanding of the uses and limits of politics in light of the modern political experiment so far.

2: Melancholy and Beyond

Croce and Gentile came to prominence around the turn of the century as part of a wider Italian cultural renewal that produced a series of avant-garde reviews and, beginning in 1909, F.T. Marinetti's futurism. Many of those involved drew on and helped spread the critique of democratic assumptions and parliamentary institutions pioneered by Gaetano Mosca and Vilfredo Pareto, who, beginning in the eighties and nineties, pinpointed the roles of elitism and myth, thereby fostering cynicism about liberal democracy.

The most weighty of the new reviews was *La critica*, which Croce launched in 1903, taking as his collaborator the young philosopher Gentile, who was only twenty-eight. Croce was nine years older and, having just published his seminal *Estetica* in 1902, was very much the senior partner at this point. For both Croce and Gentile, the immediate target was positivism, or scientism, and each embraced the tradition of philosophical idealism in the quest for an alternative. But they were always uncomfortable with the neo-Hegelian label, and Croce ended up proposing that the term *idealism* be abandoned altogether. For Croce, certainly, and in some ways for Gentile as well, the outcome of their assault on positivism was not idealism but historicism, or a radically concrete kind of humanism. Despite important differences in emphasis, each is better understood as a post-Hegelian totalizing historicist than as a philosophical idealist.

Each started with the assumption that, with Christianity in irreversible decline, the challenge was to conceive the place of human beings in a world without a transcendent God.[11] Yet none of the intellectual currents emanating from abroad by the end of the nineteenth century seemed radical enough to provide the necessary new framework. At the same time, Croce and Gentile were both frustrated with the state of contemporary Italian civic culture. It seemed time to take up again the enterprise of civic renewal that the generation of the Risorgimento had initiated – but not completed – two generations earlier. That imperative led Gentile, especially, to a lifelong concern with education, which he understood from the start as indissolubly bound up with religion and philosophy, on the one hand, and civic renewal, on the other.

Although encounter with German ideas was crucial to both Croce and Gentile – and Marx before Hegel in each case – both thinkers played up their links with a distinctively Italian cultural tradition, which they saw as their mission to bring to bear on the deepest of contemporary challenges. With his interest in literature and aesthetics, Croce found a particular kinship with Francesco De Sanctis, while Gentile, more interested in philosophy and its history, fastened upon Bertrando Spaventa, who had been De Sanctis's colleague within the notable quasi-Hegelian tradition that the generation of the Risorgimento had developed in Naples. But both Croce and Gentile traced their thinking to a common ancestor, the idiosyncratic Neapolitan Giambattista Vico, who, two centuries earlier, had recast the Italian humanistic tradition in response to the Cartesian challenge. Following Vico, Croce and Gentile agreed that this world results, endlessly, from the free, creative responses of human beings – the human spirit – in history. Conversely, the human spirit is not something given, fully formed, but is in formation, in perpetual development of itself over time, always encompassing prior stages.

The contemporary situation seemed open for Italian thinkers to make a special contribution. Already with the launching of *La critica* in 1903, Croce and Gentile sensed they were at the centre of a European-wide cultural renewal, with positivism the immediate target. By the eve of the First World War, the two thinkers claimed, on the basis of their distinctively Italian angle, to have moved to the forefront of modern thought. In developing what he came to call his absolute historicism, Croce felt he had left even his German contemporaries behind.[12] But

Gentile, especially during the war, would become even more assertive in claiming a special role for the Italian intellectual tradition that he and Croce had brought to contemporary currency. Still, even as updated for the twentieth century, that tradition bristled with questions about the human role, about the mechanisms of world-making – and ultimately about politics.

Although each of them emphasized human freedom, first Croce, and then Gentile as well, helped foster the notion that liberal democracy, as usually understood, was not congruent with the conception of the world that was emerging through their new post-Christian philosophy. Virtually from the start, Croce found the liberal ideas of 1789 to be superficial and hypocritical, and even as an anti-fascist, he never embraced the conventional justifications for liberal democracy. Seeking to eschew all forms of transcendence and hostile to the natural law tradition, he eschewed the appeal to individual rights and, for all his ongoing emphasis on 'liberty,' placed little premium on 'negative' freedom for the individual vis-à-vis the state. In fact, he was initially satisfied to relegate politics to the realm of the useful, distinguishable from the ethical; politics had a certain autonomy as power, or the quest for effectiveness. Put off during the First World War by pro-French propaganda that trumpeted conventional democratic ideas, Croce went out of his way to laud first Treitschke, for his realistic conception of the state, and then Marx, for having undercut the moralistic liberal myths of humanity and justice.[13] By implication, for both Croce and Gentile, the new Italian thought might eventually offer a more modern, convincing understanding of politics – and even pave the way for post-liberal forms of political practice.

Although Croce and Gentile continued to have much in common, their subtle differences in philosophical emphasis, evident as early as 1907, produced a public divergence in 1913. While Croce kept making distinctions – between theory and practice, knowing and doing, politics and ethics – Gentile kept trying to bring things together, to find deeper unities or identities. Croce charged Gentile with 'mysticism,' but it was this charge that led Gentile to call Croce's attention to 'that sense of profound melancholy that pervades your whole contemplation of the world.'[14] The question was what possibilities – and responsibilities – open up for humanity in a world of radical immanence, a world endlessly coming to be in history. The answers were not obvious.

Troubled by the 'melancholy' implications of Croce's position, Gentile sought mightily to show it did not exhaust the cultural possibilities that opened with the new totalizing historicism. More specifically, he sought to give an account of the world that had room for – and invited – the free, creative human agency that he had come to associate with a world of radical immanence, but that Croce seemed to delimit. Although both Croce and Gentile sought to reformulate the central insights of Christianity for a world of radical immanence, Gentile did so more radically and single-mindedly. Even after – or especially after – the death of the transcendent God, it was possible and desirable to make new sense of the spiritual conception that Christianity had posited, with human beings as free, responsible moral agents.[15] Now reality is not given, but self-creating, and humanity might come to understand its own god-like creativity as bound up with the self-creation of reality.

The question of distinction versus unity that most immediately occasioned the dispute of 1913 can seem futile indeed, given the ease of playing with both categories. And the difference between Croce and Gentile was only one of degree. Even as he accented the distinction between thought and action, Croce featured their relationship: historical knowing prepares action. And partly in response to Gentile, he would increasingly feature interconnections, affording privilege to the ethical by the 1920s. But their difference in emphasis proved to have highly symptomatic political consequences, especially concerning our way of conceiving aggregate human agency. Croce always shied away from Gentile's extreme way of fusing thought and action, knowing and what is to be known. Any such degree of unity was unnecessary – and ultimately dangerous. Conversely, as far as Gentile was concerned, no matter what adjustments Croce made, Crocean historicism left action blind, and human freedom limited, in unnecessary ways. Croce's understanding of the new Italian historicism did not invite human responsibility – did not realize human potential – in the way Gentile thought possible.

Croce's criticisms of 1913 helped Gentile clarify his emerging philosophical position, which he called 'actualism,' or actual idealism, and which he first outlined in systematic form in *Teoria generale dello spirito come atto puro*, published in 1916.[16] The central tenet of Gentile's philosophical stance is highly abstract, and on first encounter may seem simply vacuous, or merely an inconsequential move within the abstruse intellectual game that the tradition of philosophical idealism had become, or perhaps had always been. The world, he decided, is best understood as a continuous act of thought thinking. Moreover, thinking is endlessly 'actual,' in process, so the 'past' is only what we can no longer think, what is no longer thought. Gentile fastened upon thinking as the archetypal human activity, the realm of openness, or freedom of the spirit. Only in thinking do we overcome determination by being; only when we think do we, in our specifically human capacity, transcend what already is.

At first, any such priority to thinking seems merely a warrant for giddy licence, or fantasy, or 'thinking makes it so' – a more plausible charge than solipsism. But Gentile was not lapsing into the absurd notion that we can simply think away what we do not like. The key is to understand all that he encompassed by thinking – from what it means *really* to think something to what results from all that is thought at any moment. The point is not to accent thought as opposed to action, thinking as opposed to doing, but to grasp the sense in which thinking is itself creative activity – the most fundamental form – and is so bound up with action that thinking and doing cannot be distinguished. Thinking is the defining human activity only insofar as it is *not* mere passive reflection or contemplation, but creative, necessarily bound up with action, because it wants to realize itself in a double sense. It wants to be true, universal – to convince others – and it wants to help shape what the world becomes. If we really think something, we act on that basis. Indeed, *only* insofar as we seek to translate thought into action do we know we really think it. Wilful fantasy will not do, and we seek to avoid mere error for the same reason – because we want to respond to and genuinely affect the actual world. To be sure, fantasy and error have real effects, but not those intended, not congruent with thinking. We know that we have every incentive to bring action and thinking into alignment.

Gentile's way of fusing thought and action stemmed from his encounter with Vico, who had stressed the interpenetration of historical knowing and making. We are shaping history as we understand it in a certain way because any particular understanding initiates an imperative for a certain direction in practice. And our ethical capacity, our sense of responsibility, our care for the world, underpins the entire relationship, making us want whatever we think to be at once true and effective.[17] It is precisely this care that feeds our endless thinking and opens it to truth.

Although Gentile's actualism was highly abstract in one sense, no thinker has been more concerned to *deny* abstraction by connecting thinking to commitment, responsibility, and action. Indeed, laying things out philosophically was only preliminary to Gentile's ultimate aim – to invite, or draw out, our human ethical capacity and sense of responsibility as Croce apparently did not. Indeed, whatever his intentions, Croce's account of human being in a world without transcendence tended to leave action either blind – an irrational gesture – or egotistical. Or we may descend further, lapsing into passive indifference or irony. At the same time, thinking or knowing in Croce's world tends to become a mere exercise, perhaps a virtuoso performance, but irrelevant for practice. Or so it all seemed to Gentile.

In pushing on to a systematic philosophy by 1916, Gentile made the terms of the discussion even more abstract in one sense, yet the stakes of his 1913 dispute with Croce gradually became clearer. Gentile's effort to fuse thought and action through actualism responded not simply to internal problems of the idealist tradition in philosophy but to what seemed the mutually reinforcing problems of Western liberal culture and idiosyncratic Italian mores. On the one hand, he worried about the tendencies toward cynicism, indifference, and narcissism he saw around him, tendencies that, he felt, stemmed from the liberal, and generally positivist, distinctions between subject and object, inner and outer, public and private. On the other hand, he lamented what he took to be the characteristic Italian vices going back to the late Renaissance – rhetoric, most obviously, but ultimately the frivolously skeptical and detached mode of life that spawned rhetoric, and that Francesco De Sanctis had lamented in a famous lecture of 1869, 'L'uomo del Guicciardini.'[18]

Thus, both the modern liberal problem and the special Italian vice rested on separation – of words from actions, of ideals from commitments, of humanity from reality, which could too easily be talked about without genuine commitment and the action that follows from it. To posit unity, on the other hand, was to suggest that to think something – *really* to think it – is to believe it, to want others to believe it, to commit yourself to it, to conform your actions to it, to seek to shape the world in accordance with what you think. Insofar as knowledge, character, and action form this fundamental unity, we take life seriously – and take responsibility for the world.[19] The alternative can be seen in the various modern tendencies – that we might discern even in ourselves – to 'know' without acting, to embrace 'ideals' without committing ourselves to anything, to experience the world as something separate that happens to us, and that is either more serious, or less serious, than we are.

The problem was universal, but Italian idiosyncrasies meant that tensions in the development of liberal individualism and democratic politics were more pressing in Italy than elsewhere. Precisely because it was a little outside the mainstream, Italy could spearhead the solution to the general crisis of modern liberal culture. Drawing on the Italian humanist tradition, Gentile's philosophy provided the map, which pointed first to the scope for education, but then to more grandiose, concerted forms of action through the political sphere.

Gentile began systematically exploring the philosophy and practice of education around the turn of the century, near the outset of his career. At that point, of course, education had only recently become universal, compulsory, and generally recognized as a public or governmental responsibility. In positing human being as 'spiritual,' as thinking, and thus as free and creative, the new Italian philosophy conceived the individual as an ethical creature bound up with history-making. But as a practical matter it was up to education to nurture this specifically human capacity by fostering a humanistic self-awareness and the healthy sense of openness and responsibility that followed from it.[20] The capstone of education was precisely the new Italian philosophy, which was to afford students a rational understanding of the freedom and responsibility they had come to feel. But Gentile's conception also implied another step, into politics, to expand the power of the state to enhance the scope for collective world-making.

3: Divergent Perceptions, 1913–25

The political implications of their philosophical differences were hardly clear in 1913, and Croce and Gentile remained close. But they differed in subtle though significant ways during the European war when, after Italy's voluntary intervention in 1915, they found themselves called upon to explain the war's meaning for Italy.

Long identified with German culture in Italy, Croce was vilified by some as a pro-German traitor, and he sought especially to keep the war from contaminating the cultural sphere, including cultural relations among the belligerent nations. Fear that the Italians might fall into chauvinistic myth-making made Croce reluctant to specify any positive meaning of the war or to address Italy's uncertain role in it. The key for Italy was austerity, to fight without illusions or myths. Thus Croce seemed disappointingly circumspect to those who looked to him for insight into the meaning of the war for Italy.[21]

By the last year of the war Gentile was going beyond Croce to suggest that precisely in fighting without myths, the Italians manifested a new maturity that would ultimately make possible a reassertion of Italian culture and a distinctive role in Europe.[22] Gentile's wartime writings helped foster the notion that the Italian war experience was a vital intermediate step between the pre-war cultural renewal and new political forms.

Although most tried to learn from both Croce and Gentile for a while, Gentile's declaration of independence from Croce in 1913 began to make him fashionable, first especially among teachers.[23] Then, as Gentile offered his more assertive way of making cultural sense of Italy's wartime role, ever more bright young Italians began finding him more relevant than Croce. And whereas Croce had apparently finished his philosophical system before the war, Gentile published several of his major philosophical works, including *Teoria generale dello Spirito come atto puro,* during or just after the war, so his thought seemed particularly fresh and exciting. Early in 1918, he left Pisa to assume a chair at Rome, and by the early 1920s he was not only Italy's leading philosopher but also a uniquely influential political and civic educator.[24]

Whereas Croce wanted the Italians to fight the war without inspiring visions, Gentile linked the austerity and resoluteness of the army to the renewal of ordinary Italian life – a renewal that would ultimately make possible a reassertion of Italian culture.[25] In his inaugural lecture at the University of Rome in January 1918, Gentile charged that in philosophy, the cornerstone of any national culture, the Italians had for too long remained passive spectators, concentrating on absorbing the innovations of others.[26] But now Italy was mature enough to make its own contribution. Gentile warned against making a cult of the Italian past, just as, earlier in the war, he had condemned not only the German Fichte, but also the Italian Gioberti, for their artificial theories of national superiority.[27] But thanks to the austerity of the war experience itself, Italy could now come to terms with its tradition in a healthy, creative way, building on it to make, once again, a distinctive and leading contribution to European culture.

Most immediately, a task of definition and synthesis fell to Italy – and especially to those Italians who had most fully come to terms with the Germans. Although German philosophy had once been universal, absorbing and enriching the contributions of others, German culture had grown arrogant and complacent so that now, Gentile claimed, the German philosophical tradition was better understood among foreigners. And among those foreigners, of course, Gentile, Croce, and their allies were especially prominent.[28] Just as Hegel and the Germans had forged a new European synthesis a century before, it was now Italy that was situated to play a special role, taking advantage of German culture, but developing it in such a way as to be able to offer something new even to the Germans themselves.[29]

More specifically, the special Italian war experience might enable Italians to draw on their particular intellectual traditions to address ongoing uncertainties in European political culture; Italians could point beyond the present mix of political categories, which had been taken from others, and which now promised paralysis and decadence. Whereas Croce repeatedly defended the German conception of the state against the attacks of democrats, Gentile stressed the limits of both the French emphasis on abstract rights and the German emphasis on power and authority.[30] Indeed, Gentile charged that Croce's political conception, which drew on his philosophical distinctions to accent power or force at the expense of ethics, was morally debasing and threatened to compromise the Italian civic renewal that could follow from the war experience.[31]

Whereas for Croce the Italian nationalist Giuseppe Mazzini remained something of an embarrassment, Gentile felt that Italy had matured sufficiently to place Mazzini in a new perspective, and thereby to develop the viable parts of his conception, avoiding the chauvinistic excesses.[32] In invoking Mazzini late in the war and thereafter, Gentile pointed to the radical populist who had trumpeted the *duties* of man as opposed to the hallowed 'rights of man' of liberal tradition. Mazzini's vision gave a more overtly political coloration to Gentile's conception of the committed, serious, responsible mode of life, which stands opposed to any conception of fulfillment as private satisfaction or utility.

Most basically, Gentile was in the forefront of those who believed the war experience afforded the germ and the model for a new form of education and the political renewal that would follow. This notion had such force partly because it seemed to follow from the philosophy he had worked out by 1916, and that seemed, in turn, the most intriguing fruit of the intellectual revolution he and Croce had spearheaded earlier in the century.[33] It also helped that Gentile was now widely known as a philosopher of education, one who accented the moralizing potential of the educational process. Among the most influential of his immediate postwar works was a series of lectures in 1919 to the teachers of Trieste, just taken from Austria, accenting the possibilities and responsibilities that now lay before them. Though the situation in Trieste was particularly dramatic, all Italian educators faced the same challenge after the war.

By now, of course, we find it hard to take seriously any such talk of austerity and renewal. The modern political experience has left us cynical, so we have to work to reconceive the sense of possibility that Gentile felt, and that made his thinking so exciting to so many, especially among teachers and educated young people, in the aftermath of the First World War. The distinguished historian of philosophy Eugenio Garin, no partisan of Croce and Gentile, has emphasized that if we refuse to engage this cluster of wartime ideas, 'we risk not understanding the position of so many young people who, at the time of the First World War, found in Croce and Gentile two incomparable teachers' who seemed to show these young Italians 'how the course of history might converge with their ideals.'[34]

But fascism was coming, and with it precisely the rhetorical mythmaking and chauvinism that Croce had feared during the war. What intellectuals like Gentile offered proved inadequate to give form to the ideals and expectations that followed from the Italian war experience. Still, the war's meaning for Italy was not obvious when it ended in November 1918, or even after Italy's share in the peace had been mostly settled by the end of 1920. In light of all Gentile had taught for two decades, and in light of certain undoubted aspects of the Italian war experience, idealistic Italians could believe the time was ripe for a combination of political renewal and renewed cultural leadership in Europe. And many saw fascism, emerging directly from the war, as the instrument to realize that capacity for renewal.

Even with the emergence of fascism, Croce and Gentile at first remained mutually supportive, especially on the matters of educational reform that concerned both during the first years after the war. The advent of government by Mussolini gave Gentile the chance to become minister of public instruction and in that capacity, from October 1922 until July 1924, to begin translating his ideas about education into a comprehensive reform effort. He joined the Fascist party in June 1923, explaining his reasons in a letter to Mussolini. At this point Gentile associated Mussolini's government with the restoration of the pre-positivist, statist form of 'liberalism' that the *Destra Storica* – the 'Old Right' heirs of Cavour – had represented in the first years after unification. He had in mind especially those like Silvio Spaventa who had been most influenced by Hegelian notions, and who associated liberty with the authority of the state.[35] Herbert Marcuse, writing in 1934, cited this letter as a 'classic document' demonstrating the inner relationship between liberalism and totalitarianism.[36] Although Croce was more standoffish, he counselled short-term acquiescence during the first eighteen months of Mussolini's government; the liberal ruling class needed to stand back and get its house in better order. At this point it was not clear to Gentile, to Croce, or to anyone else, how radical fascism in power was to be.

But Gentile's ambitions for fascism quickly grew, and by early 1924 he was accenting its novelty and world-historical significance as the political translation of Italy's pre-war intellectual renewal and wartime maturation.[37] The crisis occasioned by the murder of the anti-fascist deputy Giacomo Matteotti in 1924 forced fascism into a more radical break with the old liberal order. Although Gentile, like the other major ministers, submitted his resignation during the crisis, he deepened his identification with fascism, for the Matteotti crisis seemed – and proved to be – the occasion for fascism to commit itself decisively to building a new, distinctly post-liberal form of state. As Gentile redoubled his efforts to show what fascism could mean, Mussolini called upon him to chair the Commission of Fifteen (later Eighteen) set up to specify the institutional changes that would carry fascism beyond its awkward, no longer tenable compromise with the old liberal regime. Gentile favoured the corporativist direction that in fact emerged from this effort – and that proved essential to subsequent fascist institutional change and self-understanding.

Croce, in contrast, committed himself unequivocally to opposition once it became clear by early 1925 that continued government by Mussolini meant a full-scale change of regime.[38] But because Croce had been even more important than Gentile in fostering the notion that liberal democracy, as usually understood, was incongruent with the new Italian anti-positivist philosophy, Gentile and other fascists continued to claim that Croce was one of them, 'a fascist without the black shirt.'[39] Forced to think more deeply about the nature of politics, Croce concluded that his own radical historicism, and not the earlier notions of utility or individual rights, afforded the only convincing basis for a modern liberal politics. In seeking to recast liberalism, he responded partly to Gentile's fascist ideas, just as Gentile, in trumpeting the virtues of fascism, continued to respond partly to Croce.

Gentile's earlier thinking was surely bound to take political form at some point, but it did not require attachment to the particular regime led by Mussolini. As he gradually committed himself to fascism, from 1922 to 1924, Gentile well understood that he was making a contingent political decision, laden with risk. Many of his followers made the same political decision, though some did not, and even a number of those who did drifted away at various points as the regime developed.[40] Several of the most important *gentiliani*, including Ugo Spirito, Delio Cantimori, and Galvano della Volpe, subsequently found their way to communism.

Gentile was too intellectual for many fascists, but he exercised a powerful role as cultural organizer within the fascist regime, serving in a remarkable array of major positions, including that of founding president of the Istituto nazionale di cultura fascista. Although his influence diminished during the 1930s, the categories he developed in his most important fascist writings, from 1924 to 1932, remained central to the fascist self-understanding.[41] Even as Mussolini's regime compromised and temporized, Gentile's prominent place made fascism seem of universal significance precisely as the political translation of the new historicist, anti-positivist culture that he and Croce had begun forging from Italian roots before the war.[42]

4: Gentile's Fascism

As Gentile explained it in numerous speeches and writings, fascism was replacing liberalism with the modern alternative foreshadowed by Mazzini and given rigorous philosophical underpinnings by Gentile himself. As a 'spiritual' conception, accenting human freedom, creativity, and ethical capacity, it also stood opposed to its major competitors for the post-liberal terrain, namely, materialistic Marxism and naturalistic nationalism or biologistic racism.

What the modern world required was not Marx's socio-economic revolution against capitalism but a two-pronged revolution against liberalism. On the one hand, that revolution was to be socio-cultural, using more broadly encompassing forms of education to develop the potential for responsibility and 'seriousness' that lies within human beings. On the other hand, that revolution was to be political and institutional, to expand the scope for collective power and responsibility. Gentile envisioned the two sides endlessly coming together as the community of responsible individuals exercised that expanded political power through a more encompassing form of state, which could be described as both 'ethical' and 'totalitarian.'[43] Bizarre as it may now seem, the notion that Mussolini's regime was leading the world beyond liberalism by creating a totalitarian ethical state was Gentile's central contribution to the fascist self-understanding. Yet how can 'totalitarian' and 'ethical' come together? Even to those comfortable with Rousseau, Hegel, and notions of the general will, Gentile's concept may seem an oxymoron at first.

It helps to start by comparing Gentile with Alfredo Rocco, the Nationalist jurist who played a central role as minister of justice during the formative years of the fascist regime, from 1925 to 1932. Although critics often lump the two together, it is crucial that Gentile, unlike Rocco, did not envision mere submission of the individual to a state that is already in place and imposes itself from above.[44] The point was not merely to get Italians to identify with the existing state and its legislation. Rather, the Italians were being *unified* with a public, political sphere that moves along with them, in the collective response through which the world is endlessly remade – or comes to be – in history.

As faith in a transcendent sphere dissipates, we adjust to a historicist perspective, and the world comes to seem *our* responsibility in a way it never quite did before. There is in principle nothing that lies beyond our sense of responsibility. But our sense of our own freedom and ethical capacity draws us into the national political sphere, for it is there that we have built institutions that concentrate power in such a way that we, collectively, may exercise that responsibility in action. Indeed, because our sense of responsibility grows in a world of radical immanence, we seek to bring the national community together more cohesively to assume the ongoing task of shaping the world. And we seek to expand the scope for power, or the political sphere, because to expand the state is to expand our freedom to act, to exercise our responsibility. The state becomes all-encompassing, totalitarian, to enable the community consciously, even rationally, to make history.

It is crucial, however, that Gentile's 'ethical state' is an ideal direction, not an empirical institution; not even the new fascist state fully realized the ideal.[45] There is an ethical state only insofar as each of us, as free, potentially creative and moral individuals, feels fully responsible for the life of the whole community, and insofar as we both concentrate power and expand its reach so that the scope for collective action is all-encompassing. Not even Gentile expected this ideal to be fully realized. The point was the possibility – and desirability – of this direction, as opposed to the liberal separation between public and private, the liberal accent on negative freedom, or 'freedom from,' the liberal solicitude for the private sphere. As Stephen Holmes has emphasized, responding primarily to more recent anti-liberals like Alasdair MacIntyre and Roberto Unger, any such accents seriously misrepresent the liberal tradition, which simply does not neglect the public sphere, or the freedom to participate, to the extent that its critics have charged.[46] But though the distinction is not as sharp as Gentile would make it, Gentilian fascism, in its priorities, its sense of human possibilities, its conception of the optimal relationship between public and private, departed from any liberalism.

For Gentile, then, concentration of power and expansion of the state do not limit our freedom, as Anglo-Saxon liberal accents lead us to assume, but enable us to exercise it more responsibly. From this perspective, in fact, my freedom and sense of responsibility *require* that there be an all-encompassing state that enables – indeed, demands – my participation. But the accent on participation raises obvious questions. It is crucial that I be able *genuinely* to participate in the exercise of that expanded power. But what scope was there for such participation in fascist Italy – or can there be within any sort of post-liberal order? Gentile could echo the arguments, familiar for a generation in Italy, that the liberal parliamentary system afforded only the illusion of participation, hiding elitism and exploitation. But even in theory, how was fascism to be different?

Some critics find Gentile concentrating power in a charismatic, dictatorial leader.[47] Although any such notion was inconsistent with the overall thrust of his thought, it is arguable that such was bound to be the practical result. By now we tend to find charismatic leadership, inviting non-rational identification with a leader, to be the only alternative to liberal democracy, revolving around the suffrage system, representation, and parliamentary politics. Perhaps in rejecting the latter, Gentile was bound to nourish the former. But if there are no other alternatives, that is clearer to us, in light of the outcome of fascism, than it was when the fascist experiment was in progress, and when Gentile and many others sought precisely to devise new forms of participation. For many of its advocates, including Gentile, the much-discussed corporativist state promised more direct and continuous forms of participation in public life than parliamentary democracy had made possible. More generally, fascism pioneered new forms of mass mobilization and organization, which served to educate and to give a public dimension to formerly private activities. The work of Emilio Gentile has shown not only how seriously this thrust – this 'sacralization of politics' – was taken at the time, but also that it was more effective than we have recognized.

But to the extent that a more direct, continuous, and intense form of participation was possible – in what sense could it be considered desirable? How does the aspiration relate to the individualism so prized in the liberal tradition? In light of the leaden images that 'totalitarianism' calls forth, Gentile's accents surprise us. Even as it expands to become totalitarian, the state need not be merely coercive, intrusive, or authoritarian, as the crucial contrast with Alfredo Rocco's brand of totalitarianism makes clear. Gentile and Rocco both envisioned a limitless expansion of the state's sovereignty, but their sense of the present challenge and imperative differed sharply. Rocco was responding to what he found the appalling vulnerability of liberal institutions, in light of the rise of the masses and the growth of powerful private associations like trade unions.[48] Gentile, in contrast, accented the positive opportunity, the scope for a qualitative departure from liberalism to more fully realize human capacities. Even as he eschewed the liberal democratic form of egalitarianism, he was seeking more genuinely participatory political forms.

From the start of his career, Gentile had sought to show how the human potential that lies in all of us could be nurtured, and how the free ethical capacity of individuals connects with the community and the political sphere. Thus his abiding concern with education and its civic implications. So as he understood it, the totalitarian state does not stand opposed to the freedom of differentiated individuals, as we tend to assume it must. That state could not be coercive or static, nor did it require an undifferentiated uniformity.[49] Indeed, it is essential that the totalitarian ethical state be *genuinely* congruent with individual freedom, that it nurture and respect the free, ethical capacity of individuals.

For Gentile as much as for any individualist, individuals differ, and each individual is a precious fount of human ethical capacity.[50] So the totalitarian state values individuation and the resulting difference of perspective.[51] Gentile insisted explicitly that participation and free discussion remain essential – not, to be sure, because individual self-realization is somehow an end in itself, but because such mechanisms are essential for change and growth.[52] But even while embracing individual differentiation and freedom, Gentile envisioned a community made up entirely of 'fascists,' in the sense that all these differentiated individuals are to exercise their responsible moral agency in the all-encompassing public world of the state.

Gentile's totalitarian fascism stands opposed not to individuation, not to debate within the state, not to dynamism and change, but to the passive indifference, the cynicism, the selfish egotism of the merely 'private' person. There is no place in Gentile's order for contemplative withdrawal, self-cultivation, or alienation. Self-cultivation is merely narcissistic; alienation is merely frivolous. Though our commitments will differ, we are to live lives of total public commitment, total seriousness, total responsibility for the world.

The alternative – freedom *from* the public world; personal, private freedom in withdrawal from the world – might make sense in terms of a transcendent dimension. But in a post-Christian world, the individual's free moral agency can realize itself only 'horizontally,' by becoming one with the public world. There can be freedom only *in* the world, with the world – only insofar as we feel at home in the world. And this means not passive acceptance of a world that comes to us from outside, about which we have no choice, but a sense of full involvement with a continuously growing world, a world that, precisely in its openness, invites our sense of full responsibility.

So in Gentile's totalitarian state, power, freedom, responsibility, and participation expand together. Genuine fascists come to experience themselves as essential components of the community of ethical agents that continually remakes the world through political action. Their sense of responsibility is continuous and limitless, and, thus, so is their involvement. The totalitarian ethical state is the continuous act by which the community of differentiated individuals forever remakes the world through the public, political realm.

5: Gentile and Beyond

Although the fortunes of Gentile's educational reform effort were mixed at best, the direction of the fascist regime by 1925 seemed congruent in important respects with his totalitarian vision. Despite all the limitations evident in retrospect, the institutions of mass mobilization and corporativism central to the fascist regime by the later 1920s were surely totalitarian in direction. To be sure, Mussolini's 1929 accord with the Catholic Church disillusioned Gentile considerably – and not surprisingly, because it was perhaps the most *un*-totalitarian measure imaginable. But even this measure was for Gentile not the occasion to abandon his effort but rather to step up the pressure – and the rhetoric. And much continued to go well, from his perspective, in the complex ongoing struggle to determine the direction of the fascist regime.

Still, by the mid-thirties, with the regime bogging down in compromise and a superficial cult of the Duce, Gentile had become much less active in fascist politics. When the Second World War broke out, he refrained from public statement for two years but began addressing its meaning after the intervention of the United States late in 1941. The culmination was his 'Discorso agli Italiani,' delivered on the Campidoglio in Rome upon the invitation of the Fascist party secretary on 24 June 1943, just a month before Mussolini's ouster. The war was to defend the ongoing promise of fascism, with its post-liberal ideals and corporativist institutions.[53] Even when Mussolini's fall signalled the end of the original fascist regime, Gentile refused to rally to the anti-fascists but rather adhered to Mussolini's rump Repubblica di Salò, in German-occupied northern Italy, until he was assassinated by a partisan in 1944.[54]

Because so much of the reality of fascism – not least, the posturing and rhetoric – flew in the face of Gentile's ideas, we may be tempted to dismiss his whole conception as irrelevant or as, at best, an instrumental myth. Moreover, as Giuseppe Calandra has emphasized, Gentile's tones of apology or triumphalism after 1929 suffocated any possibility of rational evaluation.[55] In terms of certain essential questions about fascism, Gentile's ideas are indeed but myths or window dressing, but not in terms of other such questions, especially those that deal with the origins of fascism and its relationship with wider cultural changes in the West.

In one sense, what Gentile offered was but another variation on the heady vision that we find in Hegel, the young Hegelians, and the Marxist tradition, positing a form of unification and wholeness that transcends the distinction between theory and practice, thinking and doing. For Gentile as for Marx, the scope for unifying theory and practice meant that we can begin making history lucidly, freely, responsibly, for the first time. In fact, encounter with Marxism was central to Gentile as his sense of human possibilities began to crystallize in the later 1890s.[56] He encountered Croce just as Croce had gotten caught up in his famous exchange with Antonio Labriola over the centre of gravity, and enduring import, of Marxism. Seeking to pinpoint the basis of the Labriola-Croce divergence, Gentile published a book on Marx in 1899, when only twenty-four years old. And he remained preoccupied with Marx throughout his career. It is striking that he republished this youthful work in 1937, at the height of the fascist period, noting in the new preface that Lenin had numbered the book among the best non-Marxist works on Marxism.[57] Obviously, we cannot do justice to the Marx-Gentile comparison here, but in light of essential questions about the relationship between Marxism and fascism, it is worth articulating several interlocking points about Gentile's divergence from Marx.

As we might expect, Gentile, in his early book, sought to deflate the materialism and to play up the humanism in Marxism, anticipating, up to a point, the vogue of the later Hegelian Marx that followed the publication of *The German Ideology* and *The Economic and Philosophical Manuscripts of 1844* decades later. For Gentile, 'historical materialism' was essentially an oxymoron, since history is the realm of freedom. Despite its unfortunate materialistic admixtures, Marxism rested on 'praxis,' the creative human activity through which the world is made in history.[58]

As Calandra has emphasized, Gentile was too quick to equate Marx's materialism with atomistic individualism and the notion that society is a mechanical aggregate of individuals.[59] This was essentially to attribute the deleterious features of Marxism to positivism – and it was not adequate as an account of the moment of necessity in Marxism. Still, Gentile's critique of the materialist side of Marx reflected deeper differences in their conceptions of the impediments to free human creativity – and thus of the requirements for opening that creativity.

Although 'the idea' seems ethereal and the economic factor concrete, accent on the latter may breed passivity, whereas the former invites history-making human action. The orthodox Marxist conception of the coming revolution's mental or 'spiritual' side, resting on the dialectic of total alienation and the formation of a universal class, came to seem inadequate, both in theory and practice, to an array of revisionists precisely when Gentile was coming of age. And the role of mind, consciousness, spirit, or creative thinking was never convincingly addressed within the tradition thereafter, despite all the varied efforts to clarify the dialectic of necessity and freedom. Gradually, the role for intellectuals, defined by mind or consciousness, forced itself to centre stage in Marxist thinkers from Lenin to Gramsci, but the accents that resulted never fully meshed with materialism – and especially the 'universal' role that a particular class is to play because of its objective place in the capitalist economy. As he was coming of age, Gramsci was among the many young Italians influenced by Gentile. And as the fascist experiment unfolded, he sought to think beyond Gentile about the formation of a collective will and about the role for intellectuals within that process.[60] The practice of fascism revealed Gentile's mistakes and blind spots, and Gramsci learned from them. But even in 1899, though his critique missed a good deal, Gentile pinpointed some genuine tensions concerning materialism, history, freedom, and action in Marxism.

There was room for a purely 'idealist' response and alternative to the first vogue of Marxism, and in a sense Gentile offered it in archetypal form. Yet his position vis-à-vis Marxism is not to be understand in simple dualistic terms.

We might be tempted to view Gentile, at least in his 1899 critique, as a mere throwback to the position pilloried by Marx in his famous eleventh thesis on Feuerbach: 'The philosophers have only *interpreted* the world, in various ways; the point, however, is to *change* it.'[61] For Marx, history can become – and indeed, is becoming – the realm of freedom, but it is not the realm of freedom insofar as it is made under the compulsion of capitalism or, more generally, under economic necessity and the concomitant differentiation into classes. To create the conditions of freedom, a revolutionary transformation in economic relationships is necessary. A mere reinterpretation, a different intellectual take, is not enough.

Yet though Gentile believed a new philosophy had to come first, he too envisioned changing the world – through the practical realization of that philosophy. To be sure, in 1899 he had only a glimmer of what such a practical program would entail. It was clear, however, that the key to change was not economic but educational and political, for the human capacities to be opened were being checked not by economic necessity in capitalism, but by the shadow of transcendence in liberalism and positivism. What was necessary was an assault on positivist liberalism to bring about new, more intense forms of mass education and mass politics. And the agent of change could not be defined in materialist terms as some class, its role derived from its objective place in the economy. Rather, such change comes first from a new idea, to be given rational, systematic form in philosophy. That idea realizes itself through the assent of free individuals, who come to recognize its superiority. In the Italian case, the war experience, by transcending the public-private distinction, afforded an essential preliminary.

Even with Marxist categories in some disarray, it is easy to parody Gentile's conception as conservative, ethereal, or vacuous in comparison with the Marxian emphasis on a revolutionary economic transformation. Though both Gentile and Croce pinpointed some key tensions in Marx's historical materialism, neither did justice to the force of the Marxian concept of ideology or the Marxian critique of capitalist civilization. But Gentile did not exclude economic problems from the realm that human beings might address through the expanded political sphere. The society might even deem economic problems the most important at various points. But what counts as a problem, and its degree of importance, is not objective but is rather subject to human decision. Moreover, economic impediments to human freedom continually well up anew, and we address them on the basis of the freedom that defines us now.

Even with the fascist revolutionary break, the effort that follows from Gentile's philosophy is ongoing, unfinished. In his 1899 study, Gentile found another tension in Marxism, for Marx's teleological tendency, based on his priori framework, was incompatible with the radical openness, freedom, and creativity that some of his accents suggested. To be sure, there is room for disagreement about how empty is the telos in Marx, as in Hegel. In some sense, certainly, the achievement of a classless society means not static fulfillment but the opening of free human creativity for the first time. But there remains an important difference in emphasis, for Gentile explicitly posited a species of totalist 'historicism' as opposed to the totalist telos of human emancipation he found in Marx. There is no end, no resolution, no achievement of wholeness. The human responsibility of world-making in history is never finished, nor is the ethical state, which requires ongoing education and totalitarian mobilization. Conversely, the totalitarian ethical state is not an institution of static fulfillment but an ongoing educational instrument. Gentile's sense that the tasks of education and world-building are endless helps explain the accent on ongoing activism and dynamism in Italian fascism.

The new Italian thought that Croce and Gentile developed before the war was a post-Hegelian totalizing historicism that transcended the antithesis between Hegel and the individualizing historicist tradition of Ranke, Dilthey, and Meinecke. But the political implications of such a position were hardly clear. And though the emphases of Croce and Gentile differed virtually from the start, it was only the advent of fascism that brought to the fore the central tensions and uncertainties within that larger position – and forced the political schism between the two thinkers. What was it that proved to differentiate fascist totalitarianism and liberalism within the historicist framework that Croce and Gentile shared?

We have seen that Gentile believed that the free individual, not the state, is the source of the world's ethical capacity; in this sense, he was as much an individualist as Croce was. Conversely, Croce placed no more premium than Gentile on individual self-affirmation as an end in itself. Nor was Croce any more concerned with protecting the private individual by restricting the state; he was as explicit as Gentile in criticizing the conventional liberal effort to limit the state's reach.[62] And for both thinkers, we all collaborate in the coming to be of some particular world in history. In this sense Croce, for all his criticism of Gentile, was similarly insisting on a species of unity and totality, as opposed to the earlier individualizing historicism. But for Croce what followed from the new Italian historicism was not Gentile's totalitarian inflation of politics but a new understanding of human limits – and thus a new grounding for conventional liberal procedures and institutions.

The divergence between Croce and Gentile turned on the *form* of our collective, world-making action and, still more fundamentally, on the scope for freedom and power in the immanent historicist world that both posited. As an anti-fascist, Croce was widely admired as the proponent of a 'religion of liberty,' but in a crucial sense, it was Gentile, not Croce, who sought to adumbrate such a religion in and for a world without a transcendent God. The Crocean 'religion of liberty' meant only that liberty is irrepressible, because free creative human response is built in, an attribute of human being. But human freedom remains confined to the individual, and individual moral response, in Croce's view, is lonely and idiosyncratic – even though it is to be prepared, ideally, by historical understanding.[63]

For Gentile, in contrast, we are genuinely free only insofar as we *together* can be responsible for the world. So not only must knowing, willing, and doing coalesce on the individual level, but the individual must come together with the community through common participation in expanded power. And Gentile thought it possible to bring this condition about; through a combination of education and institutional change, the ethical capacity of individuals comes together with the expanded power of the state. We can find a political form making possible full collective agency, so that in some sense we *do* know what we are doing. Only insofar as we create this new political form – this totalitarian ethical state – can there be full-scale freedom.

Even before the First World War, Gentile began to sense that Croce's distinctions left the culture not merely with loneliness and humility, but with melancholy and indifference. Without the more intensely unified sort of culture Gentile was seeking, a post-metaphysical world runs out of control, and we cannot feel – and seize – our responsibility for it. The culture gradually drifts into cynicism and egotism. In our gloomier moments, we might feel we recognize, in the condition of the polity today, some of what Gentile feared – but thought it possible to head off and transcend.

However, the outcome of fascism and the other totalitarian experiments of this century suggest that we are *not* free and responsible, that we *cannot* know what we are doing, or what is happening, in the grandiose way Gentile envisioned. The challenge then becomes precisely Croce's: to show, first, why humility, pluralism, and tolerance follow from our new sense of the human place in the world, but then why, and how, we can proceed with a modicum of confidence, rationality, and solidarity even in a world that is indeed more 'melancholy' than Gentile's, but that, as the modern political experiment has proceeded, has come to seem the only world we have.

Croce admitted that our ongoing remaking of the world always has an element of blindness to it, no matter how much we concentrate power, and no matter how successfully we require everyone to participate in that power. Thus his insistence that the maker of the world is ultimately the whole spirit; the spirit – history itself – is the only agent, and we collaborate blindly in its agency.[64] And thus his accent on the humility, pluralism, and tolerance that surround our individual commitments.[65] At the same time, however, Croce had to show why his more humble conception did not have to yield the sense of futility, the political indifference, that Gentile associated with it. And thus Croce's deepened emphasis on the enduring weight of what we do, on action as history-making, as he sought the terms of a neo-liberal politics.

Especially in his writings of the 1940s, Croce was responding not only to the ongoing totalitarian threat but also to the cultural tendencies that fed the vogue of existentialism, which he found to be a self-indulgent overreaction to the loss of transcendence and the recent political disillusionments. At the same time, he also had to struggle to retain the new historicist space against the many who, in response to the disasters of the age, were calling for a return to transcendent values, including the natural law tradition.[66] So even though he was seeking to map out a middle ground, he was engaged on several axes simultaneously, and thus, as he approached his eightieth birthday in 1946, he found himself embattled – and easily misrepresented. He left some crucial questions unanswered, and, drawn against his will to the immediate political level, he made his share of mistakes.[67] But his response invites comparison with later attempts – like that of Richard Rorty – similarly to rethink liberalism in light of the retreat from foundationalist philosophy.

To many of those who sought to reassess political possibilities during the 1940s, the world seemed to have spun out of control. Human action had come to seem futile – or to have unintended, and deleterious, consequences. For Albert Camus, who enjoyed a particular vogue in the aftermath of the Second World War, even broadly political action could only be a gesture of individual self-assertion or defiance, almost to spite history, which simply confronts us with one plague after another.[68]

Although Croce was shaken by the events of his own lifetime, his response even during the 1940s was to reaffirm and refine the historicist orientation he had gradually elaborated. But thus he drew criticism from existentialists like Nicola Abbagnano, who accused him of downplaying subjective personal experience.[69] Parrying the existentialist charge of insipid optimism, Croce stressed that for the individual, being caught up in this purely historical world was closer to tragedy than to idyll.[70] But rather than dwell on personal anxiety, we should do what we take to be our duty, understanding the role of what we do in changing the present world. In suggesting that the spirit, or history itself, is the agent of the world, Croce was not submerging individuals within some providential process, as critics like Abbagnano charged, but positing a relationship between individuality and the totality that yields a balance between commitment, on the one hand, and humility, pluralism, and tolerance, on the other.

Because our actions, in their complex interaction, produce the next moment, which becomes the basis for all subsequent moments, Croce stressed 'the immortality of the act,' the cumulative weight of what we do in the endless coming to be of the world.[71] Insofar as we care for the world and feel responsibility for it, we want what we do to last, affecting what the world becomes. It is not enough that action be authentic, or self-creating. So we experience what we do as history-making, as having enduring weight. Because we fear the sense of futility that afflicts us when our actions fail to connect with the growing world, we seek a vocation that enables us to focus our efforts and maximize our chance to respond effectively.[72]

And through historical inquiry, Croce continued to insist, we seek the understanding that prepares action, increasing the likelihood of effectiveness. So though he balked at Gentile's hyper-rationalist tendencies, Croce held to an important element of rationalism as he continued to insist on the scope for historical understanding. Thus in part his absolute historicism differed first from the existentialist premium on a gesture of authenticity, but then also from Rorty's accent on self-cultivation.

Despite the scope for knowing to prepare action, we understand that action is fraught with risk, for we can never know what will result from what we do, no matter how good our intentions. Thus we require a measure of faith to sustain us as we act. Yet all that is left to us is a mere faith in history – history stretched thin, with no implication of providence, deliverance, or even direction. In a world of absolute historicism, history entails simply Heideggerian 'gathering,' the coherence that brings actions together to produce a next moment that builds on the present, though in ways that are never totally foreseeable. But for Croce this was enough for us to feel that it matters what we do, to engage our sense of responsibility.[73]

In entrusting what we do to history, we hope that those who come after will use our legacies well, just as we feel under obligation to use well what the past has bequeathed to us. Our world has resulted from the sum of the actions of all who came before us, and a sense of kinship with them stimulates each of us to do our part, to engage and transform that world through our own present action.[74] But no matter how responsibly we have acted to transform the legacy of the past for the future, we cannot know what will happen to what we do, so we feel anxiety about how our actions will enter history. We entrust what we do to the strangers of the future, uncertain what they will make of it. In our darker moments, our faith wavers and our efforts seem futile because we risk the capriciousness of history.

Croce never neglected the troubling dimensions of the individual's relationship with history – the sense of risk, of impermanence, of futility, of tragedy – but again and again he sought to show how we endlessly surmount them.[75] So rather than accent authenticity or edification, or the scope for innocent play or endless disruption, he featured the cumulative weight of what we do, the responsible labour that serves ongoing world-building.

Turning from foundationalist philosophy a generation later, Richard Rorty came to a position that recalls Croce's in important respects, but he ended up moving in the opposite direction to accent edifying fictions, as opposed to historical truth, personal autonomy and self-creation, as opposed to identification with the wider 'public' world, and irony, as opposed to congruence with a world of nothing but history. Experiencing history as at once suffocating and capricious, he eschewed any premium on experiencing what we do as history-making. Thus, Rorty worried about our tendency to 'worship corpses' – to take some past creative 'metaphor,' or creative use of language, as today's literal truth. And though he recalled Croce in accenting the risk inherent in entrusting our acts to the capricious future, his response to the situation was different.[76] Because he found the human relationship to history to be fundamentally ironic, Rorty specified a cultural premium on literature as opposed to history, on personal autonomy, redescription, and edification, as opposed to the 'seriousness' of history-making action.[77]

Accenting the sense of futility or suffocation that the capricious historical world may entail for the individual, thinkers from Nietzsche to Camus to Rorty have suggested, as Croce did not, that individuality or selfhood must be forged in tension with history, even to spite it. And there are better reasons for such accents than Croce allowed. But especially in light of the tendencies toward extremity and overreaction, there are also good reasons for interjecting Croce's moderate, circumspect strategy into our ongoing effort to rethink our political situation after the failures of our totalitarian experiments. In light of the outcome of Gentile's fascism, Croce stood his ground, for he had begun to grasp as early as 1913 that Gentile's more grandiose reading of the new historicist humanism did not exhaust the possibilities. Even after the misguided totalitarians like Gentile have led us astray, the world is sufficiently coherent to invite ongoing questioning and work. Though it will not be in Gentile's way, the world will continually be remade through the interaction of all we do.

chapter 6

Maggi's Croce, Sasso's Gentile, and the Riddles of Twentieth-Century Italian Intellectual History

This essay was published in *Journal of Modern Italian Studies* 7, no. 1 (Spring 2002): 116–44. Michele Maggi responded in *Rivista di storia della filosofia* 58 (new series), no. 1 (2003): 87–97. I was invited by the editor, Enrico Rambaldi, to respond in turn, but I declined because of other commitments at that point. However, I have a high regard for the work of Professor Maggi, as the present article perhaps does not make sufficiently clear, in light of its particular focus and thrust. His book taught me much about the novelty in Croce's thinking in *La poesia,* for example. Still, I thought it important to go beyond his frame of reference when assessing Croce's response to the troubling events of his own time, especially if the wider ongoing relevance of Croce's thinking was to be made clear to those outside Italy. Conversely, I felt that Maggi's set of questions, useful though they were in one sense, reflected an Italian discussion that I found delimited in certain respects. It seemed to me, in fact, that his argument tended to confirm the notion that the Crocean legacy was best approached on the Italian level and lacked wider relevance. Convinced as I was of the need to show precisely that wider relevance, my task, and my challenge, in the present article had been a bit different from Maggi's, as I discussed with him when we met, cordially, in Messina late in 2002.

Aspects of my critique of Maggi here might be compared with points I raised in chapter 3. As I note there, contemporary critics were making fun of precisely the sort of serenity that Maggi accents in the late Croce. Thus, for example, Elio Vittorini, launching his review *Politecnico* in 1945, spoke sarcastically of 'a culture that consoles us in our suffering' (see note 5 in chapter 3).

I thank the editors of *Journal of Modern Italian Studies* for permission to republish the present essay.

Questioning a Distinctive Intellectual Tradition

In Italy at the dawn of the twentieth century, Benedetto Croce (1866–1952) and Giovanni Gentile (1875–1944) seized the cultural spotlight and spearheaded a remarkable intellectual revolution. And though they made lots of enemies along the way, and though they themselves split bitterly over fascism, they proved central to Italian intellectual history during the first half of the century – and in less direct but still crucial ways thereafter. Those who passed within their orbit constitute a virtual who's who among Italian intellectuals of the period, from Guido De Ruggiero, Adolfo Omodeo, Luigi Russo, and Giuseppe Lombardo-Radice to Guido Calogero, Galvano Della Volpe, Delio Cantimori, and Federico Chabod. Even those influenced less directly or consistently, from Giuseppe Antonio Borgese and Giuseppe Prezzolini to Piero Gobetti and Antonio Gramsci, cannot be addressed without reference to the tradition that Croce and Gentile initiated. So central were the two thinkers that Eugenio Garin, in his still indispensable survey of the era, decided to delete them from the index because they came up on virtually every page.[1] In its range and impact, the Croce-Gentile tradition remains unique in modern European intellectual history.

Especially through the journal *La critica,* launched in January 1903, Croce and Gentile sought to promote Italian cultural and civic renewal, in opposition, most immediately, to the reigning positivism. Although they embraced some of the categories of German idealism, they were not simply doing philosophy, operating within an established tradition, but responding to a broader challenge, not confined to Italy, bound up with modernity and especially secularization. The two thinkers gradually came to believe that, together and singly, they constituted the cutting edge of modern thought in the West. They took it for granted, in fact, that their thinking *was* modern thought.

The key was to conceive the world without transcendence – or in terms of radical immanence. There is only the concrete historical world that is forever coming to be through free, creative human response. The perpetual incompleteness of that world is a measure of our own freedom and responsibility. We come to grasp as never before the sense in which what the world next becomes is up to us. A broad cultural program seemed to follow.

The sense that they offered the ultimate in modern thought made Croce and Gentile especially exciting to Italians. And for a while their efforts attracted considerable notice abroad. Croce, especially, was among the world's best-known intellectuals during his own lifetime.[2] His *La critica*, which appeared for almost fifty years, was among the most respected journals of its kind ever published and is now to be found in virtually every major research library.[3] But the language Croce and Gentile adopted was hard for outsiders to penetrate – and by now may seem anything but modern on first encounter. Croce offered a 'philosophy of the spirit,' and Gentile's categories seem murkier still. So how to place this tradition in the wider intellectual history of the West was problematic virtually from the start. Was it genuinely innovative and modern or merely *retardataire*? It was surely distinctive, but was it thus merely idiosyncratic and even provincial?

Though they continued to share a common framework, Croce and Gentile became bitter rivals. Gentile established his philosophical distance from Croce in 1913 and over the next few years outlined his own distinctive brand of philosophical idealism, known as actual idealism, or actualism. By the early 1920s, he had become not only Italy's leading philosopher but an influential civic educator. Gentile seemed exciting partly because he, unlike Croce, found major cultural significance in the Italian war effort. He joined with fascism in 1923, becoming minister of education in Mussolini's government. His definitive split with Croce came in 1925 as Mussolini, in the wake of the Matteotti crisis, began constructing a new, specifically fascist state, soon to proclaim itself totalitarian.

Turning at last to unequivocal opposition, Croce became perhaps the world's best-known anti-fascist as he sought to offer a modern recasting of liberalism in response to the fascist challenge. Gentile, in contrast, became a major cultural power broker within the fascist regime and its most important ideologue, offering ideas central to its totalitarian self-understanding. Indeed, he was arguably the most significant intellectual to play so central a role in European fascism. And he hung on to the bitter end, even embracing Mussolini's *Repubblica di Salò* before being assassinated by a partisan in April 1944.

Although they had long seemed modern and exciting, Croce and Gentile each suffered a precipitous decline in influence in Italy with the end of the fascist era. Gentile's fate is no surprise, but Croce, too, fell from view surprisingly quickly, though he had been central to Italy's rich debate about post-fascist political possibilities. To his detractors, his thinking seemed vacuous or prejudicially conservative – a political and intellectual dead end. Some held that, despite Croce's anti-fascism by 1925, there was some deeper connection between the emergence of the overall Croce-Gentile current and the Italian invention of fascism.[4] Many among the intellectuals who had earlier embraced Croce and/or Gentile now turned to the Marxist Gramsci, whose *Quaderni del carcere* were published posthumously during the late forties. Even before he died in 1952, at the age of eighty-six, Croce was being deemed *superato*, passé. And the Gramscian turn led to a preoccupation with the ideological implications and political functions of Croce's thought.

More generally, the flight from Croce reflected a determination to break from what now seemed to have been a provincial embrace of the Italian tradition. Having been too quick to believe that the Croce-Gentile current was of universal significance, the Italians now needed to catch up to the Western mainstream. By 1978 Raffaello Franchini, the most distinguished of the last cohort of Croce's immediate followers, was lamenting that Croce had become taboo in the dominant circles of Italian culture.[5] As for Gentile, Norberto Bobbio commented in 1974 that Gentile's philosophy seemed not only dead, but literally incomprehensible.[6]

To be sure, the Crocean current remained very much alive in a few delimited circles, especially through the mediation of Franchini at the University of Naples. And still today there are major Italian scholars in every age cohort who are directly within the Crocean lineage.[7] But in the overall scheme of Italian intellectual life, the earlier tradition has remained marginal. Carlo Ginzburg developed his internationally influential version of microhistory partly in opposition to Croce. Gianni Vattimo ignored the earlier Italian tradition as he turned especially to Nietzsche and Heidegger, then, during the 1980s, attracted an international audience through *pensiero debole*, his own version of modern (or postmodern) thought.[8] It seemed that anyone seeking to be *au courant* had to engage Nietzsche and Heidegger – and stay as far from the Croce-Gentile tradition as possible.

Nor did Croce and Gentile have much enduring impact outside Italy, despite the notice they attracted at first, and despite their own sense of occupying the cutting edge. The lack of connection seemed anomalous to some. Writing in 1952, Frederic Simoni concluded that 'reference to Croce in current literature constitutes a comedy of errors.'[9] But by the early 1990s the Croce-Gentile tradition had become but a footnote, though the noted historian of criticism René Wellek found something especially curious about the neglect of Croce, who seemed to have anticipated much that was then trendy in cultural circles.[10]

When the tradition did come up, it was generally as a foil – and often subject to caricature. The most significant example is the noted encounter, or semi-encounter, between Ginzburg and Hayden White over the allegedly relativistic implications of White's thinking. Concerned about Holocaust denial and its implications for historiography, Ginzburg charged that White's position stemmed from the influence of Croce and especially the fascist Gentile, who allegedly warranted 'might makes right.' It went unremarked in the ensuing discussion that the whole confrontation rested on a particular reading (in fact, a double misreading) of the earlier Italian tradition.[11]

At about the same time, the Soviet specialist Abbott Gleason, in his penetrating survey of the notion of totalitarianism, found Gentile's conception of the totalitarian state 'extraordinary' and 'prophetic' but was quick to conflate Gentile's thinking with both 'conservative Hegelianism' and 'George Orwell's demonic visions.'[12] Still, detailed analysis of Gentile was beyond Gleason's scope, and his overall argument implicitly invited a deeper reading.

And in Italy over the last fifteen years or so there has been a revival of interest in the Croce-Gentile tradition and an effort to reassess its place. Some argued that a kind of reverse provincialism had been at work: the determined neglect of that tradition betrayed an overreaction, from exaggerated claims to excessive reticence. This was to suggest, if only implicitly, that assumptions about the Croce-Gentile tradition had remained central – indeed, that they had skewed recent Italian intellectual history.[13] But reassessment was tricky indeed. It entailed not only obviously controversial political implications but also sensitive questions about Italian culture and the wider world – questions about originality and idiosyncrasy, sophistication and provincialism, and the bases of influence, rejection, and neglect.

So how best to rethink the place of Croce and Gentile in Italy and the wider intellectual history of the West? One possibility, prominent in the recent Italian effort, is to start by revisiting the formal philosophies of the two thinkers, based on the premise that the philosophical dimension constitutes the rigorous core of any body of thought. As we noted, both Croce and Gentile found it essential to engage German philosophical idealism, and the new Italian current was known as neo-idealism or neo-Hegelianism virtually from the start. The sense of having taken the measure of that tradition was central to the self-understanding of each, but that label proved to limit their wider resonance. To many of those looking in from the outside, the thinking of Croce and Gentile came to seem a late embrace of a fading idealist tradition and thus provincial and passé, hardly the cutting edge of modern thought.[14]

Still, some sensed, at least, that the new Italian thinking was more innovative than that – for better or worse. In 1913 Ernst Cassirer noted with disapproval, even incredulity, how radically Croce had departed from the German tradition that Cassirer himself found still essential as a framework.[15] In fact, Croce explicitly rejected the neo-Hegelian label and eventually concluded that the very term *idealism* ought to be abandoned altogether.[16] Gentile remained much closer to the idealist tradition – but his thinking, too, was not so easily pigeonholed. To assume that reassessment is to start by treating their thinking as a species of idealist philosophy, thereby folding it within a prior, relatively familiar tradition, may be too easy, too safe. Such safety may tempt especially in the case of the fascist Gentile.

The place of philosophy has been central to the reassessment of cultural proportions that has marked Western intellectual history over the last century and a half or so. We hear of 'the end of philosophy,' or at least the end of metaphysics and any foundationalist role for philosophy. Insofar as it remains a cultural component, philosophy might be edifying, or therapeutic. In light of that wider framework, we should at least remain open to the possibility that Croce and Gentile, despite their idealist language, and whether individually or in tandem, might have been more radical, and thus harder to place, than the dominant understanding has recognized.

Whatever the expectations of its protagonists, however, the Croce-Gentile tradition proved distinctively Italian, not the cutting edge of modern thought – not even part of the modern mainstream, as our master narrative now has it. Questions about the Italianness of this tradition point to more general questions about idiosyncratic national traditions and their wider place. Does any such line of questioning necessarily invite a form of reductionist contextualism – and leave that tradition of no wider interest? Does distinctiveness suggest provincialism, or could it indicate an illuminating, even symptomatic 'margin' within the wider course of Western intellectual history?

Also obviously central is the relationship between Croce and Gentile – their initial collaboration, their intellectual divergence, and the continuing interplay between their cultural programs. Did their fateful political split stem merely from contingent personal assessments, or did it manifest a deeper difference in prior intellectual orientation – even a difference that might illuminate the wider experience of the era? For

Eugenio Garin, the many manifest differences between the two thinkers make it hardly legitimate to treat them together.[17] But even recognizing the crucial asymmetries, there may be scope for conceiving the two thinkers in tandem in new, more illuminating ways, as poles within a common but ultimately bifurcated Italian tradition.[18]

In short, questions about the Croce-Gentile tradition have remained central to Italian intellectual history, even as some treated it as a mere foil or wilfully turned away. Those questions have implications even for the place of Italy in the wider history of twentieth-century Europe. The recent appearance of two major books – Michele Maggi's on Croce and Gennaro Sasso's on Gentile – invites a fresh look at the scope for reassessment of that tradition. Read in tandem, the two studies raise potentially fruitful questions about the interface of the two thinkers, especially in light of fascism and totalitarianism and our ongoing attempt to learn the lessons and go beyond. But though each book has much to offer, each proves conventional and limited in crucial respects. So to take full advantage of them requires probing not only what they say but what they do not.

Maggi's Understanding of Croce's Enterprise

In *La filosofia di Benedetto Croce*, Michele Maggi, a professor of the history of philosophy at the University of Florence, eschews two contrasting approaches that he feels, quite plausibly, have long impeded understanding of Croce's intellectual centre of gravity.[19] First is the tendency we noted above – to take the Crocean corpus as a philosophical system, another variation on philosophical idealism, and to focus on internal dissection and criticism. What Croce offered, says Maggi, was not a closed 'architectural' system but something more open-ended, innovative, and even radical. The core is thus not to be grasped through formal philosophical categories, starting with the 'circle of distincts' long familiar to specialists. Lacking philosophical training, Croce had been drawn to philosophy during the later 1890s from problems encountered in everyday life and in other fields of study. And he quickly decided that the very place of what then counted as philosophy had to be questioned.

But Maggi also warns about the opposite tendency, to historicize or contextualize Croce's thinking in one of the several extrinsic ways that preclude genuine engagement – including, of course, the 'ideological' reading derived from Gramsci. Seeking to avoid either extreme, Maggi shows how Croce's effort to confront a set of European-wide cultural problems around the turn of the century led to the framework that he worked out in his more-or-less systematic works of the pre–First World War period. Croce sought to point beyond a whole set of overlapping dualisms – psychological and physical, individual and general, history and nature, fact and value – that seemed to be leading the wider culture around in circles. A radical change in the terms of the discussion seemed necessary to overcome such dualisms and the wider cultural impasse bound up with them.[20]

Even as he avoids overemphasizing formal philosophical categories, Maggi features Croce's way of addressing concerns left over from German idealism. This tack is a bit problematic because it plays down the import of Croce's encounter with Giambattista Vico, though Croce's early embrace of Vico decisively shaped his reading of the German tradition. By showing how to conceive the human world without the shadow of transcendence, Vico made it possible to bring together thought and reality, thereby overcoming, most immediately, the subject-object dualism of contemporary scientific thinking, the model for positivism. Croce concluded that the knowability of the real is not a problem; thought is fully adequate to what the world is – and to what we are, to our place in the world. To be sure, knowledge is provisional and finite; there can be no final grasp of the whole. But as human, knowledge is adequate to a world that is forever incomplete, endlessly coming to be through time, in history. Knowing, in other words, is bound up with that endless coming to be. And the key is not simply to establish the knowability of the real but actually to go about knowing it, on the basis of the new understanding of how knowing interfaces with a world that is forever coming to be.

Croce, then, was not restricting philosophy to some formal role, especially, as for some contemporary neo-Kantians, that of specifying or accounting for the methodology of the sciences. But neither was he inflating philosophy toward panlogism, some total philosophical comprehension, taken to be privileged, encompassing everything else. Rather, what Croce offered was philosophy as a cultural program, which he would eventually label 'absolute historicism.' This was philosophy as open, continually to be recast in interaction with the new problems we endlessly encounter in a changing world. In another sense, philosophy was simply the abstract moment or methodology of historiography, because it emerges from our need to understand and respond to the particular world that is forever coming to be in history. Croce recognized that even the most formal, properly philosophical dimensions of his own thinking had constantly to be clarified in light of new historical experience.

By the eve of the First World War, Croce was persuaded that his conception was novel, radical, and uniquely adequate to the modern world. Though offering only a few indications of the necessary comparisons, Maggi suggests that Croce was indeed genuinely innovative on the European level by that point.[21] He had established his distance from Kant and Hegel and had proven himself more radical than his German contemporaries. But Croce claimed no special glory for himself or for the Italian tradition going back to Vico and beyond. Although his conception constituted a kind of pivot, Croce viewed it as the harvest of a long-building European revolution – inaugurated with the Renaissance and linked to the increasing openness that he saw as the direction of the whole modern world.[22] Not only Italians like Vico and Giordano Bruno but also Cartesians, idealists, and positivists had made essential contributions. So even as he sensed his own thinking to be the cutting edge, Croce did not claim there was anything specifically Italian about it. On the contrary, he was insisting that he belonged to a common European tradition.

Because what Croce offered was not some self-contained philosophy but a broader cultural orientation anticipating ongoing adjustment, Maggi contends that its value could be assessed only through encounter with actual events. Did Croce manage to devise the concepts needed to come to terms with, and to help others come to terms with, the troubling era of the two world wars? In light of total war, fascism, and totalitarianism, can we still claim to make sense of the world and to proceed in the modern, purely secular way that Croce had outlined? His own letters and diary entries from the period indicate considerable anguish. Had he come to doubt the whole framework in light of events?

Whereas some have found rupture or dislocation, Maggi accents both continuity and the success of Croce's conception in meeting the contemporary challenge.[23] The need for clarification led Croce to radicalize some of his earlier insights, to make it clearer, especially, why his historicism led not to a premium on philosophy or some abiding logical structure but to a focus on human response, action, endless world-making.[24] But for Maggi the wider key is that Croce succeeded in showing at once the firmness of his original framework and its adaptability, its capacity to encompass even the history of this especially tortured era. As Maggi puts it in concluding, Croce could handle recent events because, in his modern secular way, he had posited Satan as intrinsic to God.[25]

Though unsystematic, Maggi's passages provide a reasonable sense of Croce's long-familiar take on fascism and Nazism, communism and Stalinism. The overall totalitarian departure stemmed from a profound spiritual crisis, entailing decadence, barbarism, a contraction of civilization and liberty. It encompassed the advent of ideologies – including a mechanical accent on race or class – that served as myths for the multitudes. It included activism and irrationalism, yet also the bogus security of a divine utopia, even an ideal of death. But Maggi concludes that, in the face of the modern totalitarian challenge, Croce's prior conception enabled him to accent the continuity of a common European culture and to specify the contemporary task that followed. The imperative was to maintain the new historical sense and thus the freedom, openness, and richness of life.[26]

Maggi's Limits

Maggi makes a convincing case against those who find some sort of *svolta*, or 'turn,' in Croce's thinking or who accent his pessimism and doubt even about the absolute historicist orientation itself. But Maggi's way of showing continuity and viability unintentionally lays bare some of the weaknesses of Croce's conception and misses some of its important strengths at the same time.

As we noted, Maggi stressed that Croce could handle recent events because he had posited 'Satan' intrinsic to 'God.' Recurring evil is part of the deal, yet we are assured of recurring moral response, welling up in the face of evil. And the imperative that follows is to go on responding morally to evil. Maggi sees this notion as consoling wisdom, but it was precisely such accents that invited the charges of vacuousness and insipid optimism against Croce by the 1940s – despite his acknowledgment that the happening of history is closer to tragedy than to idyll.[27] Still, Croce's insistence that historical understanding prepares action suggested the scope for a more specific kind of cultural resonance. In principle, at least, learning from the actual history can provide a rational framework for the essential moral response.

However, the specific categories of understanding Croce offered – barbarism, decadence, a contraction of civilization and liberty – seemed mere commonplaces. Moreover, some did not fit together well. We wonder, for example, how totalitarianism could have been 'an ideal of death' yet also bound up with activism and dynamism. Because they provided so little illumination of totalitarianism in its historical specificity, Croce's categories hardly helped contemporaries understand how best to respond or to specify alternatives. Yet Maggi simply conveys Croce's characterizations uncritically, without asking whether they could seriously serve historical questioning to prepare action.

Croce's absolute historicism opened the way to a deeper, and appropriately 'modern,' mode of historical learning that he himself did not fully develop. So though the wider framework remained firm, just as Maggi stresses, Croce's way of bringing it to bear in addressing the troubling phenomena of his own time betrayed limits in what he was prepared to ask, to hear. What is striking, then, in light of Maggi's problematic, is that confrontation with the events of the era did *not* lead Croce to a deeper understanding of the requirements for fruitful historical questioning. On the contrary, his superficial, commonplace account tended to discredit the whole orientation, diverting attention from the scope for a line of historical questioning that would be at once deeper, more fruitful, and truer to Croce's own radically historicist vision. This would even include a better understanding of the potential value of his now much disprized 'ethical-political' approach.

More specifically, there was room for a more imaginative way of probing the relationship between the advent of totalitarianism and the conditions that had led to the 'modern thought' prominent in Italy. From such a perspective, we better understand that response to the modern, crisis-laden situation might lead in a number of directions, some proving brutally negative in their consequences, even bringing to the fore the capacity for evil, the 'anti-Christ,' that Croce found in each of us in a famous article of 1946.[28] And in that light, he could have profited from a more imaginative engagement with Gentile's fascism in thinking through the totalitarian potential of 'modern thought' – and in rethinking the bases of liberalism in response. Even as they emerge in Maggi's uncritical account, Croce's diagnoses betray limits and tensions that a deeper engagement with Gentile might have helped him overcome.

For example, whereas Croce fastened upon the totalitarian embrace of 'mechanical' class or race, the totalitarian impulse has long seemed to have entailed a crucial role for something radically different, bound up with 'spirit' or 'triumph of the will.' Gentile's totalitarian conception had no place for class, race, or any other deterministic category and thus might help us grasp what else, even what may have been deeper in the overall totalitarian departure. Insofar as totalitarianism stemmed, as for Gentile, precisely from within modern thought, it could not be dismissed simply as 'anti-historicism,' yet this was the thrust of one of Croce's best-known diagnoses.[29] In the same way, we noted that Croce linked totalitarianism to barbarism and the contraction of liberty, and associated the ethical with resisting. But the opposition is too simple when we encompass Gentile, who saw the totalitarian state precisely as the expansion of liberty, as the vehicle for ongoing, and limitless, collective ethical response. Misguided, no doubt – indeed, catastrophically misguided, as practice would show. But deeper engagement with Gentile might well deepen our understanding of all that went wrong. More generally, to grasp the sources of the totalitarian catastrophe and the resulting evil may require some variation on precisely the anti-reductionist ethical-political history that Croce's conception invited in general but that he himself avoided, even precluded, when facing the difficult subject at hand.

But if Maggi's assessment is too uncritical, if Croce in fact proves disappointing in terms of Maggi's own criteria, Croce did manage to elaborate some distinctive categories that stood importantly vis-à-vis cultural tendencies inflating in the wake of fascism – and still in the mix today. Indeed, his capacity to engage contemporary cultural competitors surely confirmed his sense that he remained on the cutting edge. Although Maggi offers a few comparisons with contemporaries like Mann and Meinecke, he does not pinpoint the keys enabling Croce to maintain that, even after of all that had happened, we could proceed in a constructive spirit, avoiding totalitarian excess yet without retreating to transcendence, or wallowing in despairing angst, or lapsing into that bittersweet sense of macro-futility that seems to warrant a premium on individual edification or self-indulgence.

To show how Croce's orientation played against existentialism, for example, would require explicating, as Maggi does not, the Crocean theme of the immortality of the act. That notion warrants an experience of action as history-making that invites, in turn, a particular – rational – mode of historical questioning. The whole package stands fruitfully opposed to any accent on absurdity and futility; any premium on gesture, authenticity, edification, or self-creation. Maggi similarly neglects, on the more overtly political level, the import of Croce's argument, offered against an array from Guido Calogero's *liberalsocialismo* to Marxism, for the irreducibility of freedom and political commitments – even in the face of plausible demands for justice. And Maggi neglects the reasons for Croce's insistence – in contrast with those like Friedrich von Hayek, for example – that liberalism does not require *liberismo*, free market economics. The experience of totalitarianism need not lead us to deny our ongoing freedom to adjust economic forms through collective political choice.

As each of these examples indicates, Croce made significant, immediately relevant points by drawing out the corollaries of absolute historicism for present action. They afforded a framework for concrete response while leaving specific choices to individuals and aggregate choices to the give-and-take of liberal politics. On this level, then, we find precisely the flexibility, the capacity to proceed in light of troubling new events, that Maggi has in mind. But the force of Croce's effort on this level does not emerge from Maggi's account.

Idealist Philosophy, Italian History, and Gentile's Fascism

Though Giovanni Gentile's thinking can seem difficult, abstract, even vacuous on first encounter, a better understanding of his commitment to fascism might have much to tell us about why a culture saturated with idealism and historicism also produced the first fascism, and why it was characterized by an explicitly totalitarian aspiration. For that aspiration was surely central, whatever its realization in the practice of the fascist regime.[30] Moreover, to understand Gentile's vision might illuminate the attraction of fascism to Italians who cannot be dismissed as anti-socialist reactionaries, petty-bourgeois losers, or semi-educated adventurers. And the stakes could be wider still, for Gentile's case might enable us better to grasp whatever connections there were between antecedent intellectual innovation and the sudden, unanticipated totalitarian departure in Europe in the wake of the First World War.

In light of Gennaro Sasso's stature, the publication of his recent *Le due italie di Giovanni Gentile* is something of an event.[31] Still remarkably productive after a career spanning fifty years, Sasso is a powerful figure in contemporary Italian intellectual life. Prominent among his achievements is a massive study of Croce published in 1975.[32] He has been, since 1986, director of the Istituto italiano per gli studi storici in Naples, founded by Croce himself in 1947, and, since 1988, a member of the prestigious Accademia dei Lincei. During the 1990s, Sasso published three hefty volumes on the Italian idealist tradition, to which a fourth has recently been added.[33] When a Festschrift appeared in 1999, its girth – 919 pages – was widely seen as appropriate, in light of the generous lengths of Sasso's own works. But it also indicated the range and quality of the *scuola* that has developed around him, especially through his teaching at the University of Rome 'La Sapienza.'[34] But Sasso has long been controversial at the same time. Some find his work pretentious, and he has become known for a certain pugnaciousness, a peremptory quality that does not invite discussion.

In his lengthy new study, Sasso makes no claims to offer a full-scale assessment of Gentile's actualism, or even to summarize its basis. He assumes familiarity with Gentile's philosophy, and this is surely no book for beginners. Still, the author's concern is in one sense relatively simple – to assess, without apology or condemnation, the basis of Gentile's adherence to fascism. More particularly, did the political commitment and vision somehow derive from Gentile's philosophy, in a logical or necessary way? Such a link has sometimes been suggested, most prominently by the noted Catholic scholar Augusto Del Noce as part of his wider critical interpretation of modernity locating the source of the totalitarian impulse in secularization and atheism.[35] Explicitly against Del Noce, but also counter to Gentile's own claims, Sasso insists that actualism did not yield fascism – nor could it have for, in Sasso's view, there was simply no way to derive an account of society, law, and the state from this particular philosophy. Indeed, Sasso sometimes takes the point a step further, maintaining that there could be no genuinely philosophical account of anything properly understood as politics. For Sasso, then, Gentile's embrace of fascism was not logical and necessary but simply a political choice, the outcome of a personal passion. Gentile's own claim that actualism yielded fascism was merely ideological pretence.[36]

This is not to suggest, however, that Gentile's political choice was merely arbitrary, for Sasso's aim is to show that it was bound up with historical study and a particular understanding of Italian history. The author starts with Gentile's reading of the Renaissance, bifurcated into distinguishable cultural stands yielding two antithetical Italys – thus the book's title. The Renaissance produced the best of Italian culture in one sense, but glorious though it was, Renaissance culture was increasingly divorced from life, virtue, commitment; lacking vitality, it resulted in centuries of 'decadence.'

In Gentile's accounting, the renewal that produced the nineteenth-century Risorgimento was essentially a reckoning with the two Italys. It included intellectual innovation that reconnected with positive, specifically Italian traditions that had culminated in the thinking of Giordano

Bruno. But the Risorgimento had remained incomplete, and then its core of 'religious' idealism was gradually betrayed by the Italian ruling class. For Gentile, fascism emerged to fulfill the promise of the Risorgimento – and indeed was its necessary outcome. Although many figures of the Risorgimento era attracted Gentile's sympathetic interest, he found the most significant link in Giuseppe Mazzini – the only Risorgimento figure whom he actually labelled fascist.

Even taken to this point, Sasso's argument is neither difficult nor surprising, for the understanding of Italian history at issue is familiar, even a cliché. But the interweaving of historiographical and philosophical strands in Gentile's intellectual evolution was complex indeed, and the force of Sasso's reading stems from his way of disentangling them. Gentile certainly wanted his own philosophical effort both to reconnect with the earlier Italian tradition and to have broad civic value for his own time. So Sasso follows the internal course of Gentile's intellectual career, offering a series of detailed analyses of particular texts that he deems pivotal.

In one sense the book is thus a loosely organized set of interconnected essays. The order sometimes seems arbitrary and the connections, loose – as with the treatment of Gentile's early writings on Marx or his study of the alleged twilight of the culture of his native Sicily. As the argument builds, however, Sasso's method of interweaving disconnected episodes proves effective on one level, for the juxtapositions often prove mutually illuminating. Thus, for example, his way of moving from Gentile's historical encounter with the Reformation into his philosophical understanding of freedom and authority significantly illuminates both dimensions.

The method proves appropriate to Sasso's argument precisely because of his contention that Gentile's fascism did not result from his philosophy. Rather than a logical deployment, Sasso tells us, Gentile's course to fascism followed a tortuous path with varied strands. What emerges, then, is not the coherence but the arbitrariness and even incoherence of Gentile's overall project. In each section, Sasso's pinpoints the uncertainties, hesitations, tensions, contradictions, paradoxes, *aporie*, and even absurdities that marked Gentile's thinking as he sought to understand the two Italys – and contemporary possibilities – in interplay with his philosophical categories.

In Sasso's reading, the problems with Gentile's attempt to make sense of Italian history often boil down to the difficult relationship between logic and phenomenology – between formal philosophical categories and the understanding of historical epochs – a relationship that he finds especially problematic in Gentile. Not only could Gentile's formal philosophy not yield, or dictate, his particular political choice; neither could it underpin the understanding of particular historical epochs that proved bound up with Gentile's embrace of fascism. Had some such underpinning been possible, then an indirect but still essential link between the philosophy and the political choice would also have been possible, and something like a weaker version of the Del Noce–type argument might still hold. But for Sasso there could be no such link between philosophy and historiography, and thus the difficulty Gentile encountered in using key concepts like *decadence,* or in characterizing the actual periods of Italian history.[37]

Sasso convincingly demonstrates that Gentile's way of reading even his Italian philosophical predecessors was often arbitrary or vacillating as a result of the wider purposes that led him to construct two antithetical cultural traditions. He wanted, for example, to find early phases of both modernity and the modern Italian tradition in the thinking of the late Renaissance thinkers Bernardino Telesio, Giordano Bruno, and Tommaso Campanella, but he had problems fitting together their ways of sorting out nature and spirit. Especially illuminating is Sasso's dissection of the uncertainty and arbitrariness in Gentile's way of treating religious categories in light of his engagement with Vincenzo Gioberti, on the one hand, and mid-nineteenth-century Tuscans such as Gino Capponi and Bettino Ricasoli, on the other.[38] And the stakes were high, for at issue were abiding questions about Protestantism and Catholicism, freedom, determinism, and authority.

Though he offers no systematic account of Gentile's role within fascism, Sasso usefully suggests some conflations that must be avoided if we are to locate Gentile within the fascist mixture. Gentile was not simply a figure of the Right, a conservative or traditionalist who might be lumped together with Joseph de Maistre, Pierre Drieu la Rochelle, or Carl Schmitt. At the same time, Sasso features Gentile's difference from the various form of irrationalism or 'futurism' – wilfully turning from history altogether – that were also to be found within fascism. If anything, Sasso suggests, hyper-logical panlogism would be a more accurate charge than irrationalism. That Gentile was neither a 'traditionalist' nor an irrational futurist helps explain the opposition he drew from within fascism. At the same time, his insistence that the regime allow a measure of cultural freedom made him seem wishy-washy, less than fully committed, to certain fascist true believers. Thus by 1931, when he wrote his key essay on the Risorgimento and fascism, Gentile found himself caught up in a three-front battle against liberals, Catholics, and competing fascists.[39]

Sasso notes that as a philosopher, Gentile seemed serenely certain, betraying a certain humanistic presumption. Indeed, Sasso adds in an aside, such assurance helps explain why Gentile has been so little read in the age of doubt since the Second World War. But Sasso shows that though he was particularly loath to exhibit such doubts in public, Gentile, too, doubted and even suffered in the face of the uncertainties that leavened his intellectual enterprise.[40] Among Sasso's most intriguing pages are those devoted to Gentile's reading of the poet Giacomo Leopardi, to whom Gentile turned repeatedly – *not*, Sasso convincingly emphasizes against a common misconception, because Leopardi unified poetry with philosophy, but because of affinity with the poet's well-known tragic sense, reflecting the blindness and cruelty of nature, the omnipresence of death.

At first glance, obviously, this tragic sensibility seems antithetical to the serene confidence that Gentile's philosophy seems to convey. But Sasso displays the dialectical interpenetration of the two sides within the wider compass of Gentile's thinking. In asserting the primacy of freedom and spirit, Gentilian actualism was an overcoming of melancholy and solitude, negativity and death. In short, the philosophy was to mask the doubt. So underlying Gentile's idealism was anything but the blithe optimism to which some have reduced it.[41]

Despite this note of sympathy, however, Sasso's judgment is ultimately quite harsh. Gentile's way of sorting out the two Italys rested on prejudices, myths, and fantasies. The connections that he wanted to find – for example, between Vico and Mazzini, with Vincenzo Cuoco as bridge – were not really there. The notion that fascism was the revelation of the hidden essence or soul of the Risorgimento, with the nation to resolve itself in nationalism and imperialism, Sasso sees as naturalistic – and thus incompatible with Gentile's wider idealism.[42] Gentile's attempts to force his argument and to hide the tensions led him to awkwardness and paradox again and again.

In treating Gentile's reading of fascism, Sasso comes to favour 'absurd' to characterize Gentile's ways of forcing his pro-fascist arguments.[43] Gentile's effort to fuse thinking, willing, and acting was simply absurd, as was his call for cultural freedom within fascism. For Sasso there could be no such freedom if the state was, as Gentile claimed, the embodiment of the pure act.

Sasso's Limits

Sasso illuminates a number of episodes and dimensions, but does his way of assembling the Gentilian pieces – personal agenda, systematic philosophy, historical understanding, and fascism – make best sense of the evidence? For all its effective interweaving, Sasso's account rests on an implicit bifurcation of Gentile, and his book treats only one of the two halves – Gentile's ragged efforts to interpret Italian history and to follow his political passion. But Gentile for Sasso was also a significant philosopher, and the reverse side of Sasso's argument, never explicit but implicit on every page, is that the fascist commitment need not, should not, colour our understanding of Gentile's actualism. Sasso clearly believes in the autonomy, the intrinsic interest of philosophy, which is to be evaluated in terms of its internal rigor and the logic of its response to problems in an ongoing tradition. And though he is not concerned here to explicate, defend, or criticize Gentile's formal philosophy, by implication only such an inquiry could open the way to what was most important about Gentile's thinking.

This implicit argument reflects a concern that is appropriate up to a point – and Gentile's case especially brings it to the fore. Philosophy must be evaluated on its own terms *as opposed to* the various forms of reductionism or provincialism that lead to an accent on national origins, contextual sources, or contingent effects. Thus, in part, Sasso's reaction against Del Noce, who seemed unable or unwilling to examine Gentile's actualism apart from its alleged outcome in fascism. Especially indicative is Sasso's insistence that, on the strictly philosophical level, Germans like Kant and Hegel, and not Italians like Gioberti and Bertrando Spaventa, were the real inspirers of Gentile's thought.[44] In light of Sasso's concern with the other Gentile in the present study, we see none of that engagement with the Germans, nor do we get any sense of Gentile's significance within that wider philosophical discussion.

Sasso's conception of philosophy and its autonomy inevitably shapes his sense of how philosophy might relate to historiography, on the one hand, and political action, on the other. But that conception must itself be considered, for it points to meta-philosophical questions about the place of what we call philosophy, any philosophy, within the overall cultural economy. Assessments of that place have been changing, as we noted above, and we must ask about Gentile's concerns – and Sasso's as well – in light of that process.

Sasso remarks that ours has been an age of doubt, but his understanding of philosophy seems to ignore the way that doubt has actually played out within significant sectors of the philosophical tradition. A major concern of innovative twentieth-century thinkers from Wittgenstein and Heidegger to Derrida and Rorty has been to question that tradition from the inside. Such questioning has opened new ways of thinking about what philosophy can entail and how it might be interwoven with individual biography, with a particular historical understanding, and/or with a political departure like fascism. More specifically, the meta-philosophical question has encompassed the place of philosophy vis-à-vis history, even the longstanding philosophical distinction between logic and phenomenology that Sasso takes as bedrock.

To be sure, on one level Gentile may appear – as Croce does not – the last of the system-builders, carrying philosophical idealism to an absurd extreme in his quest for consistency and certainty. As such, it would seem, he is not to be mentioned in the same breath with the likes of Wittgenstein or Derrida. But though he was more thoroughgoing than Croce in embracing idealist categories, Gentile, too, was explicitly trying to say something radically new – not to give new answers to old questions from within a particular philosophical tradition. And, just as for Croce, the novelty entailed a particular take on philosophy and its role, bound up with Gentile's wider purposes, his underlying agenda. Thus questions arise about Gentile's centre of gravity, how we locate the formal philosophy (insofar as it is isolable at all) vis-à-vis everything else.

A central aspect of the question concerns the place in Gentile's thinking of permanent structures vis-à-vis those elements that led Emanuele Severino, for example, to characterize Gentile's actualism as a 'philosophy of becoming.'[45] Sasso leaves no doubt where he stands: Gentile's philosophy is a logical system specifying the structure of thinking as a pure, undetermined act. The act is closed in the eternity of its structure; the act itself does not develop. It is merely vacuous rhetoric to say that the pure act is the perennial creator of an ever-new world.[46] What matters about Gentile is the internally rigorous philosophical argument that, by laying out its eternal and necessary structure, tells us, shows us, that there is and always will be thought thinking as pure act. Thus Sasso denies that actualism can be understood as a philosophy of becoming, whatever Gentile himself may have thought about the matter. Indeed, for Sasso, the notion of a 'philosophy of becoming' is essentially oxymoronic.

But though made with his usual peremptory aplomb, Sasso's argument rests on a criterion that is taken a priori and invoked arbitrarily to marginalize the aspects of Gentile's thought that led Severino to characterize actualism as he did, or that led Gentile himself to suggest – to choose a passage quoted by Sasso – that 'the world is no longer what there is but what there ought to be; not what we find, but what we leave – what is born insofar as we, with the energy of our spirit, cause it to be born.'[47] In other words, the world is forever incomplete, forever in process of being (provisionally) realized through human moral response. This is one way of characterizing the continuous act that is the world.

As Gentile understood it, his own philosophy was the modern cutting edge, and to grasp it in its rigorous logic is to feel not the abiding structure but, as never before, the absence, the incompleteness of the world. What philosophy gives us, from this perspective, is a hole, an opening, compelling a more radical understanding of human freedom and a deeper, potentially all-encompassing sense of responsibility. To understand the world philosophically is thus to be propelled beyond the present through action. It is in this sense that thinking, willing, and acting come together. For Gentile, then, philosophy is *not* self-contained; there is no separating it from the human agency that is bound up with endless coming to be.

Sasso's determined denial of 'philosophy of becoming' leads to a certain blindness throughout his account. He says at the outset that he will not be treating Gentile's reading of Vico – because it is irrelevant to the question of Gentile's political commitment. Yet he notes near the end that Vico was the *Altvater* not only of the Italian philosophical tradition but also of the quest for political renewal.[48] So, in light of the problem Sasso has set himself, how can he justify neglecting Vico? In fact, without Vico, we cannot do justice to the side of Gentile's thought that Severino had in mind in labelling it a 'philosophy of becoming.'

In discussing Gentile on Bruno, Sasso features the problematic relationship between nature and spirit but does not highlight what Gentile found so exciting in the late Renaissance thinker. For Gentile, Bruno was the first to envision the world, and mind itself, as 'becoming,' as growing, developing, making itself over time, in history.[49] Sasso also says he will neglect educational philosophy and school reform because these would not add substantially to the argument.[50] But without encompassing Gentile's understanding of education, we cannot grasp his sense of the relationship between philosophy and the scope for a new, postliberal politics. Nor can we get a handle on the totalitarian content of that politics. At one point, Sasso portrays Gentile's as a philosophy of freedom, as romantic, transcending limits – but rather than explore the broadly 'historicist' implications of this view, he seeks to pinpoint another aporia: insofar as it is doomed endlessly to be/do, the act is necessity, not freedom.[51] Fine – the necessity of freedom and openness as determinism. But is this not precisely the vacuous wordplay that Sasso is quick to condemn in others?

Because he precludes 'philosophy of becoming,' Sasso is not sufficiently open to the radical novelty of the relationship between historical thinking and endless coming to be in Gentile's conception. And thus he cannot convincingly account for the tensions and especially the arbitrariness he has so well pinpointed in Gentile's reading of the two Italys. The problem was not that Gentile was missing or mishandling the classic philosophical distinction between logic and phenomenology. His rigorous philosophical account of the pure act as thought thinking did not commit him to some 'logos,' as if the actual course of things was implicit from the beginning, was determined a priori as the logical outcome of an abiding structure.

If that were true, historical understanding would indeed entail identifying some necessary sequence, deriving the actual course of things from the logic. But what in fact followed from Gentile's philosophy of becoming was a mode of presentist thinking about the actual in its endless coming to be. Actual thinking is inherently bound up with, inseparable from, that process. In addressing Italian history, Gentile was an actor or agent thinking the coming to be of the actual in his own particular way. Any such thinking is moral in freely thinking what it thinks, in genuinely believing what it thinks, but there is no scope for the moralism that comes first and shapes the historical inquiry. There is no scope for 'wishing will make it so,' no matter how genuinely ethical the wish.

But precisely here is the problem. What Gentile wanted to think, to believe, intruded in his historical thinking to yield a particular, and arbitrary, reading of Italian history. That reading was so important to him, first, because it constructed a distinctive Italian cultural tradition to which he could believe himself to be falling heir. But, even more importantly, it afforded a grasp of problems and possibilities that promised the national renewal eventually to come to fruition in fascism. So the arbitrariness in Gentile's account stemmed not from forcing a prior logic, as Sasso suggests, but from lapsing into moralistic wishful thinking.

Though they disagree about the substance of Gentile's philosophy, Sasso and Severino agree that it does not yield fascism, that it has no necessary connection with fascism. For Severino, there was a yawning gulf between Gentilian actualism, precisely as a philosophy of becoming, and fascism, as a static totalitarian state.[52] But this is to take as a given the nature of fascism, including the totalitarian state in which Gentile placed such store. There is scope for a more flexible treatment of both Gentile's thinking and the fascist totalitarian impulse, in their interaction. Could a 'philosophy of becoming' actually yield an embrace of the totalitarian state idea?

With his accent on the cleft between Gentile's formal philosophy and his political choice, Sasso never considers the basis of Gentile's vision of a totalitarian ethical state, the sense in which it might have been novel. He generally assumes a measure of continuity from nineteenth-century ideas – plausibly, at first glance, in light of the ambiguity in Gentile's initial commitment to fascism in 1923. At that point Gentile linked fascism to the particular strand of Risorgimento liberal thinking that conceived liberty as an attribute of the state, in contrast with the Anglo-French accent on individual rights. Through the agency of Silvio Spaventa, especially, that form of liberalism had fed into the *Destra Storica,* thereby influencing government in the first years after unification. Sasso tends to assume that Gentile merely offered an update of such 'freedom in the state' and 'freedom of the state' notions. Moreover, the element of 'liberalism' accounts for Gentile's accent on cultural openness within the fascist regime.

Gentile quickly made it clear, however, that realizing the promise of fascism was not simply a matter of restoring the ideals of the *Destra Storica.* In trumpeting the totalitarian ethical state, he claimed to offer a decisive admixture or update, bound up with all that was distinctive in his modern philosophy of becoming, including his way of fusing thinking, willing, and acting. But rather than seriously probing Gentile's claims, Sasso simply dismisses the key components as 'absurd.'

We need analysis on a different level, a wider frame of questions, if we are to understand the relationship between Gentile's earlier thinking and his vision for fascism. In the years since the fall of the *Destra Storica* in 1876, Italy and the West had had much new experience with liberal individualism, parliamentary government, and the expanding reach of the modern state. Gentile sensed the scope for a new politics that responded to that wider experience, and thus his novel understanding of the interpenetration of freedom, power, responsibility, and participation. Thus his novel understanding of the interaction between the state and creative individual response.

Sasso argues convincingly that Gentile was not merely a conservative traditionalist, but how might he be compared with Mussolini's minister of justice, the Nationalist Alfredo Rocco, with whom he is often lumped? To be sure, Sasso notes the difference between Gentile's idealism and the Nationalists' naturalism, a difference that emerged unmistakably during the First World War.[53] But crucial though it is, that difference does not address the role of the state, which became central as Mussolini's regime finally began constructing post-liberal institutions in 1925. Though Gentile and Rocco can both be described as totalitarian, their conceptions of the state differed in illuminating ways. To get at the contrast dramatizes precisely the novelty of Gentile's conception, its sources in the modern thought that he had pioneered with Croce.

In short, though its disastrous outcome is not in doubt, Gentile's fascism raises some big and potentially fruitful questions. The answers are certainly not obvious. But even as he eschews internalist philosophical analysis to turn precisely to the level of Gentile's fascism, Sasso's limited, peremptory approach would close off even the essential line of inquiry. Because he essentially precludes a priori any understanding of Gentile's thinking as a 'philosophy of becoming,' Sasso cannot answer convincingly his own central question about the relationship between Gentile's earlier thought and his embrace of fascism. Nor can he offer a convincing account of Gentile's vision for fascism, including especially the totalitarian ethical state.

Encompassing a Marginalized Intellectual Tradition

Though Croce and Gentile surely produced something distinctive, their international impact proved limited, and then their aggregate achievement was rejected as provincial even by the Italian mainstream. This combination of idiosyncratic outcome and marginalization could only reinforce the tendency, in Italy and abroad, to neglect the Croce-Gentile tradition thereafter. But the overall cultural episode is nonetheless remarkable, even unprecedented and unique, insofar as we encompass the whole of it – not only the content of the ideas at issue and their immediate impact, but the complex inter-layering of national dimensions and wider resonance, then and now. So we return, in light of Maggi and Sasso, to the question with which we began: how might we rethink the place of this idiosyncratic tradition, with its asymmetries and limits as well as its distinctive departures, in what we have come to take as the mainstream of modern Western intellectual history?

Concern with the bases of totalitarianism, with what went wrong and what to avoid, remains central to Western culture, as does the question of how we can best proceed in a world that has grown cynical partly as a result of the totalitarian experience. On this level, the intellectual opposition between Croce and Gentile arguably remains archetypal. The stakes for each were greater than Italian renewal, for each was addressing the question of human possibilities in the modern world of radical immanence. Understanding their divergence from within their common framework could deepen our understanding of the era, and our own ongoing possibilities. Maggi and Sasso offer much to stimulate the reconceptualization and further research we need, but each side-steps or precludes essential dimensions at the same time.

Questions about distinctiveness and wider place are implicit in both books, but neither author confronts them directly. In an aside Sasso contends that it is merely trivial to insist on asking, as Italians so often have, how 'European' Gentile's thinking was. There is always a national language. The key for Sasso, as we have noted, is that philosophy is autonomous and supranational and not to be reduced to national context. National preoccupations may betray a kind of cultural racism, on the one hand, a kind of reverse provincialism, on the other.[54]

Sasso's warning is surely well taken up to a point. But if we are to address intellectual history on the European or Western level, as opposed to settling for parallel national histories, we cannot sidestep sensitive questions about distinctiveness and idiosyncrasy, about the contingencies of influence, misreading, and neglect across national or linguistic boundaries. These issues lurk in any assessment of the place of the idiosyncratic Italian current in European intellectual history – but also in any effort to confront the question of reverse provincialism on the Italian level. *Was* the Italian tradition genuinely out front in some sense? What would be the implications of the answer, in light of the larger political and cultural trajectory encompassing fascism and post-fascism, marginalization and neglect?

In Gentile's case, even to raise such questions may appear misguided – or worse. Yet certainly the *sense* that he was offering something new and appropriately modern excited Gentile himself and helped make his thinking exciting to others. In light of the outcome, it is tempting to dismiss this syndrome as foolish, provincial, by now embarrassing. But despite all the arbitrariness Sasso has pinpointed, and quite apart from questions of internal philosophical rigor, it is conceivable that Gentile was glimpsing dangers and needs, possibilities and combinations, that no one else had. To suggest as much would not be to justify his ideas, to say they proved convincing or worth trying out. Even if it was 'cutting edge' in some sense, his vision could lead to disaster. But such an assessment would matter for understanding his appeal, for placing fascism in history, and for learning the lessons of its disastrous trajectory.

We noted that though Croce, too, believed himself to be in the forefront, he, unlike Gentile, remained determinedly cosmopolitan. It happened to have fallen to him to offer the essential 'European' solution, a convincing, usable outcome of the whole modern tendency toward openness and freedom. But Croce's sense of occupying the cutting edge entailed an implicit anticipation of wider resonance. Tensions could creep into his thinking insofar as his version of 'modern thought' was not universally recognized and embraced – indeed, was widely misconstrued or neglected. Though Croce had reason to avoid facing up to what was happening, his sense of his own place in the wider culture of his time was bound to change as the years went by. And partly at issue was the measure and the import of whatever was distinctively Italian in what he offered.

Although not quite explicitly, Croce tended to suggest, as disaster followed disaster in his own time, that the underlying problem was precisely the failure of the modern world to adjust to the new, more radically historicist perspective that he himself had outlined. Thus, for example, his noted essay 'Antistoricismo,' based on a lecture at an international philosophy conference at Oxford in 1930.[55] And as Maggi shows, Croce's confrontation with such contemporaries as Ernst Troeltsch, Friedrich Meinecke, Julien Benda, and Thomas Mann seemed to confirm the superiority of what he offered. Croce saw his own position as more radical than theirs, which he found too conventionally dualistic to respond to the current challenge. At the same time, he accented the limits of contemporary directions in European philosophy, from neo-Kantianism to phenomenology to Heidegger, again implicitly or explicitly comparing them with his own position.

Sometimes Croce could not avoid highlighting a distinctively Italian tradition, especially when he compared his own brand of historicism with the longstanding German tradition culminating in Meinecke.[56] And Maggi notes that the late Croce more single-mindedly stressed the import of Vico in pointing the way to the modern overcoming of dualism. But rather than portray Vico as central to some enduring, continuous Italian tradition, as Gentile did, Croce depicted Vico as a lonely and isolated figure – precisely as he himself was in danger of becoming. Croce resisted any emphasis on a distinctive Italian tradition because it was crucial that he remain part of a common and still cohesive European culture. To conceive or portray what he offered as distinctively Italian would have entailed the risk of being further cut off from the mainstream, of becoming marginalized as merely idiosyncratic and provincial.

Meanwhile, Croce had developed a neo-liberalism as the broadly political corollary of his absolute historicism. But though the need to respond to Gentile's challenge informed the enterprise, Croce was reluctant to face up to the sense in which Gentile had been, and even remained, a full partner in a common departure. To do so could discredit 'modern thought' as potentially fascist, but also as parochially Italian. For Gentile, of course, insisted on precisely what Croce did not – on the distinctively Italian side of modern thought. Moreover, he claimed that, properly understood, it led to fascism – indeed, that Croce himself belonged with fascism.[57] From Croce's perspective, this line of thinking entailed a kind of double provincialism that could only discredit the contemporary Italian tradition.

But there was of course a deeper difference between the two thinkers, and it is especially instructive because it emerged from within the genuinely 'modern' but distinctively Italian direction they had initiated. Indeed, even after their political split, the two remained linked, playing off each other, if not always explicitly. And the basis of the interplay and divergence is not what we might expect, in light of our usual understanding of the difference between liberalism and fascism. Gentile's conception was as attuned as Croce's to freedom and openness, to endless coming to be through creative moral response. The question was how the world gets made or, more particularly, how it could and should get made, once we have grasped anew the place of human being and the sense of opportunity and responsibility that follows. Did the modern orientation entail, as a corollary, some new way of understanding our action as collective and, on that basis, some new way of actually acting collectively?

As Maggi shows, Croce tackled the issue of the state again and again, especially in light of Gentile's argument for a totalitarian ethical state. But Maggi simply gives us Croce's argument without evaluation. To grasp the stakes of the political divergence, we need first to approach Croce from a critical perspective informed by a deeper sense of

Gentile's novelty than we find in Croce himself – or in Maggi. Neither did justice to the challenge of Gentile's conception by showing how it had emerged as one possibility from within 'modern thought.'

For Croce, the state was merely an elementary form of practical life, merely government, and not some embodiment of the ethical. Indeed, moral life constantly forces its way beyond any empirical outcome and encompasses opposition to law and government, even revolution. But such arguments did not do justice to Gentile's departure from Hegel and other earlier German ways of conceiving the state as actor and/or as the embodiment of freedom and value. The new thinking about collective action in its relation to coming to be, and the attendant new understanding of freedom and ethical capacity, might yield a new understanding of the state. For Gentile, the state in its modern totalitarian ethical form is not some fixed institution, standing apart from us, to which we give allegiance or obedience. Rather, it is at once the embodiment of our collective will to act and the mechanism that enables us to do so in a new way, congruent with our radical freedom and total responsibility. Only through such a state, as a concentration of power, do we have the capacity, and thus the freedom, to act collectively in accordance with our sense of responsibility for what the world becomes. Indeed, the necessary freedom required that the state's reach be potentially limitless. Gentile could encompass Croce's objection that moral life constantly transcends the existing, empirical state, for the Gentilian totalitarian ethical state is not static and fixed but changes precisely as moral life goes constantly beyond.[58]

Gentile insisted again and again that the state at issue was not to be conflated with the empirical government, but his point blurred in light of the inherent ambiguity of the fascist situation. The new regime was revolutionary, a pivot from one order to another, but it was also the current government of Italy. And thus the seeming contradictions of Gentile's own posture within the regime, especially the insistence on cultural freedom that Sasso finds so absurd. Despite the complexity of the situation, however, it was not contradictory to demand cultural freedom from within the new totalitarian framework. All were to understand themselves in terms of that framework, but from Gentile's perspective the totalitarian state was ethical only insofar as it drew on and absorbed the ongoing free, creative moral response of individuals. So whereas all had to be fascists, there was scope for free response, even including principled opposition to the government's specific policies.

We need not fall into apology to recognize the surprising scope for criticism that was indeed to be found *within* the fascist regime. But there was no scope for opposition to the fascist state – or even to the fascist idea of the state, as totalitarian. Indeed, in Gentile's terms, all individuals had to participate, and had to feel themselves totally responsible, all the time. It was in that sense that Gentile's ideal, though it had nothing to do with race or class, and though it reflected 'the best will in the world,' was totalitarian to the core. Indeed, precisely because it was more directly bound up with modern thought than Croce wanted to admit, his conception arguably gave the twentieth-century totalitarian temptation its archetypal expression.

Though he did not do justice to Gentile's conception, Croce sensed its dangers, and its challenge helped shape the alternative orientation he offered from within the common modern framework. And Croce surely gets the last word between the two. But to show the place of his response in our wider intellectual history, we must do better than Maggi at pinpointing its basis.

Maggi is concerned with the adequacy of Croce's framework by the 1940s, but insofar as it did *not* hold, what would that mean, how would we know? From the start, the essential premise of modern thought was radical immanence – the need to conceive the world without transcendence. But in light of fascism and totalitarianism, it is not surprising that many, in Italy and throughout the Western world, sought to retreat precisely to the transcendence, including the natural law tradition, that modern thought had seemingly left behind.[59] So part of Croce's challenge was simply to hold firm, to show that there was no turning back, even as he also continued to insist that longstanding religious categories could assume new meaning from within the modern framework.

We saw that Sasso concluded from Gentile's attraction to Leopardi that Gentile was seeking some rigorous assurance of the endless overcoming of negativity and death. For the loss of transcendence was of course two-edged; the possibility of nothingness or meaninglessness accompanies our deepening sense of freedom and creativity in the modern world. But what Gentile felt was required was not, as Sasso implies, merely a consistent philosophy displaying the enduring world of free spirit. What was required, rather, was a new mode of collective action – the totalitarian ethical state – which was necessary to warrant what proves an essential sense of mastery. Though the possibility dawns, the world does not spin out of control with the loss of transcendence insofar as we find this new totalitarian way to seize collective responsibility for it. But if we fail to create the means for this collective freedom to act, drawing out and focusing the human sense of responsibility and power, the individual may lapse into cynical passivity, or mere self-indulgence, or melancholy – the worrisome melancholy that Gentile found pervading Croce's whole sense of the world when their philosophical divergence became public in 1913.[60]

In charging melancholy, Gentile had glimpsed the tendencies in Croce's thought that would lead him to accent humility, pluralism, the idiosyncrasy of individual response, and a very different understanding of the human place in a world that is forever coming to be. Up to a point that understanding did indeed entail the implications Gentile feared. The Crocean world cannot be mastered in the way Gentile envisioned; there is no way to climb higher within the process by creating a new instrument for collective action. There is no escaping a sense of futility, even tragedy, for we can never foresee the results of our actions. Moral response remains irreducibly personal, idiosyncratic, lonely.

Croce's challenge was to specify, still from within the common modern framework, an alternative that avoided the totalitarian temptation but that also headed off the cynicism, the self-indulgence, the sense of futility that Gentile feared from the modern break. At the same time, the totalitarian experience itself deepened the challenge that Croce faced in an indirect way, for whatever might have seemed the possibilities at the outset, its disillusioning outcome tended to breed, as one of several directions, a new disillusionment and cynicism, a premium on private satisfactions as opposed to responsible world-making.

What Croce sought to show, most basically, was that though the coming to be of the world was not masterable in the Gentilian sense, neither was it simply absurd. The key was then to draw out the implications of this middle course for broad societal priorities and for concrete individual lives. Thus the import of the several Crocean themes that we found lacking in Maggi's assessment of Croce's response to his own time. To show the scope for responsible world-making was to head off any premium on self-affirming gesture or edification; to show the scope for genuinely learning from historical questioning was to head off any warrant for cynical political reductionism or instrumentalism. To insist on the primacy of freedom even over justice was to warrant a democratic order in which none could claim privilege and all were to be taken seriously.

As we have seen, it was Croce's ability to address the challenge on this level that confirmed his sense that, despite all that had happened, his framework was uniquely adequate to the challenges of his own time. But in light of the dilemmas surrounding what proved the idiosyncrasy of the Italian tradition, Croce found it ever more difficult to place his contribution in wider perspective as he neared the end of his life. Though what he offered was not the last word, it was surely a distinctive strand – yet in its distinctiveness it ended up marginalized. By now Croce's historicist neo-liberalism is a classic 'margin' that could fruitfully be encompassed in the ongoing conversation about how we proceed after both transcendence *and* totalitarianism. For we have certainly not surmounted the challenges Croce faced by the 1940s.[61]

Sasso considers the basis of Gentile's fascism; Maggi considers the adequacy of Croce's response to the era. Though the overlapping questions at issue do not encompass all the reasons for interest in Croce and/or Gentile, those questions have been central to Italian modes of engagement with the Croce-Gentile tradition – and they point to one basis for reconnection to the wider mainstream of Western intellectual history. But the riddles of distinctiveness and provincialism have continued to make it especially difficult for Italians to reassess the Croce-Gentile tradition in ways that would invite reconnection with the wider culture. Though they are only implicit, such concerns helped lead both Sasso and Maggi to turn from the dimensions we have explored. And it is those dimensions that suggest why there is much potential value to re-engagement with a tradition that proved idiosyncratically Italian but modern and quite sophisticated in its own distinctive, and sometimes troubling, way.[62]

chapter 7

How Not to Think about Fascism and Ideology, Intellectual Antecedents and Historical Meaning

This essay was published under this title in *Journal of Contemporary History* 35, no. 2 (April 2000): 185–211 © SAGE Publications, 2000. I am grateful to the publisher, SAGE Publications, Ltd, for permission to republish this article in the present form. In an effort to assist present readers, I have restored the section titles that were in my original but that were dropped from the article as published.

1: Fascist Ideology and Contemporary Scholarship

What is the place of Italian fascism within the contours of Western cultural and political development since the Enlightenment? The answer would surely encompass not only outcomes but also the originating aspirations that produced fascism in the first place, whether or not those aspirations bore fruit in the practice of Mussolini's regime. At issue are questions about the relationship of fascism to antecedent intellectual innovation *and* to the subsequent intellectual framework – the framework from within which we seek to place the fascist experience today. And those questions lead quickly to the slippery issue of 'ideology.'

It was long held that Italian fascism had no ideology, that it could be adequately placed in terms of opportunism, bourgeois reaction, and petty bourgeois *ressentiment*, that it was merely authoritarian and thus of secondary interest vis-à-vis the full-blown totalitarianism of German Nazism. Some specialists have long challenged that view, however, and a body of recent scholarship has taken Italian fascism, even as totalitarian, newly seriously, inviting a fresh look at matters of content, ideology, and historical place.[1] Especially prominent has been a genre focusing on aesthetics and rhetoric, ritual and spectacle, virility and 'the body,' variously taken as keys to understanding. And though each rests, implicitly or explicitly, on a certain way of conceiving 'ideology,' these approaches tend to play down the sort of substance that might stem from antecedent intellectual innovation and take form in articulated ideas. I will suggest that these contributions, even as they illuminate undeniably important dimensions of fascism, mislead us about its proportions, and thus its wider place, because of inadequacies in that conception of fascist ideology.[2]

When confronting matters of ideology, students of fascism typically refer to the Israeli scholar Zeev Sternhell as the authority – but also as a foil. The author of several major works on fascist ideas in France, Sternhell was immediately influential when he turned to Italy in *Naissance de l'idéologie fasciste,* published in French in 1989, then in English as *The Birth of Fascist Ideology* in 1994.[3] Sternhell takes the ideology of Italian fascism very seriously indeed – as the key both to its origins and its wider historical meaning.

So we have, on the one hand, a cluster of fashionable approaches resting on a certain understanding of fascist ideology and content and, on the other, the work of Sternhell, who has influenced our understanding of ideology in general and Italian fascist ideology in particular. By treating the two sides in tandem, we can clarify the content of Italian fascism and deepen our understanding of the place of intellectual antecedents and ideology in such political departures.

A reconsideration of fascist ideology in light of Sternhell's influence is fruitful partly because of the postmodern turn, which I take to entail not some aestheticist blurring of 'history' and 'fiction' but a suspicion of binary categories and master narratives that opens the way to a deeper, more reflexive mode of historical questioning. The self-understanding of liberal democracy derives partly from the whole twentieth-century political experience, including its unforeseen anti-democratic extremes, with their disastrous outcomes. Yet a certain triumphalism, and perhaps a certain nervous reticence, have delimited our engagement with that earlier experience, aspects of which were quickly marginalized, with ideas neglected and aspirations explained away.[4] A better sense of what fed the anti-democratic experiments, including Italian fascism, might deepen our sense of the possibilities and limitations of modern politics. In taking ideology seriously, Sternhell seems to be raising the right questions, but he ends up foreclosing the sort of inquiry we need.

Sternhell insists that on the level of ideology, there was a radical distinction between Italian fascism and German Nazism, with its basis in racist biological determinism.[5] Though it is possible to take a different tack even in light of this crucial difference, Sternhell's insistence on the distinction is surely plausible. To follow him is to recognize that Italian fascism might have been important on its own terms – for its own reaction against the liberal parliamentary political mainstream, and not merely as a lesser partner of Nazism, with its particular racist agenda. It would be perverse indeed to suggest that because Italian fascism was *not* based on biological racism, it was somehow less innovative – and thus less interesting, less revelatory, even less troubling.

Like A. James Gregor in a series of books from 1969 to 1979, Sternhell recognizes that the longstanding tendency to trivialize Italian fascism, partly by denying that it had any coherent ideological basis, is facile, even self-serving because it warrants sidestepping real challenge. But Gregor seemed to have an a priori agenda that led him to overdo the coherence and significance of Italian fascism – as a distinctive form of radical politics, as the archetypal developmental dictatorship.[6] And it is clear in retrospect that Gregor's way of taking fascism seriously tended to throw us off in a double sense. Most basically, his accents seemed to suggest that taking ideology seriously meant crediting the regime's achievement in practice, even justifying the regime. Moreover, whereas Gregor was taking Italian fascism seriously in one way, the terms of the import he assigned it – as a developmental dictatorship – arguably marginalized it in another. For this was to play down the sense in which Italy was not merely playing catch-up but was a full participant in the modern European political and cultural mainstream. It had experienced decades of parliamentary government, and its sophisticated intellectual tradition was deeply attuned to, among other things, the performance of parliamentary liberalism. Yet Italy was also idiosyncratic in important respects, so its political experience and its variations on the intellectual currents of the time included certain distinctive features. The key, from this perspective, is that this distinctiveness cannot be explained away in term of relative backwardness; rather, it entailed a particular angle on more general features of modern liberal culture and politics.[7]

Sternhell implicitly agrees that the way to locate fascism – via ideology – is not as a product of relative backwardness, as if fascism was simply an extraordinary means of catching up. Yet Sternhell, too, is forcing the evidence on the basis of an a priori agenda, and like Gregor he ends up leaving us worse off than before – though he offers a diametrically opposed interpretation. For Sternhell's aim is not to credit Mussolini's regime but to deepen his critique of the wider European cultural revolt against the Enlightenment that he had addressed in his earlier work.

Like Gregor, Sternhell seeks to assemble the pieces to show that Italian fascism did indeed have a coherent ideology, as coherent as Marxism or liberalism, that demands to be taken seriously. It grew from that anti-Enlightenment revolt, which encompassed much of the avant-garde that was questioning positivism, rationalism, and mass democracy by the turn of the century. But the core of fascist ideology developed from relatively delimited strands within that wider revolt, notably the integral nationalism of Charles Maurras and the revolutionary syndicalism of Georges Sorel, each of which emerged in France around the turn of the century and then, through French influence, spread to Italy, where they found the context to germinate, producing the first fascist movement and regime.[8] Growing from the revision of Marxism that gathered force in the 1890s, syndicalism came together with nationalism to form the ideology of fascism, which was essentially in place by the time Mussolini became prime minister in October 1922.

It has long been known that syndicalists were prominent among the creators of fascism, though many have assumed that they were part of an ephemeral early Leftist strand that was quickly marginalized with fascism's apparent turn to the Right by 1921. Confirming the findings of a handful of earlier scholars, Sternhell shows that the relationship between the syndicalist tradition and Italian fascism was much deeper, more enduring and significant. He follows the pre-war syndicalist current as it evolved, in gradual, piecemeal fashion away from orthodox Marxism and toward nationalism – or Nationalism, in the specific version of the Italian National Association, founded in 1910. Merging with the Fascist party in March 1923, Nationalism provided the regime with a number of major functionaries and ideologues, including the single most important architect of the new fascist state, the jurist Alfredo Rocco.

But as Sternhell shows, syndicalism gave fascism figures of comparable importance. Although some leading syndicalists split off, the majority of the current's leaders, some primarily ideologues, others active as labour organizers, ended up major fascists, from Michele Bianchi and Edmondo Rossoni to Sergio Panunzio and A.O. Olivetti. With their roots in the pre-war subversive Left and their revised blueprint for change, these veteran syndicalists were able to gave younger fascists a framework for conceiving problems and potential solutions. They thereby helped establish the parameters for the fascist departure from both parliamentary democracy and Marxist socialism.

For Sternhell, then, Italian fascism had deep roots, a coherent ideology, and wider – profoundly negative – significance as the first full-blown political manifestation of the wider cultural revolt against the Enlightenment tradition, with its rationalism and humanism. Whereas in France this cultural fascism hardly managed to transcend its literary incarnation, in Italy, where democratic traditions were weaker, the revolt could actually take political form. At the same time, however, precisely because it could become a genuine political movement and even come to power, Italian fascism had to make compromises with the establishment, especially during the years of the fascist regime. So the relationship between Italian fascism and the wider cultural revolt blurred in practice. Thus, Sternhell holds to his earlier argument that fascism remained purer, closer to the ideal type, in France – precisely *because* there it could not compete for power and thus was not forced to compromise. Yet he manages to have it both ways. With Italian fascism having bogged down in compromise, Vichy France, in its first 'national revolution' phase, proved the clearest, archetypal political translation of fascist ideology.[9]

Whatever their conclusions about its nature, most specialists would hesitate to conflate Italian fascism with the Vichy regime. The dualism of Sternhell's framework gives pause. Indeed, though Sternhell is convincing in insisting on intellectual substance, he reads the Italians in terms of an a priori dualistic framework, and his whole of way of conceiving 'ideology' throws us off. Yet even Stanley Payne, while accenting the virtual non-existence of fascism on the political level in France, is quick to credit Sternhell's overall argument: 'Zeev Sternhell has conclusively demonstrated that nearly all the ideas found in fascism first appeared in France.'[10] Such testimony, from perhaps our most authoritative expert on European fascism, is surely impressive, yet the notion is curious on the face of it – for it assumes we already know what fascism was. But Sternhell, when deciding that fascism had been born in France, had not yet done the analysis of Italy that he did later. And without tracing the genesis of Italian ideas in their own context, rather than assuming he already knows fascism from France, how can he be sure what the ideas meant, what the relevant categories were, how they meshed, and in what proportions?

At issue is not the outcome of fascism, or even whether it was a good idea in the first place. Those matters are settled, as far as I am concerned, and my argument has nothing to do with them. The fascist experiment produced a coercive yet still shoddy, in some ways superficial, regime. At issue is where fascism came from, why the creators of fascism came to view the world and conceive the possibilities as they did, and how it was caught up in wider processes that are still at work. A deeper approach to such questions results not in justification or rehabilitation but enables us to learn more deeply from this negative episode within our own continuing history.

2: It Happened in France

In one sense, Sternhell is still caught up in a tradition that has at least become suspect with the postmodern turn. His proves a Manichean struggle, with the rational universalistic Enlightenment tradition, underpinning liberal democracy, under assault by the counter-tradition that took cultural form by the end of the nineteenth century and eventually led to fascism. The Enlightenment tradition entails a cluster of themes that apparently fit neatly together, and the elements of the counter-tradition, such as anti-materialism, myth, elitism, and a cult of violence, similarly coalesce seamlessly. But if there is one deeply simple thing we have learned from the postmodern turn, it is to question any implication that things are ever that simple, that easy.

Although Sternhell obviously values the Enlightenment tradition, he does not analyze it as such, so we are not quite clear what combination affords his standard for assessment. To be sure, that tradition entails rationalism, humanism, universalism, and liberal democracy, self-recommending at first glance, but even these are not unproblematic, especially as we stir in other elements that come up crucially in Sternhell's account. He seems to deplore market capitalism, yet that surely was bound up with the demand for individual freedom in the Enlightenment tradition. Do the rationalism and universalism he values entail 'materialism,' the first target of his proto-fascists? Does humanism necessarily entail materialism, or an assault on private property? The connections are not obvious, yet these are just a few of the questions that Sternhell's juxtapositions and oppositions suggest. And of course, looking at the Nazi side, we have come to recognize that some of those who, at the time, could plausibly claim to be the most rational and enlightened proved culpable of what we now see as the worst crimes, evils.[11]

Sternhell's narrowly dualistic model suggests that the good, or reason, or humanity is given once and for all – at least from the time of the Enlightenment dispensation – so that challenge could only come from irresponsible intellectual malcontents. Yet early in the book, when he is seeking to establish the intellectual credibility of the oppositional national syndicalist tradition, his argument seems to recognize the scope for questioning the liberal political mainstream as it had settled out by that point. In the thinking of Mosca, Pareto, and Michels, for example, we seem to have not just tiresome cultural despair but an unsentimental effort to get beyond the rhetoric of popular sovereignty and the rights of man to reveal the actual workings of democratic institutions, in light of experience. Whatever its claim to have applied reason to the problems of the eighteenth century, the Enlightenment had not settled, for an age of mass politics, the cluster of issues concerning leadership, elitism, mass participation, political motivation, and bureaucracy that concerned these intellectuals. In light of their findings, it would have been irrational for contemporaries *not* to have raised new questions about democratic politics, and thus aspects of the Enlightenment legacy.

The same is true with respect to Marxism, which was encountering ever more insistent questions about strategy and even centre of gravity by the 1890s. Here again, Sternhell initially seems to appreciate the bases for revision in light of, most immediately, the apparent successes of the capitalist economy, which seemed incongruent with Marx's projections. At least by implication, Sternhell recognizes that it made sense, in light of that fact, to raise new questions about agency – and thus about will, commitment, values. If the proletariat was not getting worse off, the basis of its universal role, tricky in any case, became even more difficult. Did the industrial workers, or some subset thereof, have to be afforded a privileged role in any revolutionary transformation? At the same time, there were plausible questions about Marxist internationalism in light of differential capitalist development and about the factors responsible for the limits to such development – in Italy, for example. Here again, it would have been irrational *not* to have raised new questions in light of experience.

But though Sternhell seems to recognize the plausibility of such questioning, the answers, as he understands them, conflate with categories long familiar in the interpretation of fascism: authoritarian discipline; a certain take on elitism, violence, and myth; an effort to preserve private property behind a facade of change and participation, class collaboration and national solidarity.[12] This outcome seems surprising in light of the apparent plausibility of the proto-fascist questioning along the way. Things have come together a little too quickly. Questioning positivism slides into an aesthetic of violence; questioning the liberal parliamentary system seems necessarily to reflect a 'fear of the masses.'[13]

Part of the problem is that Sternhell is reading the Italian case in terms of the French-based framework he had established in his earlier works. That syndicalism emerged first in France is clear, and the Italian syndicalists were surely indebted to the French to some degree. By the middle of the first decade of the century, there was much interchange between the French and Italian currents. But Sternhell overemphasizes French influence on the Italians and thus misconstrues the implication of categories like myth, violence, elitism, and nationalism that were central to the syndicalist evolution.[14] In forcing his dualistic framework, he misses the scope for a more genuinely historical analysis, more attentive to context, with subtler attention to those categories as responses to new, genuine, and open questions that cannot be framed in simple binary terms.

Myth is especially tricky because even Sorel's concept is widely misread as a manipulative notion, whereas for Sorel it entailed a kind of primitivism; bound up with pre-rational commitment and belief, myth could only well up from below.[15] Familiar though it is, the notion of elites consciously using myths to mobilize masses was absolutely antithetical to Sorel's notion. Yet Sternhell treats myth precisely in this erroneous way, as a manipulative concept, linked to elitism.[16] To be sure, the Sorelian idea could be taken from its original context to stimulate others – Mussolini, for example – to make manipulative use of myth. But the distinction is important to any attempt to understand the connection between intellectual innovation and subsequent political departures, and Sternhell simply glosses over it.

As for the Italian syndicalists, Sternhell attributes myth to them unproblematically, ignoring the testimony from major syndicalists like Arturo Labriola, Sergio Panunzio, and Enrico Leone warning against irrationalism and explicitly criticizing or playing down even Sorelian myth, properly understood.[17] He goes on to conclude that 'faith in the power of myth ... is the key to the Fascist view of the world.'[18] Though it is plausible to associate myth with Mussolini, it gives pause, in light of Sternhell's insistence on the unity of fascist ideology, that neither the category nor the orientation it denotes was central to the thinking of any of the three most important fascist ideologues, Rocco, Panunzio, and Giovanni Gentile. Indeed, each was a rationalist in a sense that Sorel would have criticized, repudiated. There is, however, a deeper sense in which myth was at work in Italian fascism – though it was not as a direct result of Sorelian influence, and Sternhell cannot get at it. We can best consider that sense below, after discussing Gentile.

As with myth, Sternhell's treatment of violence is murky even in its pristine Sorelian context, and violence is then overemphasized in Italian syndicalism – and thus in fascism as well.[19] He finds a cult of violence as a permanent value for fascism while ignoring, for example, the warnings of Agostino Lanzillo – the Italian syndicalist closest to Sorel – against violence in the fascist context.[20] That fascism was born in violence is clear, but to assess proportions, we must be able to distinguish a willingness to acquiesce in violence, as a moment in radical change, from some cult of violence as a permanent value.[21] Whereas the fascist institutions that grew from national syndicalism were surely totalitarian in direction, they had nothing to do with violence or even irrationalism, but aimed to expand the state as the sphere of law. A good example is the Magistracy of Labour, established in 1926, which extended the sovereignty of the state over labour relations, an area subject, under the liberal dispensation, to the potentially violent clash of private interests.

We would not expect those who assume that fascism had no ideology, or that its 'discursive content' was secondary, to grasp the relationships and distinctions at issue, for they, of course, would not have read Panunzio and Lanzillo and Rocco. But Sternhell claims to have read them. The problem is that he has done so a priori, forcing his categories.

'Elitism,' too, is hardly univocal, and here again, Sternhell is fuzzy even on the Sorelian level. It is certainly true that both Sorel and the Italian syndicalists thought in terms of differentiation, an aristocracy of labour, since what matters is not simply objective place in the economy but subjective values, bred of organizational membership and activity. As an empirical fact, some workers were more 'syndicalist' than others – more militant, more committed, more disciplined – and thus the element of 'elitism' in the original syndicalist conception. And it is also true that such values were bound up with an accent on authority and discipline. But Sternhell is too quick to conflate these themes with what he takes to be subsequent fascism. For Sorel, as for the Italian syndicalists, the initial accent was not on some hierarchical control but on the *self*-discipline and even individual initiative that result from trade union membership and activity.[22] In the same way, the fact that the syndicalists featured virtues they saw developing first only in certain sectors of the working class conflates all too quickly with 'fear of the masses' in Sternhell's account.[23] But fully to grasp the problem with Sternhell's use of elitism, we must look more closely at the Nationalist-syndicalist convergence, which was subject to fundamental tensions over precisely this category.

3: Syndicalism, Nationalism, and Corporativism

The most obviously heterodox outcome of the syndicalists' revision of Marxism was a species of 'nationalism,' which they embraced on the basis of a serious rethinking of the relevance of Marxist internationalism in light of the concrete Italian situation. But the political implications of a generic nationalism can be disparate indeed, and Sternhell's way of positing a nationalist-syndicalist synthesis is misleading. At issue is the relationship between the syndicalist concern with the national dimension and the particular form of nationalism propounded by the Italian Nationalist Association.

After positing nationalist-syndicalist convergence by the time of intervention and carrying it through the advent of fascism, Sternhell finally introduces the most important Italian Nationalist, Alfredo Rocco, near the end of the book, noting, correctly, that he had supplanted the more literary Enrico Corradini as the association's leading spokesman as early as 1914.[24] Even as they embraced their particular form of nationalism, the syndicalists differed considerably even from Corradini. But Rocco gave Nationalism greater doctrinal depth and coherence, and it is especially when he becomes the focus that we encounter the most important questions about the nationalist-syndicalist interface.

First, to what degree was Rocco's thinking congruent with Sternhell's understanding of the wider cultural revolt underlying Italian fascism? Certainly Rocco was explicitly hostile to 'the ideas of 1789,' which had produced liberalism, democracy, and socialism, and his aims were overtly elitist. But though Rocco surely fits in part, Sternhell does justice neither to the force of Rocco's thinking nor to the deep differences between the Nationalist and the syndicalist understandings of fascism.

Sternhell notes that the essence of Rocco's thought was 'a mystical and organic view of the nation' entailing the 'supremacy of the collectivity over the individual.'[25] It is certainly true that Rocco posited the supremacy of the nation over the individual, but this emphasis serves Sternhell as a warrant to subsume Rocco's thinking within the wider French-based package – including myth. Whatever we think of Rocco's priorities, his conception of the relationship between individual and society was no more 'mystical,' no less rational, than the ideas of 1789.

It is not clear what was 'rational' even as the Enlightenment tradition freed the individual from traditional limitations. There was still much thinking to be done – and thus, for example, the space for Durkheim, who was committed to the democratic Third Republic, but who posited a new and in many ways post-liberal understanding of the relationship between individual and society to help deepen the identification of individuals with that Republic. It was a relationship of subordination in one sense – but it was not to be conflated with Rocco's conception, which occupied one extreme among efforts to rethink this uncertain, contested relationship. Yet the outcome for Rocco was a legal rationalism diametrically opposed, most notably, to the Nazi conception of law, based on mystical race, blood, and the will of the Führer.[26]

At the same time, however, Rocco's accents differed radically from those of Panunzio, the most powerful syndicalist thinker, though the difference had nothing to do with rationalism, mysticism, and law. Yet Sternhell continues to assume a neat convergence even when he finally gets around to bringing Rocco to centre stage, whereas in fact the nationalist-syndicalist interface, though indeed crucial to Italian fascism, was riddled with tensions that severely compromised the effectiveness of the regime. At issue, on the institutional level, was corporativism, which was central to fascism's self-understanding and claim to a world-historical role.

Sternhell correctly pinpoints the nationalist-syndicalist synthesis as the basis for the corporativist direction chosen once the regime committed itself to a deeper raison d'être and thus to significant institutional change in light of the Matteotti murder of 1924. But when he treats fascist corporativism, it is not in its Italian genesis but simply as an aspect of the overall anti-Enlightenment, Sorelian culture that he finds almost ubiquitous by the 1930s.[27] So rather than consider major Italian corporativists like Rocco, Panunzio, Giuseppe Bottai, Ugo Spirito, and Arnaldo Volpicelli, Sternhell repairs to such figures as Henri De Man and Marcel Déat. They are interesting, to be sure, but we cannot make sense of the Italian embrace of corporativism through reference to what figures like these were arguing about nation or class. Because of the generality of his inquiry, Sternhell could not possibly find any features in Italian corporativist thinking that pointed away from his a priori syndrome, encompassing elitism, anti-humanism, and free-market economics. In his most pointed characterization, he finds corporativism to have been one manifestation of an overall fascist reduction of socio-economic problems to matters of psychology; corporativism produced the *feeling* of change, of participation, without any real change in socio-economic structures.[28] In fact, the corporativist thrust in fascist Italy was far richer, partly because of the incompatibility of some of the priorities that had emerged as the syndicalists and Nationalists rethought the relationship between economics and politics.

The two groups had fundamentally different reasons for rejecting parliamentary democracy and positing corporativism in its place.[29] Although each envisioned expanding the sovereignty of the state to encompass the sphere of production, they differed, most basically, over the quality of the participation that would become possible through the newly politicized economy. Sternhell's dismissive characterization of corporativism, as a means of sidestepping problems, utterly misrepresents the conception of old syndicalists like Panunzio and Olivetti. In the same vein, Sternhell notes that democracy had been an object of disdain for the French and Italian syndicalist intellectuals, who 'had always been extremely doubtful about the capacity of people to govern themselves.'[30] Certainly the Italian syndicalists were hostile to parliamentary democracy, but it seemed possible to pinpoint the sources of its apparent inadequacies and, on that basis, to imagine other bases for 'people to govern themselves.'

There are varieties of anti-democracy just as there are varieties of elitism. Rocco occupied one pole, explicitly advocating a new governing elite as the antidote to mass-based parliamentary government, which invited electoral pandering, corruption, and a premium on short-term interests. For Rocco, corporativism was, most obviously, a means of disciplining the unions, but ultimately also of mobilizing and regimenting Italians for production – and imperialism. But syndicalists like Panunzio and Olivetti differed explicitly, portraying corporativism as a system for enhancing popular political capacity through more constant and direct involvement in public life. Mosca and Pareto had shown that, despite the rhetoric of popular sovereignty, politics had remained elitist and exploitative under the liberal parliamentary system. But it was possible to do better, especially by politicizing the workplace and expanding state sovereignty, diffusing political decision-making into economically based groupings growing from the trade unions that had attracted the syndicalists in the first place. For the syndicalists, then, corporativism afforded at once an alternative venue for political participation and a new institutional framework for addressing concrete socio-economic problems.

Make no mistake: this understanding of corporativism was overtly totalitarian; now even economic roles were to be experienced as political, and the public participation would be direct and constant, like it or not. But the conception was still not rigidly elitist like Rocco's. The system demanded the participation of all producers in institutions that would enjoy greater autonomy than Rocco envisioned, and that would have serious things to do as they exercised the expanded power of the state. As with the original syndicalist vision, this totalitarian corporativist framework would allow for autonomous individual decision and initiative, as opposed to mere regimentation. Unfamiliar juxtapositions, to be sure, yet these were the ones at issue for fascist corporativists – and only insofar as we grasp them can we understand why so many of those seeking change in Italy after the First World War could have believed in the innovative potential of fascism.

In light of the uncertain dynamic that resulted from the nationalist-syndicalist interface, there was much pulling and tugging as corporativist institutions developed. Seeking to avoid exclusive identification with any of the contending factions, Mussolini tended to balance personnel and innovations in order to foster a facade of consensus.[31] But significant public polemics, such as the notable exchange between Panunzio and Carlo Costamagna in 1926, made the underlying differences clear.[32] And by the early 1930s old syndicalists like Olivetti were often sharply and publicly critical of the top-down functioning of corporativist institutions, which meant lack of autonomy and genuine participation.[33] Although the outcome by this point accorded more with the Nationalist script, the struggle continued, as did the institutional innovations. No one could be sure of the outcome, and the somewhat ramshackle outcome in fact was not quite what anyone had envisioned when fascism's long voyage began in earnest in 1924.

Many have misinterpreted the origins and place of Italian fascist corporativism because of a priori assumptions about the relevance of ideas, keeping them from bothering to read the thinkers Sternhell finds important. Hard-headed inquirers who insist on practice as opposed to mere theory would deny that what Panunzio and Olivetti were saying could tell us anything significant. But Sternhell insists, correctly, that their ideas mattered then and should matter to us, insofar as we seek to understand the aspirations, the sense of problems and the scope for solutions, that led the fascist regime in a corporativist direction in the first place. Yet though he continued to accent the syndicalists' intellectual pedigree and ongoing centrality, he apparently no longer bothered reading them once he got past 1922. He relies instead on a prior framework that keeps him from grasping, or admitting, what they were in fact saying about the tricky matters at issue. Because he seems to have engaged these ideologues yet has not really done so, the reading he offers is worse than no reading at all.

4: Economics and Politics

The whole syndicalist revision, and not just its corporativist outcome, entailed an effort to rethink the web of relationships involving politics, anti-politics, and economics. Yet those relationships are a source of confusion throughout Sternhell's account, even over how to characterize the original syndicalist vision.[34] The most salient issue concerns the place of free-market economics, including private property and free trade, in the initial conception, the evolution, and the fascist outcome. For Sternhell, the syndicalists' early *liberismo* – their hostility to protectionism, plausible on orthodox Marxist grounds – slides into defence of private property as the underlying purpose.

At issue is why, and in what measure, the syndicalists turned from the classical Marxian assault on free-market capitalism. Crediting the economic theories, revolving around 'hedonism,' of the syndicalist intellectuals Arturo Labriola and Enrico Leone, Sternhell portrays the syndicalists as defenders of capitalism, the market economy, and private property based on what they concluded were the 'universal laws of economic activity.'[35] Only when he finishes discussing their economic thinking does he point out, somewhat grudgingly, that neither of these two syndicalist intellectuals became a fascist.[36] But rather than considering the possibility of some different axis, Sternhell carries this alleged accent into fascism, with syndicalism a key source of the free-market orientation notable in Mussolini's early statements.[37] And though subsequent fascist practice did not conform to Mussolini's early position, Sternhell finds that free-market accent even underlying corporativism. By overemphasizing the free-market side of syndicalism, he ends up reinforcing the commonplace notion that from the start, on all levels, corporativism was a mere subterfuge to protect narrow bourgeois interests, to preserve the market economy and private property, in response to the threat of socialism.[38]

By the time fascism was on the agenda, the syndicalists had indeed decided that frontal assault on private property was not the issue, but neither were they embracing classical free-market economics. For those like Panunzio and Olivetti who turned to fascism, there was greater scope for political-economic experiment than Labriola and Leone, with their accent on objective economic laws, allowed. So the corporativism that grew from syndicalism was an attempt to redo the liberal relationship between politics and economics in a non-socialist way, in light of experience so far with the combination of capitalism and parliamentary democracy. It sought to transcend the antithesis of market economics and collectivism through a kind of productivist self-regulation of the economy. And though it is well known that some of fascism's economic innovations of the 1930s were not specifically corporativist but pragmatic responses to the depression, the wider fascist context of experiment facilitated even these.[39] Indeed, the whole sense of openness and experiment, the scope for political intervention, was precisely an aspect of the anti-materialism that Sternhell sometimes accents.

Commonplace though it is, the view of corporativism as a conservative subterfuge is surely worth considering, especially in light of the outcome. But precisely because he started by taking ideology seriously, Sternhell had access to evidence that at least challenges any such narrowly reductionist interpretation of origins and purposes. Insofar as corporativism in practice ended up serving business interests, this outcome stemmed not from the syndicalist-based ideology but from the whole dynamic of the regime, in which syndicalist ideas and business interests were both at work. Whereas those who discuss corporativism in wilful ignorance of intellectual antecedents have an extremely restricted sense of the possible meanings of the categories in play, Sternhell understands the import of the syndicalist revision for the advent of corporativism. But rather than let that evidence open and challenge, he offers a restrictive and misleading treatment, even as he seems to be taking newly seriously the underlying ideas.

The syndicalist transition to fascism obviously entailed a kind of reversal in one sense, for the priority changed from an assault on capitalism to a political revolution to transform the liberal state. But Sternhell's accent on the 'primacy of politics' may mislead if not differentiated, for politics encompasses an array of possibilities.[40] And fascist corporativism retained some of the syndicalists' original anti-political vision of a self-governing society of producers without parliamentary politics, which seemed inherently self-serving and short-sighted. In the new fascist state, based on economically based groupings, political participation was to grow not from citizenship but from economic roles as producers. From my perspective, the syndicalists were overreacting in reducing political values and conflicts to matters of economic interest or expertise, but the sense, if any, in which politics is to be understood as an autonomous arena for value conflicts remains contested even today.[41]

Within fascism, the tension-ridden web of relationships involving economic roles, technical competence, anti-materialist will, and political-ethical capacity was in almost continual dispute. It is crucial that even while embracing corporativism, Giovanni Gentile, the single most important fascist ideologue, criticized any emphasis on technical expertise or economic interest at the expense of the primary ethical capacity of individuals, to be realized in and through the totalitarian state. On these central issues, ideas were indeed significant, and we find serious, sometimes challenging, impulses at work from each angle. But we find fundamental differences among the major fascist ideologues at the same time, so those ideas hardly formed a neat synthesis. Because Sternhell forces the evidence though his a priori dualism, he does not get at the essential axes. Yet only insofar as we do so can we make sense of the regime's dynamic and understand the wider place of the whole fascist experience.

5: And Gentile?

Whatever the import of Sorel, syndicalism, and nationalism, any effort to take fascist ideology seriously must come to terms with the philosopher Giovanni Gentile, who, in several major roles, was central in specifying the regime's totalitarian self-understanding and direction.[42] Even before fascism had coalesced as a political movement, Gentile's grandiose, philosophically grounded vision of renewal attracted many of Italy's best and brightest as they sought to make sense of the possibilities that seemed to open after the First World War. And that vision soon led Gentile and a number of his followers to fascism. Among his many roles as the regime's cultural arbiter, Gentile wrote the theoretical portion of Mussolini's 'Doctrine of Fascism,' published in 1932, the closest thing to an official statement of ideology that fascism produced. At the same time, even as he exerted considerable influence, Gentile attracted criticism from fascists who understood and disliked the implications of his vision for fascism.[43]

In an earlier work, Sternhell notes that among European fascist intellectuals only Gentile produced a body of ideological writings comparable in quality to French fascist literature and thought.[44] And in turning systematically to Italy in *The Birth of Fascist Ideology*, Sternhell mentions Gentile periodically, seemingly taking his centrality for granted. So how does Gentile mesh with what Sternhell takes to be the key to fascist ideology, the national syndicalist synthesis derived from French influences?

Satisfied with his French-based framework, Sternhell offers no sustained analysis of Gentile's philosophy, his path to fascism, or his impact within the regime. It is presumably enough that Gentile falls within anti-materialism, one of the impulses central to the syndrome Sternhell assembles. Perhaps, reading between the lines, we are to surmise that Gentile moved from philosophy to politics and fascism because of the diffuse influence of the Nationalist-syndicalist synthesis, with its anti-materialism and myth. In light of Sternhell's overall framework, it would seem that only thus could a major intellectual have embraced fascism and offered a totalitarian vision.

But Gentile, together with Benedetto Croce, was central to a tradition of historicist neo-idealism that looked initially to Germany, not France, and that ultimately accented an indigenous Italian tradition traced back to Vico and even to Renaissance humanism. The two thinkers believed they had recast for the modern secular world the Italian humanistic tradition based on radical immanence, and on that basis they questioned the conventional justifications for liberal democracy. Whatever we might conclude about the force of their critique of the Enlightenment tradition, any convincing effort to explain the genesis of fascist ideology would have to analyze this cultural departure on its own terms, even if only to assess the relevance of national traditions and influences.

Though it had some of the same targets, Gentile's historicist anti-materialism owed nothing to Sternhell's French counter-tradition, so unless we analyse Gentile's thinking on its own terms, our conception of the basis for fascist anti-materialism will be too limited. In the same vein, Sternhell's readers can only surmise that Gentile, as the leading fascist ideologue, was part of the 'antihumanistic rebellion' that Sternhell attributes to fascism.[45] But Gentile's vision for fascism, though explicitly totalitarian, stemmed from arguably the most radical form of philosophically grounded humanism we have known. What he offered was a philosophy of action, even a kind of activism, though it did not entail irrationalism or myth, let alone anti-humanism. Yet his novel way of bringing together individuality, freedom, responsibility, participation, power, and action led him to claim that we *require* a totalitarian state to exercise our human capacities in the modern world.

Gentile's way of assembling the pieces defies our usual categories again and again, and it is extraordinarily difficult to penetrate today.[46] Unless we do so, however, we cannot pretend to have confronted 'the birth of fascist ideology' or to have understood the sources of the cultural revolt against liberalism and positivism that led to fascism. Yet there is no way we could do so from within Sternhell's restricted dualistic framework.

6: The Myth of Italian Fascism

Only once we have Gentile on the table can we seriously confront the relationship between Italian fascism and 'myth,' the category so central to Sternhell's reading. It is true and important that the emergence of fascism, the sense of what it could accomplish, entailed something of the original Sorelian concept, though Sternhell does not get at the relationship. What Sorel, like Pareto, anticipated was something like fascism – the welling up of a new movement, based on strong group values and willing to use violence, in response to the inadequacies of the whole liberal culture that had grown from the Enlightenment. Insofar as we can distinguish Sternhell's ideologues from the early fascists – war veterans and political outsiders with an inchoate image of renewal – the Sorel-Pareto moment, having provided a prior sense of how radical change could take place, led these intellectuals to valorize the eruption of fascism, including the moment of violence. They believed in the potential of fascism partly because of the way it emerged in violence from the war. But their faith entailed neither an ongoing cult of violence nor a premium on ongoing mobilization through what were known to be myths. The priority for the syndicalists was institutional change to foster productivism and new modes of participation, decision making, and societal administration, and as the syndicalists themselves outlined them, these new modes were neither more nor less rational than parliamentary representation or bureaucracy.

Still, the distinction between intellectuals and mass movement breaks down in a crucial sense, for there was a mythical aspect to the whole business, bound up with the overblown sense of grandiose possibility in Italy after the war. Thanks partly to the war experience, Italy could leapfrog over the apparently more advanced countries and offer a global antidote to the inadequacies of liberal-positivist culture and politics. During the First World War, Croce had warned against the growing tendency toward such inflated claims, which he noted in his collaborator Gentile among others, and which could have unfortunate cultural and even political consequences.[47] Partly because of the terms in which they viewed early fascism, many of the intellectuals who embraced it failed disastrously to gauge its real prospects for significant change. They were not advocating or fostering myths but thinking in mythical terms themselves.

The inflated sense of possibility bound up with the advent of fascism was fed by intellectual antecedents that overemphasized the significance of indigenous Italian traditions, but it was not, and could not have been, from direct Sorelian influence, because lucid, purposive myth-making is an oxymoron. In other words, myth in its Sorelian guise is experienced as truth, reality, by those caught up in it, and the point in this case is that the fascist agents believed it. So the relationship eludes Sternhell's point, bound up with elites and mobilization. Even 'faith in the power of myth' implies lucidity on the part of the agents; the prior articulated ideology – now a blueprint in place – includes a role for myth as one of its components. So though myth proved central to the fascist dynamic, it was bound up with antecedent intellectual innovation in more complex ways than Sternhell suggests. Sorel's category can help us understand the mythical dimension, but it was not the immediate source of that dimension.

Disparate though their visions were, ideologues like Gentile, Rocco, and Panunzio offered new ideas in response to genuine uncertainties, and the prospects for significant change were not clear in 1924. So the grandiose sense of possibility bound up with the advent of fascism was not entirely groundless; myth grew from genuine intellectual innovation. But as the regime wore on and the original aspirations met frustration in practice, the mythical potential inherent in fascism inflated, and fascism became its own myth. And thus the superficiality of the later emphases – on *Romanità*, on empty ritual, on the cult of the Duce. But because Sternhell's idea of myth is so limited, and because he pulls back from any effort to sort out the actual dynamic of the regime, he offers no analysis on this level, crucial though it is to any effort to connect origins, including ideology, with outcomes.

7: Thinking Historically – Even about Fascism

Our approach to 'ideology,' with all it *may* encompass, affects how we conceive everything about Italian fascism – origins, dynamic, and wider significance. Sternhell has gotten much right in insisting that fascism had serious intellectual antecedents and that we cannot understand it apart from them. But though he leaves the impression that he has seriously confronted the essential intellectual dimension, with results that conveniently confirm many of our prior assumptions, he has not really done so. Insofar as we believe that, thanks to Sternhell, we understand fascist ideology, we need not further probe intellectual antecedents or follow the relevant ideas in the regime. But unless we are more attentive to unfamiliar meanings and novel juxtapositions, we misconstrue the content and thus the role of the ideological dimensions at work.

For more recent scholars, having Sternhell available, whether as authority or as foil, becomes an excuse to marginalize 'ideology,' ideas, content. Either Sternhell has told us what we need to know about ideology and antecedent ideas, which can thus be taken as given, or his treatment suggests that ideological themes are secondary, whether because of the inadequacies in his account or because of the fascist compromises in practice that he accents. Playing off Sternhell warrants turning from any engagement with fascist ideas to focus on dimensions readily opposed to ideational content, such as aesthetics, ritual, spectacle, rhetoric, virility – mutually reinforcing categories now widely taken to be the keys to understanding.

Although Jeffrey Schnapp departs from Sternhell in accenting ideological instability and tension, the fact that he takes Sternhell as the authority on ideology proves significant to his overall approach, which privileges spectacle in a way that renders unnecessary any engagement with the texts, the ideological elements in play. Because, contrary to Sternhell, they are easily shown to have been *not* unified, they are a tissue of contradictions that cannot have been very important to the regime and perhaps not even serious to their proponents. What matters is the aesthetic overproduction through which the regime sought 'to compensate for, fill in, and cover up its unstable ideological core.'[48] Because Sternhell's insistence on a unified prior ideology does not convince, we can neglect such ideological elements altogether and focus on the aesthetic admixture.

Even as he pulls back from Sternhell to accent ideological instability, Schnapp assumes that thanks to Sternhell we know what the confused elements were. So we need not confront them and consider how, whatever the tensions and contradictions, they might still have been central, not only as originating aspirations but as components within the dynamic resulting in the eventual outcome. But because he has relied on Sternhell, Schnapp has only a limited idea of the ideological elements in play, so he cannot really know what it would take 'to compensate for, fill in, and cover up.' And thus he cannot convincingly assess proportions – including the import of any particular episode within the regime. So whereas Schnapp tells – and tells well – a significant story about fascist spectacle, his accent on the aesthetic dimension, on form as opposed to content, misleads about fascism's overall dynamic and wider place.

For Mabel Berezin, Sternhell functions more clearly as a foil, and she criticizes him explicitly on a few particulars – for his overemphasis on violence, for example. But her approach, too, has been limited by engagement with his argument.[49] The coherence of Italian fascism, she tells us, was not on the level of ideology, but in its style and emphasis on action. Its ends malleable, fascism 'repudiated the word and the text' and replaced argumentation, explanation, and rational discourse 'with the primacy of feeling and emotion.' And because what matters is performance as opposed to text, analysis of ritual action affords the best access to the fascist project.[50]

Even while minimizing the role of ideology, Berezin goes on to discuss several key fascist texts, essentially to buttress her point about form devoid of content.[51] But her treatment of these texts is shallow and misleading because in approaching them she did not know the categories at issue. Several of the statements analyzed entail Gentilian language, but she has no sense of the Gentilian content or where it comes from. Is an emphasis on fascism as a 'spiritual idea,' or as a 'religious conception of life,' rhetorical or substantive? How do such accents relate to reason, will, action, even 'feeling'? Even when she turns to the more down-to-earth Labour Charter of 1927, Berezin simply does not know what is at issue, where the ideas come from, what they meant in context. There was more than ritual at work in this document's discussion of relations of production. Though she notes, more generally, that corporativism was understood as an alternative basis for participation, she has no idea of the issues – and treats the point in one sentence.[52]

Before she could convincingly assign priority to ritual, Berezin would need more seriously to assess the content, having a look at those who were articulating the categories – in texts, in stuff written down. But she need not bother with such discursive evidence, for Sternhell has already done so, though not very convincingly – and not in a way that would invite ongoing engagement with the substantive dimension. Thus she can safely focus on ritual. The alternative we need is not a mere reversal, affording a priori privilege to content over ritual, but a more open-ended inquiry asking how the ongoing and contested ideational content plays into or against the undeniably significant element of ritual.

For Barbara Spackman, Sternhell has his place – but his contribution is almost trivial. He settles for showing that the texts he accents were fascist, when the key, now that we can take content for granted, is to understand how they work as fascist. The issue is not the substance – and how it responded to whatever it responded to – but fascist rhetoric and its cultural sources. To understand fascism, we must study the rhetoric in order to grasp how the ideology actually functioned.[53]

Up to a point, Spackman's argument is unassailable. The study of rhetoric, always promising, is especially necessary in the case of Italian fascism, the advent of which manifestly entailed a change in rhetoric, including the intensification of masculinist themes. And, just as she suggests, we must probe this dimension to understand how the ideological elements worked in practice. But Spackman's approach takes ideology as at once unproblematic – its content given, transparent – and instrumental. We need a deeper engagement with the unstable and contested ideational elements, as they play into and through the rhetoric she features. But having Sternhell as her source has kept her from the more balanced approach necessary.

In focusing on spectacle, ritual, and rhetoric, these and other scholars have illuminated important dimensions of fascism, but by sidestepping encounter with ideas, they mislead regarding origins, proportions, dynamic, and wider meaning. The most basic imperative is to avoid conceiving intellectual or discursive content as some sort of finished ideology, or as theory that might be opposed to practice.[54] Whether as a blueprint or as mere window dressing, 'ideology' tends, as for Sternhell, to be taken as a coherent whole. By breeding essentialism in this way, we miss the mutual implication of theory and practice, ideas and actions. The practice is neither an attempt to implement a blueprint nor sheer opportunism behind an ideological facade, but a contingent and open dynamic in which ideas, the meaning of categories of understanding, were centrally involved, and contested, along with much else.

Insofar as we do not settle for reduction to opportunism, petty bourgeois resentments, or class reaction, we recognize that the aspirations motivating the creators of fascism stemmed from a novel sense of the world – a sense of possibility, even responsibility – vis-à-vis antecedent conceptions and practices. The Enlightenment tradition, though not irrelevant, had not afforded some privileged 'rational' blueprint to guide those seeking to make their way in light of secularization, democratization, and industrialization. Indeed, subsequent development revealed tensions and uncertainties within the creases of that tradition, and those we call intellectuals responded by articulating tensions and rethinking categories in light of the new experience. And just as the Enlightenment was not a completed set of answers, the implications of such new ideas could not be fully thought through all at once. Emerging from within the creases, such categories were contested, their scope for combination uncertain. Even when they claimed to offer a full-blown theory or ideology, intellectuals simply put into play various bits and pieces that then played out contingently in practice in unforeseeable ways.

So how was fascism, as an unexpected and rather extreme departure from the Enlightenment tradition, caught up in the play of categories? The question is crucial for origins, but of course the play of categories continued – not only within the dynamic of the regime but also thereafter, as the fascist experience itself affected subsequent political thinking and historical questioning. The categories continue to be questioned, contested, refined today as we seek to make deeper sense of the eruption of fascism as a chapter in the continuing political experiment. As part of that process, we are coming better to understand that we cannot grasp what fed into fascism insofar as we engage it, place it, only in terms of our present categories, reflecting our knowledge of the outcome.

Writing on postmodernism and historiography in 1989, Jane Caplan found it anomalous that in the ongoing debate about the fascist sympathies of Martin Heidegger and Paul de Man, there was, as she put it, 'a virtually complete silence on both sides about the actual premises and texts of fascist or Nazi ideology: as if this were coherent, already known, yet somehow insignificant.'[55] She went on to propose that the insights of deconstruction might open the way to a riskier, but deeper, more illuminating approach to European fascism. This would entail, she suggested, letting the binary oppositions at work in the discussion of fascism – rational/irrational, for example – themselves be at issue, so that we might open the standard dichotomies, questioning their positive terms.

The alternative to Sternhell requires no specific embrace of deconstruction, narrowly defined; indeed, the orientation Caplan advocates partakes at least as much of the hermeneutic circle. Inquiry into intellectual antecedents is essential to widen our frame of expectation so that we might hear what the agents were saying as opposed to what we expect, based on our contemporary categories, reflecting our knowledge of the outcomes. In approaching Italian fascism, it has been especially hard to recognize the novel cluster of ideas at work because of the limited range of what we are prepared to hear, to grasp. Thinking in terms of reason versus myth, or elitism versus egalitarianism, or totalitarianism versus individualism as undifferentiated dualisms, our grid has been too coarse to enable us to catch and sift the novel ideational elements in the mix. To expand the frame, to refine the grid, we have to engage the earlier intellectual innovations – in their genesis and ensuing contest – to open those categories *for us.*

Thus the value of grasping, for example, how a different understanding of humanism emerged, or how ways of relating economics and politics changed, or how a totalitarian corporativism could seem more genuinely participatory than representative democracy. Virtually all the Enlightenment categories – reason, egalitarianism, freedom, cosmopolitanism, in tandem with an array of variations and contraries – were at work in light of the questions that experience had forced to consciousness. And unless we recognize the openness of the questions at issue, we fail to understand the exciting sense of possibility among the creators of fascism, the sense that Italians, having addressed uncertainties in the liberal tradition that had found particularly explicit form in Italy, could create a wholly new form of state buttressed by a whole new political culture.

At the same time, because we cannot adequately grasp the implications of the categories at issue apart from practice, an inquiry into fascist ideology cannot stop in 1922, on the grounds that thereafter the ideological essence now in place could only be compromised through interface with an 'establishment' that was still in place. Rather than distinguishing theory and practice, we must recognize that actors were thinking and thinkers were acting in the same field of conflicted categories. Thinking does not stop when action kicks in, and contest over the open-ended categories was quite obviously central to fascism in practice. Because much that nobody had yet fully articulated remained open, the contest could result in the refinement of ideas, or in disillusionment and rethinking, even as some ideas won out and other were marginalized along the way. Thus, the fact that the ideological elements did not mesh neatly but rather constituted an unstable mixture is not a warrant to take one or more of the several 'non-discursive' dimensions as more important. Despite the increasing tendency toward myth and overblown rhetoric, the contest of ideas remained central to the fascist regime, and the strands in contest remained relatively coherent. So to understand the course of the regime, we have to keep listening to arguments, reading texts.

For all the undeniable importance of ritual and rhetoric, those who have found ways to marginalize ideas prematurely simply cannot understand the overall dynamic and shape of the fascist regime. Most fundamentally, the contradictions among the founding impulses helped produce the impasse that in turn fed the superficiality of the regime's later phase, especially the increased centrality of the cult of the Duce. Now spectacle and ritual also became more central, almost ends in themselves, effective on one level, but only superficially, as Berezin has emphasized. And as the original ideological elements bogged down, ever more grandiose rhetoric inflated the achievements of the regime to the level of myth.

Fascism was a messy mixture, and its centre of gravity changed as the regime evolved. We can find ritual and rhetoric, virility and the body, but we can also find, written down, in texts, serious debate over the meaning of corporativism, serious rethinking of the Hegelian ethical state for a mass age, serious discussion of the scope for new forms of education, serious reassessment of the legacy of Giuseppe Mazzini in light of the outcome of Marxism. Unless we engage those texts, we cannot assess sources and proportions – and we will not even know what we are missing. No matter how sophisticated the treatment of fascist style, no one who has failed to grasp what Panunzio had against liberal democracy *and* how he differed from Rocco has understood Italian fascism. Nor has someone lacking any sense of Gentile's totalitarian vision, the basis of its response to liberalism and its interface with the Rocco-Panunzio axis.

Although Sternhell seems to be addressing precisely the necessary dimensions, his way of treating fascist ideology proves counterproductive. He does not engage even his own sources in the open-ended way that would enable him to deepen our understanding as opposed to confirming his prior interpretation. And in positing a finished ideology in place by 1922, but then pulling back from further inquiry, he makes things too neat; he misses tensions and raggedness – and thus the real dynamic of the long fascist experiment.

8: Political Mistakes and Historical Learning

In line with Sternhell's earlier work, the epilogue to *The Birth of Fascist Ideology* makes it clear that his target is the whole intellectual tradition, spanning two or three generations, of those who either prepared the ground for fascism or became 'fellow travellers' during the fascist period. Within the latter category, such prominent intellectuals as Emmanuel Mounier and Henri De Man get plenty of play, but in one sense archetypal, and subject to Sternhell's particular criticism in this Italian context, is Benedetto Croce, the most noted Italian intellectual of the era, indeed, in the words of a longtime antagonist in 1937, 'the most famed Italian abroad, at least in the scholarly world, since the days perhaps of Galileo.'[56]

Although Croce would end up a liberal – and arguably the world's best-known anti-fascist – his position with respect to fascism has always been controversial. In the first years of Mussolini's government, before it had a definite direction, Croce was among the many prominent Italians who adopted a wait-and-see attitude, based on a sense that the liberal political elite was exhausted – and that the alternative to Mussolini was likely to be worse.[57] Indeed, Croce was slow to pull away even in the face of the Matteotti murder of June 1924, although he committed unequivocally to opposition early in 1925, when it became clear that continued government by Mussolini meant a full-scale change of regime. Still, because Croce, prior to fascism, had been even more important than Gentile in suggesting that liberal democracy, as usually understood, was incongruent with the new Italian anti-positivist philosophy, Gentile and other fascists continued to claim that Croce was one of them, 'a fascist without the black shirt.'[58] And despite his anti-fascism, Croce's effort at historical explanation after the fact was notoriously weak; his interpretation of fascism as a mere 'parenthesis' still serves widely as a foil. Nor was he entirely forthcoming in assessing his own earlier role.[59]

Sternhell, alert to any deviation from enlightened democratic orthodoxy, is quick to heap scorn on Croce first for having questioned that tradition, then for not having grasped the 'true nature' of fascism – in June 1924, just after the Matteotti murder.[60] Moralistic second-guessing is all too easy in this context, but the point is not to defend Croce's political judgments. He certainly made his share of mistakes – not only in the context of early fascism, but also after the Second World War. Our concern, rather, is the wider intellectual framework, the continuing trajectory from the Enlightenment to us, and what might be learned from the responses of intellectuals within it. Is the key, as for Sternhell, that Croce criticized the Enlightenment and was slow to condemn fascism, or might we learn more deeply about the overall trajectory, and especially about the contours of post-Enlightenment politics, by focusing on the other side, asking why Croce ended up repudiating fascism despite his anti-Enlightenment stance – and what he learned, and offered, as he did so?

The challenge of fascism, especially his erstwhile collaborator Gentile, forced Croce to think more deeply about the nature of politics, including the basis of his own earlier opposition to conventional liberal democracy and his current rejection of fascism. But rather than simply turning back to the Enlightenment tradition, saying he must have been wrong all along, he tried to push on to a post-fascist understanding in response to experience. Precisely because he too had questioned the Enlightenment tradition, he knew the points of tension and ambiguity – and he knew that Gentile was seeing beyond the culture of liberalism and positivism in important respects. In this sense, he took fascism seriously, even while refusing to admit it. And thus he was able to offer a renewed understanding of liberal democracy – beyond the somewhat frayed, uncertain Enlightenment tradition, which he found inadequate to sustain liberal democratic procedures and institutions in a world that has known fascism and the totalitarian temptation in its seductive Gentilian form. He concluded that his own radical historicism, not conventional notions of individual rights or utility, afforded the only convincing basis for a modern liberal politics.

Though Croce's neo-liberalism entailed some notable blind spots, it had new things to say about the reach of the state, the bases of political decision, the relationship between freedom and justice, the place of reason and ethical response, the sense in which there is and is not equality. Above all, it posited limits, humility, pluralism – and openness to the input of everyone, as they are now, even as they fail to conform to abstract ideals of freedom, reason, or justice.[61] In the face of those like Friedrich von Hayek who found as the lesson of totalitarianism the need to ward off wider statist tendencies, Croce accented openness and flexibility in the relationship between the political and economic spheres. The point was not a priori limits on the state, nor did liberalism have to entail *liberismo,* or free-market economics. The economic realm was secondary to the ethical-political: economic arrangements are up to us, and there was room for much variation, depending on the society's choices. What mattered was how those choices were made.

But Croce is only an example. Whatever the merits of his recasting of liberalism, his example suggests the scope for a more genuinely historical approach to earlier intellectuals and their role in the ongoing contest of categories than Sternhell's dualistic approach provides. In affording the Enlightenment tradition special purchase on reason, freedom, and humanism, so that any questioning conflates with fascism, Sternhell does not just miss, but precludes even considering, what someone like Croce derived from the long encounter. By locating fascist ideas, anti-fascist ideas, and our own modes of questioning within the continuing play of categories, a more genuinely historical approach opens the way to a renewed political understanding in light of fascism's catastrophic trajectory. Conversely, we deepen our self-understanding insofar as we avoid both the a priori dualism and the aestheticist reduction that preclude serious encounter with fascist ideas.

chapter 8

Croce, Crocean Historicism, and Contemporary History after Fascism

This is a slightly modified and augmented version of a paper I presented in Italian under the title 'Croce, lo storicismo crociano, e la storia contemporanea dopo il fascismo' as part of the conference 'Croce filosofo: Convegno internazionale di studi in occasione del 50 anniversario della morte' (Croce Philosopher: International Conference on the Occasion of the Fiftieth Anniversary of His Death) in Naples on 27 November 2002. The paper was published in Giuseppe Cacciatore, Girolamo Cotroneo, and Renata Viti Cavaliere, eds., *Croce filosofo: Atti del Convegno internazionale di studi in occasione del 50 anniversario della morte (Napoli-Messina 26–30 novembre 2002)* (Soveria Manelli: Rubbettino, 2003), 2:557–68. I am grateful to the editors for permission to republish this essay here, where it appears in English for the first time.

In writing the present essay, I frankly had forgotten that I had taken up some of the same issues, in a very preliminary way, in chapter 3 here, which dates from 1981.

The recent reassessment of the bases of the postwar Italian Republic has necessarily entailed a re-examination of the pivotal 1940s, when Italy first sought to come to terms with the fascist past and to find a post-fascist orientation. The result has been renewed controversy over what was confronted and what was sidestepped in the supercharged atmosphere of recrimination, shame, hope, and expectation that characterized that decade. Much rested on how to apportion national versus supranational and historically specific versus ahistorical factors in accounting for the emergence and disastrous trajectory of fascism. Obviously prescription for the future depended on the diagnosis of what had gone wrong.

The same problem of coming to terms and moving on in light of fascism, Nazism, or totalitarianism has of course been a massive preoccupation for much of Europe since the Second World War.[1] Not surprisingly, national sensitivities and political concerns have been central in the countries most immediately involved, sometimes yielding a certain self-absorption and a neglect of wider questioning. Yet we often assume that on some level totalitarianism, fascism, and the Holocaust remain problems for all of us in the West, not just for the countries from which they emerged.

More generally, the whole notion of 'coming to terms' entails uncertainties about criteria, about what reorientation in light of the experience at issue would have to entail. Is it a matter of learning specific lessons so that we actively root out or guard against this or that, or is it more a matter of digesting that earlier experience, putting it in historical perspective, so that we can move on, no longer traumatized? Dissolving the weight of a traumatic past seems very different from probing its place in ongoing processes to help us respond more effectively to the present. Or perhaps understanding leads to forgiveness – and then invites the danger of rehabilitation.

Benedetto Croce was of course central to the Italian effort of the 1940s. Indeed, whereas intellectuals like Meinecke and Jaspers sought to offer leadership in Germany, Croce's situation, and opportunity, were surely unparalleled. Yet he was quickly subjected to critiques not only from the expected enemies but also from some once within his orbit. Among other things, Croce seemed too quick to make Italian fascism a manifestation of a wider pan-European totalitarian tendency, a mere parenthesis on the Italian level. To some he was thereby sidestepping the need for significant change to root out the forces responsible for fascism. At the same time, Croce himself seemed to grow disillusioned, leading some to infer that he had come to doubt even the overall intellectual orientation he had worked out over the previous fifty years. At any rate, what Croce was prepared to offer somehow was not meshing fruitfully with the wider effort of his time to come to terms with the past and prepare for the future.[2]

Caught up in a dramatic role at an advanced age, Croce faced immediate pressures and difficult choices on the practical level, and few deny that he did not always respond to best effect.[3] But intellectuals often make poor politicians, and there would seem scope for distinguishing his practical responses from the wider relevance of his overall historicist framework. Having been an intellectual fixture for close to fifty years, he could seem old-fashioned, but his thought was still evolving, especially in response to the disasters of his own time, and many of those now declaring him *superato* were demonstrably misrepresenting his thinking. It is possible that the relevance of Croce's ideas *even for the immediate challenge* might have been especially hard to grasp under the tortured circumstances of the time. It is also possible that Croce himself left ambiguities that might more readily be addressed now. Recent political and cultural changes invite a fresh look at what Croce did and did not do, what he might have done and what still might be done on the basis of Crocean insights.

Croce began almost immediately to try to account for fascism historically once he unequivocally repudiated Mussolini's regime early in 1925. But at this point his erstwhile collaborator Giovanni Gentile and others were claiming that Croce was 'a fascist without the black shirt.'[4] For Gentile, fascism was the political fruit of the distinctively Italian humanist intellectual tradition that he and Croce had by then made relevant to the challenges facing the contemporary West. Resisting any such notion, Croce began playing down the specifically Italian side of fascism by accenting a more generic totalitarian departure that ultimately encompassed Nazism and Soviet communism. As a manifestation of this wider totalitarianism, fascism was not a specifically Italian phenomenon – or problem. Moreover, it was not, as for Gentile, the modern forefront, but essentially the opposite, an especially troubling manifestation of a wider incapacity to adjust to the modern historicist world, the political corollary of which, Croce increasingly emphasized, was liberalism, newly reconceived on that modern historicist basis.[5]

By the 1940s, Croce had developed a repertory of interpretive categories based on this line of analysis. While admitting that totalitarianism had not been devoid of ideals, he attributed it primarily to an antihistoricist quest for security, for a utopian end of history, which was ultimately an *ideale di morte.* The embrace of naturalistic race and class categories merely manifested this wider denial of historical openness and freedom. Totalitarianism reflected a profound spiritual crisis, a moral depression, a weakening of the will, the contraction of civilization and liberty, the advent of barbarism and decadence.[6] In offering categories largely congruent with Erich Fromm's 'escape from freedom,' J.L. Talmon's 'security of a prison,' and Karl Dietrich Bracher's intolerant 'tyranny of the majority,' Croce was helping to establish a familiar interpretive tradition.[7] These categories suggested that something like totalitarianism remained an ongoing danger in the modern world, whatever the defeat of the fascist and Nazi strands of its contemporary incarnation.

Versus those playing up Croce's pessimism and doubt, Michele Maggi recently insisted that Croce's underlying orientation proved adequate for understanding even the disturbing events of his own time. Croce, of course, had consistently stressed that, whereas we can and do know the world as history, we must continually return to the philosophical moment in historiography to re-fashion the categories in order to come to terms with new historical experience.[8] And Maggi concluded that, despite anguish and difficulty, the late Croce managed the necessary conceptual clarification, which underpinned the account of totalitarianism we noted.[9] What seemed necessary was a deeper grasp of the historical role of the negative and evil, including even what Croce called 'the anti-Christ that lies in each of us.' As Maggi put it, Croce could make sense even of troubling recent events because he had made Satan intrinsic to God. Conversely, all his reflection on the period confirmed his philosophy, its capacity to encompass history.[10]

As Maggi sees it, Croce was thus able to offer a kind of consoling wisdom.[11] But we must flesh out Maggi's argument a bit to make clear what the consolation at issue does and does not entail. Counter to a longstanding criticism, Croce was not simply assuring us that, watching passively, we can understand after the fact how any novel phenomenon came to be and grasp that it was necessary for our present world to be as it is. Rather, what Croce offered was a call to action, a charge of responsibility. Though new, ever 'richer' evils come to be as the world grows, new ethical response wells up in response. To be sure, even ethical response can be misguided, producing fanaticism or reducing to mere personal gesture. But as Maggi noted, Croce derived a duty of rationality from the way human beings are caught up in history. Our capacity to understand even so troubling a novel experience as totalitarianism enables us to respond in a responsible, rational mode.

It may well be true that Croce's way of rethinking categories eased his own anguish, but the potential for intellectual leadership and the claims of his wider cultural program suggest questions about criteria of adequacy that seem to carry beyond Maggi's assessment of what Croce offered. Maggi found confirmation of the capacity of Croce's philosophy to encompass history – even history that now includes our experience of totalitarianism. But what does it mean to 'encompass' in this case? Maggi found Croce's way of refurbishing categories adequate to make sense of that experience. But what level of detail is required?

Although his interpretive categories offered some indications, Croce did not attempt a systematic, full-scale history of fascism or totalitarianism. Even while defending, in principle, the scope for writing the history of one's own time, he noted that the task that had fallen to him had been to abhor the fascist regime, not to write its history.[12] Yet his well-known accents on contemporary concerns in historiography and the centrality of historiography in preparing action might seem to suggest that a more systematic effort to make sense of fascism historically would have been central to the present effort to come to terms. In fact the orientation Croce offered rested on historical understanding only in the most general sense. Rather than seeking to transcend history through some secure but death-like completion, we are to think and live historically. And insofar as we do so, we mesh with the ever-growing world through historical understanding and ethical response. In themselves, these assurances and imperatives did not illuminate the present situation in its historical genesis, yet that would seem the key to orienting for action in light of new experience.

Many of his contemporaries found Croce's offering too thin, too vague, to afford the orientation his cultural program seemed to promise. Though the point was never to claim the last word and stop the discussion, can his account be considered adequate if it failed to convince others to this extent? In Croce's terms we can indeed get some things settled and move on, but we surely still have not done so in the case of fascism and totalitarianism. Though disagreement and contest will continue, and though the level of consensus cannot be specified in advance, we cannot speak of adequacy, or a capacity to encompass recent history, until we have a historical understanding that yields a deeper consensus about the place of fascism and how it relates to us. On that basis we can better grasp present challenges and possibilities and thus proceed more productively.

In one sense, the process of providing orientation in Croce's terms was multi-layered and bound to take time, so it is not surprising that he did not complete the enterprise. At the same time, however, certain conflicting pressures compromised his effort even to show the way. Moreover, even his sense of what was required to prepare the way, in light of this particular novel experience, betrayed certain limitations. Let us consider these three layers of difficulty in turn.

From one perspective, the Crocean notion that history prepares action is merely formal and descriptive and entails no particular imperative or prescription. We must orient ourselves by thinking in order to act coherently at all. Situations are understood only in their genesis, and orientation for action means simply that we have a sense of how the situation to which we must respond came to be. On that level, we always have the historical understanding we need because we decide what we need, selecting on the basis of some contemporary concern. Early on, in response to Renato Serra's laments about what seemed the inherent inadequacy of any historical account, Croce contended that 'we know at every moment all the history that we need to know' ('noi, a ogni istante, conosciamo tutta la storia che c'importa conoscere').[13] This suggests that understanding is always adequate. And in one sense it is; some historical sense of the present world underpins our continuing moral response. But Croce's accents often pointed beyond, in a prescriptive vein. And in fact our present understanding may be inadequate – even an impediment to fruitful action – and thus open to criticism.

Even in the best of circumstances, the cultural effort to orient for present action in light of new experience seems bound to entail an intervening moment of uncertainty, inadequacy, and friction. As we seek to determine how to question the new experience, we will disagree even about the utility of existing categories. Indeed, the effort to come to terms can take place only within a framework of contest at all levels. For a while the contest itself may be largely futile, with people talking past rather than seriously engaging each other, producing a fusion of horizons and thus growth. So whereas we have everything we need in one very general sense, in another we certainly do not.

The necessary re-elaboration after fascism took place from within such a multi-layered and contested framework, in which not only the actual history but the categories for questioning the history and wider cultural priorities were all at issue. In his effort to provide orientation, Croce had to engage all layers of the debate. On the level of the categories, many during the 1940s and thereafter tended to treat fascism in reductionist terms, invoking big capital, petty bourgeois losers, or ahistorical character types. From this perspective, it was sufficient to adapt such relatively familiar categories to come to terms with the new experience. Croce continued his longstanding critique of all such forms of reductionism, most prominently in his polemics against Marxism. And on the level of the wider frame, he redoubled his efforts to prescribe his absolute historicist orientation against an array of competitors, including, most obviously, Marxism, Christianity, and existentialism. That historicist orientation showed how to proceed in a certain spirit that alone would make it possible to come to terms with the recent past.

To grasp in a Crocean way how we are caught up in history is to feel the prescriptive dimension, beyond what we necessarily do. To fulfill our duty of rationality, we ought to formulate the questions that seem most likely to illuminate the situation to which we are called upon to respond in action. And we ought to be open to genuine stretching and learning; we ought to be open to truth, as opposed to merely 'usefully' confirming prejudices or making propaganda points, serving some existing cause through what Croce called 'party history.'[14] At the same time, the willingness to question and learn requires reflexivity, a capacity for self-criticism, a recognition that our beliefs are implicated in our historical inquiries.

Croce was surely reflexive when he candidly implied that having lived through fascism, he hated it too much to write its history. Though his reasons were surely understandable, this was implicitly to recognize in himself the practical impulses that would compromise the essential openness to learning and truth. Not only would it have to wait for others to write the history, but even Croce's way of re-elaborating categories and formulating new questions might well be compromised as a result. In fact his abhorrence both reflected and fed a combination of reductionism and ahistorical moralism that impeded the deeper historical understanding his wider framework demanded.

That reducible impulses were at work goes without saying, and Croce's earlier understanding of the useful or economic side of the practical could account for them up to a point. But something new had come into the world with totalitarianism, so even as he criticized the a priori reductionist approaches of others, he found it a priority to re-elaborate the useful or economic to encompass 'vitality,' even the place of evil, to account for the troubling novelty. But to fasten upon the negative and evil in history was to repair to the ahistorical at the expense of more risky questions about the historical specificity of the human responses at issue. The approach was ultimately too moralistic to make sense of totalitarianism in its historical specificity.

Though such impulses are never pure, the key, from the wider Crocean perspective, is to probe for whatever free ethical-political responses were at work, to assess their proportions, and to seek to understand the resulting historical trajectory on that basis. Insofar as we settle too quickly for moralism or reductionism, our framework is too limited to understand response as ethical-political. We fall into error in Crocean terms and fail the imperative of reorientation.

Croce specified that if he were to have written a history of fascism, it would not have been all black. In light of his dictum that history traces the positive, the point was partly that even Italian fascism had provoked positive effects – the discipline of the Resistance, for example. But to concentrate on the positive in that sense is to miss the scope for learning more deeply about our own situation. Whatever effects they produced, the responses at issue may have stemmed from, and may illuminate, historically specific conditions of possibility that remain in place. Croce got closer when he noted that in focusing on the fascists themselves he would cite their generous sentiments and good intentions, even while noting that, as youthful and immature, they had lacked the essential critical admixture.[15]

This was a start, but *what* intentions and sentiments, and why these, in light of the wider, historically specific situation? Insofar as they could be taken as ethical-political, they did not manifest mere 'moral depression,' so how did they relate to the impulses he had long associated with *antistoricismo*? Croce had noted that liberty, as central to the ethical-political impulse, always strives to re-establish the socio-political conditions for a more intense liberty.[16] Was it possible to conceive even totalitarianism as such a quest for freedom? And though his reference to youthful exuberance afforded some indications, how could any such ethical-political aspiration lead to myth-making and such travesties as the cult of the Duce and the racial laws?

Croce had noted that history could find the reasons behind every event and the place of every event in its wider epoch.[17] So totalitarianism had a place in a wider, historically specific period, the contours of which, by definition, continue in some measure. And the key to assessing aspirations, proportions, and the disastrous trajectory is precisely to place the phenomenon historically, in terms of those wider processes. To grasp the aspirations as ethical-political requires understanding the novel, historically specific situation to which they were responding. But though Croce's understanding of the texture of a world of radical immanence might have offered particular insight into that dimension, he himself did not probe totalitarian aspirations on this level. And this was true partly, at least, because he found it a priority to oppose two contrasting but complementary cultural tendencies that the disasters of the era were now bringing to particular prominence: on the one hand, existentialist angst; on the other, the longing, in light of recent suffering, for some definitive order through science.[18]

To counter both, Croce played up the sense in which the present world is what it always has been – and thereby minimized the depth of the modern break and the novelty of the challenges it had occasioned. What he and his contemporaries had just suffered was not qualitatively different from what people had suffered before. Living history entails tragedy, not the sweetness of an idyll, and we have no right to expect any better than our predecessors. But the impossibility of some definitive peace and harmony was no warrant for existentialism, which portended self-preoccupation, loss of nerve, at best mere gesture. Neither the scientistic nor the existentialist tendency was true to the terms of a historicist world, with its ongoing sense of responsibility. Under the circumstances, opposing them both had to be central to Croce's effort to provide orientation.

But though the texture of the historical world remains the same in one sense, history includes moments of crisis, of pivot, of change on extraordinary levels. Croce had recognized the cultural import of the waning of traditional religion and the drama of adjusting to a historicist perspective in response. Indeed, he explicitly called it the task of his generation to show the way.[19] Not all generations face comparable challenges. But Croce's sense of the range of new experience and response that became possible within the absolute historicist universe proved too limited. As he saw it, those who did not embrace his own version of the new historicist perspective could only be dreaming of some 'dead' completeness or some scientifically ordered society – or perhaps lapsing into existentialist self-indulgence. He was not prepared to probe the sense in which the totalitarian departure was itself an effort to respond positively as part of the same big adjustment to the loss of transcendence.

The new sense of the human place in history seemed to invite, even to require, new modes of collective action to mobilize energies and make history in light of what seemed the limits of the mainstream Enlightenment dispensation, including liberal democracy. But the effort opened the way to an array of unforeseen disasters. We had not known, could not have known, that modernity entailed such possibilities and dangers. And the imperative is not simply to respond to evil or to beware the fascist psychological types but to deepen our understanding of the terms of the modern historicist world, the continuing challenges and dangers it entails. That is what orientation requires.

At the same time, Croce's sense of the theoretical moment, in light of this historically specific novelty, was too limited, even formulaic, and this, too, tended to restrict his range of questioning. In *La storia* Croce said that historiography requires rigorous definition of categories like baroque, materialism, democracy, or Renaissance, though they are never found in pure form.[20] In the case at hand, the comparable categories might include fascism, totalitarianism, ethical state, and myth. But rigorous definition of such categories is not sufficient for us to know how to question the novelty in this case. To formulate such categories, even to formulate the questions, requires a sense of precisely the recent history that we do not yet understand. The philosophical moment had to entail wider reflexive thinking, more open-ended than establishing rigorous definitions or expanding our sense of what the four moments of the spirit can encompass. Theoretical reflection enables us fruitfully to question, to probe the ongoing challenges, possibilities, and dangers of the historically specific, absolute historicist world to which we are still adjusting. This more reflexive approach enables us better to understand how historical questioning can yield orientation for action in light of the especially troubling experience of fascism and totalitarianism.

What Croce offered as orientation in light of fascism seemed slippery, moralistic, even self-serving, partly because it did not engage the totalitarian experience in a more genuinely historical way. But though he left much undone, the process of coming to terms continues, and Crocean historicism still offers essential aspects of the framework as we continue our struggle to understand the history. Croce showed not only what to look for but also the spirit in which we can question, learn, and proceed more fruitfully.

On the basis of a Crocean history we can better assess the proportions of fascism as at once national and supranational. We can better assess the relative import of historically specific yet supranational factors as opposed to ahistorical factors, from Crocean vitality to what Umberto Eco has called ur-fascism. And, insofar as we take totalitarianism as modern, we can better assess the degree to which, and the sense in which, it stemmed from conditions of possibility that remain ongoing, as opposed to confined to an era now completed, thanks not least to the experience of totalitarianism itself. So though the process of reorientation is in a sense unfinishable, there remains scope for taking advantage of Croce's wider frame to dissolve the weight of a disastrous past and more fruitfully orient ourselves for action to shape the future.

chapter 9

Crocean Historicism and Post-Totalitarian Thought

This is a slightly expanded version of the paper I presented in Italian under the title 'Lo storicismo crociano e il pensiero post-totalitario' as part of the conference 'Benedetto Croce 50 anni dopo / Benedetto Croce 50 év után,' organized by János Kelemen and József Takács in December 2002, with sessions first at ELTE University in Budapest, then at the Hungarian Academy in Rome. At the invitation of the organizers, I presented the paper twice, first in Budapest on 6 December, then in Rome on 12 December. The present version was then published in both Italian and Hungarian in the acts of the conference, *Benedetto Croce 50 anni dopo / Benedetto Croce 50 év után,* ed. Krisztina Fontanini, János Kelemen, and József Takács, 503–16 (Budapest: Aquincum Kiadó [l'Istituto Italiano di Cultura per l'Ungheria], 2004), I thank the editors for permission to include it here, where it is published in English for the first time.

The unexpected decay of communism in east-central Europe was bound up with a good deal of innovative thinking about how the system functioned, how it might be overcome, and how best to proceed into the future in light of what the late communist experience had revealed. Such key intellectuals as the Poles Adam Michnik and Jacek Kuroń, the Hungarians Miklós Haraszti and George Konrád, and the Czechs Milan Kundera and Václav Havel became known in the West even before the fall of the communist regimes. And though their accents sometimes differed considerably, they seemed to Western observers to occupy the same post-totalitarian universe.[1]

Sympathetic observers abroad found promising the claim of these intellectuals that totalitarianism in the Soviet bloc manifested totalizing tendencies characteristic of modernity itself, tendencies that had taken heightened, garish form in decaying communism but that were, if anything, still more insidious in the seemingly more successful West. And of course that wider totalism would continue even as totalitarianism itself proved subject to decay and end. So the alternative for east-central Europe was not merely to catch up to the West, confirming liberal capitalist triumphalism. And the opportunity for unforeseen modes of response in east-central Europe might show even the West how to overcome dehumanizing aspects of modernity.

An influential example of such thinking in the United States was Jeffrey Goldfarb's *Beyond Glasnost: The Post-Totalitarian Mind*, first published in 1989. In seeking to draw out the wider relevance of this east-central European current, Goldfarb showed how it paralleled, and extended, the earlier thinking of Hannah Arendt, who had similarly worried that totalitarianism, even in its earlier form, manifested ongoing totalizing tendencies.[2] All these thinkers are part of a continuing tradition seeking the implications of the totalitarian experience for the modern self-understanding. The premise is that merely to embrace the conventional Western understanding of liberal capitalism cannot be sufficient in light of all that totalitarianism revealed about modernity itself.

It is no secret that Benedetto Croce has not been part of this discussion, though a number of his mature categories – including his historicist recasting of liberalism – emerged in response to the totalitarian departures of his time. Still, even many Italians found him passé by the mid-forties, so it is not surprising that he attracted little attention among the major east-central European figures. Yet insofar as we now have a tradition of post-totalitarian thought, we might ask what happens if we return to Croce in light of the late communist experience and the rethinking of possibilities and priorities that it spawned.

Croce offered a cultural program – summed up as history as thought and action – that entailed a premium on action prepared by historical understanding and experienced as history-making. Yet in the east-central European reading, the totalitarian experience reinforces wider modern cultural tendencies that seem to undercut any such accents. The question is what the Crocean embrace of history might mean, how it might still be relevant, in light of the east-central European concerns.

In a short space, I believe I can make my point by focusing on Kundera and Havel among the east-central European thinkers. Though they had come to represent quite different – even conflicting – perspectives by the late 1970s, their diagnoses and prescriptions had enough in common that Goldfarb, for example, could plausibly draw on both. Though in different ways, Havel and Kundera were each concerned with a cluster of intersecting themes including lightness and weight, personal and political, memory and forgetting, innocence and responsibility, power and modes of resistance in what increasingly was coming to seem a purely secular world. Croce addressed the same cluster, partly because he, too, had lived through a novel and disillusioning political regime.

In exploring our collective and individual relationship with history, Kundera played up one familiar aspect of totalitarianism – control of memory, of the past itself, partly through enforced forgetting. Even photographs become lies as important individuals are airbrushed out.[3] But such totalitarian practice seemed simply to reveal in ludicrous form a wider modern tendency, for, as Kundera put it, 'perhaps our entire technical age does this, with its cult of the future, its cult of youth and childhood, its indifference to the past and mistrust of thought.'[4]

In a noted section of *The Book of Laughter and Forgetting*, Kundera examines the layers of lightness and forgetting by moving back and forth between the Czech communist experience and the fate of Tamina on an island populated only by children.[5] Gustav Husak, installed by the Soviets in 1969, was the 'President of Forgetting,' builder of a world without memory. Embracing children as the future, he advocated never looking back, never allowing memory to weigh down the future.[6] For Kundera, children have no past but rather magical innocence, and humanity itself is becoming ever more childlike.[7] Crucial to that transition is the return of music to its primeval state, manifested in the amplified guitar of youth-oriented popular music, which Kundera found stereotypical and monotonous.[8] This is music without memory, affording the bland, immediate happiness of an eternal present. Husak understood that such music complemented the communist political order when he made it a priority to persuade the pop singer Karel Klos to return to Czechoslovakia.

Kundera found the image of the children's island in communist youth organizations. A site of innocence, without memory, without weight, the island seemingly offers the forgetting that Tamina thought she wanted. But the idiotic music, accompanying the absurdly sensual dancing of the children, induces in Tamina the sense of nausea that emanates from weightless things. Lightness itself becomes a terrifying weight, leading her to try to escape, sustained only by the weight of her own body and by a craving for life itself. Yet she dies in the process; for Tamina, at least, there was no escape.

In *The Unbearable Lightness of Being*, the communist experience brings into sharp relief the texture of the historical world and the stuff of which we construct its public memory. It is a world of capriciousness, contingency, unintended consequences, in which street names change, the police make unforeseen uses of our photos and the truths we tell them, and the public dimension forever escapes our control.[9] Under the circumstances, public and private are mutually implicated, and communication itself becomes problematic as words fail to convey what was intended. For Sabina, 'having a public in mind means living in lies.' There can be truth only in private, even in secret.[10]

As Kundera sees it, this texture means that history – whatever sense we have of being caught up in history – is anything but the source of the weight we might seek. On the contrary, 'history is as light as individual human life, unbearably light, light as a feather, as dust swirling in the air, as whatever will no longer exist tomorrow.'[11] Insofar as history is the mode of remembrance as opposed to forgetting, it conflates with public lies, with 'official memory,' as 'written by the victors.' Instead of weight we have what Kundera calls 'kitsch' in the original sense, excluding shit, contradiction, everything unacceptable.[12] Though it takes garish form with Husak, the children, and the bland immediacy of pop music, kitsch is by no means confined to late communism. In the modern world, kitsch is what becomes of everything we do, including all politics.

In *The Unbearable Lightness of Being* Kundera was especially concerned with 'The Grand March' – shorthand for one especially prominent form of political kitsch. Although it sometimes seems to encompass any accent on history, faith in the Grand March characterizes especially the leftist orientation to which Kundera himself had subscribed, but that proves to rest on the facile assumption that all good things fit together, that there could be liberty and justice for all.[13] Having once produced communism, the modern Grand March now yields an equally simplistic anti-communism. Thanks to kitsch, the Left was able sheepishly to reclassify the Soviet Union as a obstacle to the Grand March and move on.[14]

Kundera was playing down any premium on political response or, more generally, any self-understanding in terms of history-making. But what instead? Responding to the tendency of well-meaning German admirers to view her art as political protest, Sabina insists that her enemy is kitsch, not communism.[15] Futile though it will no doubt prove, an effort to resist or undercut kitsch is valuable for Kundera, essentially as a gesture of truth-telling and self-affirmation. Also redeeming are simple acts of kindness, contrasted with grandiose, often grandstanding political gestures that lead who knows where. It is more important to rescue a half-buried crow than to send petitions to the president.[16]

When decaying totalitarianism brings the texture of the public, historical world garishly to the fore, responsibility itself becomes a dead weight. Thus Tomas is relieved to abandon all sense of mission or vocation, to experience the blissful lightness of forgetting and indifference.[17] Yet such personal lightness, reflecting the weightlessness of history, is itself sometimes unbearable, so through his characters Kundera moves back and forth among modes of response, exploring the paradoxical interplay of lightness and weight, naïveté and cynicism, autonomy and interdependence, mind and body. Balancing the modern kitsch of feel-good forgetting is the scope for modes of action that either resist, like Sabina's art, or that are sufficiently immediate and personal to stand alone, like rescuing a half-buried crow.

For Kundera, the experience of decaying communism was only the latest phase of an extremely concentrated history that has enabled Central Europe to see beyond the modern mainstream; there, most basically, 'a lucid form of skepticism has arisen in the midst of our era of illusions.'[18]

Though Havel was less cynical, less overtly anti-political, many of his accents pointed in parallel directions. Underlying the present crisis is the arrogant anthropocentrism that has resulted from our unprecedented departure from God, our loss of metaphysical certainties. That anthropocentrism has yielded an impersonal, irresponsible juggernaut of power that produces the sometimes obvious, sometimes hidden mechanisms of totality. Modern totalizing power tends to reduce individuals to helpless, undifferentiated cogs by means of advertising, manipulation through television, and a consumerist value system that literally 'demoralizes,' undercutting any sense of societal responsibility.[19] From within this framework, even stable categories and written histories tend to become instruments serving the power of the victors.[20]

This mechanism was producing comparable alienation under state socialism and capitalism, though Havel found the lurid forms of decaying totalitarianism especially revelatory – and a warning to the West. At the same time, there was no evidence that Western democracy could offer a satisfactory alternative for east-central Europe. Indeed, said Havel, people are manipulated in infinitely more subtle ways in the West. Even parliamentary democracy could be no more than a transitional step; in light of all that the east-central European experience had revealed, it was essential to think beyond mainstream Western mechanisms.[21]

Although his references to power and victors sometimes suggested the familiar bifurcation of dominator and dominated, Havel came to recognize that everyone is both powerful and powerless, both victim and supporter of the system. Thus, even totalitarianism entails universal complicity and responsibility. In his famous greengrocer example, individuals behaving *as if* they believed in it actually become the system, as everyone going through the motions pressures everyone else to do the same.[22] But thus Havel's now-familiar but once-revolutionary premise – the seemingly powerless have the power to undermine the system simply by living the truth.

Whereas Leszek Kolakowski, for example, found the soil for religious renewal in the move beyond totalitarianism, precisely as a move beyond the arrogant modern anthropocentrism, Havel implied that there could be no turning back from the secular side of modernity.[23] But the self-momentum of impersonal power was now in crisis – most obviously in east-central Europe, where people had begun to see through the mechanisms and thus to grasp their own power to withdraw from complicity.[24] The greengrocer simply ceases playing the game, performing rituals in which he does not believe. The seemingly powerless of east-central Europe were thereby showing the modern West that we all have the power to stop being reduced to cogs. So as we come to grasp the mechanisms, the antidote is resistance, living the truth, which is constantly to disrupt systems of power. Renewal, said Havel, is a task confronting each of us at every moment.[25]

Reacting against Kundera's cynical devaluation of the historical sphere, Havel insisted explicitly that we all contribute to the making of history.[26] He was not advocating, in other words, that we simply pull back to some 'inner freedom,' as if truth is possible only in private, or even in silence, as Kundera sometimes suggests. Rather, Havel envisioned a sense of positive responsibility to and for the whole. But in light of modern consumerist demoralization, engendering this sense of responsibility would require, Havel noted explicitly, a kind of existential revolution, the moral reconstitution of society.[27] And something along those lines might seem what Giovanni Gentile and other totalitarians had had in mind in the first place. So how is it possible to resist power, reconstitute society, and avoid lapsing back into totalitarian utopianism at the same time?

For Havel, the key is to hollow out and defuse power by simultaneously reconstituting civil society. Restoring the human dimension requires decentralization and self-management in the economy and small-scale, ad hoc organizations in lieu of bureaucracy.[28] At the same time, congruent with his intellectual beginnings, Havel sometimes characterized such resistance in quasi-existentialist terms, as a gesture of authenticity. We must avoid the trap of tactical disputes, he tells us, and simply live the truth; 'the purity of this struggle is the best guarantee of optimum results.'[29]

These are all surely noble-sounding imperatives. Who, after all, would venture to oppose civil society or living the truth? The question is how well they cohere to afford an alternative to arrogant anthropocentrism.

What, then, of Croce in light of these east-central European concerns and prescriptions? Obviously Croce was no guide to the specifics of consumer society or the manipulations of TV and advertising. Even during his own post-totalitarian moment, his account of fascism and totalitarianism seemed weak, slippery, even self-serving. And some today would no doubt carry the point further, arguing that Croce is not merely irrelevant but represents precisely what must be left behind once we embrace the post-totalitarian thinking of those like Kundera and Havel. Most obviously, Croce's accent on 'history as the story of liberty' seems to suggest the kitsch of the long march. Indeed, he might even seem precisely one of those victors whose categories justify whatever has happened.[30]

I argue that, on the contrary, placing Croce alongside Kundera and Havel indicates that his mode of post-totalitarianism, though surely incomplete, makes an essential contribution to the wider frame necessary to contain even these later post-totalitarian insights. As offered, they have tended to reinforce wider recent cultural tendencies toward excess and overreaction. Though his diagnosis of totalitarianism itself was somewhat shallow, Croce was operating on precisely the level at issue, showing how we might adjust to a purely human world without the arrogance that came to trouble Havel. Croce's way of doing so addressed precisely the issues of power, weight, lightness, memory, responsibility, and futility at issue for east-central European post-totalitarian thought. Even while remaining true to the secular frame and eschewing the totalitarian alternative, he found a more affirmative, reconstructive way of addressing those issues, not least in an effort to counter tendencies toward overreaction already at work.

In characterizing 'history as the story of liberty,' Croce was not positing some 'grand march' or lapsing into liberal triumphalism. Far from moving toward some definitive triumph, liberty is simply an ongoing human attribute, adequate to the ever-new challenges we face. There is always scope for fresh overcoming through free ethical response, buttressed by historical understanding. And even with its accent on liberty, the Crocean orientation does not deny but encompasses precisely the unacceptable that, in Kundera's reading, modern kitsch denies. Indeed,

Croce tackled head on the sense of futility, the absurdity of unintended consequences, that led Kundera to posit the weightlessness of history.

At first glance, however, Croce's antidote, his way of imputing the necessary weight, may seem thin, naïve, in light of Kundera's often brilliant explorations – and the further historical experience to which they responded. Croce posited a combination of immortality of the act and faith in history. What we do lives on, helping to shape the next moment, and thus becomes the foundation for subsequent response.[31] Kundera seems to be mocking any such notion when he observes in *The Book of Laughter and Forgetting* that 'our only immortality is in the police files.'[32]

But Croce had reason to claim that, though we have no grand march, we have a measure of historical coherence and continuity that makes a decisive difference. Our sense of temporal continuity connects us with those who came before, nurturing a feeling of responsibility for the world they have bequeathed to us. Our care for what the world becomes invites some particular vocation as we seek to mesh our talents with present needs and possibilities. And though action is fraught with risk, our sense of care and responsibility leads us to experience what we do as 'history-making' – as affecting what the world becomes.

Moreover, the world is sufficiently coherent to be open to historical understanding. To be sure, we have *only* historical understanding, a finite, provisional grasp of a finite, provisional world; there can be no shortcut, nothing that tells us what to do with scientific certainty. But that merely historical understanding is adequate to prepare action in the sense of affording a rational frame for ethical response, so that what we do is neither a mere shot in the dark nor a mere gesture of personal authenticity. Whereas for Havel, as we saw, the purity of the struggle itself 'is the best guarantee of optimum results,' for Croce the sense of the potential weight of what we do prompts historical questions, opens us to learning and understanding, and thereby enables us to proceed in a more rational way as we judge the historical outcomes so far.

Yet we construct our histories at least partly from evidence that, in Kundera's universe, seems fatally compromised. Tomas, recognizing that the place might be bugged, fears that the police will twist his words, quoting him out of context. And thus he notes that he has no ambition to be quoted by future historians.[33] History becomes light for Kundera partly because we reconstruct historical accounts on the basis of such dubious evidence as this.

It is surely true that history as orientation becomes much more complex as the stakes of historical memory become clearer and people are airbrushed out. We may generate the evidence for later historians partly with the aim of influencing them. But the mechanisms that concerned Kundera do not undermine the Crocean sense of the scope for true historical understanding. What opens us to truth is not the public grandstanding prominent in Kundera's account but a sense of responsibility for action that entails a duty to question and to learn. We may have reason to lie even to ourselves, but we have the capacity to open to truth, and we do so insofar as we feel the weight of the human place in the historical world – both our debt to the past and our responsibility for the future. On that basis we simply become more critical in our use of evidence as we continue – even in light of Kundera.

Though Havel recognized that on some level power and complicity are universal, his accents suggested that the problem is power itself, with its own impersonal, totalizing momentum. Any outcome of power is a 'victory' – and thus illegitimate domination. Insofar as all resultants are comparably dehumanizing, disruption becomes the archetypal expression of the ethical. But any such notion is subject to the objection that has been raised against Michel Foucault's thinking, which betrays, as Richard Rorty put it, a 'crippling ambiguity' between power as a neutral, descriptive category and power as pejorative, as illegitimate domination.[34]

There may be good reason for a premium on resistance or disruption under certain circumstances, but insofar as power is not merely an impersonal totalizing force but the neutral glue making possible any world at all, disruption cannot be the privileged priority if we are to have constructive, world-making objectives. So whereas Havel also offered some more constructive imperatives, they mesh uneasily with his tendency to conceive power in the pejorative sense and to privilege mere disruption. Partly as a result, those more constructive imperatives seem at once utopian and vague. Insofar as we want an existential revolution that leads to a positive sense of moral responsibility for the whole community, even living the truth will not suffice. We will have to focus and exercise power in what we determine to be a constructive way.

If we seek the basis for positive, history-making social construction without totalitarian excess or anthropocentric arrogance, the question is how we are to conceive our individual and collective place in the ongoing process through which power is created and, through its exercise, our world is endlessly remade. For Croce freedom is bound up with constructive responsibility so it cannot be merely negative, mere 'freedom from' – pursued by disrupting, resisting, or extricating from systems of power. Rather, freedom is positive, 'freedom to,' and thus is inherently bound up with the exercise of power. The issue is how, in a humble and pluralistic way, we are to act together, using power, even through the much-disprized state with its much-disprized but inevitable bureaucracy.

Are Kundera's cynicism and Havel's premium on disruption based on experience and reflection that simply carry beyond Croce, or do they manifest certain limits, even a failure fully to grasp the terms of the ongoing secular adjustment and the range of possibilities that have so far emerged from within it? The tradition of post-totalitarian thought reflects a plausible concern to find an alternative to triumphalist liberal capitalism and, in its recent phase, an understandable eagerness to accentuate the import of the east-central European experience. But these have contributed to a prejudicially delimited sense of the overall framework from within which both the totalitarian departure and our efforts to proceed in the aftermath have taken place. Without a better understanding of the wider modern frame, we cannot do justice to the place of lightness and weight, innocence and responsibility, and the interplay of the historical, the political, and the personal.[35]

As it happened, the east-central European response, eagerly embraced by the disaffected in the West, contributed to a characteristic overreaction based on noble-sounding but dubious conflations, as when Kundera's Mirek says in the aftermath of the Prague Spring, 'The struggle of man against power is the struggle of memory against forgetting.'[36] More generally, that response came to reflect and reinforce prejudicial postmodern understandings of the human relationship with history – and thus of the scope for collective or political action.[37] Indeed, the familiar contemporary ways of conflating history with the grand march, of insisting that power controls memory, that history celebrates the victors, that coherence is domination, and that the ethical lies in disruption – all this, I suggest, constitutes the latest intellectual kitsch. Such notions enable us to feel superior even as they also seem to justify delimiting our sense of responsibility for the world to certain delimited channels – channels sufficiently delimited to enable us to sidestep wider questions about ongoing collective action.

No one would claim that Croce merits the last word; he offers only certain strands for the wider frame we need. But though he could not have foreseen much that rightly preoccupies us today, he made his contribution on the level that remains most deeply in question, and his effort to show how we might stay on a modern even keel remains relevant as we try to surmount the same challenges fifty years after his death.[38] Croce outlined an orientation that invites the weight of ongoing affirmative yet humble world-making while resisting the overreactions and conflations that have yielded the latest kitsch.

chapter 10

What Is Living and What Is Dead? Ginzburg's Microhistory, Croce's Historicism, and the Search for a Postmodern Historiography

I delivered this lecture in Italian under the title 'L'eredità di Croce e la critica della storiografia postmoderna' (The Crocean Legacy and the Critique of Postmodern Historiography) at the invitation of Professor Renata Viti Cavaliere, and under the auspices of the philosophy department (Dipartimento di filosofia A. Aliotta), at the University of Naples (Università degli studi di Napoli Federico II) on 11 May 1998. As is so often the case, I was asked to specify the title well before I had decided on the precise focus for the lecture, and the title I came up with was generic indeed. So I have substituted here a title that I think better reflects the contents of the piece. I had treated the noted pioneer of 'microhistory,' Carlo Ginzburg, as one especially innovative and influential exemplar of contemporary historiographical practice, in my book *Nothing but History,* but I was led to probe the relevant subset of issues more deeply in preparing a review essay, taking off from Mark Poster's stimulating *Cultural History and Postmodernity,* for *History and Theory.* My thinking led me to the Ginzburg-Croce pairing – or antithesis – and I was invited to lecture at Naples shortly after completing the review essay.

I shared the widespread admiration for Ginzburg's microhistory up to a point, but I also found something a little wayward or excessive in it. Indeed, some of the excess seemed to me to reflect assumptions and preoccupations that were becoming all too common – and too little questioned – among historians. Although Ginzburg himself had been admirably lucid and reflexive in articulating how he had come, in reacting against Croce, to his premium on 'what is really dead' in the past, I thought I noted unwarranted conflations and misplaced assumptions in his way of doing so. And these seemed to me to portend deleterious cultural consequences. By this point anglophone historians had lost contact with Croce, so even those who followed Ginzburg's meta-reflections were not likely to recognize the sense in which Croce was being misconstrued, had become a straw man. Nor could they see how, with just a modicum of recasting, he could at least challenge Ginzburg's assumptions, even as they were becoming almost articles of faith for many in the historical profession.

Although I was treated most cordially by my friends in the philosophy department at Naples, I was struck on this occasion, too, with the difficulty of fostering dialogue between philosophers and historians from within the Crocean tradition. The philosophers in my audience (I did not detect any historians) seemed to conclude simply that Ginzburg did not understand Croce's philosophical concept of the historical judgment. Because Ginzburg was philosophically naïve, Crocean philosophers need not concern themselves with him. But Ginzburg was quite influential in Italy and beyond, fostering an utterly anti-Crocean conception of historiographical priorities, so there seemed scope for dialogue addressing him and his influence on that wider level, concerning the cultural uses of historical understanding. Conversely, it was especially a broader view of the Crocean legacy that seemed to show the way to boxing out certain excesses in Ginzburg's position.

I did not seek to publish this essay, however, because I had already begun exploring another aspect of Ginzburg's reading of Croce. In a 1990 symposium on representing the Holocaust, Ginzburg had invoked Croce in a most particular way as he offered what became a noted critique of Hayden White. I came to believe that, in light of the stakes of this encounter and the overall range of ancillary references – including, among others, Tolstoy, Nietzsche, Benjamin, and Kracauer – in Ginzburg's use of Croce, the two essays might form the core of a book. But as circumstances had it, I found it appropriate, not to say expedient, to prepare the Ginzburg-White-Croce material separately, and it is included as chapter 11 in the present volume. I still believe that these two essays are usefully considered in tandem, and I bring them together here for the first time.

1

I am most grateful to Professor Viti Cavaliere for the invitation to speak at this distinguished and historic institution, which has influenced even my own intellectual development significantly, if indirectly. As a second-year graduate student at the University of California at Berkeley, I took the seminar of Professor Carl Schorske, the well-known student of fin-de-siècle Vienna. His topic that year was 'universities and museums,' and I chose to write on the University of Naples in the age of the Risorgimento. Studying the remarkable generation of Francesco De Sanctis,

Bertrando Spaventa, and Luigi Settembrini, I came to ponder for the first time the place that the Neapolitan intellectual tradition might assume in the new Italy. In that sense, this institution helped focus my commitment to the study of modern Italian culture, and for me, over thirty years later, the opportunity to speak at the University of Naples is a special one indeed.

For half a century and more, we have seen remarkable innovation in historiography – from the *Annales* school and the hegemony of social history to microhistory and *Alltagsgeschichte.* In its recent forms, at least, this innovation has some relationship with the wider cultural direction that has come to be known, *faux de mieux,* as postmodernism. Although such influential historians as Emmanuel Le Roy Ladurie in France and Natalie Zemon Davis in the United States have produced notable examples of the genre, microhistory has been above all an Italian current, associated with the journal *Quaderni storici* and a notable series published by Giulio Einaudi. Carlo Ginzburg has been the most influential microhistorian, but Giovanni Levi and Eduardo Grendi have also been central. Even as it strongly disputed certain contemporary cultural tendencies, this current seemed characteristic of postmodernism by the 1980s, when it came to enjoy a considerable vogue.[1]

There is much that I applaud in the postmodern turn in historiography, but I also find overreaction, precluding other modes of historical understanding that do not partake of the discredited side of 'modernism.' Because of the resulting polarization in the historical profession, historians have not managed to seize the opportunity, with the receding hegemony of social science, to play a more central cultural role. And I will suggest that a perspective derived from the thinking of Benedetto Croce can help us both to head off the overreaction and to clarify the possibilities before us.

This suggestion may seem simply bizarre at first glance, for Croce rarely comes up in postmodern discussion, and when he does, especially in connection with historiographical practice, he seems to represent precisely the 'modern' tendencies that we have fortunately left behind. First, he has seemed to posit an almost providential telos – the triumph of freedom and reason. Though his portrayal of 'history as the story of liberty' at the height of fascism was inspirational, and not only in Italy, by now the notion seems quaintly old-fashioned, suggesting a master narrative. Second, his emphasis on ethical-political history seems elitist and utterly incongruent with the expansion of the historiographical focus associated with social history over the past half century or so. And his way of featuring the origins of the present, of what in fact came to be, in any past moment has seemed too obsessively presentist, precluding taking the past on its own terms. His history of the baroque era is only the most notorious example.

There is point to these objections, but there is more to the story. The anomalies in Croce's eclipse since his death in 1952 were noted with much acumen and some bitterness by Raffaello Franchini in his *Intervista su Croce*, published in 1978, and reiterated by the noted historian of criticism René Wellek as recently as 1992.[2] It is striking that during his lifetime Croce was internationally famed as an anti-positivist innovator stressing the active role of the present historian who, on the basis of some contemporary concern, constitutes a history from the documents. Croce explicitly denied that there is some stable past 'reality,' a sphere of fact that exists independently of the inquirer. But he was so radical that in the United States, for example, even innovative historians like Carl Becker and Charles Beard, who embraced his thinking in part, only dimly understood what he offered.[3]

In recent years many of the same issues have come up again with the turn toward postmodernism in historiography. Yet Croce went into eclipse, even in Italy, while the French *Annales* paradigm, about as distant from Croce as possible, assumed a kind of hegemony in historiography by the early 1970s. In an astute study of the origins of that French current, Massimo Mastrogregori showed that, because of provincialism on both sides, the Italian and French traditions failed to engage each other – and unfortunately so, for each could have learned from the other.[4] But with the ascendancy of the French, the Italian tradition around Croce was marginalized – *before* its possibilities had been worked out. So the Crocean perspective was not part of the mix when the next generation sought to move beyond the *Annales* paradigm and structuralism to post-structuralism, microhistory, and postmodernism. Yet though his limits are undeniable, Croce would seem worthy of a fresh look in light of the new cultural situation that has emerged since his eclipse by the early 1960s. With a retreat from social science, a linguistic turn, and much that suggests a kind of reduction to history, we can now understand that he was not a retrograde humanist resisting the modern scientific world but a pioneer proposing a radically new cultural framework, 'absolute historicism,' for a post-metaphysical world.

In suggesting how a Crocean perspective might help us better to align postmodern historiographical insights, I will focus especially on Italian microhistory, but I will also refer to the influential American Mark

Poster, who includes microhistory among the fruitful postmodern departures, but who particularly values the new cultural history associated with those like Roger Chartier and Michel de Certeau in France. Although these historians differ sharply on matters of relativism and truth, they clearly operate within the same universe of new approaches that we have come to term postmodern.[5]

2

Carlo Ginzburg occasionally refers to Croce – and unfavourably, so these passages suggest an illuminating comparison. I emphasize, however, that much of microhistory has usefully carried historiography beyond Croce. Still, because there has been uncertainty about this current's purposes and principles of selection, the vogue of microhistory has reinforced the blurring and overreaction that has marked the postmodern discussion in historiography.

As Ginzburg has explained, Italian microhistory followed François Furet and Jacques Le Goff in reacting against the longstanding historiographical focus on such large-scale processes as modernization, economic development, the rise of the bourgeoisie, and the affirmation of national identity. Such processes had seemed to afford a principle of unity and a sense of proper scale, but by the late 1960s they had come to seem limited, Eurocentric, teleological. There seemed reason to focus instead on ordinary people as shapers of their own lives, quite apart from – even in tension with – what had seemed mainstream developments. Ginzburg showed convincingly how traditional historiography had 'filled the gaps in the narrative to form a polished surface.' And he suggested that attention to both the gaps in the documentation and 'the hesitations and silences of the protagonists' affords not simply an antidote but an expansion of what we can learn through historical inquiry.[6]

Most obviously, microhistory entails an experimental reduction of scale – with unpredictable results. As Levi has put it, 'phenomena previously considered to be sufficiently described and understood assume completely new meanings by altering the scale of observation. It is then possible to use these results to draw far wider generalizations.'[7] In the same way, Ginzburg embraced an implicit or explicit comparative perspective as he confronted the obvious questions about criteria of selection. Microhistorical focus on the anomalous as opposed to the analogous affords a different angle on proto-industrialization, say, or on the advent of the modern state.[8] In the same vein, Levi noted that whereas the earlier functionalism in social science had emphasized social coherence, microhistory concentrates on the contradictions within normative systems, and thus on the fragmentation and plurality that make all systems fluid and open. So by altering the scale to focus on minute and localized actions, the microhistorian pinpoints the gaps left open by the inconsistencies in the system and thus better accounts for change.[9]

It would seem that even this sort of inquiry must start with some contemporary concern in order to know where to look among the scraps of history. Even insofar as we settle for ahistorical comparison across time, the aim is to bring back to and deepen our understanding of some process to the present. So up to a point, microhistory might seem congruent with Croce's presentism, which affords the essential focus, the criterion of selection. To be sure, Croce himself had a limited notion of what the dominant processes might entail. Thus, as I have argued elsewhere, his conception is usefully supplemented by Hans-Georg Gadamer's insistence, derived from Heidegger, that concealment accompanies every disclosure.[10] This was to recognize, as Croce did not, the significance of the holes, the absences, the lost possibilities inherent in the ragged process through which a particular world endlessly comes to be over time. We deepen our understanding if we study actualizing, or coming to be – of the industrial world, for example – in tandem with what was being lost or marginalized along the way.

But here we begin to encounter tensions and further questions about cultural uses and criteria of selection, for the microhistorians have not settled for a more reflexive and inclusive presentism. At work in microhistory is a more complex relationship between present and past, even privilege to dimensions that defy the presentism that seems necessary to provide a principle of selection. An apparent premium on difference led the microhistorians to seek out what seemed most opaque and uncanny, most opposed to the dominant processes that had led to us. But why was there something privileged about defying presentism and process? Why had it become so important to focus upon those hitherto lost to history?

The radical American scholar Keith Luria suggests that one of Ginzburg's major themes is to 'bring to light those forms of knowledge or understanding of the world which have been suppressed or lost. This hidden or forbidden knowledge [has] subversive possibilities, given the elite's attempt to define and control access to "valuable knowledge."'[11] In some ways Ginzburg's thinking is more nuanced than this; he has warned against what he called easy leftist or feminist attitudes.[12] But questions about positive aims and uses remain, and, in any case, Ginzburg has not been immune to impulses like those Luria features.

In an interview with Luria and Romulo Gandolfo, published in 1986, Ginzburg referred to Croce in articulating the key questions: 'After all,' he asked, 'why should people be interested in obscure men and women? I don't have an answer.' When he started studying history in Italy, Ginzburg explained, it had been fashionable, thanks to the Croce-Gramsci legacy, to seek what was contemporary, or had immediate political relevance. But Ginzburg himself had been restive. In a pivotal passage explaining his early responses, he recalled a discussion of the title of Croce's once-famous 1906 essay *What Is Living and What Is Dead in the Philosophy of Hegel* (*Ciò che è vivo e ciò che è morto della filosofia di Hegel*): 'I said, polemically, that I was interested in what was dead in history not in what was alive. And then when some years later I found that insistence on gaps in history, by Foucault, for instance, that insistence against the notion of continuity, I felt very sympathetic. In fact, I think that I was fascinated by a lot of things which could not be related to the present – I mean things which were really dead.' At first, Ginzburg went on, people thought he was mad, but then at a certain moment the intellectual atmosphere changed, and what he was trying to do was accepted as relevant.[13]

Picking up on this passage, Edward Muir, a leading American student of early modern Italy, suggests that to Ginzburg 'the proper goal of the historian is not to explore the historical implications of a contemporary theory or problem, but to write about things that are totally forgotten and completely irrelevant to the present, to produce a history that is "really dead."'[14] Referring to the ideologically charged Italian academic world, Muir suggested that microhistorians like Ginzburg accented difference and sought to *dis*connect the past moment from any process to the present precisely in order to find a mode of historical inquiry that does *not* serve some present concern, which would entail getting caught in contemporary political squabbles.

But surely such immediate anti-political impulses do not provide the whole explanation. Recognizing that questions about selectivity and concerns about triviality have accompanied the turn to microhistory, Muir explained that the ablest microhistorians 'have been struggling to eliminate the distortions produced by the giantification of the historical scale, which has crushed all individuals to insignificance under the weight of vast impersonal structures and forces.'[15] Some strands of the *Annales* school, when asking certain kinds of questions, played up impersonal structures and the *longue durée*, but lurking in much postmodern discussion is a conflation of 'modern' with Hegel. Thus, for example, Levi invokes Heidegger and a 'hermeneutic of listening' as he seeks to allow the dead of the past to remain 'other,' which, as Levi sees it, is to depart from the Hegelian knowing subject, dissolving others into itself.[16] The opposition here is typical of much postmodern thinking, from Jean-François Lyotard to Mark Poster. 'Modern' historiography somehow entails 'Hegel' – progress, telos, closure through totalization, the historian as stable knower of a stable, objective world.

Insofar as Hegel is the alternative, such solicitude for the Other may well seem self-justifying. But let us recall that Croce, at least, was not only anti-positivist but also decidedly post-Hegelian, so the premium he placed on process to the present was weak and non-teleological. Yet the mainstream of postmodernism has been quick to preclude consideration of any such possibilities as it features those hitherto lost to history, lost insofar as we feature the processes that have led to us, resulting in our present world. So, again, why such privilege to the dead as opposed to the living? There seems more to it than an unnecessary anti-Hegelianism.

3

Concluding his introduction to *The Cheese and the Worms*, Ginzburg recognized that in one sense his protagonist, the sixteenth-century miller Menocchio, has a place in a line of development to the present that we can construct in retrospect. In that sense, Menocchio is one of our forerunners – one whom, to be sure, Croce would not have included, though an expanded Crocean framework could and should encompass those like him. But Ginzburg's accent finally falls on the other side of the coin as, to conclude the introduction, he invokes a well-known passage from Walter Benjamin's 'Theses on the Philosophy of History.' For though Menocchio *can* be connected to us, Ginzburg tells us, he

> is also a dispersed fragment, reaching us by chance, of an obscure shadowy world that can be reconnected to our own history only by an arbitrary act. That culture has been destroyed. To respect its residue of unintelligibility that resists any attempt at analysis does not mean succumbing to a foolish fascination for the exotic and incomprehensible. It is simply taking note of a historical mutilation of which, in a certain sense, we ourselves are the victims. 'Nothing that has taken place should be lost to history,' wrote

> Walter Benjamin. 'But only to redeemed humanity does the past belong in its entirety.' Redeemed and thus liberated.[17]

This remarkable passage, revolving around such categories as 'arbitrary,' 'unintelligibility,' and 'mutilation,' requires our particular attention. There is a point to those categories that defies Croce's orientation, but there is also something single-minded about Ginzburg's priorities here. What sense of the world does such language reveal – and what is being precluded? Once we grasp the alternatives, are we persuaded that a postmodern historiography entails such privilege to the dead at the expense of the living – which is us, in our finitude, with all we have lost, as we have become a certain way, *necessarily* precluding all the other ways we have not become? At the very least, what is the relationship between 'what is living and what is dead'?

Lurking in microhistory and much of postmodernism is a sense that 'history' is the totality of past lives and that the outmoded 'modern' approach, with its implicit privilege to the present, does violence to them by making them part of *our* stories. It follows that the aim of historical inquiry is somehow to reproduce past reality, lived experience, as opposed to understanding some process through which our present has resulted. Indeed, even continuity comes to seem bogus, serving to legitimize the present situation; we must feature discontinuity since reality is *really* somehow discontinuous.

4

Ginzburg recognizes a particular debt to Tolstoy, who managed to integrate the lived experience of a whole array of participants with a great event. Indeed, Ginzburg identifies with Tolstoy's ideal – to reconstruct and interweave the activities, experiences, and memories of every participant. But he also recognizes that any such enterprise requires invention precluded to the historian. So Ginzburg has consistently allowed, even invited, a tension. Even as he notes, with appropriate professional circumspection, that microhistory 'accepts the limitations while exploring their gnoseological implications and transforming them into a narrative element,' he admits that the Tolstoyan ideal has more directly informed his own activity as a historian. In fact, *The Cheese and the Worms* 'can be considered a small, distorted product of Tolstoy's grand and intrinsically unrealizable project' of putting everything in, connecting everything, including the lived experience of all the participants.[18]

Ginzburg finds the issue of levels, discontinuities, and completeness confronted in archetypal form in Renato Serra's 'Partenza di un gruppo di soldati per la Libia' (1912), which was central to Serra's richly problematic relationship with Croce before Serra's death in the First World War in 1915, just after Italian intervention.[19] Writing to Croce in November 1912, Serra referred specifically to Tolstoy and noted that Croce's way of handling the problem of contemporary history and of historical knowledge left Serra himself unsatisfied. At issue was the totality of lived experience, which Croce seemed to dismiss too easily as the mere historical 'thing in itself.'[20]

In 'Partenza di un gruppo di soldati,' Serra was concerned with the apparent gulf between the lived experience of the participants and the later historical account of the events taking place.[21] Even the documentary record fails to bridge that gap, for documents are generated for particular practical aims. As Serra put it, 'There are people who imagine in good faith that a document can be an expression of reality ... As if a document could express something different than *itself* ... A document is a fact. The battle is another fact (an infinity of other facts) ... Between the two there can be no relationship of identity, of adequacy.' Thus the anomaly of 'the massive faith that with all those pieces together reality itself can be reconstructed!'[22]

There is indeed a kind of disjunction between the momentary experience of those marching off to war or fighting a battle and their place in the larger event, the outcome of which these participants cannot possibly know. And insofar as that immediate experience of the event is not simply evanescent, a novelist like Tolstoy is almost certainly better able to get at it, to convey what it was like actually to live the moment in question. But we need to sort out our diverse purposes in asking historical questions and to ponder the difference between asking about experience and asking about outcomes. To what extent do we need the former to grasp the latter? Why may history aim at something *other than* recapturing lived experience? Why might the ideal *not* entail inclusiveness or completeness?

5

When Croce comes up at all in postmodern discussion, it is often in simplified, stereotyped fashion, and Ginzburg, in discussing the Serra-Croce dispute, typically provides only a brief passage from Croce that can easily seem ridiculous. Whereas Serra, attuned to real experience, probed the reasons for the inherent inadequacy of any historical account, Croce countered blithely that 'at every moment we know all the history that we need to know' – a notion that seems to confirm the image of Croce as at once extravagant and blandly optimistic, even vacuous.[23] Although this passage comes from an essay that concerns precisely what is at issue for Ginzburg, Ginzburg embraces Serra, and even Tolstoy, without seriously considering Croce's point.

Tolstoy is among the targets in Croce's critique of the idea of 'universal history' that he first offered in 1912, then revised for inclusion in the book that reached definitive form as *Teoria e storia della storiografia* in 1917.[24] Concerned first to undercut the skeptical notion that unless we know everything, we know nothing, Croce ended up addressing the more fundamental problem of historiographical purpose in light of what human beings are and do – and what we need, to do what we do. In some of our moods, we think we would like completeness, the whole historical record laid out to us. But Croce invites us to imagine having all our historical questions answered to infinity. Then what would we do? Such completeness would lead to madness, for what we need, as Croce put it, is not that infinity that expands every time we touch it, but rather the finite, the concrete that becomes the base of our existence, the point of departure for our actions. So even if such infinity or completeness was somehow within our grasp, we would still concentrate on the particular, finite strand that responds to an active, living problem – and forget the rest.

Tolstoy was stuck on the notion that we cannot truly know how a battle went, even just after it is over, because an artificial, legendary account begins to crystallize immediately. Professional historians merely pile fantasy upon fantasy. Croce insisted, in response, that we all forget most of our thoughts and actions. The point, however, is that we remember some of them and that sometimes, when we need to, we manage to bring others back. And thus the Croce passage that Ginzburg quoted: 'At every moment we know all the history that we need to know.' The rest, precisely because it is not important to us, we lack the conditions for knowing, but those conditions change as our priorities change. If we are uneasy about this insistence on the inherent finitude and incompleteness of historical understanding, it is only because we are misled by the eternal phantom of the 'thing in itself,' which is but our fantastic projection of the infinite.

At issue is the human place in the historical world and our present purposes in constructing histories. For Croce, a total history is inconceivable, but that is not what we need. We have access to the finite historical understanding we do need, as present individuals called upon to respond to the present situation, the result of history so far. Historical understanding pertains to the coming to be of the actual, which is the universal as concrete, particular, determined. In this sense, history is knowledge of the eternal but ever-provisional present.[25]

Serra's reference to 'reconstruct reality' indicates an aspiration that also lurks in Ginzburg and much recent historiography. From a Crocean point of view, the point is *not* to reconstruct past reality, a nonsensical notion that would lead to madness. Rather, we construct a *history*, some particular, finite connection or process, which affords the mode of understanding we need for response to the present. At the same time, Croce played down lived experience – as ephemeral – and accented what he called the immortality of the act instead.[26] The world grows, and the next moment is as it is, as a result of all we do today.

Still, Croce, with his presentist historicism, was quick to preclude other modes of relating to a world of nothing but history. And Serra's concern about forgetting, loss, and the disjunction between lived experience and the historical account pointed toward one of those modes. But in Serra, as in the more recent stress on the past moment, or past experience, as opposed to some larger event or process, plausible quasi-religious impulses mix with a tendency to misconstrue the sort of constructive, presentist alternative that might be derived from Crocean historicism.

In the passage from *The Cheese and the Worms* that I quoted above, Ginzburg's language – 'arbitrary,' 'respect its residue of unintelligibility,' 'mutilation,' 'victims' – betrays a deep restiveness with finitude, concreteness, the fact that the world continually comes to be in some particular way. Croce, like Nietzsche and Heidegger, was determined to think through the sheer finitude of a purely human and historical world, but he differed from these more extreme thinkers in his way of unifying human being with finitude, with the endless particularizing of the world. Whatever happens, we are caught up in this particularizing, and thus marginalizing, even as we ask the historical questions we do – even as, with Ginzburg, we choose to feature what is dead. For Croce, all the rest, all that does not become part of the next moment, is dark, even dead – at least at present, so far. From his perspective, preoccupation with what is lost or dead can only stem from futile nostalgia or resentment.

There are better reasons than Croce allowed for a relationship to all that came before us that defies his own brand of reconstructive historicism, with its accent on history as thought that serves history-making action, but there are also better reasons for that Crocean orientation, as an alternative postmodern strand, than those like Ginzburg have allowed. In fact, they afford an a priori privilege to the dead past, thereby precluding even *postmodern* presentist alternatives, which they conflate with modern master narratives. Thus any alternative to an orientation privileging 'what is dead' seems illegitimate, serving hegemonic power, justifying present domination.[27]

Not that Croce was immune to the 'populist,' even religious, sentiments discernible in the priorities of both Serra and Ginzburg. I have frequently quoted the passage that concludes his once-noted essay of 1930, 'Antistoricismo' (Anti-historicism). After arguing that the only religion left to us is a kind of historicism, a religion of history, he noted that we experience a sense of kinship and collaboration not only with our contemporaries but with all those who came before us, whose responses have resulted in our world, the world entrusted to us:

> Whoever opens his heart to the historical sensibility is no longer alone, but united with the life of the universe, brother and son and comrade of the spirits that formerly laboured upon the earth and that live in the work that they completed, apostles and martyrs, ingenious creators of beauty and truth, decent and humble people who spread the balm of goodness and preserved human kindness; and to all of them he makes entreaty, and from them he derives support in his efforts and labours, and on their lap he aspires to rest, pouring his labour into theirs.[28]

The historicist populism in this passage contrasts markedly with the elitist accents of Crocean 'ethical-political history.' Although some have a disproportionate influence in certain spheres, we are *all* historical actors helping to shape what the world becomes at the next moment. And for all his presentist accent on 'what is living' in the past, Croce was hardly inviting, in E.P. Thompson's famous phrase, 'the enormous condescension of posterity.'[29] On the contrary, he posited a kinship with *all* our predecessors and invited our gratitude to them, for we understand that our world has resulted from the whole past, the totality of their actions. But as Croce emphasized in his essay on completeness, we cannot – and need not – tell that whole story. Rather, we are true to our predecessors insofar as, feeling responsible for the world they have bequeathed to us, we take up and transform their collective legacy. That ethical principle leads us to seek the particular historical understanding we need to orient us for action in the present.

So we are true to our predecessors insofar as we open ourselves to a true historical understanding of what is living. We need not seek to resurrect all of them, a futile aspiration that can only breed paralysis, or even to feature those of the dead, like Ginzburg's Menocchio, who happen to turn up in the documents left to us. Nor, to deepen the point, need we seek revenge on finitude, particularizing, actualizing, by affording a kind of a priori privilege to those outside what proved the dominant processes of coming to be. Any such privilege to disruption reflects our own present resentments, and these, too, are merely paralyzing, rather than serving the endless task of world-building.

For Croce, we can know the past as a true history precisely insofar as we orient ourselves toward the future – to endless reconstruction. Conversely, precisely because the point of historiography is not 'to reconstruct reality,' getting at how it really was, there is no basis for the skeptical conclusions that Ginzburg, like Serra, draws from the apparent disjunction between how things *really* were and how they come to be remembered or related.[30] As Croce charged, preoccupation with any such disjunction betrays the chimera of the historical 'thing-in-itself,' some stable past reality, the totality of past experience. At the same time, to say that the objective of our historical inquiries is not simply *ricostruire la realtà* does not mean licence to play with the historical record, or to make history up as it suits us. Croce's distinctions help us see how certain practical concerns may contaminate our quest for historical understanding, just as the ethical desire for free response may serve it. But once we grasp what sort of understanding we need and why we can have it, in light of what we are, we grasp the sense in which our historical understanding can be true but never complete, universal. Though always finite and provisional, that understanding is sufficient in light of our need to respond to specific, finite situations. And thus, again, Croce's apparently extravagant notion that 'at every moment we know all the history that we need to know.'

6

In their 1986 interview, Luria and Gandolfo asked Ginzburg, 'Does your interest in the dead of history allow you to pay the proper respect to the people you are studying, as opposed to trying to make them seem like us in some way?' To which Ginzburg replied, 'I think that is true in the sense that anachronism is a kind of conscious or unconscious will to impose your own values and also your own existence on a people.' And he went on to observe that difference, not similarity, is what is most interesting.[31] It is certainly true that anachronism remains a danger, but this exchange betrays the limited, dualistic way of framing of the alternatives that constantly marks the postmodern discussion. It would seem that unless we accent difference, leaving the past dead, we illegitimately make our predecessors like us – and eviscerate historical study at the same time. Postmodernists like Mark Poster repeatedly suggest that we bring those of the past to us, understanding them in terms of our needs, simply to gain a spurious sense of mastery, to confirm our political views, or to justify some present situation. But this is to blur the alternatives unnecessarily, as attention to Poster's critique of Lawrence Stone's account of the emergence of the modern family will indicate.[32]

Poster convincingly shows how a telos of affective individualism and a corresponding denial of difference limits Stone's account. In the face of evidence of parental indifference to their children in the eighteenth century, Stone provides an alibi, foreclosing the possibility that 'love' meant something different or that something other than love was at work in the familial relationship at issue. And this move, for Poster, is typical of mainstream 'modern' historiography. At those points where the past was different and strange, the historian, wanting our predecessors to have been like us, seeks ways of understanding them in our terms, thereby erasing threatening differences. For Poster, this is to preclude the alternative, with Foucault, of holding onto the difference in order to undercut the seeming naturalness of present practices.

But Poster's contention that 'historians, by explaining changes, erase the difference between the past and the present' is simply fallacious.[33] It is the process of change that comes to erase the difference, for by definition the difference does somehow get erased as the present situation emerges. For Poster, too, there was indeed a change in child–parent relations, and there is a dominant present configuration that is later than the prior. The nuclear family, based on affective individualism, has come to be taken as normal and thus privileged. To understand that present situation, it helps to question where it came from. So we seek to account for the change – to understand it, as best we can. We may then criticize, opening the way to alternatives.

To understand how some present situation emerged historically, through a continuous narrative from past to present, is not in itself to justify that present situation. On the contrary, precisely because 'historical' means *not* natural or metaphysically sanctioned, historical understanding opens the present to further change. To gain this understanding, we start by doing justice to difference, but we then probe the process of change through which the provisional present situation got constructed, came to be. That situation resulted from the earlier different situation through a process that was continuous – but weakly continuous, jagged, not smooth, precluding this as it enabled that. And as I noted earlier, we surely must attend, as Croce did not, to the elements of disruptive tension, the contingencies and preclusions and losses, as we seek to understand the present in its historical genesis. But our purpose is to understand the weakly continuous process through which the present dominant conception emerged. And that understanding can be more destabilizing, enabling more effective criticism, than fixation on difference.

7

The tendency of postmodernism has been to miss the scope for a reflexive but still constructive historiography, with purposes more positive than those that have led to the present emphasis on difference, deadness, otherness, or ritualistic disruption. But postmodernism also invites us to take a fresh, more reflexive look at our own intellectual history, attending precisely to the contingencies and margins. We have come to sense that an appropriately renewed historiography could play a more central cultural role, but through such contingencies, Croce was lost to the discussion while others managed to set the terms of the debate. From the French triumph, which set the parameters for Ginzburg's range of questions, to Hayden White's linguistic turn, that dominant outcome has enabled much, but it has also precluded certain possibilities.

In light of this outcome so far, Croce is a hole, a margin – but one with whom we might fruitfully reconnect in dialogue.[34] Not that his legacy is to be accepted whole, but he, uniquely, derived an affirmative, reconstructive role for historiography from a broadly post-metaphysical orientation. And although Croce himself neglected them, a Crocean framework can easily absorb the new themes that, as Ginzburg notes, Le Goff had proposed in 1973, including the family, gender relations, and the body. We can and should ask about whatever concerns us, about how it came to be, as we seek orientation for present action. The range of possible questioning is as wide as human experience. The choice is always up to us.

I note with great interest that Professor Viti Cavaliere, starting not with historiography but with contemporary problems in philosophy, has come to what I believe are comparable conclusions about the potential import of the Crocean legacy for contemporary culture. I thank her again for the opportunity to share my ideas and, I hope, to help foster renewed interest in the Crocean legacy in Italy.

chapter 11

The Stakes of Misreading: Hayden White, Carlo Ginzburg, and the Crocean Legacy

This is a slightly revised and augmented version of the keynote address I delivered under this title on 18 November 2002, to the conference 'Benedetto Croce Fifty Years Later: His Historical, Aesthetic, and Philosophical Legacy,' organized by Massimo Verdicchio at the University of Alberta in Edmonton. It was published (in English) as part of the acts of the conference (re-entitled 'Benedetto Croce Fifty Years Later: An Assessment for the Future') in *Rivista di studi italiani* 20, no. 2 (December 2002): 1–30, then republished (also in English) in the Italian journal *Storiografia* 9 (2005): 61–86. I thank Professor Verdicchio and the editors of *Rivista di studi italiani* for permission to republish this essay here as well.

During the fall of 2001, after having developed an interest in this overall topic but before preparing the essay, I was contacted by Herman Paul, a doctoral student in the Netherlands, about his interest in Hayden White and White's use of Croce. I let him know what I had done, and envisioned doing, in this general area, and we then corresponded further after I had published the present article. Paul went on to complete a doctoral dissertation entitled 'Masks of Meaning: Existential Humanism in Hayden White's Philosophy of History' under the direction of Professors Frank Ankersmit and Chris Lorenz at the University of Groningen in 2006.

I am grateful to Dr Paul for letting me know of a relevant paper by White that I had missed: 'The Italian Difference and the Politics of Culture,' originally a response to a paper by the Italian thinker Mario Perniola in 1983, published in *Graduate Faculty Philosophy Journal* 10, no. 1 (1984): 117–22. I wish I had known of this article when preparing the present essay, though it would not have changed the thrust of my argument.

Hayden White and Carlo Ginzburg have been two of the most influential figures in Western historiography over the past half century. White is widely credited with reorienting theoretical discussion through a linguistic turn, focusing on the construction of historical texts in narrative language, after the analytical philosophy of history seemed to have reached a point of diminishing returns by the late 1960s. But many practising historians found White's innovations threatening; he seemed to invite a blurring of fact and fiction and thus to breed skepticism and relativism. During the same period, Ginzburg became one of the most revered practising historians of his generation by showing, through his innovative 'microhistory,' how to use neglected evidence to illuminate hidden aspects of the past.

In making their contributions, both White and Ginzburg were reacting against none other than Benedetto Croce, once noted even in the English-speaking world as a radically anti-positivist philosopher of history, though he has been almost forgotten over the last three decades.[1] In using Croce as a foil, White and Ginzburg inevitably contributed to his marginalization as they themselves moved to the forefront. Yet they rejected Croce for reasons that seem almost diametrically opposed: for Ginzburg, Croce was too presentist, too concerned with those dimensions of that past that had lived on, leading to us, whereas for White, Croce tended to make history dead because he was not presentist enough.

Meanwhile, Ginzburg launched a bitter assault on White in 1990 over White's alleged relativism in the context of concerns about Holocaust denial. And though White, by this point, almost never mentioned Croce, Ginzburg traced what he found to be the waywardness in White to an abiding Crocean influence. But Croce, as Ginzburg saw it, had been merely a conduit for the influence of Croce's one-time collaborator Giovanni Gentile, who had departed from the liberal Croce to become a fascist – and arguably the most important European fascist thinker. What White had taken from Croce, then, was nothing less than fascism, read in a particular way, boiling down to 'might makes right.' But Croce had been a bitter critic of fascism – and of Gentile's fascist notions in particular. What relationship between Croce and Gentile was Ginzburg claiming – and what plausibility is there to his charge against White, who claimed to foster pluralism and tolerance as he invited a more active, relevant role for historians?

At issue is a perplexing but potentially instructive web of encounters featuring Ginzburg and White, each highly influential, yet at odds over some of the most sensitive matters in contemporary historiography, and each in interaction with the earlier Italian tradition revolving around Croce and Gentile. Yet even as Ginzburg's assault on White elicited much comment, Croce's role drew no sustained analysis. And I suggest that the whole discussion rested on layers of misreading of the Italian tradition, with important costs for our understanding of contemporary cultural alternatives.

Assaulting Croce

At first glance, it might seem obvious why recent innovators like White and Ginzburg would reject Croce, who, especially in connection with historiographical practice, seems to represent certain 'modern' tendencies that we seem fortunately to have left behind. Among other problems, his way of featuring, in any past moment, the origins of the present, of what in fact came to be, has seemed too obsessively presentist, precluding taking the past on its own terms by focusing on the actual lived experience of our predecessors. Indeed, his way of accenting 'what is living' tended to preclude other modes of relationship between present and past that his overall historicist orientation might seem to warrant. We think especially of the more dialogical relationship that Hans-Georg Gadamer specified.[2] But whereas Croce certainly does not merit the last word, there were aspects of his conception that White and Ginzburg missed, even actively precluded for reasons of their own, aspects that we can still usefully ponder.

Famous as a philosopher of history by the 1930s, Croce accented the active role of the present historian in constructing any genuinely historical account. Indeed, he insisted that 'all history is contemporary history,' because some contemporary concern leads the inquirer to pose some particular historical question, and thereby to forge some particular connection between present and past.[3] Thus, though constrained by the documents, the historian is not disinterested but plays an active role. At the same time, the historian never simply copies or represents some stable, 'given' past reality, some sphere of fact that exists independently of the inquirer. It was crucial for Croce that there is no such thing.

These notions made Croce intriguing to innovative historians like Carl Becker and Charles Beard in the United States. But even they were nervous about the apparently relativistic implications of his extreme presentism. And others, from Maurice Mandelbaum to Siegfried Kracauer, became active critics. Writing in the 1960s, Kracauer explicitly attacked

Croce's accent on present interest. 'Instead of waiting for what the sources may wish to tell him,' said Kracauer, the Crocean historian 'forces [them] to answer his questions.' The danger, as Kracauer saw it, was that passionate engagement would yield mere exhortation or some 'feel-good' myth. The antidote was of course detachment, 'love of the past for its own sake.'[4] Ginzburg later embraced Kracauer explicitly as he, too, rejected Croce's presentist concern with what is living in the past.

When he started studying history in Italy, Ginzburg explained in 1986, it had been fashionable, thanks to the legacies of Croce and Antonio Gramsci, to seek what had contemporary political relevance. But he himself had been restive. Recalling a discussion of the title of Croce's 'What Is Living and What Is Dead in the Philosophy of Hegel,' first published in 1907, Ginzburg specified his own orientation with particular force: 'I said, polemically, that I was interested in what was dead in history not in what was alive. And then when some years later I found that insistence on gaps in history, by Foucault, for instance, that insistence against the notion of continuity, I felt very sympathetic. In fact, I think that I was fascinated by a lot of things which could not be related to the present – I mean things which were really dead.' Ginzburg was studying sixteenth-century heretics, for example, not in connection with the coming of the Enlightenment but precisely in their *lack* of connection with what came later.[5]

Ginzburg invoked not only Kracauer but also Leo Tolstoy, Renato Serra, and Walter Benjamin to explain his anti-Crocean emphasis on 'what is dead.' Even as he recognized that Tolstoy's ideal in *War and Peace* – to interweave the experiences and memories of every participant in a great event – requires invention precluded to the historian, Ginzburg noted that his own best known work, *The Cheese and the Worms*, 'can be considered a small, distorted product of Tolstoy's grand and intrinsically unrealizable project.'[6] Croce, in contrast, had criticized Tolstoy and the ideal of completeness in an essay of 1912.

Ginzburg also identified with Renato Serra, a brilliant young Italian intellectual who, though in one sense within Croce's orbit, had taken Tolstoy's part against Croce at precisely that point, in 1912.[7] Writing to Croce that November, Serra charged that Croce, with his accent on contemporary concerns, was too quick to dismiss the totality of actual lived experience as some mere historical 'thing in itself.'[8] In a rumination that same year on the departure of soldiers for Italy's imperialist war in Libya, Serra explored the issue of levels, discontinuities, and completeness in a way that Ginzburg found archetypal. At issue was the apparent gulf between the lived experience of the participants and the later historical account of the events taking place.[9] Even the documentary record fails to bridge that gap, said Serra, for documents are generated for particular practical purposes. Thus he found anomalous the 'massive faith that with all these pieces together one can reconstruct reality!'[10]

In taking Serra's side in this encounter, Ginzburg provided only a brief passage from Croce, but it may seem sufficient to make the case. Whereas Serra, attuned to past experience, showed the inherent inadequacy of any historical account, Croce countered blithely that 'we know at every moment all the history that we need to know,' a notion that seems at once extravagant and too blandly optimistic.[11] Ginzburg viewed his own innovative approach as a way of defying the Crocean presentism that provides a principle of selection at the expense of any focus on the totality of the experiences of all who lived before.

Concluding his preface to the Italian edition of *The Cheese and the Worms,* Ginzburg revealed much about his underlying purposes, especially as he invoked a passage from Benjamin's 'Theses on the Philosophy of History' of 1940. Ginzburg noted that though his own protagonist, the sixteenth-century miller Menocchio, *could* be connected to us, he is also

> a dispersed fragment, reaching us by chance, of an obscure shadowy world that can be reconnected to our own history only by an arbitrary act. That culture has been destroyed. To respect its residue of unintelligibility … is simply [to take] note of a historical mutilation of which, in a certain sense, we ourselves are the victims. 'Nothing that has taken place should be lost to history,' wrote Walter Benjamin. 'But only to redeemed humanity does the past belong in its entirety.' Redeemed and thus liberated.[12]

Lurking in microhistory and much of postmodernism is a sense that the 'modern' approach does violence to past lives by making them part of *our* stories. The aim of historical inquiry should thus be to reproduce past reality, lived experience, *as opposed to* understanding some process through which our present has resulted. Indeed, even the notion of continuity seems inherently to legitimize the present situation. Some suggest that by featuring discontinuity instead, we might undercut that sense of legitimacy and invite action.[13] Ginzburg himself, however, eschewed any such present political relevance. As his use of Benjamin suggests, to find discontinuity and leave the past suspended was apparently to serve some deeper, almost religious need.

Though many found microhistory characteristic of postmodernism, Ginzburg bitterly criticized the tendency toward relativism that the postmodernist direction seemed to invite – and that, he felt, had seriously infected contemporary historiography.[14] At first glance, his insistence on the scope for cognitive differentiation and truth might seem fully congruent with his premium on 'what is dead,' which suggests detachment and thus objectivity, as opposed to an engaged presentism. But he was well aware that the relationship between the epistemological question and the dichotomy of living and dead, or present and past, was more problematic than that. Though he had started, he said, with a positivistic notion of truth, he had come to recognize that the rules, too, have been constructed, necessarily by those with power. To avoid positivist naïveté, that power dimension had to be addressed explicitly. But, as Ginzburg put it, 'can you look for the implications of power in every kind of intellectual exchange or symbolic exchange without falling in a kind of skeptical trap? This is a problem.'[15] Ginzburg's solution was explicitly paradoxical. He advocated, even for his own readers, the creative misreading he imputed to his protagonist Menocchio, even as he himself still believed in a right meaning and, at the same time, recognized that many were coming to find the very notion of a right meaning heretical.[16]

Like so many of his contemporaries, Ginzburg was seeking a way beyond the dichotomy of 'authoritarian' 'positivism' – the notion that there is a single right way of representing the past 'as it actually happened' – and the 'anything goes' relativism that would pluralistically let a thousand stories be told. Such pluralism might invite, as one among all the others, a story about European Jews that denied the Holocaust. It was concern over this issue that prompted Ginzburg's attack on Hayden White.

White was seeking a more innovative role for historiography – just as Ginzburg was. But far from suggesting a premium on 'things which were really dead,' White's innovations seemed to warrant an extreme presentism instead. White was reacting against what he took to be the neutering bourgeois realism that had proven the norm as history became a recognized professional discipline by the late nineteenth century. His path-breaking *Metahistory*, published in 1973, examined the construction of historical accounts in narrative language and thereby forced renewed attention to the historian's active role. So, when compared with Ginzburg, it is not immediately clear what White had against Croce, the presentist who had focused on what was living in the past.

Indeed, White began as a Croce partisan, proclaiming 'the abiding relevance of Croce's idea of history' in an article published in 1963.[17] Nothing in English had better shown why history for Croce transcends naturalism to become the story of liberty, or why Croce's historicism entails broadly liberal implications. In his pivotal essay 'The Burden of History,' published just three years later, in 1966, White's sense of the active contemporary role history might play still reflected his Crocean background; indeed, it seems unlikely that he could have conceived the challenge and the possibilities as he did had he not been so well versed in the Crocean tradition. Thus he insisted, for example, that 'the contemporary historian has to establish the value of the study of the past, not as an end in itself, but as a way of providing perspectives on the present that contribute to the solution of problems peculiar to our own time.'[18] In another passage he noted that Hegel, Balzac, and Tocqueville 'did not see the historian as prescribing a specific ethical system valid for all times and places, but they did see him charged with the special task of inducing in men an awareness that their present condition was always in part a product of specifically human choices, which could therefore be changed or altered by further human action in precisely that degree. History thus sensitized men to the *dynamic* elements in every achieved present.'[19]

Yet though he had proclaimed Croce's abiding relevance just three years before, White mentioned Croce only briefly, neutrally, in his essay of 1966.[20] And in the passage just quoted, he went on to lament that by the later nineteenth century, as history was becoming a professional discipline, historical culture had lost sight of that dynamism and begun justifying the status quo.[21] This had happened during Croce's own time, and the alternative White was beginning to formulate was already taking on an anti-Crocean spin.

As White saw it, historians had become self-satisfied – and irrelevant. The present burden was to make the historical discipline consonant with the purposes of the wider intellectual community and thereby to enable the historian to participate actively in liberating the present from the burden of history itself.[22] 'Only history,' said White, 'mediates between what is and what men think ought to be with truly humanizing effect. But history can serve to humanize experience only if it remains sensitive to the more general world of thought *and* action from which it proceeds and to which it returns. And as long as [history] refuses to use the eyes which *both* modern art and modern science can give it, it must remain blind.'[23] History had much to learn from contemporary art and science especially, because both had come to recognize the provisional character of the metaphorical constructions they used to comprehend a dynamic universe. One key charge against Croce would soon be explicit: not only was he by now too old-fashioned to serve the essential dialogue with the innovative art and science of 1966; he had been blind to the most innovative art and science even of his own time.

White's characterizations of wider thinking that defied the mainstream historical understanding suggested the anti-Crocean cultural direction he was coming to find desirable. He identified with Sartre, who believed, as White put it, that, since the past has no existence aside from our consciousness of it, 'we choose our past in the same way that we choose our future. The historical past, therefore, is, like our various personal pasts, at best a myth, justifying our gamble on a specific future, and at worst a lie, a retrospective rationalization of what we have in fact become through our choices.'[24] White also found positive indications in Burckhardt, who came to grasp, partly via Schopenhauer, 'that every attempt to give form to the world, every human affirmation, was tragically doomed in the end, but that individual affirmation attained to a worth of its own insofar as it succeeded in imposing upon the chaos of the world a momentary form.'[25]

Indeed 'chaos' was becoming central to White's sense of the human relationship to history, and his conception of the historian's task was becoming anti-Crocean especially in that light. 'The historian serves no one well,' said White, 'by constructing a specious continuity between the present world and that which preceded it. On the contrary, we require a history that will educate us to discontinuity more than ever before; for discontinuity, disruption, and chaos is our lot.'[26] For Croce, in contrast, the premium on showing how some present situation had emerged from the past required constructing precisely the sort of continuous process White had come to deplore.

The priorities White had begun to outline in 1966 informed his critique, three years later, of Croce's influential account of Vico.[27] Croce had sought to marginalize precisely what, for White, was by now the most relevant side of Vico – the proto-structuralist social science, encompassing a pioneering understanding of the scope for scientific laws in the study of society. In *Metahistory* four years later, White went much further, featuring Croce as the sterile culmination of nineteenth-century historiographical traditions.[28] Whereas other rhetorical strategies had afforded historiography a certain cultural resonance earlier in the nineteenth century, Croce heralded the 'ironic' mode that henceforth characterized the professional discipline.

The irony lay first in the disjunction between present and past that enabled the historian to assume a stance of superiority. Peering into the past, the historian understands what was happening in a way the participants themselves did not. Our sense of presentist superiority feeds our assumption that we can render what has happened in a coherent, realistic historical account. Thus the ironic disjunction between present and past was bound up with the assumption, central to historiography as an autonomous discipline, that realistic representation of the past is possible.[29]

But this outcome proved ironic in a second sense, because the assumptions of present superiority and realistic representation breed a passive acceptance of the present. In making history coherent, even 'beautiful,' through a realistic narrative form, we make it come out 'right.' So the historical account not only affords aesthetic satisfaction but justifies the present outcome.[30] Confined to the temple of art, historiography was severed from the broadly political world of present action. Yet also lurking, for White, was the deeper ironic sense that because the historical account is a narration in language, it cannot really grasp and fix what has happened; it is not adequate at all, but *merely* 'beautiful.' This sense reinforces the ironic disjunction between what, from this perspective, is only the pretence of understanding and the scope for action.[31]

Croce had explicitly assigned history to the realm of art as opposed to science. Moreover, he was notably unsympathetic to the contemporary artistic avant-garde as it was breaking fruitfully from realistic representation. Thus, especially, White could link Crocean historiography to realism, a particular, mimetic conception of art – and thus with the passive acceptance that White associated with mainstream historiography.

At the same time, in associating history with art, Croce was separating it from science and thus, for White, the search for usable general knowledge. In this sense, too, Croce was denying history any present political import. Indeed, wrote White, 'it is difficult not to think of Croce's "revolution" in historical sensibility as a retrogression, since its effect was to sever historiography from any participation in the effort – just beginning to make some headway as sociology at the time – to construct a general science of society.'[32] So in settling for an aesthetically satisfying realism that afforded the pretence of definitive understanding, Croce was both undercutting creative action and denying the scope for a usable social science.

Though White rarely addressed Croce explicitly as he refined his ideas after *Metahistory*, Croce lurked as a foil in his subsequent essays –

as Ginzburg had occasion to emphasize.[33] But White came to portray Ranke as representing the defining orthodoxy of the historical discipline – though in essentially the same terms, bound up with aesthetic realism, that had characterized Croce in *Metahistory*. And certainly White's own abiding aims emerged clearly from his two-sided critique of Croce.[34] The major aim was to foster openness, creativity, and presentist relevance in historiography, which could come to serve human freedom and mastery as it had earlier, before the advent of the ironic relationship between present and past. But an underlying concern for structure and order lurked as well.

Most basically, White sought to show that historical accounts are actively constructed in language through particular rhetorical strategies that stem from broadly political concerns and have broadly political implications. Irony was not the only mode of emplotment, nor need it be privileged. Indeed, it was merely one of four such strategies evident in nineteenth-century historiography and classifiable in terms of the four tropes of neo-classical rhetorical theory. By de-privileging irony and showing how historical discourse works like fictional narrative, White hoped to sensitize us to our freedom to choose historiographical strategies based on our present, life-serving concerns.[35]

White elaborated on his ideal of openness in a number of follow-up essays, one of the most arresting of which, 'The Politics of Historical Interpretation' (1982), proved especially important for Ginzburg. Here White sought to clarify what was entailed, and what was marginalized, as history underwent disciplinization during the later nineteenth century. Most fundamentally, this process entailed suppression of an earlier 'sublime' historical consciousness that was now subordinated to the beautiful – and thus tamed or neutered. The sense of historical chaos that White found in Schiller, anticipating Nietzsche, engendered a feeling of human freedom, even serving, as White saw it, the vision of a perfected society and thus devotion to utopian politics.[36] The dominant modern ideologies, in contrast, 'impute a meaning to history that renders its manifest confusion comprehensible to either reason, understanding, or aesthetic sensibility. To the extent that they succeed in doing so, these ideologies deprive history of the kind of meaninglessness that alone can goad living human beings to make their lives different for themselves and their children, which is to say, to endow their lives with meaning for which they alone are fully responsible.'[37]

Addressing concerns about relativism, White recognized that historical inquiry presupposes an archive of information and a naked chronology; we cannot invent documents or change dates. But the sphere in which the distinction between truth and fiction is relevant to historiography lies at a relatively low level and can essentially be taken for granted. What required attention was the process through which historical writing transforms information and chronology into a specifically historical, and inherently interpretive, kind of knowledge through the narrative mode of representation.[38] From the same historical subject matter, it is always possible to construct a variety of narratives – and thereby to confer different meanings. And whatever the meanings they confer, historians construct plots using the same rhetorical strategies, or modes of linguistic figuration, that imaginative writers use.[39]

Although the essentials of White's argument about narrative emplotment were unassailable, a number of sophisticated theorists found the argument unnecessarily extravagant in certain respects. In the wake of White, they sought to make deeper sense of the distinguishing characteristics of specifically historical discourse.[40] But their accents differed considerably, and the issues have yet to be settled.

Even as he invited a more creative role for historians, White sought to specify a frame of order and structure, at least partly to head off the excess that his own accent on openness might seem to invite. He was troubled by what he found to be the potential for excess in post-structuralism, which, especially in Derrida's version, he found to represent an 'absurdist moment' in contemporary discussion.[41] Thus the abiding interest in the scope for some sort of science of society that had underpinned his critique of Croce's Vico, and thus he continued to accent some version of the structural tropology central to *Metahistory*. Even as he pulled back from suggesting some quasi-naturalistic 'deep structure,' White still found it crucial that modes of emplotment stemmed from a finite – in some sense stable and a priori – set of possibilities specific to each culture.

In important respects, then, White was seeking a middle ground within the wider humanistic discussion, at least as it has played out over the last forty years, the period of Croce's eclipse. But did he find it? Writing in 1980, one of White's major allies, Hans Kellner, noted an abiding tension in White's work. Even as he seemed to invite freedom and openness, White pulled back to make the theory of tropes a bedrock of order. The problem, as Kellner put it, was that 'the determinism of the system seems to contradict the sense of human freedom which ... is White's primary goal in *Metahistory*.'[42] At about the same time, Dominick LaCapra found a comparable tension, for White seemed to grasp, yet found too disconcerting to face, the insight into 'bottomlessness,' the absence of any stable grounding, the endlessness of contest, that had informed Derrida's assault on structuralism.[43] And thus, again, White's reluctance to jettison structure and system.

The points at issue in these critiques obviously recall White's double argument against Croce. On the one hand, White sought greater historiographical openness and found Croce, with his putative realism, to represent precisely the problem to be overcome. On the other hand, Croce had also resisted scientific system. But did Croce's orientation really present a double obstacle or rather an alternative moderate post-realism, perhaps more consistent than White's? And how does the issue between Croce and White relate to the matters of truth and relativism that concerned Ginzburg?

Ginzburg's Critique of White

That concern led Ginzburg to attack White explicitly in the context of a symposium on representing the Holocaust in 1990. If modes of emplotment are all ultimately 'political' in some sense, were not those of a Robert Faurisson, denying the essentials of the Holocaust, as good, in cognitive terms, as any other? Whatever White's professed aims, Ginzburg found White's orientation to leave us with nothing but effectiveness, power, 'might makes right' as the criteria for differentiating among historical stories.[44]

White was clearly sensitive to the challenge of Holocaust denial in his own contribution to the same symposium. Without responding to Ginzburg directly, he proposed retreating to an intransitive 'middle voice' reflexively integrating the level of the inquirer and the level of the participants. But as the intellectual historian Martin Jay promptly pointed out, White seemed to be pulling back from what had made him so challenging.[45] Yet neither, from Jay's perspective, was White's effort to nuance his position likely to satisfy Ginzburg.

As Ginzburg saw it, the problem stemmed from White's appropriation of the Italian tradition centring on Croce. At first glance, however, Ginzburg's treatment of Croce in light of White seems contradictory. On the one hand, he accepted White's notion that Croce represented an outmoded realism; White himself had reacted beyond it. But on the other hand, Croce had helped pioneer the post-realist historiographical relativism that Ginzburg so deplored.[46] But for Ginzburg, the inconsistency was in the thinking of Croce himself. While accepting the widespread characterization of Croce as a neo-idealist, Ginzburg found

Croce's neo-idealism to have been, as he put it, 'rather peculiar'; indeed, 'critical positivism' was perhaps a better characterization.[47]

Ginzburg explained the alleged awkwardness by referring to Croce's complex relationship with Giovanni Gentile, who had been Croce's junior partner in the assault on positivism during the first years of the century. Gentile proved more systematic as a neo-idealist philosopher and eventually, of course, diverged from Croce to became a major fascist ideologue.[48] The two thinkers disagreed publicly in 1913 over philosophical matters that, though rarefied indeed, proved to adumbrate their later political split. However, the implications of that philosophical disagreement for action, relativism, and truth were – and are – less clear.

For Ginzburg, Croce's thinking could entail outmoded realism yet still feed relativist overreaction because it included a poorly integrated Gentilian idealist admixture. As Ginzburg saw it, Gentile had proposed a particularly activist version of idealist subjectivism, positing spirit as the transcendent subject that creates reality.[49] By implication, that idealist subjectivism had led Gentile himself to fascism, whereas in the less consistent Croce it had remained an undigested component. And White, in reacting against Croce's aesthetic realism, had embraced the undigested Gentilian subjectivist elements in Croce's thinking even as he thought he was rejecting Croce altogether. And thus White, too, ended up implicitly trumpeting the putatively fascist notion that power is the only criterion, that 'might makes right.'[50]

Ginzburg found support for this linkage in White's article on the 'historical sublime,' where White himself had noted that

> the kind of perspective on history that I have been implicitly praising is conventionally associated with the ideologies of fascist regimes. Something like Schiller's notion of the historical sublime or Nietzsche's version of it is certainly present in the thought of such philosophers as Heidegger and Gentile and in the intuitions of Hitler and Mussolini. But ... we must guard against a sentimentalism that would lead us to write off such a conception of history simply because it has been associated with fascist ideologies. One must face the fact that when it comes to apprehending the historical record, there are no grounds to be found in the historical record itself for preferring one way of construing its meaning over another.[51]

White was obviously not suggesting that sublime orientations *must* lead to fascism, but neither did he find it a priority to address the basis of the differentiation from within the post-realist universe.

Subsequent comment clarified the stakes of Ginzburg's assault, though certain categories were taken over without analysis. Citing Ginzburg's 'astonishing political claims,' Jay noted that underlying Croce, in Ginzburg's reading, was Gentile,

> whose fascist politics were intimately connected to his antihistoricist philosophy of pure action. For Ginzburg, despite all the obvious differences, White's radical subjectivism and skepticism about historical truth echo Gentile's sinister position. Rather than leading to tolerance, it betrays a tacit concession that might makes right, which in historical terms means accepting Faurisson's version of the Holocaust if it ever becomes 'effective.'[52]

Commenting several years later, Jeremy Varon suggested that White, in conceding the affinity of his proffered 'historical sublime' with fascism, was inviting the use of history as myth for political ends.[53]

Seeking to point beyond White while still eschewing mere realism or positivism, Ginzburg again invoked Renato Serra against Croce, now understood, of course, as encompassing an element of Gentile's subjectivist activism.[54] For Ginzburg the only way to head off relativism was to afford privilege to the dead, to conceive the ideal, the measure, to be Tolstoy's aggregate of lived experience and to preclude the Crocean, crypto-Gentilian basis for an alternative accent on those aspects of the past that lived on.

Jay nicely pinpointed Ginzburg's strategy: Serra's Tolstoyan answer to Croce, said Jay, was also Ginzburg's to White – 'that our macronarratives can be ideally constructed as the sum total of all the micronarratives of the historical actors.' As Jay noted, Ginzburg found the Serra-Tolstoy accent on the testimony of witnesses to afford greater balance between the powerful living of the present – us, in other words – and the helpless dead. Ginzburg invoked Serra against Croce partly, as Jay put it, to embrace

> Tolstoy's utopian project of collecting the memories of everyone involved in an event, testimonials which might provide the only proof for a subsequent historical interpretation. Here the power relationship between the form-giving historian in the present and the residues of the past preserved by survivors is rendered more nearly in balance than it is in the Gentilean historiography Ginzburg attributes to White.[55]

From this perspective, the asymmetry between present and past means that we must find ways of countering the power relationship between us of the present and the dead past. Jay and others assume that even without the overt activism attributed to Gentile, we want to impose ourselves on those who actually experienced all that became part of our history. If, as with Gentile's alleged subjectivism, we carry that activist presentism to its absurd extreme, we give ourselves free reign, and the historical account tends to become 'myth,' precisely as for Varon.

For Ginzburg, then, to head off relativism requires a premium on 'what is dead,' on what it was like for those who lived through it, *as opposed to* any premium on process to the present. To accent 'what is living,' or what lived on, is to impose ourselves on the dead, forcing them into our stories. Though we can never attain the Tolstoyan ideal, insofar as we recognize the inevitability of our own present role, we can resist making the dead part of our stories and find ways of leaving them disconnected from us.

Though Jay credited Ginzburg's argument up to a point, he noted that we still cannot see how Ginzburg proposes to bridge the gap between the testimony of witnesses and the later historical reconstruction. Though that testimony is essential, 'no accumulation of memories will yield the historical account.'[56] Jay concluded that though we must eschew both mimetic representation and subjective imposition in our approach to the past, all we can do is to 'foreground the tension between the historian's reconstruction and what is being reconstructed, rather than smooth it over in the name of an impersonal middle voice.' We can thereby 'paradoxically acknowledge the limitations on the historian's capacity to refashion the past on his or her own terms, thus avoiding the Gentilean subjectivism Ginzburg finds so troubling in White's work.'[57]

For Jay, then, there was something excessive in Ginzburg's privilege to the dead, yet White's effort at adjustment was not convincing either. Jay proposed his own solution, based especially on 'the professional institutionalization of communicative rationality.' But his call to 'foreground the tension between the historian's reconstruction and what is being reconstructed,' though not so deliberately paradoxical, recalled what Ginzburg had advocated in other contexts. Moreover, Jay's characterization of the power relationship between dead past and living present had not done justice to the Italian tradition, which arguably could still contribute to the framework from within which we might better address the overall problem.[58]

Varon took Ginzburg's charge against White still more seriously, though he found even less merit in Ginzburg's solution. As Varon saw it, White had been too quick to lump together under 'bourgeois realism' any accent on objective meaning or on the scope for a commitment to truth. So some sort of enabling myth had come to seem the only alternative to a stultifying realism. In his 1982 article, especially, White had jumped to equating explanation with justification. Varon insisted that what serves a quest for change is not to posit the past as inscrutable but to provide a historical account, which may enhance repugnance and illuminate repressed possibilities.[59]

Even as they criticized in part, Jay and Varon tended to accept the characterizations of the Croce-Gentile tradition that White and Ginzburg had offered, including Ginzburg's implication that Gentilian subjectivism, bound up with fascism, was the coherent harvest of that tradition.[60] Though Varon usefully focused on White's overreaction, he lacked the independent sense of the Italian tradition necessary to assess what White was doing in using first Croce, then Gentile, as he did. Yet surely such an assessment might have served Varon's effort both to head off what he found the debilitating overreaction in White and to specify a more constructive alternative.

Intersecting with the Croce-Gentile Axis

Ginzburg's argument rested first on his way of embracing, even forcing, White's account of Croce, accenting 'realism.' It is surely true that idealism is not right to characterize Croce's position – as Croce himself came to emphasize.[61] But neither is realism, in the mimetic sense that first White, then Ginzburg, had in mind. Ginzburg seems to have been prepared to conceive the alternatives only in such restrictive dualistic terms. At the same time, he was quick to accept 'realism' as the basis for White's rejection of Croce. Insofar as realism was not really what Croce was about, White's repudiation becomes more complex and interesting.

In reacting against positivism, Croce and Gentile did return to the idealist tradition, but they found it essential to work beyond the idealist problematic if they were to address the contemporary cultural challenge. Especially through a creative recasting of Vico, they claimed to offer a uniquely relevant cultural orientation, best understood as a radical and thoroughgoing historicism. For both, the key was to show how the world could be understood without transcendence. Through a full embrace of radical immanence we overcome *both* realism and idealism as heretofore conceived. We are left with a world that is forever coming to be in history.

Though Gentile, unlike Croce, did not explicitly repudiate the idealist label, even he was not positing spirit as a transcendental subject that creates reality. Any such characterization misses Gentile's Vichian departure from Kant and the difference it makes to posit an immanent subject. And to differentiate Gentile from Croce's alleged realism on the basis of conventional idealism is to neglect what the two thinkers continued to share. In positing a purely immanent spirit, each was at once denying any thing-in-itself or unknowable residue while at the same time meshing human creativity with the self-creation of the real through history. So to link Gentile to the more familiar categories of philosophical idealism can only misconstrue the basis of his difference from Croce – and thus also the basis of his fascism and whatever he might have in common with White.

Jay referred, in connection with Gentilian subjectivism, to 'the historian's capacity to refashion the past on his or her own terms.' And Gentile surely did posit that capacity in some sense – as, of course, did White. The question, however, is what the historian's 'own terms' might entail. For Gentile, the openness at issue did not warrant, as even Jay seems to assume, creating whatever past happens to suit us, as if willing makes it so – at least insofar as we have the power to impose our will. For Gentile, everything rests on freely thinking; what we think is what we genuinely believe to be *true*. And what we can and do think is living and present, and shapes what we do. As early as 1914 Gentile specified the need and the scope for truth, in contrast with fantasy or fiction, in light of radical immanence.[62] In contrast, 'what is dead' is what we can no longer think, which is precisely 'the past.' So Gentile, like Croce, continued to posit the scope for true understanding of the historical world. The split between Croce and Gentile did not rest on the matters of truth, power, and 'effectiveness' that led Ginzburg to focus on the relationship between the two thinkers.

What Gentile did posit, and what Croce denied, was the scope, and the need, for a certain kind of culture based on a certain way of unifying thinking, willing, and acting. That was what led Gentile from liberalism to fascism. Put differently, the Croce-Gentile split concerned not idealism versus realism but broadly political possibilities and priorities within a historicist world of radical immanence. For both thinkers that world warranted a new understanding of human freedom entailing a more lucid sense of responsibility for the endless remaking of the world in history. But they differed over how that endless world-making happens, or could and should be made to happen. Though he did not begin drawing out the political implications until later in the First World War, Gentile's way of unifying thinking, willing, and acting foreshadowed a new mode of history-making through the collective exercise of human responsibility. Gentile was in one sense more optimistic about the mode of world-making that now became possible, but his insistence on a certain mode of unity seems to reflect a deeper underlying pessimism or concern at the same time. As they diverged in 1913, Croce found 'mysticism' in Gentile's insistence on unity, whereas Gentile called Croce's attention to 'that sense of profound melancholy that pervades your whole contemplation of the world.'[63] It seemed that only a certain 'sublime' mode could overcome that tendency toward melancholy in a world without transcendence.

Gentile was seeking an antidote to bourgeois liberalism and positivism, so his target was certainly close, at least, to White's, summed up as bourgeois realism. And Gentile's direction, when compared to Croce's, was 'sublime' on something like the basis White had in mind when he noted the kinship. But we saw that White, in his key 1982 essay, casually lumped together versions of the historical sublime, and these must be distinguished if we are to address Ginzburg's concern. Even as he paralleled Gentile in embracing a 'sublime' alternative, White was looking in Nietzsche's direction, not Gentile's. At the same time, the Crocean alternative was not mere bourgeois realism but a competing post-realist orientation. That orientation, however, was not sublime but mundane, even melancholy, just as Gentile noted. So it contrasts with both sublime strands. What we have in Croce, Gentile, and White is a kind of triangular relationship within the quest for post-realist cultural forms. And Gentile, even as he embraced one sort of sublime orientation, was not only seeking an alternative to the post-realist but melancholy Croce; he was also, at least implicitly, seeking to head off the particular kind of sublime orientation White later propounded.

In their different ways, Croce and White each claimed to offer an alternative sufficient to invite individual responsibility, but for Gentile neither could be adequate. Indeed, in a mass secular age, Nietzschean sublime and Crocean melancholy were likely to interpenetrate and contribute to the same deleterious cultural syndrome: irony, cynicism, indifference, perhaps mere consumerism – anything but the sense of collective history-making that breeds responsibility for the whole and for the future. So even as he, too, departed from realism or positivism,

Gentile had no place for either Croce's moderate humility or White's alternative sublime. Indeed, he would transcend both by educating individuals, marshalling and channelling their ethical capacities, leading them to share in the sense of total ongoing responsibility, and making them want to be part of the collective will. Though it did not entail wilful activism or 'might makes right,' the Gentilian sublime led archetypally to totalitarianism. And White, who was proposing anything but fascism, would have repudiated Gentile's totalitarian vision just as surely as Croce did.

Gentile, then, was not the source of the problem Ginzburg found in White. But that still leaves the question of the basis of White's rejection of Croce if it involved something other than realism and idealism. When we grasp the real basis of White's rejection of Croce, we better understand what should in fact have been the focus of Ginzburg's concern.

Croce in Light of White

We noted that White accused Croce of actively resisting contemporary artistic and scientific innovations – seemingly for conservative purposes. But this line of attack raises two sets of questions. First, was engagement with the latest innovations in art and science really the key to the essential post-realist renewal of historiography? That historians might learn from artistic and scientific innovations is undeniable, but White was quick to credit both art and science, as if each was on a secure path in a post-realist world. The alternative that he thereby tended to preclude was to rethink the autonomy of history, the nature of the specifically historical dimension of our experience, in light of the wider cultural changes that were also affecting art and science. Second, was Croce in fact merely reactionary in his response to the art and science of his own time, or was he engaging the innovations in those spheres, but in a particular way, precisely as part of his effort to specify an alternative culture of history?

Croce constituted a double challenge for White because he actively sought to undercut *both* the bedrock of order and the sublime direction that White found to be cultural priorities. And White, in accenting Croce's alleged aesthetic realism, seems almost wilfully to have neglected the basis of Croce's argument against both. Indeed, he was arbitrarily conflating ideas taken out of context to attribute to Croce a conception of history as 'art' that was diametrically opposed to Croce's own.

In assigning history to the sphere of art, Croce was neither embracing 'realism' nor warranting passive acceptance of historical outcomes.

We saw that White associated both Croce and Ranke with the sterile realistic-aesthetic orientation that came to characterize professional historiography. But Croce explicitly repudiated Ranke, who seemed engaged, as he put it, in the fine art of embalming a corpse.[64] For Croce, then, Ranke could indeed be associated with art and even death, just as for White, but that was precisely why Croce, too, rejected Ranke. Like White, Croce was seeking a more central cultural role for historiography in light of post-Rankean, post-realist premises. And he, too, posited a kind of middle way, but one that transcended White's disparate imperatives – sublime/utopia and science.

Any association of Croce with 'realism,' the notion that history seeks to 'represent reality,' is particularly misguided. As we noted, denial of even the shadow of some 'thing in itself' to be represented was central to the Croce-Gentile claim to have moved to the modern forefront. Writing history is a creative act, reflecting the contemporary concern of the historian, who fashions one of the infinite number of particular histories that the documentary archive allows. In an article published just before *Metahistory*, White himself recognized that history as art for Croce was not to be conflated with mimetic realism. Croce and Hegel, wrote White, differed from most of their successors in holding that 'history, like other formalizations of poetic insight, was as much a "making" (an *inventio*) as it was a "finding" of the facts that comprised the structure of its perceptions.'[65]

That 'making' happens in language, which, Croce well understood, is not neutral but inherently rhetorical. Indeed, he anticipated the basis for White's 'bedrock' point that the various ways of emplotting a given set of facts reflect characteristic rhetorical strategies.[66] For White, of course, it was important that works of history can be classified in terms of the rhetorical strategies they use to form a coherent, convincing story. As White saw it, Croce had come close to the same insight – and priority – but somehow had pulled back. Treating Croce alongside Hegel and Nietzsche, White noted that 'in his analysis of the bases in speech of all possible modes of comprehending reality, he came closest to grasping the essentially tropological nature of interpretation in general. He was kept from formulating this near perception, most probably, by his own "ironic" suspicion of system in any human science.'[67]

Croce did indeed have his doubts about any such system, but they entailed neither irony nor conservatism. He denied White's bedrock of order in terms that anticipate, in a rudimentary way, the post-structuralist challenge to structuralism, as derived from Saussure. The key, Croce felt, was to explore the implications of the fact that creativity and novelty continually overflow what at any one moment affords some structure. Addressing Saussure in passing in 1946, Croce made the historicist point that had been implicit in his treatment of language even in the *Aesthetic* of 1902: the linguist, he said, can only be a historian. He or she can only do the history of vocabulary and transformation and must renounce the temptation from the earlier era of positivism to be a 'scientist,' '*somigliare fisico.*'[68] That was why, from Croce's perspective, there was little to be gained by laying out some proto-White tropology.

In the same way, White seems deliberately to have ignored Croce's sustained premium on ongoing action, his sustained accent on human creativity and the scope for novelty. Historical understanding does not preclude action but is bound up with it, for the need to act underlies the effort to understand. What was most immediately at issue between Croce and White was not action or passivity but the *mode* of action, *how* action is bound up with both the human ethical capacity and the scope for truth.

In the wake of his *Aesthetic* of 1902, some of Croce's would-be followers, imbued also with Nietzsche and anticipating, it would seem, White's sublime, utopian side, initially read Croce as advocating almost precisely 'aestheticism,' entailing not so much art as a haven within which we contemplate the beauty of history, but 'life as literature,' the scope for self-creation.[69] But in clarifying his position in the *Logic* and the *Philosophy of the Practical* by 1909, Croce deflated those expectations by showing that action was to be experienced more broadly, not as self-creation but as history-making, and was to be disciplined by historical understanding, the measure of rational response in a historical world.

The question of the criteria of such discipline and rationality lead us back to the sensitive matters of presentist purpose and truth that concerned Ginzburg. For Croce, once we grasp the human relationship with history in radically post-realist terms, we begin to see that truth is possible precisely because, in questioning the past, we have a present interest, linked to ongoing action. Indeed, we have an ethical responsibility to discipline ourselves by opening to learning and truth.

As ethical creatures who care what the world becomes, we seek the historical understanding that uniquely can orient us for responsible action in response to the present, the resultant of history so far. Insofar as historical inquiry stems from this ethical sense, we seek genuinely to learn, and we are vehicles for the happening of truth. The scope for true knowing is simply an attribute of human being; 'truth' is our term for what happens when we relate to the world in a certain mode. As Croce emphasized in a key passage against pragmatism, it is precisely because of the practical stakes of our inquiries that truth is possible.[70] The scope for truth is thus bound up with our presentist interest in what is living in the past, in what led to and illuminates our present, as opposed to what is dead.

Though openness to truth is ethical, a merely 'moralistic' purpose – questioning history to serve some prior moral or political aim – does not qualify because any such purpose compromises the openness to learning that makes truth possible. In fact, purposes compromising the scope for truth will always be present to some extent, and we cannot be certain that some particular account is true.[71] Truth is not suprahistorical but merely historical – always provisional, finite, incomplete, weak. So historical understanding, too, is necessarily provisional, finite, incomplete – and contested. Croce, then, posited the scope for understanding without the definitive meaning, completeness, or suprahistorical justification that would warrant White's concerns about passivity. Once we grasp how we are caught up in history, we realize that we are capable of the true historical understanding we need – but also that we need it not smugly to contemplate the historical outcome but to go on responding to that outcome in action.

We noted that in turning against Croce in the 'The Burden of History,' White used terms like chaos, discontinuity, and 'tragically doomed' to characterize the human relationship with history. But wherein lay the difference from Croce that seemed to warrant such language? For Croce, too, it was axiomatic that we never attain completion, that we never establish why, on some ultimate level, things have happened as they have and our world is thus as it is. So far as we can tell, there is no such level of meaning. But once we adjust, we recognize that to characterize our situation in terms like White's is an overreaction – and invites further overreaction. We cannot overcome finitude and provisionality, but we do not need completeness or some transcendent sanction to navigate within our particular, concrete world. What we need is not 'a history that will educate us to discontinuity,' as White put it, but a history that orients us by showing how the present came to be. For though it has no *transcendent* reasons for being as it is, that present has *historical* reasons for being as it is.

As his earlier Crocean sense of the challenge dissipated, White pointed toward a premium on edification, as opposed to the disciplined inquiry, open to learning, that might serve to overcome the burden of this or that particular historical outcome.[72] Feeling ourselves 'tragically doomed' in the absence of settled meaning and any transcendent sanction for this particular world, we discharge ourselves of the burden by affirming ourselves vis-à-vis the 'chaos' of history as a whole. But we may well end up acquiescing in the particular outcome as a result. For Croce, in contrast, we do not expect to make definitive sense, find definitive meaning. The burden is particular, and thus we pick and choose, reacting against this or that outcome that seems an obstacle to our freedom. And we make some necessarily provisional but adequate sense of that outcome by constructing a continuous process from past to present. The continuity in the historical account is indeed constructed – and from an overtly presentist perspective at that. But it could be deemed 'specious' only on the basis of residual realist premises.

In challenging the contemporary claims of social science, Croce was not resisting modernity, as White implied, but anticipating one strand of post-modernism. To be sure, variations on the anti-modern charge against Croce were widely heard in Italy by the 1950s, and by that point his influence had indeed retarded the Italian embrace of contemporary social science. But by the late 1960s, precisely as White began attacking Croce on the issue, social science was being deflated from several angles in Western culture, most notably hermeneutics and post-structuralism, and it was pulling in its horns on its own.[73] From our present perspective, White's implication in 'The Burden of History' and after that historians needed to jump onto the social science bandwagon appears dated at best.

Croce sought to delimit social science because, from his perspective, it was being oversold, skewing cultural priorities by muddying our understanding of particulars, generalizations, and the uses (and limits) of knowledge for action in a radically historical world. Science serves action by providing rough-and-ready generalizations from particular historical instances, but it is ultimately some particular situation that we seek to understand, because we need to act in response to some determined, particular case. Conversely, those particular instances do not merely constitute the raw material for a science that could serve action in a more determinate way. In making this argument, Croce was not ignoring contemporary science but incorporating the insights of innovative, philosophically oriented scientists like Ernst Mach and Henri Poincaré.

The question of art is trickier; Croce was indeed quick to dismiss contemporary artistic innovations as irrational or irresponsible, just as White suggested. Even from a wider Crocean perspective, there is more room for experiment and innovation in dealing with historical material than Croce himself seemed to invite. But he had reasons for keeping his distance from contemporary artistic innovations.

A Crocean would welcome new modes of emplotting history that served the quest for understanding to prepare action. But insofar as new modes foster disruption, evoke uncanniness, or serve sublime edification, to embrace them is to compromise the scope for truth. If we were actually to create a surrealist or actionist historiography, as White proposed in 'The Burden of History,' the results might well be worthy as art, which often deals with historical material – but art *as opposed to* history. Or does that difference itself dissolve? If lines are still to be drawn, where do we draw them in particular cases, and on the basis of what criteria? Those, of course, are the questions. Croce found some of the intellectual and artistic innovation of his own time to entail confusion over precisely these issues – and thus to portend overreaction into 'decadent' self-indulgence. So his treatment of modern art was not a manifestation of conservative realism, but simply an aspect of his quest for a post-realist orientation, one that proves to elude White's restrictive categories.

Even as White denied that he was lumping history with fiction, his dualistic way of conceiving the possibilities led him to blur, if not undercut altogether, any premium on truth in historiography. We saw that in advocating a return to the historical sublime, he claimed to be seeking an alternative to the dominant modern ideologies, which 'impute a meaning to history that renders its manifest confusion comprehensible to either reason, understanding, or aesthetic sensibility.' So comprehensibility itself conflates with the strong truth that justifies the present situation and renders us passive. Conversely, to deny such comprehensibility, to remain truer to history's 'manifest confusion,' was allegedly to 'goad living human beings ... to endow their lives with meaning for which they alone are fully responsible.' This was to suggest that any premium on true understanding, with its implication of definitive meaning and justification, is incongruent with seizing responsibility. But only a very particular kind of responsibility can be fostered if, through conflation with justification and acceptance, we play down the role of historical understanding. In tending toward personal edification, White's alternative precludes the wider historicist responsibility that would warrant disciplined historical inquiry.

In fact, White rejected Croce not as realism but as a competing post-realism, bound up with a different sense of responsibility that entailed both discipline and humility. Croce saw beyond the ideal of getting the story straight, but he also sought to head off the extravagant excess that seemed to threaten if we do not make deeper sense of the insight that 'the past' is open to the historian's creative will. By conflating Croce with realism, White did not have to engage the mundane Crocean alternative and could more readily trumpet his own sublime course as the appropriate post-realist direction.

From the perspective of Ginzburg's concern, the problem with White was not that he was too Crocean but that he was not Crocean enough. His premium on self-creation, his way of accenting will with no link to the scope for truth in a post-mimetic mode, could indeed contribute to the relativistic blurring in historiography that Ginzburg deplored.

Croce in Light of Ginzburg's Concern with Relativism

But, turning in the other direction, if Croce posited truth as weak and our historical accounts as finite, incomplete, and provisional, he, too, might seem to foster relativism and feed Ginzburg's concerns. However, Croce himself insisted that *only* his absolute historicism could overcome the concerns about relativism that were bound to accompany the retreat from transcendence, realism, and subject-object dualism. Gadamer's comparable claim of 1971 essentially recapitulated the argument Croce was making by 1915.[74] It is precisely in a realist, mimetic mode that skepticism is unavoidable, partly because realist assumptions entail an implicit demand for completeness. Relativism dissolves once we understand any particular historical account not as a copy or representation of reality, but simply as one among the infinite possible ways of connecting the present to what came before.

We saw that Ginzburg, in criticizing Croce, fastened onto Croce's statement of 1912 that 'we know at every moment all the history that we need to know' – a notion that may seem extravagant indeed at first glance. But Ginzburg was quick to invoke Serra and Tolstoy without seriously considering Croce's point. Provisional and incomplete though they are, our histories are adequate to our relationship with our fundamentally historical world. Conversely, from a Crocean perspective, Ginzburg, in invoking Tolstoy, Serra, and the ideal of completeness, was not resisting relativism but inviting it.

In the argument that includes this passage, Croce was both criticizing Tolstoy's ideal of completeness and specifying what we need – and do – instead.[75] In some of our moods, we think we would like the whole historical record laid out to us. Indeed, we may fall into the skeptical notion that unless we know everything, we know nothing. But Croce invited us to imagine having all our historical questions answered to infinity. The quest for such completeness leads to madness, for that infinity, as Croce put it, expands every time we touch it. What we need is not some incomprehensible completeness but rather the finite and concrete that affords the point of departure for our actions. So even if such completeness were somehow within our grasp, we would still concentrate on some particular, finite strand that responds to a living problem and forget the rest.

Renato Serra, in making the anti-Crocean argument that Ginzburg embraced, assumed that the aim of historical writing is to 'reconstruct reality,' a realist aspiration that still lurks in Ginzburg as well, informing his ideal of encompassing the whole past. From this perspective any accent on process to the present conflates with forcing past lives into our stories. But from a Crocean perspective, again, the point is not to *re*construct past reality but to *construct* a history, tracing some particular, finite process connecting us with what came before. Thus there is no basis for the skeptical conclusions that Ginzburg, like Serra, drew from the apparent disjunction between how things *really* were – the actual lived experience of everyone – and how they come to be remembered or related.[76]

In accenting 'what is living' in the past, Croce was not inviting 'the enormous condescension of posterity,' so famously deplored by E.P. Thompson.[77] On the contrary, he posited a kinship with *all* our predecessors and invited our gratitude to them, for we understand precisely that our world has resulted from the whole past, the totality of their actions.[78] But we cannot – and need not – tell that whole story. Rather, we are true to our predecessors insofar as, feeling responsible for the world they have bequeathed to us, we take up and transform their collective legacy. We serve them not by featuring their difference, or by privileging their lived experience, but by tracing the process through which our present emerged from what they did – so that we can go on from here.

Although, coming later, we are privileged in the obvious sense that we can know, as our predecessors could not, the outcome so far of all they experienced first hand, we come to grasp how weak and fleeting that privilege is. In making them part of our stories, we do not fix the meaning of their experience for good but only for us, in light of our present concerns. Those who follow will necessarily start with what we have made of that past experience, but they will build upon our understanding in light of their somewhat different concerns. Moreover, our measure of presentist privilege does not warrant willfully erasing difference and *forcing* our predecessors into our stories. On the contrary, it leads us to take difference more seriously than ever as we come to feel we have nothing but history for orientation. Although Croce's own way of probing 'what is living' in his historical works was surely too limited, Brook Thomas, for example, has shown how attention to the excluded other, standing in tension with and threatening to disrupt some dominant process, may deepen what we can learn from historical inquiry and thereby serve the wider aim of presentist reconstruction.[79]

In misconstruing Croce, Ginzburg missed the sense in which Croce's mode of presentism, in contrast to White's, might actually serve the effort to box out relativism. Conversely, a premium on getting at the dead past may warrant not disciplined detachment, as might first seem the case, but a blurring with fiction, insofar as the aim is not to orient for present action but to engender a certain quasi-religious sensibility.

Misreadings and Margins

That White and Ginzburg have each made contributions of enduring value is undeniable. And the fact that each thinker raised the questions he did by bouncing off Croce might suggest the culturally productive 'strong misreading' that Harold Bloom featured and Richard Rorty endorsed.[80] Indeed, some such misreading may seem precisely what we expect and want in our post-realist or postmodern age. I surely risk ridicule insofar as I have suggested that the misreadings of White and Ginzburg can be measured against some more authoritative reading – especially the one that I have implicitly claimed to offer. But it remains possible to invoke the documentary archive, what Croce actually wrote. And we may ask whether White and Ginzburg engaged what he wrote or simply jumped to conclusions on the basis of assumptions about such familiar categories as realism, idealism, subjectivism, and historicism. Taken as part of the landscape by the sixties and seventies, Croce was easily stereotyped, and thus White and Ginzburg could disassemble his legacy, using this or that as a foil as they pursued their own agendas. Their misreadings thus furthered the marginalization of a voice – even a tradition – the absence of which has delimited recent humanistic discussion, and thus our own self-understanding.

A different postmodern theme invites us to incorporate precisely such margins as part of a fresh, more reflexive look at our own intellectual history – at how we have come to conceive the alternatives as we have. In doing so, we see that, indispensable though their contributions have been, White and Ginzburg each fed a wider cultural tendency toward overreaction precisely as each eschewed deeper engagement with Croce. Ginzburg's way of privileging what is dead reflected a misreading of what a contrasting focus on what is living can entail; White's premium on a mode of presentism that could invite political instrumentalism or feel-good edification reflected his conflation of Croce's alternative presentism with merely conservative realism. Croce not only stands up to the criticisms of White and Ginzburg but fruitfully challenges what each interjected as an alternative. The orientation he articulated entails precisely what recent discussion has tended to preclude: first, the scope for moving beyond 'authoritarian' or neutering realism without the blurring of truth and fiction that feeds relativism; and second, the scope for purposes more constructive than those underlying the present premium on disruption, discontinuity, difference, and deadness.

Croce specified repeatedly, as explicitly as could be wished, that he offered not some finished system but only, as he put it, 'an instrument of labor' for those who followed.[81] And certainly we cannot simply invoke some canonical passages from his writings to answer the questions currently at issue. But what Croce offered has yet to be fully digested, and cutting through the tensions in more recent innovators like White and Ginzburg suggests that fifty years after his death, his legacy remains an essential instrument of labor.

chapter 12

Postmodernism and History: An Unfinished Agenda

This article was invited by the Italian journal *Palomar*, to be included in a special issue on the present state of historiography. The essay appeared under the title 'Il postmoderno e la storia: Un agenda incompleta' in *Palomar*, no. 26 (July 2006): 6–25. I am grateful to the editor, Daniela Coli, for permission to publish the article here in its original English version.

As I noted in the introduction to the present volume, I refer only minimally to Croce in this piece, but it will be obvious that the orientation I advocate owes much to the Crocean legacy. Conversely, any suggestion that the encounter between postmodernism and history has passed seems to me premature, to put it charitably, partly because Croce has remained neglected. But the scope for a deeper, more fruitful discussion remains.

Missed Connections

In the anglophone world, we have experienced a flurry of discussion over 'postmodernism and history' over the past fifteen years or so, producing much rancor but also some soul-searching, at least for a while. Many believe the peak of the encounter now to have passed. 'The theory wars are over,' proclaimed Michael S. Roth in 2004, noting that Keith Jenkins's postmodernist manifesto *Rethinking History* was to be reissued as a Routledge Classic. As Roth saw it, the time had come to write the history of postmodernism.[1] But polarization continues even among practising historians as some embrace 'theory' of one sort or another, while others remain resolutely a-theoretical. And postmodernism has arguably affected the priorities of historians in ways not fully examined.

Indeed, the whole encounter between postmodernism and historiography has been somewhat pallid. Writing *In Defense of History*, Richard Evans showed convincingly that postmodernists like Jenkins tend to caricature the self-understanding and the actual practice of mainstream historians, but in focusing on such tendentious enthusiasts as Jenkins, Evans had it too easy and ended up caricaturing the postmodern challenge – and opportunity.[2] Whereas historians continue to do much fine work illuminating this and that, a multitude of questions about the place of historical inquiry and understanding, in light of wider cultural changes, have yet to be adequately addressed.

'Postmodernism' is a notoriously slippery term that is made to encompass the most bewildering variety of notions, some of them not mutually consistent. It certainly has something to do with the waning of foundationalist philosophy and the loss of transcendent, suprahistorical grounds of appeal. That we have experienced something like a postmodern turn is hard to deny, and despite Roth's suggestion that the postmodern moment has passed, the implications of that turn are still being sorted out. Partly because postmodernism has entailed a certain extravagance, some of its tenets have seemed particularly to threaten the self-understanding of practicing historians. In stressing, for example, that moral and/or political choices channel the rhetorical strategies of historians, one generally postmodern strand might seem to warrant histories that serve personal edification or some political cause, thus undercutting the scope for truth. Defenders of conventional practice have tended to repair to a residual realism, often combined with an appeal to disciplinary standards. Of course we are finite and limited, they say; of course we never tell the whole story or get it exactly 'straight,' but we do the best we can to 'represent reality,' the past as it actually happened. And even if there is no settled epistemological ground of appeal, we have disciplinary standards, hammered out over a long period, that enable us to distinguish among historical accounts.

The debate over postmodernism and history has been relatively superficial especially because of a lack of intellectual historical depth. Although 'reflexivity' is much bandied about as a postmodern imperative, it has tended mostly to mean a sort of up-front, first-person self-consciousness that becomes almost narcissistic on occasion. It has not meant situating ourselves in light of serious engagement with earlier figures who articulated the changing cultural situation that we now see as the postmodern turn. The diagnoses and prescriptions of such thinkers must be part of any fruitful framework for debate.

Certainly the discussion has encompassed some of the bits and pieces of our recent intellectual history. We find much interest in, for example, Walter Benjamin's 'Theses on the Philosophy of History,' but this example raises the question of who gets adopted, who gets marginalized or forgotten, of how and why it has been decided which figures from the past we need to engage. The lack of reflexivity and depth has itself warranted selective borrowings and tendentious readings. Why the infatuation with Benjamin, for example, when his characterization of the situation is so obviously tension-ridden, in light of his residual 'modern' accent on 'historical materialism'? Insofar as we revisit our place in our continuing intellectual history, we may find it possible to place the influence of Benjamin in better perspective and even to reconnect with marginalized ideas.

Although others could surely be adduced as well, I have found it illuminating to focus on what Nietzsche, Croce, and Heidegger had in common in departing from earlier thinkers, from Vico to Hegel to Dilthey, often associated with some sort of break into 'modern historical consciousness.' Nietzsche, Croce, and Heidegger suggested that the world, as particular and finite, comes to be through history, that we in a sense belong to history, and that the place of historical understanding must be reassessed in that light. But from within that new space, Nietzsche, Croce, and Heidegger proposed radically divergent cultural strategies, and subsequent thinkers added further layers, sometimes by responding to the insights of these pioneers. Hans-Georg Gadamer, departing from Heidegger, showed how historicism takes on ontological weight in light of Dilthey's limits and the ensuing 'crisis' of the earlier historicism. The framework expanded with Gianni Vattimo's appropriation of Nietzsche and Heidegger, the deconstructive notions of Michel Foucault and Jacques Derrida, and the updated pragmatism of Richard Rorty.

Not that we must passively accept this or any other lineage of earlier thinkers. Rather, we must approach our own intellectual history critically, accounting for overreaction and excess. On that basis, we can develop a deeper sense of the framework in which we operate. As it is, we tend not even to consider where our assumptions and priorities have come from, why we have embraced them, the sense in which, the degree to which, they themselves are historically specific – and thus how they might be assembled differently. All our debates about objectivity and relativism, the status of historical knowledge, and the place of language and narrative tend to lead us around in circles. Conversely, through a deeper, more reflexive understanding of our own intellectual history, we can better grasp what has fallen away with the postmodern turn and better reconceive what is left, including the place for historical inquiry and understanding.

Aspects of the Postmodern Challenge

Of the several aspects of postmodernism, the most immediately threatening to practicing historians has been the linguistic turn, which, in stressing the role of structured and/or figured language, called into question the scope for realistic representation in historical writing. Whereas that turn had many sources and has many dimensions, it affected historiographical discussion most directly through the narrativist argument of Hayden White, who foreshadowed his argument in a pivotal article, 'The Burden of History' (1966), developed it systematically in *Metahistory* (1973), and clarified and extended it in numerous follow-up essays.

One of White's major disciples, Hans Kellner, was typically provocative in insisting that we historians are not getting the story straight, according to the old objectivist or realist ideal, but getting it 'crooked' in one way or another as we emplot our histories from within the finite array of rhetorical conventions that our culture makes possible.[3] In a world of indeterminacy and flux, we may find, as White himself sometimes seemed to, a structuralist-scientific (and thus distinctly 'modern') 'bedrock of order' by mapping the modes of doing so. But White's accent was on the scope for more innovative historical writing, once we recognize that moral/political choices necessarily inform our rhetorical strategies as we construct our histories. The openness that White invited was to warrant a 'sublime' historical sense, which had anticipations in Schiller and even in Nietzsche, Heidegger, and Giovanni Gentile.[4] This was to be an essentially postmodern orientation in its departure from the defining nineteenth century modes of historical emplotment that, as White saw it, had reached an ironic dead end on the philosophical level with Croce. Trapped in their impossible realistic framework, historians had been turning in the same groove thereafter; as a result they had become ever more marginal to the culture.

Even to some who welcomed some aspects of the postmodernist reaction against 'modern' ways of conceiving history, the linguistic turn seemed to dissolve the hard reality of history into mere language, 'discourse,' and thereby to promote relativism. Dispute on this, above all, makes it clear that we have had anything but homogeneity and consensus even among those most attuned to new historiographical approaches in light of the postmodern turn. The pioneering microhistorian Carlo Ginzburg made it clear he disliked the skepticism and relativism that seemed to follow from postmodernism, then leveled a highly symptomatic assault on White, whose relativistic implications seemed to leave historiography with no grounds of appeal beyond mere 'might makes right.'[5]

But the challenge of postmodernism has not been limited to the linguistic turn, especially insofar as questions of cultural connection are at issue. In some of its more extreme formulations, postmodernism has seemed to suggest that 'there really is no such thing as history' and to dissolve any premium on thinking historically in a world of 'slippage' and unstable categories. Instead there is mere flux, upon which we impose our histories, whether to serve power and legitimation or to find an antidote to 'the primitive terror' we feel in the face of the real nothingness of the flux.

There has been much interest in Reinhart Koselleck's point that the possibility of conceiving history in the singular – as unified, in some sense 'total' – emerged only in the eighteenth century. Previously there had been only particular histories of this or that.[6] As part of the break into modernity, this notion was itself merely historical, historically specific, even contingent – and bound up with hopes for a better world, even with salvationist aims. To unify history, making it total, was apparently to posit an a priori meaning, some telos of freedom, justice, and redemption.

The generally postmodern turn from the mainstream modern mode of historical-mindedness has stemmed largely from our disillusioning historical experience itself. The disturbing, unanticipated sequence of events from the First World War at least through the Cold War seemed to undermine the notion of a unified progressive history and occasioned a wider cultural tendency to denigrate historical approaches. Thus, for example, the oft-heard notion that only literature can do justice to the experience of the two world wars.

The Holocaust, especially, seems to have shattered any notion of a unified, meaningful history. Reflecting on what seemed the special European path 'from Athens to Auschwitz,' the German classicist Christian Meier was explicit that Auschwitz 'best highlights the challenge that has arisen for our self-definition in terms of history.' The Holocaust marked the end of the special European path, and special role, that had been bound up with assumptions of a continuous and unified European history.[7]

Indeed, in light of our ongoing tendencies to feature what seems good and progressive in history, some have concluded from the Holocaust that our priority must be to disrupt any attempt at historical understanding. Lawrence Langer noted that what he called 'humiliated memory,' one mode evident in survivors' testimony, sabotages our ongoing quest to find value for the future in the Holocaust experience. This mode thereby undermines 'one of the foremost impulses to historical inquiry, which is life-promoting insofar as it mirrors insights from the past that enable us to confront the future with a more informed sense of ourselves as human beings in time.'[8]

At the maximum, this reaction conflates all 'modern' notions of history with something akin to Hegelianism – or, only slightly weaker, with belief in a progressive master narrative. Such beliefs now draw withering scorn. In his 'Theses on the Philosophy of History,' Benjamin mocks 'the angel of history' as he notes how 'progress' leaves wreckage upon wreckage, with the dead as victims unredeemed in and by history even as we project into the future.[9]

So strong has been the reaction against the putatively modern historical sense that even any concern with continuous process becomes suspect. Process seems to conflate with 'the historical process,' and thus some master narrative, if not full-blown Hegelianism. Thus, for example, Mark Lilla notes that 'commitment to seeing history as "process" usually means that the account of origins will be tailored to make the present appear, if not foreordained, then at least anticipated from the outset.'[10] As a related aspect of the overall reaction, we have the widely heard notion that history is necessarily written by the victors, and thus entails justification of the outcome.

For Milan Kundera, history conflates with public lies, with 'official memory' – again, as 'written by the victors.' We tend to airbrush out what is no longer convenient. In a world of contingency, capriciousness, and unintended consequences, history comes to seem 'unbearably light, light as a feather, as dust swirling in the air, as whatever will no longer exist tomorrow.'[11] Even the archive comes to seem corrupt, for we never can be sure who or what has been airbrushed out. To be sure, we cling to a residual modernism, but Kundera dramatizes the absurdity of faith in the 'long march' of history. Instead of weight we have what he calls 'kitsch' in the original sense, excluding shit, contradiction, everything unacceptable.[12] Such kitsch would surely encompass the tendencies, so bitterly opposed by Langer, to find in the Holocaust some variation on 'the triumph of the human spirit.'

A contrasting postmodern direction is the notion that we as a culture no longer need to be, or want to be, 'historical' in a world that seems to flatten out into a 'post-historical' 'fluctuating steady state.' This sensibility is loosely bound up with globalization, which seems to entail the end of history as we have known it in the modern period. Accelerating technological change makes innovation routine, and the advent of new media seemingly alters our relationship with both space and time.

Taken together, these disparate strands suggest that the specifically modern form of historical-mindedness that became possible in the late eighteenth century has by now dissipated – or should dissipate. 'Might it not be,' asks Massimo Mastrogregori, 'that the idea of having to or being able to know the past has become hollow, and another possibility looms on the horizon, where the past is pure discontinuity, a storehouse of incomprehensible fragments?'[13] But where do we find ourselves in light of all these cultural changes? Is the lesson for historians simply to turn off their computers and get on with life in a post-historical mode, or does historiographical practice somehow serve liberation from the weight of the past, even from history itself? Whereas some in the wider culture turn from history altogether, a number of historians find it worthwhile to focus precisely on the discontinuities and fragments that Mastrogregori mentioned. These historians seek to keep us from constructing stable meanings and reassuring connections between the past and the present.

Changing Priorities in Historiographical Practice

Indeed, the reaction against 'modern' historical-mindedness has channeled historiography toward certain approaches, starting with those that disrupt on some level. The United States, especially, has seen an extraordinary vogue of Foucault, with his implication that whatever results from history is an instance of power/knowledge and thus domination. More generally, we find a widespread focus on the underdogs, the perceived 'victims,' even if ultimately to feature their 'agency,' or at least 'negotiation,' to invoke two of the buzz-words of the 1990s, and thus to deny their victimhood. The vogue of subaltern and postcolonial studies remains symptomatic.

A measure of editorializing about power and powerlessness, about our tendency to misuse our privilege of 'coming later' by misreading the past for our own dubious purposes, has become almost de rigueur among practicing historians. In her illuminating recent study of villager agency in the face of baronial and bureaucratic pressures in the early modern Papal States, Caroline Castiglione forcefully articulated what seems to many the historiographical imperative. Speaking of one of her ordinary villagers, she noted that 'for me, Iezzone provides a lesson, however unintentional: that we would do well to facilitate the reading and writing of texts from the powerless who constitute most of the world's people, and to consider the possibilities for meaningful change they offer, rather than read them defensively or exclusively as threats to our rights and privileges, or merely as a side road taking us away from our grander and more telegenic ideologies."[14]

Such priorities have been especially clear in the impact of microhistory, as pioneered in Italy by Carlo Ginzburg, who developed a considerable following in the United States. A good recent example of the genre is a prize-winning book by Thomas V. Cohen, which, after offering a series of vignettes illuminating aspects of life in sixteenth-century Rome, nicely summarizes the uses and strategies of microhistory.[15] Most basically, such microhistories seek to get at meaning – meaning *for them*, their lived experience, in defiance of our tendencies to make them part of our stories or to make them like us. In other words, zeroing in on discrete microhistorical episodes attunes us to difference, to strangeness. Pursuit of this goal, Cohen suggests, has nurtured innovative strategies both for avoiding presentist misreadings and for accessing past experience in its difference. We learn to attend to unspoken presuppositions; we penetrate the meaning of gestures, or non-verbal forms of communication. We attend not only to communication but to transformations and transfers *within* modes of discourse, which illuminate both the form and the edges of agency and negotiation.

Carlo Ginzburg suggested explicitly that microhistory, in pulling back from and even disrupting any sense of a single progressive history, is congruent with Leo Tolstoy's notion, explored in *War and Peace*, that the totality of lived experience *is* the history. From this perspective, there is still, in principle, a historical totality, but it would be, precisely as for Tolstoy, the totality of lived experience. In some of its formulations, the notion that literature trumps history in light of the sequence that began with the First World War similarly suggests Tolstoy's conception of history. However, Ginzburg was also explicit that any such conception is unrealizable – at least from within history itself. That unrealizability helps explain the element of indeterminacy, of bafflement, that Cohen finds inherent in the microhistorical effort to get at meaning *for them*, in their difference.

But for Ginzburg the unrealizability is bound up with a quasi-religious sense of the significance of historical inquiry, as is evident in his way of invoking Benjamin's 'Theses.' Explaining his purposes in writing his best-known work, *The Cheese and the Worms*, Ginzburg noted that though his protagonist, the sixteenth-century miller Menocchio, *could* be connected to us, he

> is also a dispersed fragment, reaching us by chance, of an obscure shadowy world that can be reconnected to our own history only by an arbitrary act. That culture has been destroyed. To respect its residue of unintelligibility that resists any attempt at analysis does not mean succumbing to a foolish fascination for the exotic and incomprehensible. It is simply taking note of a historical mutilation of which, in a certain sense, we ourselves are the victims. 'Nothing that has taken place should be lost to history,' wrote Walter Benjamin. 'But only to redeemed humanity does the past belong in its entirety.' Redeemed and thus liberated.[16]

Microhistory fed the wider turn to 'the new cultural history,' which has similarly partaken of certain postmodern insights, and which has seemed the historiographical cutting edge for the last fifteen years or so. A good example, partly because of its explicit and somewhat aggressive postmodernism, is Patrick Joyce's *Democratic Subjects*, which treats the construction of democratic identities in Victorian England. As a postmodernist Joyce sought explicitly to subvert the distinction between representation and the real. We find no given essences, no pre-existing, independent reality to be represented, but only the making of meaning, a central human activity. And it takes place in language, which is necessarily creative, though metaphoric, as we always say something new in terms of something old.[17]

This was to feature the centrality of culture and discourse as opposed to a prior reality – productive relations, for example – that culture and discourse merely grow from and reflect. Experience and even productive relations cannot be understood beyond discourse. Even poverty, insecurity, are not primary, do not give us direct knowledge of the real. More traditional historians have been troubled by such 'new cultural' accents, which seem to dissolve the hard reality of history into a soft haze of shifting discourse. Joyce was seeking to point behind any such hard-soft dichotomy, though he admitted that doing so was troubling as well as liberating.

In starting with culture, the new cultural history was usefully questioning the assumptions even of social history, which had comparably emphasized 'history from below.' Thus Joyce treated the construction of identities without reifying, without taking 'class,' for example, as real and privileged. We find the beginnings of democratic identity as individuals came to feel themselves to be part of the people, quite apart from class differentiation. But that identity involved a complex, unstable interplay between a certain understanding of self and a certain understanding of society; in a crucial sense they constituted each other. The sense of belonging was bound up with a sense of the scope for 'independence,' a situation of individual freedom and self-reliance to which all could aspire, though it depended on character, found within. Emerging only as it came to be imagined in this complex way, 'democracy' was uncentered, unstable, and tension-ridden. But precisely *as* imagined, it became eminently real and powerful.

Compared with social history, the new cultural history has been more deeply anti-reductive and dialogical, respecting difference, and more deeply reflexive, recognizing how we are caught up in the history we seek to understand. Following the noted intellectual historian Dominick LaCapra, Lloyd Kramer stressed the value of historical investigation that unearths the many submerged voices that contest our 'metaphysical' desire for unified, unambiguous meaning.[18] This imperative is of course congruent with those of both Ginzburg and Joyce. And LaCapra's dialogue imperative had been drawn partly from Gadamer. Moreover, LaCapra noted that such dialogue may lead us to change our mind – may enable us genuinely to learn, in other words. So at least in some of its manifestations, the new cultural history reflects precisely the reflexive engagement with our own intellectual history that we need.

But certain assumptions have channeled the new cultural enterprise, and we must ask whether its reflexive self-understanding is broad enough to grasp its own cultural role – and also the place for somewhat different lines of questioning from within a generally postmodern framework. Some manifestations of the new cultural history, embracing the 'thick description' pioneered by the noted anthropologist Clifford Geertz, tend to favor synchronic slices and to denigrate any concern with change over time, as if any such concern necessarily leads to a justifying master narrative. At the same time, the worthy imperatives of openness and dialogue, based on respect for earlier voices, seems sometimes to warrant an almost exclusively disruptive mode of historical inquiry, with privilege to experience that seems most to disrupt the expectations and desires that putatively lead us to construct certain kinds of narratives.

Weak Totality

Many of these new directions have been invaluable, but we noted some open questions and axes of contest. And whereas some such contest is surely inevitable and healthy, the terms of the ongoing contest in historiography have reflected confusion and overreaction that have produced, in turn, tendencies toward imperialism and delimitation. A premium on disruption or past lived experience is not the only alternative to a master narrative or to the 'modern' notion of history as meaningful and unified in the loaded sense. At issue is not meaning or meaninglessness but distinctions among modes of meaningful and modes of unified. 'Getting the story crooked' is not the only alternative to getting it straight. What needs discussion is not objectivity versus subjectivity but the basis for distinctions among modes of subjectivity.

We noted that some postmodernists and recent historians pick up on Koselleck's point that it became possible to conceive history in the singular, as unified and in some sense 'total,' only in the eighteenth century. The conception was thus itself historically specific, and surely it could indeed come to an end. Whether it in fact does, or should, in light of our subsequent experience and thinking is another matter, and the present conflations make it difficult to assess the possibilities. In fact, an awareness that the idea of a single unified history is specifically modern changes nothing. It seems decisive only insofar as we are still thinking in terms of the philosophical foundations or transcendent sanctions that we claim to have left aside. The progressive or redemptive gloss has surely fallen away, but not necessarily the idea of a single unified history itself. Before proclaiming that this too falls away, we must conceive more broadly what it might entail, *other than* progress, redemption, or some suprahistorically privileged master narrative.

Despite all the premium on disruption, a sort of Benjamin-Tolstoy ideal has seemed – explicitly for Ginzburg, and implicitly for others – a desirable alternative to the Hegelian or more weakly progressivist vision of historical totality that putatively remain as legacies from our modernist past. But these do not exhaust the ways of understanding the world, or the human place in the historical world, in light of the postmodern turn. A deeper sense of our situation suggests, most basically, the scope for thinking in terms of what we might call, borrowing loosely from Gianni Vattimo, 'weak totality.' Although this perspective does not exhaust the postmodern field, thinking through its basis and implications suggests how to deepen the encounter between postmodernism and historiography.

Even as they sensed that no transcendent privilege attaches to the historical process, those pioneers who departed from both Hegel and Dilthey saw that the world is endlessly coming to be some particular way through history, as human beings continually respond to what the world has come to be so far. At each moment, the range of possible responses to every particular aspect of the whole is infinite, but we respond in this way and not that. We ask these historical questions and not those and thus construct these historical narratives and not those. And the world endlessly becomes some particular way as we do so. The totality of response upon response just *is* the world we have to deal with.

So the loss of grounding or transcendence leaves us not with a heap but with a particular world, *this* particular world, which is surely a totality, though the totality is 'weak' in a double sense. First, it has no suprahistorical sanction; there is no 'good' or necessary reason for its being as it is. On the contrary, it has come to be as it is only through the 'dread accident' of history, as Nietzsche understood archetypally. And he found appalling, on first encounter, the mechanisms of a purely historical world, which have left us, so far, with this particular world, the only world there is. Although his *response* to this realization was also archetypal in one sense, we will see below that it was idiosyncratic and certainly did not exhaust the field. Second, the totality is weak because it is ever provisional and incomplete, ever slipping. The lack of necessity and the endless provisionality are simply the reverse side of the human capacity for creative response and the world's capacity for novelty.

We come to feel that 'everything' has come to be through history, even that everything is constructed and thus, in a sense, that there is 'nothing but history,' as, borrowing from Croce, I once proclaimed in a book title – a title that Giuseppe Galasso then borrowed from me.[19] The phrasing was hyperbolic, as I emphasized, though some critics seemed to miss the point. The hyperbole suggested a tendency, and thus also a challenge, as the range of the historically specific expands *almost*, it seems, to become all-encompassing. With the postmodern turn, in other words, the world comes to seem more deeply historical as opposed to given, or grounded in some 'metaphysical' way.

But do we implicitly posit 'just another metaphysics' if we speak of 'weak totality' – or use any such postmodern or post-metaphysical characterization of 'what there is'? Critics take delight in charging as much, but the charge proves merely an excuse to avoid serious engagement with the alternatives at issue. Such terminology is merely a way of saying how the world, and the human place in it, has come to seem to us now, partly in light of the analyses of earlier thinkers who contributed to the postmodern turn. It does not entail a metaphysics because it does not claim to specify how things are once and for all; it takes seriously its own provisionality. But it is able to see beyond the dualistic overreaction that posits mere fun and games as the alternative to any claim to definitive specification and closure.

If the world is more deeply historical than even the 'moderns' had realized, then contrary to the notion that history becomes irrelevant or goes limp with the postmodern turn, we face new questions about the potential cultural uses of a specifically historical mode of understanding. To assess the possibilities requires considering more deeply our place in history and thus how and why we ask historical questions; it requires considering more deeply the place of language and the scope for learning and even truth, in light of a fresh understanding of our need to think historically.

Dualism and Language

If the world has come to be this particular way and not some other way, though a process that was this particular way and not some other way, there is certainly an 'actual,' as is so important to those who cling to realism. And what purports to be history-writing cannot violate it. But that is no warrant for saying that we simply represent it – as best we can. The linguistic turn raises questions about how we represent what actually happened in language. Moreover, the realist ideal of rendering history 'as it actually happened' would entail an impossible completeness. So what do we do, what do we want and need to do, instead?

If the language in historical writing does not simply 'represent reality,' what *does* it do? We note, first, that postmodernism itself points us away from the dualistic assumptions that make the linguistic turn seem threatening; we come to understand, most basically, that language does not mask reality or impede understanding but discloses. To speak of 'disclosure,' however, may seem a form of mystification. To get clearer on what *disclosure* means, in light of the interface between postmodernism and history, we must first back up a bit.

The historian does not 'represent reality' most basically because the historian's enterprise necessarily entails a more creative, constructive dimension. And it is undeniable that an essential dimension of that creative construction lies in narrative emplotment. We will long remain indebted to Hayden White for bringing the overall issue so forcefully to our attention. But the contingencies of his particular way of doing so, the priorities he had in doing so, need to be pondered as part of our intellectual historical self-understanding. Even White's set of insights is better embedded in a wider vision of human creativity and the role of language than he himself provided, starting as he did with his sublime ideal on the horizon.

Based partly on his reading of Heidegger and Gadamer, Richard Rorty conveyed the deeper, more general notion in explaining why 'being that can be understood is language.'[20] Although this notion may initially seem extravagant to historians with realist assumptions, it does not warrant mere fun and games but brings home the seriousness of what we do – or have the potential to do. We come better to understand that a turn from realism does not necessarily invite White's sublime orientation, which accents the latitude we have for constructing histories for whatever ethical-political purpose, including personal edification, so that history-writing tends to converge with the creative, aestheticist mode of re-description explored in Alexander Nehamas's *Nietzsche: Life as Literature.*

Put differently, to say that 'being that can be understood is language,' or that we dwell in language, points us away from the usual debilitating dualism of language and reality. There is simply no point in insisting either that language has real referents or that it does not, but thus there is no implication that language is somehow inadequate to 'reality,' let alone merely arbitrary. *Reality* is itself a word, functioning, and meaningful to us, only as part of language. Even humanity, society, and nature are constructed, not given, 'just there,' apart from our naming of them, and thereby distinguishing them, in the particular ways we have done so. And *as* we have done so, a particular world has disclosed itself to us. So language does not limit us but makes our world possible.

In itself, this sense of being caught up in language changes nothing about what we historians do; its implications for our self-understanding are not in themselves radical or threatening. It does not undermine the scope for truth. Indeed, the fact that we perform our role in language proves distinctly secondary. But, as I have suggested, wider aspects of postmodernism do have significant implications for what we do – or might do.

Past, Process, and Historical Learning

If we recognize no master narrative and if, conversely, we could narrate the historical construction of seemingly anything at all, from 'accuracy' to 'Africa' to our present understanding of gender relations, we wonder how we decide what is worth asking and whether the openings surrounding the postmodern turn have affected our criteria. Although in principle we might envision a species of 'dada' history, with topics for historical inquiry selected by chance, and/or with scraps from the past assembled as in a Kurt Schwitters collage, historians do not in fact operate that way. Even insofar as we claim to privilege 'margins,' we seem far more interested in some margins than others (for the range of margins is of course infinite). Does the imperative of respect for voices that resist the interpretations we would like to place on them apply, for example, to fascists? How have we decided, and how might we decide? Modes of presentism are necessarily at work as we decide about focus and priorities, and such questions lead us to the need and the scope for distinctions among those presentist modes. And these distinctions suggest that misplaced or tendentious assumptions, resulting at least in part from confusions surrounding the postmodern turn itself, presently tend to delimit our range of questions and modes of inquiry.

Centrally at issue is the interrelationship of past, present, and process. To pinpoint the key issues, it helps initially to ask simply whether history is about the past or about process. In other words, is historical inquiry simply to focus on the past moment, on some past experience, or does it seek to trace some process by featuring in any past moment whatever seemed to lead to the next moment? It is hard even to raise the question because, as we noted, any mention of process seems to conflate with 'the historical process,' and thus some master narrative, if not full-blown Hegelianism.

But process can be weak, indeed is necessarily weak in a postmodern world that affords no basis for a claim to a supra-historical grasp of what is happening or has happened. Those quick to associate justification with any focus on process fail to distinguish finding merely historical reasons from finding the supra-historical or transcendent reasons that would indeed afford justification. Nietzsche remains archetypal on the difference, yet many, even as they invoke this or that aspect of his legacy, miss precisely the Nietzschean point that we noted above. What most struck Nietzsche was how the particular world comes to be, historically, contingently, for no 'good' reason, affording justification. In its weakly postmodern guise, historical inquiry merely indicates how the world became this way as opposed to some other, how we got from then to now – or some delimited segment of that transition.

Whatever the focus, the process at issue will not be 'special' in some transcendent sense. Mark Lilla's characterization, quoted earlier, misses precisely the sense in which process can be weak. In the same way, Christian Meier, in stressing the impact of Auschwitz, conflates historical-mindedness in general with belief in a special path for European culture, a special role that has now been lost. The self-understanding in terms of history does not fall away; we simply have, as the result of our continuing history, including Auschwitz, a different understanding of our place in that history.

But once we get beyond the unwarranted conflations, a deeper issue of focus is indeed central. And some of the reasons that astute postmodernists like Mark Poster give for turning from any focus on process are compelling, up to a point. No matter how successful we are in eschewing teleology, insofar as we seek the seeds of the next moment in the past, we may indeed tend to play down difference as we engage those who came before us. Perhaps we must feature discontinuity to keep ourselves from portraying them as having been like us, or as trying to be like us, or to keep ourselves from taking their only historical meaning to be in leading up to us. Thus our fastidious insistence that history is about *their* experience. Starting with this concern, we find an array of reasons to focus on history as past *as opposed to* process.

But though we must surely take care to be true to the past in its difference, our concern to eschew any imputation of a master narrative leading to us need not require privilege to, let alone an exclusive focus on, discontinuity. We need not leave, for example, the figures in Richard Cohen's microhistories in their strangeness, as if defamiliarizing was the privileged purpose of historiography. We wonder, if only implicitly, how we got from there to here, from their modes of experience to our own. And only by focusing on process, asking how the world came to be as it is, can we orient ourselves to respond to some aspect of the present provisional outcome, and thereby create the next moment. Precisely because it entails a deeper sense of the historicity of things, postmodernism invites historical questioning that can provide such orientation, even though the resulting understanding cannot specify what we ought to do. And whereas the concern for creating the next moment certainly entails projection into the future, such projection does not posit predictability and control, as Mastrogregori, for example, implies that it must.[21]

We noted that new cultural histories tend to focus on particular past episodes or synchronic slices for fear of forcing our predecessors into our stories. Yet Patrick Joyce noted that a somewhat different understanding of the interface between democracy and personal identity, bound up with a different conception of selfhood and the social, had emerged by the early twentieth century. He was not concerned with that process, but his insights into the creation of the earlier meanings of democracy, and of the tensions in those meanings, can illuminate change and even the terms of the wider ongoing democratic political experiment. We wonder how the tensions played out. What implications did the particular way of playing out have for later political departures? On the basis of such questions, we generate a continuous narrative of process toward the present. Conversely, to grasp the sense in which our predecessors *are* part of our stories does not warrant presentist imposition.

Stemming from a present concern, an inquiry into process seeks 'what is living' at each moment in order to understand outcomes, not, however, to celebrate or justify but first simply to understand. From there we may possibly criticize and seek to overcome. Indeed, such inquiry opens the way to deconstructing anything that has gotten constructed and even for reconnection with what had gotten marginalized along the way from then to now. So our quest for orientation may lead to the sort of radical, deconstructive historical questioning that Nietzsche attempted in *The Genealogy of Morals.* But this example reminds us that we need to be clear on what it means to learn, as opposed to serve some a priori agenda.

Subjectivity and 'creativity' are inevitable, and some generally moral-political agenda guides our questioning. Moreover, we always have an infinite number of ways of making sense, even an infinite number of *true* ways of constructing processes and thereby accounting for how the world has become as it is. But not just any way of making sense will satisfy us, insofar as we are genuinely concerned to learn how the world has come to be in order better to respond to it in action. Insofar as we seek such orientation, our historical inquiries are open to dialogue, to risking our presuppositions, and to adjusting our perspective on the basis of the ensuing encounter. In this mode, we are open to learning, which entails a disclosure that we can usefully call 'true,' in distinction from its several contraries. Truth is simply the outcome of inquiry in a certain mode. Nor does the lack of a single, stable, unified truth dissolve the distinction between truth and its contraries. At the same time, grasping, with Kundera, the potential corruption of the archive leads us not to turn away altogether but simply prompts us to a more critical posture as we seek historical understanding.

But though in principle we can distinguish the mode of inquiry that opens to learning from those that serve other purposes, no instance of historical writing is pure; thus the place of truth remains problematic. Although professional disciplinary standards afford a kind of winnowing-out process, Richard Evans reminds us that such standards have their limits; the presence of a community of trained historians in Nazi Germany did not prevent what now seems a most tendentious reading of history by its members.[22] Ultimately, the scope for truth depends simply on the need and desire of the individual historian genuinely to learn. This goodwill may seem a thin reed, but it is more likely to be grasped if the stakes and alternatives that emerge from a postmodern framework are made clearer. It stems from our sense of moral responsibility, which is nurtured by our sense of involvement with our continuing history. And as the essential complement to disciplinary standards, it is ultimately more convincing than Evans's residual realism.

Varied Ways of Relating to History

But if history as process has been marginalized prejudicially with the postmodern turn, it has no exclusive claim in a postmodern world, which opens us to a variety of modes of orientation toward history and the past, and thus invites a variety of cultural roles for historical inquiry and understanding. To approach the issue, again focusing on the interplay between past and process, let us recall Croce's observations on history as 'anecdote' and ask how they do and do not apply to Carlo Ginzburg and microhistory. Even as he insisted that genuinely historical inquiry starts with a contemporary concern, Croce recognized that we also have other reasons for delving into the past. History as 'anecdote' keeps alive varied manifestations of humanity. Such inquiry gets at something that did in fact happen and can yield truth, because we want 'to know not possible but effectual occurrences, in fact to know what has been the real capacity of humanity for action and suffering in good and evil conditions, and thence infer in the future what can be done and suffered or reasonably expected.' The transition between anecdote and the historical novel is gradual, not absolute; the degree of imagination varies. But as Croce saw it, such 'anecdotal' inquiry is not genuinely historical because the episode in question is not placed in terms of historical development. Still, he found both anecdote and history to be necessary; indeed, he deemed them complementary.[23]

Croce, then, was recognizing that we have different purposes in dealing with historical materials, though his major accent was always on process. Ginzburg noted explicitly that he came to his premium on what is 'really dead' in the past precisely in reaction against Croce's emphasis on 'what is living,' or what led to the next moment.[24] And Ginzburg's reasons for that premium transcended the reason Croce gave for a focus on 'anecdote.' Microhistorians like Ginzburg focus on scraps and margins not simply to enhance our sense of what to expect but to disrupt our tendency to construct meaningful processes. And as we saw in Ginzburg, this latter priority was bound up with a quasi-religious solicitude for individuals and experiences marginalized by history.

If we become clearer on the diversity of purposes, in light of the postmodern turn, that lead us to ask historical questions, we can better grasp the uses of both 'history as past' and 'history as process' and eschew the imperialistic implication that one is illegitimate because it is not the other. Indeed, we come to understand the fruitful tension between them. Conversely, greater clarity on the basis of the tension would help us better to understand both sets of aims.

Just as no transcendent sanction attaches to any historical resultant, neither are there transcendent grounds for *condemnation* just because *any* outcome will have been an instance of power, marginalizing other possibilities, and thus can *always* be construed as domination. So disruption, as opposed to reconstructive deconstruction, is not privileged a priori. Making such determinations is up to us, as part of our ongoing response to what the world has come to be so far. At the same time, focus on process, necessary though it is, reflects only a partial human relationship to the historical world, and those modes of history-writing that, in their varied ways, focus on the past in its difference, distance, or real deadness enhance our experience and broaden our overall orientation to the world.

We find an example of fruitful interplay between past and process in an especially innovative area in American historiography over the last fifteen years or so, focusing on Native Americans, or – as is again respectable usage – Indians, especially in the eighteenth century. At first, this focus was part of a laudable effort to understand colonial America on its own terms and not as a step toward the emergence of the United States. And this effort was partly to disrupt the longstanding, celebratory master narrative that posited America as an empty 'virgin land' before the Europeans came. Innovative historians showed that the eighteenth-century experience very much encompassed the Indian experience and above all the interaction of Indians with those of European and, especially in some regions, African ancestry. But from there historians began reconnecting the colonial and early national periods though a much more complex understanding of the process of transition, which included the marginalization of Indians to American life by the early decades of the nineteenth century.[25] It mattered, in ways historians had heretofore neglected, that the place of Indians had become radically different. And getting at *why* it mattered required grasping the process through which the situation became so different.

It is not surprising that the recent discussion, with its various – legitimate and illegitimate – reactions against process, has had little to say about the kinds of process that might be at issue as we seek understanding in light of the postmodern turn. As basic assumptions that once seemed grounded or transcendent come to seem historically specific, our quest for orientation demands that we try out historical questions on higher levels of abstraction. The narratives that result need not be *master* narratives, yet historians, unlike some philosophers, have been reluctant to question on such levels, partly, no doubt, because of the accent on archival research and monographic publication in the historical profession, but also, it seems, because of conflation with master narratives and even justification of outcomes. Yet such expanded historical questioning might illuminate – and possibly unsettle – our own assumptions, categories, and priorities in unexpected ways.

Modes of 'Liberation' from History

A better sense of the interplay of present, past, and process would enable us better to sort out 'lightness,' 'weight,' and modes of 'liberation' in terms of a generally postmodern orientation toward history. Massimo Mastrogregori explicitly suggested that the postmodern condition makes possible freedom from the past, whether it is because we no longer *have* to think, or because we are no longer *able* to think, in the historical way we once did.[26] Nearer the outset of the postmodern break, Hayden White was similarly pondering the scope for liberation from 'the burden of history' as he turned from Croce to invite a freer, 'sublime' historiography in the mid-1960s. Weight and lightness was an essential polarity in Nietzsche's ruminations on the historicity of the world, a polarity that Kundera explored as he wove his novel *The Unbearable Lightness of Being* around his own musings on Nietzsche's historical sense. However, Kundera did not do justice to the complexity and layering of Nietzsche's response to the uncanniness of a merely historical world. Kundera's partial misreading of Nietzsche is symptomatic of our ongoing problems in characterizing generally postmodern possibilities with respect to 'history.'

On the one hand, Nietzsche found it appalling, 'the greatest weight,' that we have only this finite particular world that has no supra-historical reason for being as it is. Yet he also found that world precious, as the only world we have. Even as he found only 'dread accident' at the source of our world, his response in his late works suggested neither some ongoing history-making engagement with the world nor a mere turning away. He sought a mode of affirmation of the finite particularity of the world, experienced precisely as a totality. The mode of 'eternal recurrence' entailed willing, affirming not only all the world ever has been but all it ever will be. This mode of experience entails lightness, 'dance,' because the scope for novelty, and thus the scope for human responsibility and guilt, is denied. Only in this mode, insisted Nietzsche explicitly, do we experience the 'innocence of becoming.'

Heidegger offered a contrasting extreme response, a mode of disengagement, in light of a comparable sense of the finitude of the actual particular world that comes to be through history. Though their responses were diametrically opposed, Nietzsche and Heidegger both envisioned a mode of liberation from the weight of a world that had come to seem more deeply historical. Each was reacting against 'historicism,' or a cultural premium on history-making, on active engagement with the world to help shape the future. But whatever the symptomatic value of these contrasting extremes, such ongoing historicist engagement remained a possibility as well.

From this last perspective, we are necessarily caught up in the happening of history; we belong to history in its particularity, finitude, and provisionality. So we achieve only the illusion of liberation from the weight of the past insofar as, with Nietzsche, we simply affirm the totality or, with Heidegger, simply disengage from it. Liberation requires the action, informed by historical understanding, that overcomes some present resultant of history to which we object. But of course the weight returns because history continues to afford us fresh challenges. However, insofar as we grasp our place in the world, we continue to rise to them. From this perspective, to accent either lightness or some full-scale liberation from history betrays one side of the irresponsible overreaction that critics have found in postmodernism.

But, again, the history-making orientation can claim no monopoly. Although they do not go to the outer edges explored by Nietzsche and Heidegger, the defamiliarizing and even disruptive strategies, bound up with an emphasis on past as opposed to process, operate within the space that these two 'prophets of extremity' blocked out. And those strategies remain an essential counterpoint to the history-making orientation that emphasizes process.

Conclusion: The Three Cultures and the Historicist Revolution

The place and status of 'history' have long been scrutinized – and have long seemed oddly ambiguous. To some extent we remain caught up in the assumption of 'two cultures,' the literary and scientific, as famously juxtaposed and distinguished in C.P. Snow's *The Two Cultures and the Scientific Revolution,* published in its original form in 1959. Even Richard Rorty, thinking big in 1980 about changing cultural priorities, posited a comparable bifurcation and similarly implied that these two modes exhaust the field, even if, as he saw it, a mode of 'textualism' was waxing in a way that earlier observers like Snow had not recognized.[27]

The place of historical inquiry and understanding vis-à-vis each of 'the two cultures' has long been at issue. In recent years, both theorists and practitioners of history have been more concerned about its interface with literature than with science, but in the wider culture, the longstanding question of the status of history vis-à-vis science surely remains equally important. Is history 'the soft stuff' because it cannot do what science does? Is it thus merely a form of literature? Conversely, is history so beholden to 'facts' – to what actually happened, and to the evidence we happen to have – that it can never approach the level of imaginative construction and synthesis we find in literature, even as it also lacks the precision and predictive value of science? Stuck with the worst of both worlds, history might seem doomed to remain a cultural stepchild.

In his pivotal article of 1966, 'The Burden of History,' Hayden White sought to open historical culture beyond 'realism' and other essentially nineteenth-century modes to dialogue with the most advanced thinking in art and science. And certainly White had his own strategy as he turned from Croce to embrace Jean-Paul Sartre, Northrop Frye, Roland Barthes, and others, including a certain side of Vico. In light of the contingencies of our own intellectual history, then, the generally postmodern challenge, and invitation, to historians came from a certain angle, entailing a certain way of relating history to innovative thinking stemming, above all, from literature.

Although the linguistic turn in historiography got us over certain historically specific scientific hang-ups, it did so in its own historically specific way, a way that invited certain possibilities but neglected others. And as a result it seemed all the more extravagant to traditionalist historians. The reaction among them then took the form of a renewed, if weak, embrace of science, based on notions of realism, representation, and objectivity. But thus the ensuing discussion was channelled in certain restricted directions as each side found it easy simply to engage the other's delimited points and thus to assume not only superiority but also that the postmodern challenge and opportunity had thereby been addressed. At the same time, much of the polarization in the historical profession stems from the assumption that science, bound up with a certain role for language, and literature, bound up with a quite different range of roles for language, are the two possibilities. The historians prove eager to nest with one side or the other of 'the two cultures.'

As debate has continued along certain delimited axes, the scope for alternatives has tended to get marginalized. But our overall intellectual history of course continued after 1966, producing a dramatically different cultural situation. At that point, after all, the key works of Kuhn and Gadamer were just beginning to have an impact, the post-structuralist assault on structuralism was just beginning to gather force, and the social sciences were just beginning to become more deeply self-critical. As a result, earlier figures like Nietzsche, Heidegger, and, yes, even Croce began to appear in a new light. And the scope for a deeper rethinking of the place of history, and thus a richer debate, began to emerge.

Such a deeper rethinking suggests the need, and the scope, to transcend the art/science binary altogether and to specify the autonomy and significance of history in a new way. We might even begin to think in terms of three cultures, now including the historical alongside the artistic and scientific, in light of what we might call, paralleling Snow, the historicist revolution that has been bound up with the postmodern turn. Although historical approaches to both art and science are of course valuable, this is not to warrant some imperialism on the part of history. Art and science surely retain their autonomy; there is no need to claim superiority for any one of three approaches.

Heralds of postmodernism like Lyotard have often been simplistic in addressing history and its cultural place. Yet such would-be mediators as

Richard Evans and Ernst Breisach, assuming that a residual realism is the key, are too limited to tell them what they are missing. On the basis of a fuller understanding of the third culture, historians can engage the most innovative in other cultural spheres from a position of greater confidence, neither clinging to the old-fashioned skirts of 'common-sense' realism nor falling in behind the literary culture, as if we are all just making up stories. We thereby at once diminish the polarization among historians, foster more fruitful dialogue between historiographical 'theory' and 'practice,' and promote a deeper connection with the wider culture.

Notes

Introduction

1 David D. Roberts, *Benedetto Croce and the Uses of Historicism* (Berkeley: University of California Press, 1987). For Alexander J. De Grand's review, see *American Historical Review* 94, no. 1 (February 1989): 178–9. Although De Grand was (and is) not only a highly respected Italianist but also a personal friend, and although I appreciated his quite favourable review, he was no intellectual historian, as he was quick to admit in private communications. And he was surely not the one to articulate whatever wider import my recasting of Croce might have had, in terms of the historiographical discussion nearing a sort of mini-peak at that point. See also Stephen Bailey's review of John Michael Krois, *Cassirer: Symbolic Forms and History*, in *American Historical Review* 98, no. 4 (October 1988): 1008–9.

2 Hannah Arendt, *The Origins of Totalitarianism* (Cleveland: World [Meridian], 1958), 256–60. For Ernst Nolte's way of taking Italian fascism more seriously, see his *Three Faces of Fascism: Action Française, Italian Fascism, and National Socialism*, trans. Leila Vennewitz (New York: Holt, Rinehart and Winston, 1966).

3 Karl Heussi, *Die Krisis des Historismus* (Tübingen: Mohr, 1932). Especially symptomatic was Friedrich Meinecke's 'Deutung eines Rankeswortes,' in *Aphorismen und Skizzen zur Geschichte*, 2nd ed., enlarged (Stuttgart: Koehler, 1952), 119–29.

4 Chester McArthur Destler, 'Some Observations on Contemporary Historical Theory,' *American Historical Review* 55 (1950): 504, 517.

5 Giuseppe Antonio Borgese, *Goliath: The March of Fascism* (New York: Viking, 1937), 23, 295–302. See 23, 297–8, 299, for the passages quoted. Borgese taught Italian at the University of Chicago; Salvemini taught

history at Harvard. For references to Salvemini and further discussion of the overall issue, as it played out in the United States, see pp. 100–1 in the present volume. See also Ulisse Benedetti, *Benedetto Croce e il fascismo* (Rome: Volpe, 1967), for a scathing post-mortem on Croce's overall stance vis-à-vis fascism.

6 On Croce's politics, and especially his myriad anti-fascist activities, see Fabio Fernando Rizi, *Benedetto Croce and Italian Fascism* (Toronto: University of Toronto Press, 2003).

7 E.J. Hobsbawm, 'The Great Gramsci,' *New York Review of Books*, 4 April 1974, 39. Hobsbawm was referring to the culture from which Antonio Gramsci had emerged, around the time of the First World War.

8 Giovanni Gentile, *Che cosa è il fascismo* (Florence: Vallecchi, 1925), 153–61; Gioacchino Volpe, *Guerra dopoguerra fascismo* (Venice: La Nuova Italia, 1928), 293–9.

9 Benedetto Croce, 'Frammenti di etica,' in *Etica e politica* (Bari: Laterza, 1967), 167–8. See also Benedetto Croce, *Ultimi saggi* (Bari: Laterza, 1963), 223–4 (1926).

10 I adapt the next four paragraphs from my book *The Totalitarian Experiment in Twentieth-Century Europe: Understanding the Poverty of Great Politics* (London: Routledge, 2006), 133–4. See 130–42 for an account of the overall emergence of Gentile's thought.

11 Gabriele Turi, *Giovanni Gentile: Una biografia* (Florence: Giunti, 1995), 72–4, 117–18, 128–9, 145, 147, 208.

12 Giovanni Gentile, *'Veritas Filia Temporis'* (1912), now in his *Il pensiero italiano nel rinascimento*, 3rd ed., rev. (Florence: Sansoni, 1955), 337–9.

13 Ibid., 347, 350–4.

14 Giovanni Gentile, *La riforma della dialettica hegeliana*, 3rd ed. (Florence: Sansoni, 1975), 1–65, 237–40; see especially 36–9.

15 This is the title of the new translation by Colin Lyas published by Cambridge University Press in 1992. It is surely superior to the more familiar *Aesthetic as Science of Expression and General Linguistic*, as rendered in the standard translation by Douglas Ainslie. Unlike some of Croce's Italian titles, this one – *Estetica come scienza dell'espressione e linguistica generale* – surely does not lend itself to elegant translation.

16 'Croce and Beyond: Italian Intellectuals and the First World War,' *International History Review* 3, no. 2 (April 1981): 210–35.

17 Benedetto Croce, *Conversazioni critiche*, 2nd ser. (Bari: Laterza, 1950), 67–95; Giovanni Gentile, *Saggi critici*, 2nd ser. (Florence: Vallecchi, 1927), 29.

18 Though it had been commissioned in 1974 for the collaborative volume later published as *Who Were the Fascists*, this article was not published until

1980 because of delays the editors encountered in putting the collection together. It finally appeared as 'Petty-bourgeois Fascism in Italy: Form and Content,' in *Who Were the Fascists: Social Roots of European Fascism*, eds. Stein Ugelvik Larsen et al. (Bergen: Universitetsforlaget, 1980), 337–47.

19 Zeev Sternhell, with Mario Sznajder and Maia Asheri, *The Birth of Fascist Ideology: From Cultural Rebellion to Political Revolution*, trans. David Maisel (Princeton: Princeton University Press, 1994; original French ed. 1989); Zeev Sternhell, *Neither Right nor Left: Fascist Ideology in France*, trans. David Maisel (Princeton: Princeton University Press, 1996 [1st ed. of English trans. 1986; original French ed. 1983]).

20 Stanley G. Payne, *A History of Fascism, 1914–1945* (Madison: University of Wisconsin Press, 1995), 291.

21 This is perhaps the occasion to recall a memorable conversation with my friend Paolo Bonetti, as we were crossing the Strait of Messina one evening late in November 2002, about the place I had come to assume – by happenstance, not remotely by design – in the Italian discussion of the Crocean tradition. My task from there was to try to make the most of my odd position to show the wider ongoing relevance of Croce's historicism.

22 As revised and augmented, these were subsequently published as *Una nuova interpretazione del pensiero di Croce: Lo storicismo crociano e il pensiero contemporaneo* (Pisa: Istituti Editoriali e Poligrafici Internazionali, 1995). Invited again by Mario Corsi, I returned to the Scuola Superiore Sant'-Anna in Pisa for a second set of three lectures in 1994. These culminated in a discussion of Giovanni Gentile but first explored the wider relevance of idiosyncratic Italian angles in light of such disparate figures as Vilfredo Pareto and F.T. Marinetti. This set of lectures was later published, unrevised, as *Giovanni Gentile e la politica italiana*, ed. Mario Corsi (Pisa: Edizioni ETS, 1999).

23 Presented 28–9 April 1997, these were entitled 'Lo storicismo crociano e la filosofia contemporanea: Due lezioni.' I did not seek to publish these lectures because I understood that the institute would be publishing them. However, parts of the second lecture found their way into chapter 5 here.

24 'L'eredità di Benedetto Croce nel secondo dopoguerra in Italia: Presenze e assenze' ('The Legacy of Benedetto Croce in Italy since the Second World War: Presences and Absences'), presented as part of a conference organized by Franco Manni, sponsored by the City of Brescia and entitled 'Un'Italia che va? Trasformazioni reali e trasformazioni immaginarie nell'Italia della seconda metà del XX secolo,' 15 May 2004. The other presenters at the conference were Franco Sbarberi, Gianni Vattimo, Padre Saverio Cannistrà, and Sebastiano Vassalli. Lucio Russo was also on the

program but had to withdraw at the last minute. I would especially like to have included this paper here, but I concluded that it overlaps too much with chapters 1 and 2. Thanks to the efforts of Professor Manni, excerpts of my lecture were published in *Stilos: Il settimanale dei libri* 6, no. 32 (17 August 2004): 6.

25 Girolamo Cotroneo, 'Croce e Nietzsche,' in his *L'ingresso nella modernità: Momenti della filosofia italiana tra Ottocento e Novecento* (Naples: Morano, 1992), 193–209. Cotroneo was trained by Raffaello Franchini, the most influential of the last generation of Croce's immediate followers. See the introduction to chapter 2.

26 A more recent essay on Croce and Nietzsche by another distinguished representative of the Croce-Franchini school, Renata Viti Cavaliere, suggests precisely that wider reach. See her 'Croce e Nietzsche: Antimetafisica e storia,' in her *Saggi su Croce: Riconsiderazioni e confronti* (Naples: Luciano, 2002), 93–108.

27 Giuseppe Calandra, *Gentile e il fascismo* (Rome: Laterza, 1987), vii, 4, 12–13, 113, 156.

28 See, for example, Herbert Marcuse, *Reason and Revolution: Hegel and the Rise of Social Theory* (Boston: Beacon, 1960; first pub. 1941), 402–12, especially 407–8, for the former reading, and Franz Neumann, *Behemoth: The Structure and Practice of National Socialism, 1933–1944,* 2nd ed. (1944; New York: Harper & Row, 1966), 75–6, for the latter. The influential American journal *Foreign Affairs* published a translation of one of Gentile's key essays as 'The Philosophic Basis of Fascism' in January 1928 (vol. 6, 290–304).

29 Emilio Gentile, *The Sacralization of Politics in Fascist Italy* (Cambridge: Harvard University Press, 1996), 58.

30 Abbott Gleason, *Totalitarianism: The Inner History of the Cold War* (New York: Oxford University Press, 1995), 19. See also 9, 94–5.

31 Just as Croce informs the overall argument of my *Nothing but History,* Gentile informs my more recent *The Totalitarian Experiment in Twentieth-Century Europe.* I treat Gentile most explicitly on pp. 130–42, 183–7, and 299–305.

32 'Ogni filosofo, alla fine di una sua ricerca, intravede le prime incerte linee di un'altra, che egli medesimo, o chi verrà dopo di lui, eseguirà. E con questa modestia, che è delle cose stesse e non già del mio sentimento personale, con questa modestia che è insieme fiducia di non aver pensato indarno, io metto termine al mio lavoro, porgendolo ai ben disposti come strumento di lavoro.' Benedetto Croce, *Filosofia della pratica: Economia ed etica* (Bari: Laterza, 1963), 406.

33 In certain respects my *Totalitarian Experiment* is obviously, if never explicitly,

an effort at that sort of post-Crocean book. The conclusion, especially, is Crocean, reflecting, in a sense, Croce's victory over Gentile from within the same framework. But I believe my overall debt to others, especially Hans-Georg Gadamer, is also clear.

34 Giuseppe Galasso, *Croce e lo spirito del suo tempo* (Rome: Laterza, 2002); Giuseppe Galasso, *Nient'altro che storia: Saggi di teoria e metodologia della storia* (Bologna: Il Mulino, 2000).

35 Jeffrey C. Goldfarb, *Beyond Glasnost: The Post-Totalitarian Mind* (Chicago: University of Chicago Press, 1991). Goldfarb developed his ideas further in such works as *After the Fall: The Pursuit of Democracy in Central Europe* (n.p.: Basic Books, 1992); and *Civility and Subversion: The Intellectual in Democratic Society* (Cambridge: Cambridge University Press, 1998).

36 Peter Novick, *That Noble Dream: The 'Objectivity Question' and the American Historical Profession* (Cambridge: Cambridge University Press, 1988).

37 David D. Roberts, 'Postmodernism and History: Missing the Missed Connections,' *History and Theory* 44, no. 2 (2005): 240–52. Ernst Breisach's *On the Future of History: The Postmodernist Challenge and Its Aftermath* was published by the University of Chicago Press in 2003. The reprint edition of my *Nothing but History* was published by the Davies Group in 2007.

38 The overall title for the session was 'Studying Italian History in the Twenty-First Century: Challenges and Changes to the State of the Field.' Chaired by John A. Davis, the session took place in Philadelphia on 7 January 2006.

39 In the area of fascism and totalitarianism, this has meant leaving out most significantly:

a. 'Petty-bourgeois Fascism in Italy: Form and Content,' cited above.

b. *Nazism, Fascism, Totalitarianism: The Layers of Historical Understanding*, a thirty-six-page pamphlet that grew from a lecture I presented at the invitation of Professor Wolf D. Gruner at the University of Rostock, Germany, in 1996. After revision, the lecture was published as volume 10 in the *Rostocker Beiträge zur Deutschen und Europäischen Geschichte*, edited by Wolf D. Gruner. Rostock: Universität Rostock, Philosophische Fakultät, Historisches Institut.

c. invited comment on Roger Griffin's article, 'The Primacy of Culture: The Current Growth (or Manufacture) of Consensus in Fascist Studies'; my comment appeared in *Journal of Contemporary History* 37, no. 2 (April 2002): 259–93.

d. 'Comment: Fascism, Single-Party Dictatorships, and the Search for a Comparative Framework,' *Contemporary European History* 11, no. 3 (2002): 455–61; this was an invited comment on an article by Antonio Costa Pinto that appeared in the same issue of this journal.

e. 'Understanding Fascism as Historically Specific,' *Erwägen Wissen Ethik (EWE)* 15, no. 3 (2004): 347–8; and 'Roger Griffin, Ernst Nolte, and the Historical Place of Fascism,' *Erwägen Wissen Ethik* 15, no. 3 (2004): 411–13. These are my two contributions to an international exchange on fascism based on a lead article by Roger Griffin. The entire issue of the journal was devoted to this exchange. It has been republished in book form as *Fascism Past and Present, West and East: An International Debate on Concepts and Cases in the Comparative Study of the Extreme Right*, eds. Roger Griffin, Werner Loh, and Andreas Umland (Stuttgart: Ibidem-Verlag, 2006).

f. 'Rethinking the Problem of Totalitarianism,' lecture at the invitation of Professor Karl Acham, Institut für Soziologie, Karl-Franzens-Universität Graz, Austria, 2 June 2005 (unpublished).

In addition to those published in Italy, and mentioned in note 22, a couple of lectures on Gentile remain unpublished, and it was tempting to include at least one of them here. However, they proved in a sense preliminary, even as they helped me work out my account in essays 5 and 6 and in my book *The Totalitarian Experiment.* I particularly profited from the discussion that followed from three of these earlier papers:

a. 'Croce, Gentile, and the Problem of Italian Fascism,' presented at the annual meeting of the American Association for Italian Studies in Toronto, 11 April 1986. Here I first to begin to develop my interpretation of Gentile's fascism, and I especially thank Edmund Jacobitti for his comments in the aftermath.

b. 'Fascism and Philosophy: The Case of Giovanni Gentile,' presented at the Institut für Zeitgeschichte of the Leopold-Franzens University in Innsbruck, Austria, 19 April 1995, thanks to an invitation from Michael Gehler and Rolf Steininger.

c. 'Giovanni Gentile,' presented as part of the academic session of the Society for Italian Historical Studies, held in conjunction with the annual meeting of the American Historical Association in San Francisco on 5 January 2002. The session, chaired by Walter Adamson, was entitled 'Italy from Liberalism to Fascism: The Biographical Approach.'

In the area of historicism and historiography, I have had to leave out especially:

a. 'Straight Stories, Crooked Histories, and Vichian Possibilities,' *New Vico Studies* 8 (1990): 79–88. This is a review essay taking off from Hans Kellner's *Language and Historical Representation: Getting the Story Crooked* (Madison: University of Wisconsin Press, 1989).

b. 'Suffocation and Vocation: History, Anti-History, and the Self,' in *Alternative Identities: The Self in Literature, History, Theory*, ed. Linda Marie Brooks (New York: Garland, 1995), 109–38.

c. 'Postmodern Continuities: Difference, Dominance, and the Question of Historiographical Renewal,' *History and Theory* 37, no. 3 (1998): 388–400. This is a review essay taking off from Mark Poster's *Cultural History and Postmodernity: Disciplinary Readings and Challenges* (New York: Columbia University Press, 1997).

d. 'History as Thought and Action: Croce's Historicism and the Contemporary Challenge,' in *The Legacy of Benedetto Croce: Contemporary Critical Views*, ed. Jack D'Amico, Dain A. Trafton, and Massimo Verdicchio (Toronto: University of Toronto Press, 1999), 196–230.

e. 'Characterizing Historicist Possibilities: A Reply to Claes Ryn,' *Humanitas* 13, no. 1 (2000): 68–88. This is a response to Claes G. Ryn, 'Defining Historicism,' *Humanitas* 11, no. 2 (1998): 86–101, a review essay on my *Nothing but History*. Ryn responded to my response in his 'History as Synthesis,' *Humanitas* 13, no. 1 (2000): 89–102. The place of Croce is central to this exchange.

f. 'Postmodernism and History: Missing the Missed Connections,' cited in note 37.

I would also like to have been able to include:

a. 'Croce and Beyond: Italian Intellectuals and the First World War,' cited in note 16.

b. 'Frustrated Liberals: De Ruggiero, Gobetti, and the Challenge of Socialism,' *Canadian Journal of History* 17, no. 1 (April 1982): 59–86.

Chapter 1

1 The examples are legion, yet there seems little interest in them today. For one such example, see Paul Einzig, *The Economic Foundations of Fascism* (London: Macmillan, 1933), which vehemently contrasted corporativist fascism with German Nazism, deemed merely barbarous and destructive.

2 Writing in 1937, the exiled Italian scholar Giuseppe Antonio Borgese, by now a long-time antagonist, found Croce 'the most famed Italian abroad, at least in the scholarly world, since the days perhaps of Galileo.' See his *Goliath: The March of Fascism* (New York: Viking, 1937), 295–6.

3 Chester McArthur Destler, 'Some Observations on Contemporary Historical Theory,' *American Historical Review* 55 (1950): 504, 517.

4 Frederic S. Simoni, 'Benedetto Croce: A Case of International Misunderstanding,' *Journal of Aesthetics and Art Criticism* 11 (September 1952): 7–14. The quoted passage is from p. 9.

5 Franz Neumann, *Behemoth: The Structure and Practice of National Socialism, 1933–1944*, 2nd ed. (1944; New York: Harper & Row, 1966), 75–8; Herbert Marcuse, *Reason and Revolution: Hegel and the Rise of Social Theory* (1941; Boston: Beacon, 1960), especially 402–9, on 'Fascist "Hegelianism,"' for his critique of Gentile.

6 Marcuse, *Reason and Revolution*, 411–12.

7 Raffaello Franchini, *Intervista su Croce*, ed. Arturo Fratta (Naples: Società Editrice Napoletana, 1978), 5.

8 Bobbio also noted that not so long before, intelligent, idealistic young Italians had found Gentile's thinking exciting and inspiring. Bobbio's two-sided characterization is cited, and endorsed, in Maurizio Ferraris, 'Il Gentile di Garin,' *Aut Aut*, n.s., no. 247 (January–February 1992): 26. Though there is much force to Bobbio's point, Gentile certainly had not disappeared altogether, thanks partly to the continuing interest of earlier followers like Ugo Spirito, who had turned from Gentilian fascism to communism, and to the continuing efforts of Gentile's publishing house, G.C. Sansoni in Florence. It is striking that on its cover *Giornale critico della filosofia italiana*, one of the most distinguished journals of its kind in Europe, continued (and continues) to indicate Gentile as its founder. Gentile had started the journal in 1920.

9 See, for example, Pietro Rossi, 'Max Weber and Benedetto Croce,' in *Max Weber and His Contemporaries*, ed. Wolfgang J. Mommsen and Jürgen Osterhammel (London: Allen & Unwin, 1987), 447–67. On Hughes's debt to Rossi, see H. Stuart Hughes, *Consciousness and Society: The Reorientation of European Social Thought, 1890–1930* (New York: Random House [Vintage], 1958), 432–3. Although sympathetic to Croce up to a point, Hughes's account was deeply inadequate as an account of Crocean historicism. See chapter 4 here, p. 101.

10 Fulvio Tessitore, *Dimensioni dello storicismo* (Naples: Morano, 1971), 74–82, 87–95, 105–11. See also Fulvio Tessitore, 'Brevissime note su Croce e lo storicismo,' in *Benedetto Croce trent'anni dopo*, ed. Antonino Bruno (Rome: Laterza, 1983), 261–4.

11 See especially Raffaello Franchini, *Esperienza dello storicismo* (Naples: Giannini, 1953), 20–8, which specifies clearly the inadequacies that had produced the crisis of German historicism – and insists explicitly that Croce offered the solution. See also 39–58, 166–7; and Raffaello Franchini, *Metafisica e storia* (Naples: Giannini, 1958), 51–2, 59, 64–5, 69, 70, 281–3, for further indications of the German–Italian relationship.

12 Hans-Georg Gadamer, 'Replik,' in Karl-Otto Apel et al., *Hermaneutik und Ideologiekritik* (Frankfurt: Suhrkamp, 1971), 299. Although he made the

argument repeatedly, Croce offered his classic statement about relativism in 1915 in his 'Contributo alla critica di me stesso,' now in his *Etica e politica* (Bari: Laterza [Edizione economica], 1967), 350.

13 Hannah Arendt, *The Origins of Totalitarianism* (Cleveland: World [Meridian], 1958), 478. A leading authority on Arendt, Margaret Canovan, has argued persuasively that totalitarianism was central to the whole of Arendt's political thought, the centre of gravity of which is unfathomable otherwise. Indeed, Canovan shows that the eruption of totalitarianism persuaded Arendt that our traditional categories had been inadequate for understanding the nature and meaning of politics in general. See Margaret Canovan, *Hannah Arendt: A Reinterpretation of Her Political Thought* (Cambridge: Cambridge University Press, 1992), 86–7, 102–3.

14 To be sure, Arendt was departing, just like Croce, from traditional conceptions of philosophy as foundational and potentially coercive, but she still ended up with a different sense of the possibilities, including the respective roles of philosophy, thinking, action, and history. For one bit of testimony, see Hannah Arendt, 'On Hannah Arendt,' in *Hannah Arendt: The Recovery of the Public World*, ed. Melvyn A. Hill (New York: St Martin's, 1979), 303–6. See also Canovan, *Hannah Arendt*, 268–9.

15 David D. Roberts, *Benedetto Croce and the Uses of Historicism* (Berkeley: University of California Press, 1987), 189–98.

16 See especially Jeffrey C. Isaac, *Arendt, Camus, and Modern Rebellion* (New Haven: Yale University Press, 1992).

17 I think especially of the pioneering work by Jeffrey C. Goldfarb, *Beyond Glasnost: The Post-Totalitarian Mind* (Chicago: University of Chicago Press, 1991), e.g., 16–17, 25–6, 129–31.

18 Milan Kundera, *The Book of Laughter and Forgetting*, trans. Aaron Asher (New York: HarperCollins Perennial Classics, 1999), 120.

19 Milan Kundera, *The Unbearable Lightness of Being*, trans. Michael Henry Heim (New York: HarperCollins [Perennial], 1991), 218.

Chapter 2

1 Raffaello Franchini, *Intervista su Croce*, ed. Arturo Fratta (Naples: Società Editrice Napoletana, 1978), 5. Franchini found greater reason for optimism when he briefly surveyed the situation again near the end of his life, at a time when interest in the Crocean legacy seemed to be reviving. See especially his 'Premessa,' 5; and 'Il significato della filosofia di Croce,'

28–9, in Raffaello Franchini, Giancarlo Lunati, and Fulvio Tessitore, *Il ritorno di Croce nella cultura italiana* (Milan: Rusconi, 1990).

2 Giuseppe Antonio Borgese, *Goliath: The March of Fascism* (New York: Viking, 1937), 295–96.

3 On Croce's impact in the United States, see David D. Roberts, 'La fortuna di Croce e Gentile negli Stati Uniti,' in 'Croce e Gentile un secolo dopo,' special issue, *Giornale critico della filosofia italiana*, 73, nos. 2–3 (May–December 1994): 253–81. A slightly revised and expanded version of the Croce portion of this essay was published as 'Croce in America: Influence, Misunderstanding, Neglect,' *Humanitas* 8, no. 2 (1995): 3–34. [See chapter 4 in the present volume.]

4 René Wellek, the distinguished historian of criticism, noted that in movements influential since Croce's death – from Russian formalism and structuralism to hermeneutics and deconstruction – Croce 'is not referred to or quoted, even when he discusses the same problems and gives similar solutions.' And for Wellek this was anomalous in the extreme, for Croce had been arguably the most erudite and wide-ranging figure in the history of criticism. René Wellek, *History of Modern Criticism* (New Haven: Yale University Press), 8:187, 189. See also 6:63.

5 Richard Rorty, *Contingency, Irony, and Solidarity* (Cambridge: Cambridge University Press, 1989), 108.

6 Franchini, *Intervista su Croce*, 13, 31.

7 Ibid., 138.

8 From *Corriere della Sera*, 2 November 1985; as quoted in Domenico Settembrini, *Storia dell'idea antiborghese in Italia* (Rome: Laterza, 1991), 459–60.

9 Franchini, *Intervista su Croce*, 129. Among the examples are 'Croce e Gentile un secolo dopo'; Jader Jacobelli, *Croce Gentile: Dal Sodalizio al dramma* (Milan: Rizzoli, 1989); and Michele Ciliberto, ed., *Croce e Gentile fra tradizione nazionale e filosofia europea* (Rome: Riuniti, 1993).

10 E.J. Hobsbawm, 'The Great Gramsci,' *New York Review of Books*, 4 April 1974, 39.

11 Massimo Mastrogregori, *Il genio dello storico: Le considerazioni sulla storia di Marc Bloch e Lucien Febvre e la tradizione metodologica francese* (Naples: Edizioni Scientifiche Italiane, 1988).

12 Franchini, *Intervista su Croce*, 129.

13 Michele Ciliberto, in his introduction to *Croce e Gentile*, x.

14 Franchini, *Intervista su Croce*, 11. See also 16, 57, 110–11, on the autonomy and indeterminacy of action, which responds not to metaphysical abstractions but to particular, historically determined problems.

15 Ibid., 107.

16 For indications of the interface of history as thought and action with *polit-*

ica and *etica,* see ibid., especially 106, 110–11. For Franchini's more systematic discussion, which provides some of the best gloss on Croce's conception that we have had, see his *Esperienza dello storicismo* (Naples: Giannini, 1953), and *La teoria della storia di Benedetto Croce,* 3rd ed., ed. Renata Viti Cavaliere (1966; Naples: Edizioni Scientifiche Italiane, 1995).

17 Franchini, *Intervista su Croce,* 14, 57, 110. See also Raffaello Franchini, 'Croce interprete di Hegel,' in his *Croce interprete di Hegel e altri saggi filosofici,* 3rd ed. (Naples: Giannini, 1974), 3–51 (1963).

18 I have in mind Carlo Ginzburg, Hayden White, and Giuseppe Mazzotta, each of whom invokes Croce primarily as a negative foil. But I also include the conservative thinker Claes Ryn, who uses Croce sympathetically but to my mind a bit misleadingly. By playing up the place of universals in Croce's thought, Ryn makes Croce's strategy less radical, and safer, than Franchini does. Thus Ryn inadvertently reinforces the tendency to dismiss Croce altogether in circles less conservative than his own. See my 'Characterizing Historicist Possibilities: A Reply to Claes Ryn,' in *Humanitas* 13, no. 1 (2000): 68–88; and Ryn's reply in the same issue, 89–102.

19 Renata Viti Cavaliere, 'Il liberalismo nella filosofia politica di Hannah Arendt,' in *Critica della ragione liberale,* ed. Ernesto Paolozzi (Naples: Alfredo Guida, 2000), 63–91.

20 I think especially of the pioneering work by Jeffrey C. Goldfarb, *Beyond Glasnost: The Post-Totalitarian Mind* (Chicago: University of Chicago Press, 1991), e.g., 16–17, 25–6, 129–31.

21 Hannah Arendt, *The Origins of Totalitarianism* (Cleveland: World [Meridian], 1958), 478. A leading authority on Arendt, Margaret Canovan, has argued persuasively that totalitarianism was central to the whole of Arendt's political thought, the centre of gravity of which is unfathomable otherwise. Indeed, Canovan shows that the eruption of totalitarianism persuaded Arendt that our traditional categories had been inadequate for understanding the nature and meaning of politics in general. See Margaret Canovan, *Hannah Arendt: A Reinterpretation of Her Political Thought* (Cambridge: Cambridge University Press, 1992), 86–7, 102–3.

22 See Arendt, *The Origins of Totalitarianism,* 256–60, 308–9, 325, on Mussolini's regime, and 458, 462–6, 470, on the centrality of 'ideologies of motion,' which posit a mode of human fulfillment through change over time.

It is increasingly recognized, in Italy and abroad, that Gentile was a symptomatic figure who is thus potentially highly instructive. In his penetrating survey of the uses of the concept of totalitarianism, the Soviet specialist Abbott Gleason found Gentile's conception of the totalitarian state 'extraordinary' and 'prophetic' while concluding that 'Gentile deserves to be called the first philosopher of totalitarianism.' See Abbott Gleason, *Totalitarianism: The Inner History of the Cold War* (New York: Oxford University Press, 1995), 19. On p. 9 Gleason notes that 'the philosopher Giovanni Gentile, operating in the highly abstract vocabulary of conservative Hegelianism, produced a brilliant and premonitory justification of the totalitarian state that seems amazingly like Hannah Arendt's and George Orwell's demonic visions of the later 1940s, only with the value signs inverted.' See also 94–5, where the basis for the link to Orwell is clearer: Gentile's totalitarianism was to be internalized and willed by all.

In Italy, scholars from Augusto Del Noce, in a seminal essay of 1968, to Emilio Gentile (no relation), in several more recent works, have posited a place for Gentile that would seem to demand the attention of anyone seeking to understand the wider totalitarian direction of the era. For Emilio Gentile, Gentile was 'the chief theologian' as fascist Italy pursued a radically new, overtly totalitarian 'sacralization of politics.' Emilio Gentile, *The Sacralization of Politics in Fascist Italy* (Cambridge: Harvard University Press, 1996), 58. See also Augusto Del Noce, *Giovanni Gentile: Per una interpretazione filosofica della storia contemporanea* (Bologna: Il Mulino, 1990), 123–94; and Emilio Gentile, *Il mito dello stato nuovo dall'antigiolittismo al fascismo* (Rome: Laterza, 1982), 231–61. Still, the sources, implications, and significance of Gentile's totalitarian vision remain hard to pin down. Even Gabriele Turi, in his comprehensive and fair-minded biography, falls into unconvincing commonplaces when confronting the ideas that Gentile brought to fascism – as, for example, when he suggests that Gentile offered 'a static and authoritarian vision of society.' See Gabriele Turi, *Giovanni Gentile: Una biografia* (Florence: Giunti, 1995), 244–5. Indeed, there remains much point to Norberto Bobbio's comment of 1974 that even in Italy, Gentile's philosophy seems not only dead, but literally incomprehensible. Yet Bobbio also noted that not so long before, intelligent, idealistic young Italians had found Gentile's thinking exciting and inspiring. Bobbio's characterization is cited, and endorsed, in Maurizio Ferraris, 'Il Gentile di Garin,' *Aut Aut*, n.s., no. 247 (January–February 1992): 26.

23 Though fundamental in certain respects, even Croce's noted essay 'Antistoricismo,' originally a lecture at the seventh international congress of philosophy, held at Oxford in 1930, is disappointing in its diagnoses. See Benedetto Croce, *Ultimi saggi* (Bari: Laterza, 1963), 251–64. Near the end of his life, Croce confessed that he hated fascism too much to write its history; see Benedetto Croce, *Terze pagine sparse*, 2 vols. (Bari: Laterza, 1955), 1:115–16. The problem was that, in his own terms, he was thereby

pulling back from any possibility of understanding fascism and the wider political universe from which it had emerged.

24 Giovanni Gentile, *Saggi critici*, 2nd ser. (Florence: Vallecchi, 1927), 28–9.

25 Gennaro Sasso, *Filosofia e idealismo*, vol. 2, *Giovanni Gentile* (Naples: Bibliopolis, 1995), 383–97, especially 393–4.

26 This is not to suggest that encounter could have yielded some sort of synthesis; their respective cultural orientations were radically disparate. But Croce and Heidegger were each seeking to respond to the several cultural tendencies at work with the advent of a modern, secular culture, and the thinking of each could have been sharpened by engagement with the other. By treating Crocean absolute historicism as a paired opposite with Nietzsche, Heidegger could more fully have characterized what, for him, was the contemporary 'nihilism' requiring an antidote – to be found, he concluded, through a kind of disengagement from the actual. Heidegger tended to conflate the despised reign of technology with historicism, as for example, when he insisted in 1946 that 'historicism has today not only not been overcome, but is only now entering the stage of its expansion and entrenchment. The technical organization of communications throughout the world by radio and by a press already limping after it is the genuine form of historicism's dominion.' See Martin Heidegger, *Early Greek Thinking: The Dawn of Western Philosophy* (San Francisco: Harper & Row, 1984), 17. For an approach to Heidegger in light of Croce, see David D. Roberts, *Nothing but History: Reconstruction and Extremity after Metaphysics* (Berkeley: University of California Press, 1995), especially 135–52.

Croce, of course, mentioned Heidegger a few times but tended simply to conflate him with Gentile. Coming a few years later, Franchini was better able to put Heidegger in perspective, even as Heidegger's thinking continued to develop. Franchini noted that Heidegger seemed to be seeking a mode of life emptied of content, of concrete living, yet somehow thereby opening to something ecstatic and mystical. See especially Franchini's 1955 essay on Heidegger in his *Metafisica e storia* (Naples: Giannini, 1958), 15–47, but note also the discussion of Heidegger on pp. 63–4, 68–9.

27 Daniela Coli has accented Croce's sense, by about 1914, that he had gone well beyond what his German contemporaries were doing. See Daniela Coli, *Croce, Laterza e la cultura europea* (Bologna: Il Mulino, 1983), 61–100, on Croce's relationship with German culture, and especially 77–80, 85–6.

28 Franz Neumann, *Behemoth: The Structure and Practice of National Socialism, 1933–1944*, 2nd ed. (1944; New York: Harper & Row, 1966), 75–8; Herbert Marcuse, *Reason and Revolution: Hegel and the Rise of Social Theory* (1941;

Boston: Beacon, 19601), especially 402–9, on 'Fascist "Hegelianism,"' for his critique of Gentile.

29 Marcuse, *Reason and Revolution,* 411–12.

30 Benedetto Croce, *Discorsi di varia filosofia,* 2 vols. (Bari: Laterza, 1959), 2:15–17 (1945).

31 An influential diagnosis was Karl Heussi's *Die Krisis des Historismus* (Tübingen: Mohr, 1932). For Croce's review, see *Conversazioni critiche,* 5th ser., 2nd ed., rev. (Bari: Laterza, 1951), 169–72. On p. 172, Croce remarks explicitly that all this had been confronted earlier in Italy, from about 1900, and that the process had been in a sense completed by 1915. Indeed, Croce suggested gently, the Italians had dealt with the crisis more systematically and effectively than had the Germans – and Heussi's book offered at least a suggestion to that effect.

32 As Franchini explained in *Esperienza dello storicismo,* 34–5, Croce sought to defend himself from accusations of 'historicism' (*istorismo*) prior to World War I because he understood it as positivistic and objectivist, as expressed, for example, in the famous Ranke imperative to get at the past *wie es eigentlich gewesen* – as it actually happened.

33 Benedetto Croce, *La storia come pensiero e come azione* (Bari: Laterza [Edizione economica], 1966), 72. See 72n3 for comparable criticism of Meinecke and the entire section 'Lo storicismo e la sua storia' (53–72), which addresses the confusions surrounding the term. In addition, see Croce's appendix to Friedrich Meinecke, *Senso storico e significato della storia* (Naples: Edizioni Scientifiche Italiane, 1948), 115–16. This is a translation of Meinecke's *Vom geschichtlichen Sinn und vom Sinn der Geschichte* (1939).

34 On the contrast, see Franchini, *Esperienza dello storicismo,* 18–28, 44, 166–8; and especially *Metafisica e storia,* 235–42. This latter is a critique of Pietro Rossi's *Lo storicismo tedesco contemporaneo* (Turin: Einaudi, 1956), which Franchini found inadequate on Troeltsch and Meinecke, confused on the place of Weber, and thus, not surprisingly, misleading on contemporary cultural options. Rossi made his preference for the German variety of historicism most explicit in *Storia e storicismo nella filosofia contemporanea* (Milan: Lerici, 1960), 285–330; see especially 303–5, 309–11, 314.

35 In addition to the above, see Pietro Rossi, 'Max Weber and Benedetto Croce,' in *Max Weber and His Contemporaries,* ed. Wolfgang J. Mommsen and Jürgen Osterhammel (London: Allen & Unwin, 1987), 447–67. It is worth noting that the American H. Stuart Hughes recognized a major debt to Rossi in *Consciousness and Society: The Reorientation of European Social Thought, 1890–1930* (New York: Random House [Vintage], 1958), 432–3. In the English-speaking world, this was the most influential work of

modern European intellectual history for a generation and more – and though sympathetic to him up to a point, it was deeply inadequate as an account of Croce. See Roberts, 'La fortuna di Croce e Gentile,' 271.

36 Fulvio Tessitore, *Dimensioni dello storicismo* (Naples: Morano, 1971), 74–82, 87–95, 105–11. See also Fulvio Tessitore, 'Brevissime note su Croce e lo storicismo,' in *Benedetto Croce trent'anni dopo*, ed. Antonino Bruno (Rome: Laterza, 1983), 261–4.

37 See especially Franchini, *Esperienza dello storicismo*, 20–8, which specifies clearly the inadequacies that had produced the crisis of German historicism – and insists explicitly that Croce offered the solution. See also 39–58, 166–7; and Franchini, *Metafisica e storia*, 51–2, 59, 64–6, 69, 70, 281–3, for further indications of the German–Italian relationship.

38 Although later Germans interested in the earlier historicism, such as Herbert Schnädelbach, Reinhart Koselleck, and Jörn Rüsen, have made significant contributions to the ongoing discussion of these issues, they do little or nothing with the earlier Italian tradition – especially because the transnational connection was not made at the pivotal moment.

39 Hans-Georg Gadamer, 'Replik,' in *Hermaneutik und Ideologiekritik*, ed. Karl-Otto Apel et al. (Frankfurt: Suhrkamp, 1971), 299. Although he made the argument repeatedly, Croce offered his classic statement about relativism in 1915 in his 'Contributo alla critica di me stesso,' now in his *Etica e politica* (Bari: Laterza [Edizione economica], 1967), 350.

40 There are no bannisters, as Margaret Canovan puts it (Canovan, *Hannah Arendt*, 173–4, 184–5); there is no 'heavenly searchlight,' as Croce put it in 1945, responding to Guido De Ruggiero's suggestion that Croce's conception had proven too empty, in light of fascism and the wider crisis of the era. See Benedetto Croce, *Nuove pagine sparse*, 2 vols. (Bari: Laterza, 1966), 1:155–56. In addition, see Roberts, *Benedetto Croce*, 141–5.

41 Hannah Arendt, 'What Is Freedom?' in *Between Past and Future: Eight Exercises in Political Thought* (New York: Viking, 1968), 151; Hannah Arendt, 'Freedom and Politics,' in *Freedom and Serfdom: An Anthology of Western Thought*, ed. Albert Hunold (Dordrecht: Reidel, 1961), 198; Canovan, *Hannah Arendt*, 178, 213.

42 For Arendt, 'Marxism could be developed into a totalitarian ideology because of its perversion, or misunderstanding of political action as the making of history.' Hannah Arendt, 'The Ex-Communists,' *Commonweal* 57, no. 24 (20 March 1953): 597. See also Canovan, *Hannah Arendt*, 71, 164–5. Especially as mediated by sympathetic commentators like Canovan, Arendt's sense of action and history led toward prejudicial conflations. On p. 165, Canovan notes that for Arendt, 'the notion of *making* history,

taking one's future in one's hands and shaping it, always entails violence. Fabrication is a violent business.' Or, on p. 166: Arendt sought 'to present a version of humanist republicanism *without* the model of fabrication, without means-ends thinking, without the sanctification of violence.' See also Canovan, *Hannah Arendt*, 76–7, for the same tendency toward conflation.

43 To be sure, Arendt was departing, just like Croce, from traditional conceptions of philosophy as foundational and potentially coercive, but she still ended up with a different sense of the possibilities, including the respective roles, and relationships among, philosophy, thinking, action, and history. For one bit of testimony, see Hannah Arendt, 'On Hannah Arendt,' in *Hannah Arendt: The Recovery of the Public World*, ed. Melvyn A. Hill (New York: St Martin's, 1979), 303–6. See also Canovan, *Hannah Arendt*, 268–9.

44 Here I follow especially Canovan's characterizations, which usefully distill Arendt's accents. See especially Canovan, *Hannah Arendt*, 142, 154, 250–2. Note also the interface between individual agency and history in Hannah Arendt, *The Human Condition* (Chicago: University of Chicago Press, 1958), 181–8.

45 See especially Croce, *Ultimi saggi*, 263–4 (1930).

46 Adapting a theme from Harold Bloom, the contemporary American neopragmatist Richard Rorty has recently explored this sense of risk and its implications. As contemporary agents, we will be redescribed in contingent ways by those who come after us. On the basis of their particular agendas, they will perform their own 'thus I willed it' on the meaning of what we do – just as we are doing to the actions of our predecessors. See Rorty, *Contingency*, 41. Our dependence 'on the kindness of all those strangers out there in the future' affects our sense of our own relationship with history, and in my view Rorty's concerns led him to a prejudicially extreme position, including a measure of resentment toward history itself and concomitant strategies for one-upping it. I have suggested elsewhere some ways of understanding the sources of such impulses and their interplay with the more constructive relationship with history that Croce delineated. See Roberts, *Nothing but History*, chap. 9, for my reading of Rorty, and pp. 242–3 for the point at issue here. Some of the same line of thinking is to be found in my *Una nuova interpretazione del pensiero di Croce: Lo storicismo crociano e il pensiero contemporaneo* (Pisa: Istituti Editoriali e Poligrafici Internazionali, 1995), 46–51, 83–4, 106.

47 Roberts, *Benedetto Croce*, 189–98.

48 See especially Jeffrey C. Isaac, *Arendt, Camus, and Modern Rebellion* (New Haven: Yale University Press, 1992).

49 Franchini, *Metafisica e storia*, 51–2.

Chapter 3

1 Robert Wohl, *The Generation of 1914* (Cambridge: Harvard University Press, 1979), chap. 6. For a gloomy assessment of Croce's eclipse since the war by a distinguished disciple, see Raffaello Franchini, *Intervista su Croce,* ed. Arturo Fratta (Naples: Società editrice napoletana, 1978).

2 Ranuccio Bianchi Bandinelli, *Dal diario di un borghese e altri saggi,* 2nd ed. (Milan: Il Saggiatore, 1962), 61, 79–80, 242.

3 Guido De Ruggiero, *Il ritorno alla ragione* (Bari: Laterza, 1946), 13–16.

4 David D. Roberts, 'Benedetto Croce and the Dilemmas of Liberal Restoration,' *Review of Politics* 44, no. 2 (April 1982): 214–41. Most of the substance of this article found its way into chap. 5, 'Historicist Politics,' of my *Benedetto Croce and the Uses of Historicism* (Berkeley: University of California Press, 1987).

5 Elio Vittorini, 'Una nuova cultura,' *Il politecnico,* 29 Sept. 1945, 1; Nicola Chiaromonte, 'Pangloss redivivo,' in *Benedetto Croce,* ed. Giuseppe A. Borgese et al. (Boston: Edizioni 'Controcorrente,' 1946), 48; De Ruggiero, *Il ritorno alla ragione,* 3–41. Edmund Jacobitti echoes many of the standard criticisms in his *Revolutionary Humanism and Historicism in Modern Italy* (New Haven: Yale University Press, 1981); see especially 151–5.

6 For examples from Croce's later years, see *Discorsi di varia filosofia* (Bari: Laterza, 1959), 1:125–8; *Il carattere della filosofia moderna* (Bari: Laterza, 1963), 21–2, 100–3; and *Scritti e discorsi politici (1943–1947)* (Bari: Laterza, 1973), 2:203–5. See also Croce's responses to De Ruggiero in *Nuove pagine sparse* (Bari: Laterza, 1966), 1:151–9; *Scritti e discorsi politici,* 2:169–72; and 'Agli amici che cercano il "trascendente,"' an appendix to *Etica e politica* (Bari: Laterza, 1967), 378–84.

7 Benedetto Croce, *Cultura e vita morale* (Bari: Laterza, 1955), 250.

8 Croce, *Etica e politica,* 191; Croce, *Nuove pagine sparse,* 1:358; Benedetto Croce, *History of Europe in the Nineteenth Century,* trans. Henry Furst (1932; New York: Harcourt, Brace & World, 1963), 362.

9 See Croce, *Scritti e discorsi politici,* 2:422–3, for an indication of his hostility to the ideology concept.

10 See especially Enzo Paci, *Esistenzialismo e storicismo* (Milan: Arnoldo Mondadori, 1950), 28–9, 135–9, 210–41, 268–9, 296–9. It is not possible here to consider Croce's new concern with 'vitality' in the 1940s, a concern that owed something, at least, to the existentialist challenge. See Antonino Bruno, *La crisi dell'idealismo nell'ultimo Croce* (Bari: Laterza, 1964), on this aspect of the late Croce.

11 Nicola Abbagnano, *Critical Existentialism,* trans. Nino Langiulli (Garden

City, NY: Doubleday [Anchor], 1969), 1–18. See also Antonio Santucci, *Esistenzialismo e filosofia italiana* (Bologna: Il Mulino, 1959), 160–227.

12 Mario Sansone, 'La cultura,' in *Dieci anni dopo: Saggi sulla vita democratica italiana*, Achille Battaglia et al. (Bari: Laterza, 1955), 530–1.

13 Croce, *Discorsi di varia filosofia*, 1:127–8.

14 Benedetto Croce, *Indagini su Hegel e schiarimenti filosofici* (Bari: Laterza, 1967), 168; Croce, *Scritti e discorsi politici*, 2:207.

15 Croce, *Discorsi di varia filosofia*, 2:269–70; Benedetto Croce, *History as the Story of Liberty*, trans. Sylvia Sprigge (New York: Norton, 1941), 187–8, 293. See also Raffaello Franchini, *La teoria della storia di Benedetto Croce* (Naples: Morano, 1966), 143, 163–6. [This last, a fundamental work by Franchini, is available in a third edition, edited by Renata Viti Cavaliere (Naples: Edizioni Scientifiche Italiane, 1995).]

16 Croce, *Etica e politica*, 225–34, especially 232–3. See also Giuseppe Galasso, *Croce, Gramsci e altri storici* (Milan: Il saggiatore di Alberto Mondadori, 1969), 31–47, 66–7, on the rupture in Croce's historiographical thinking.

17 Croce, *History as the Story of Liberty*, 161–2.

18 See, for example Eugenio Garin, *Intellettuali italiani del XX secolo* (Rome: Riuniti, 1974), 60–5, on the excesses of political commitment that can be seen in Croce's histories, if they are viewed from a rigorously historicist point of view.

19 Croce offers a start in *History as the Story of Liberty*, 179, 182.

20 Benedetto Croce, *Terze pagine sparse* (Bari: Laterza, 1955), 1:115–16.

21 For Croce's 'parenthesis' argument, see especially *Scritti e discorsi politici*, 1:7–16; and 2:156–7, 174, 361. See also Luigi Russo, *Il dialogo dei popoli*, 2nd ed. (Florence: Parenti, 1955), 347 (1953), for evidence of frustration with Croce's interpretation; and Denis Mack Smith, 'Croce and Fascism,' *Cambridge Journal* 2 (March 1949): 343–56, for a scathing indictment from abroad.

22 Sandro Setta, *Croce, il liberalismo e l'Italia post-fascista* (Rome: Bonacci, 1979), 103–14; Vittorini, 'Una nuova cultura,' 1.

23 Alberto Asor Rosa, *La cultura* (*Storia d'Italia*, 4, *Dall'unità a oggi*, 2) (Turin: Einaudi, 1975), 1535.

24 In the lecture of 1950, cited above, Croce admitted that a genuine history of fascism would have more room for the positive; see *Terze pagine sparse*, 1:115–16. See also Nino Valeri, *Da Giolitti a Mussolini: Momenti della crisi del liberalismo* (Milan: Il Saggiatore, 1967), 225–6; and Croce, *History as the Story of Liberty*, 200, on this issue.

25 Russo, *Il dialogo dei popoli*, 301.

26 Ibid., 282–361. For some further observations about Croce's rigidity, see

Guido Calogero, *Difesa del liberalsocialismo e altri saggi*, new ed. (Milan: Marzorati, 1972), 40; and Calogero's remarks in *Benedetto Croce: A Commemoration*, Gilbert Murray et al. (London: Istituto italiano di cultura, 1953), 13, 35–6. On the other hand, for observations about the superficiality of the encounter of younger intellectuals with Croce after World War II, see Eugenio Garin, 'Quindici anni dopo,' in *Cronache di filosofia italiana, 1900/1943* (Bari: Laterza [ed. Universale], 1975), 2:537; and Vittorio Enzo Alfieri, 'Croce e i giovani,' *Rivista di studi crociani* 1 (January–March 1964): 58–9, 71.

Chapter 4

1 Giuseppe Antonio Borgese, *Goliath: The March of Fascism* (New York: Viking, 1937), 295–96.

2 Near the end of Croce's life, Gian N.G. Orsini, a Crocean who would become a distinguished professor of Italian literature at the University of Wisconsin, noted with some exasperation the failure of American intellectuals to engage Croce, who, Orsini argued, had anticipated by decades several of the apparently most innovative currents in American intellectual life. See [Gian] Napoleone [G.] Orsini, 'Note sul Croce e la cultura americana,' in *Benedetto Croce*, ed. Francesco Flora (Milan: Malfasi, 1953), 359–66. Although it suffers from important omissions, Ernesto G. Caserta's *Studi crociani negli stati uniti: Bibliografia critica (1964–1984)* (Napoli: Loffredo, 1988), provides a useful critical assessment of much recent work on Croce.

3 René Wellek, *History of Modern Criticism* (New Haven: Yale University Press, 1992), 8:187, 189. See also 6:63.

4 The most significant exception was Patrick Romanell (born Pasquale Romanelli), who followed his 1937 Columbia dissertation on Gentile with a number of books and articles, some focused on Croce, some comparative. See also Merle S. Brown, *Neo-Idealist Aesthetics: Croce-Gentile-Collingwood* (Detroit: Wayne State University Press, 1966). The best studies of Gentile published in the United States were by accomplished philosophers who were comfortable with the idealist tradition; each understood that Gentile was a rigorous idealist in a way that Croce ultimately was not. See Roger W. Holmes, *The Idealism of Giovanni Gentile* (New York: Macmillan, 1937), and H.S. Harris, *The Social Philosophy of Giovanni Gentile* (Urbana: University of Illinois Press, 1960).

5 Although comparison with the British case is illuminating, the ready

exchange of ideas between Britain and the United States blurs the contrast somewhat. Not only were English translations of Croce by the Britons Douglas Ainslie and R.G. Collingwood widely available in the United States, but so was the important early study by Herbert Wildon Carr, *The Philosophy of Benedetto Croce: The Problem of Art and History* (London: Macmillan, 1917). In Carr's book, Americans at least had access to an informed and sympathetic account of Croce's thought up to that point. However, another widely available work from Britain, Angelo Crespi's *Contemporary Thought of Italy* (New York: Knopf, 1926), was hostile to both Croce and Gentile. A lecturer at the University of London, Crespi produced the book for the 'Library of Contemporary Thought,' published first in Britain. Writing from a Christian perspective, he took a critical view of Italian neo-idealism, with its effort to purge all transcendence, and found it deeply implicated in present problems, including nationalism and fascism. See especially 246–9.

6 See, for example, *My Philosophy and Other Essays on the Moral and Political Problems of Our Time* (London: Allen & Unwin, 1949), 19.

7 Benedetto Croce, *Discorsi di varia filosofia*, 2 vols. (Bari: Laterza, 1959), 2:15–17 (1945).

8 Frederic S. Simoni, 'Benedetto Croce: A Case of International Misunderstanding,' *Journal of Aesthetics and Art Criticism* 11 (September 1952): 7–14. The quoted passage is from p. 9. Simoni found especially damaging an early review of Croce's *Estetica* by George Santayana, to be discussed later. Simoni's essay was promptly published in translation in Francesco Flora, ed., *Benedetto Croce*, an important anthology on Croce's thought and influence; 345–57.

9 Ransom to Tate, 25 June 1927, in *Selected Letters of John Crowe Ransom*, ed. Thomas Daniel Young and George Core (Baton Rouge: Louisiana State University Press, 1985), 175.

10 Seeking to explain why Croce did not receive the recognition he deserved in the United States, Italo De Feo noted that Croce declined several opportunities to come to the United States, though he travelled frequently in Europe. See Italo De Feo, *Croce: l'uomo e l'opera* (Milan: Mondadori, 1975), 636–42. De Feo also noted that the Italian language was an obstacle, and certainly it is true that American scholars were less likely to read Italian than French or German. Still, major early students of Croce like Joel Spingarn and Irving Babbitt did read Italian.

11 See Gian N.G. Orsini, *Benedetto Croce: Philosopher of Art and Literary Critic* (Carbondale: Southern Illinois University Press, 1961), 49–50, 304–6, 320n2, on the English translations of Croce. Perhaps the most praisewor-

thy are Arthur Livingston's translation of a selection from Croce's *Frammenti di etica*, published as *The Conduct of Life*, and Frances Frenaye's rendering of Croce's *History of the Kingdom of Naples.* Moreover, what other thinker has found so illustrious a translator as R.G. Collingwood, who brought out English versions of Croce's *Autobiography* and *Philosophy of Giambattista Vico*?

12 Marshall Van Deusen, *J.E. Spingarn* (New York: Twayne, 1971), 19, citing a Spingarn letter of December 1899 to Croce. I have sought, without success, to locate Croce's letters to Spingarn. In correspondence, Professor Van Deusen told me that he possessed English translations, provided by Arthur Collins, but not the Italian originals. I would be grateful for further information. [Note my reference, in the introduction to this essay, to Emanuele Cutinelli-Rèndina's edition of the *Carteggio Croce-Spingarn* (2001).]

13 See 'Notes,' *Nation* 71 (15 November 1900): 386; and 75 (25 September 1902): 252–3.

14 G[eorge] Santayana, 'Croce's Aesthetics,' *Journal of Comparative Literature* 1 (1903): 191–5.

15 See especially two of the essays collected in Santayana's *Obiter Scripta: Lectures, Essays and Review* (New York: Scribner's, 1936), 30–4, 72–3. Santayana's longstanding hostility was important to Croce's fate in America. It was also a bit ironic, because Santayana lived in Rome for much of the 1930s and had the opportunity to probe Italian culture at close range.

16 The lecture was delivered at Columbia on 9 March 1910 and published as *The New Criticism* (New York: Columbia University Press, 1911). On Spingarn's use of Croce, see Van Deusen, *J.E. Spingarn,* which includes numerous references to Croce; and Wellek, *A History of Modern Criticism,* 6:61–3.

17 As Spingarn paraphrased Croce, 'Every poet re-expresses the universe in his own way, and every poem is a new and independent expression.' The question about any particular work of art was not how well it has conformed to some prior model or ideal, but what that work has sought to express and how completely it succeeded. See Spingarn, *The New Criticism,* 24.

18 *The Book of the Opening of the Rice Institute,* 3 vols. (Houston: [The Rice Institute, 1912]). See 2:430–517 for Croce's 'The Breviary of Aesthetic.' The same translation was then published in England under the title *The Essence of Aesthetic* (London: Heinemann, 1921). Subsequently the American scholar Patrick Romanell published a new translation under the title *Guide to Aesthetics* (South Bend, IN: Regnery Gateway, 1979), with a useful introduction.

19 Raffaello Piccoli, *Benedetto Croce: An Introduction to His Philosophy* (New York: Harcourt, Brace, 1922), iii–x.
20 Ibid., 303–4.
21 Spingarn collected many of these essays in his *Creative Criticism and Other Essays,* now available in an enlarged edition (Port Washington, NY: Kennikat, 1964). See 162–78 of this edition for his response to what was becoming the familiar set of objections to Croce.
22 Croce reviewed Dewey's *Art and Experience* in *La critica* in 1940; reprinted in *Discorsi di varia filosofia* 2:112–19. This review was then published in English translation as 'On the Aesthetics of Dewey,' *Journal of Aesthetics and Art Criticism* 6 (March 1948): 203–7, with a follow-up note by Dewey, 'A Comment on the Foregoing Criticisms,' 207–9. Croce responded in 'Dewey's Aesthetics and Theory of Knowledge,' *Journal of Aesthetics and Art Criticism* 11 (September 1952): 1–6, a piece collected in Croce's *Indagini su Hegel e schiarimenti filosofici* (Bari: Laterza, 1967).
23 Croce, 'Dewey's Aesthetics,' 1, 6.
24 De Feo, *Croce,* 636–9. Even before the Croce-Dewey exchange, William Savery suggested that Dewey's conception, emphasizing the individuality of things, amounted to a kind of historicism that might be 'allied to the romantic philosophies of Croce, Bergson, and Spengler.' See William Savery, 'The Significance of Dewey's Philosophy,' in *The Philosophy of John Dewey,* ed. Paul Arthur Schilpp (Evanston, IL: Northwestern University Press, 1939), 497–8.
25 See, for example, Croce, *Indagini su Hegel,* 290–302. Reviewing Max A. Fisch, ed., *Classic American Philosophers,* in 1951, Croce found pragmatism on the right track, but generally superseded in European philosophy by the early twentieth century.
26 John Dewey, *Art as Experience* (New York: Minton, Balch, 1934), 294–5.
27 Croce, 'Dewey's Aesthetics,' 5–6.
28 George H. Douglas, 'A Reconsideration of the Dewey-Croce Exchange,' *Journal of Aesthetics and Art Criticism* 28 (Summer 1970): 497–504. This brief article is among the best works on Croce in English; on pp. 501–2, Douglas is especially good on the Crocean notion of 'intuition,' which caused such problems for Croce's American commentators.
29 Thomas M. Alexander, *John Dewey's Theory of Art, Experience, and Nature: The Horizons of Feeling* (Albany: State University of New York Press), 1987), especially 1–13, 25–6, 281–2n25.
30 Croce is barely mentioned in, for example, the recent study by Robert B. Westbrook, *John Dewey and American Democracy* (Ithaca, NY: Cornell University Press, 1991). While completely neglecting Croce, Richard Rorty has

recently noted his own kinship with the Italian *pensiero debole* of Gianni Vattimo et al. See Rorty's introduction to *Essays on Heidegger and Others* (Cambridge: Cambridge University Press, 1991), 6.

31 De Feo, *Croce*, 641. See also 636–9 on Croce and America.

32 Gian N.G. Orsini, *Benedetto Croce: Philosopher of Art and Literary Critic* (Carbondale: Southern Illinois University Press, 1961). On the import of Orsini's work, see Dante Della Terza, 'Croce in America,' in his *Da Vienna a Baltimora: La diaspora degli intellettuali europei negli Stati Uniti d'America* (Rome: Riuniti, 1987), 197–205. See also Brown, *Neo-Idealist Aesthetics*; and Giovanni Gullace, introduction to his translation of Croce's *La poesia* (1936), *Benedetto Croce's Poetry and Literature: An Introduction to Its Criticism and History* (Carbondale: Southern Illinois University Press, 1981), xiii–lxxiv. Patrick Romanell contributed, among others works, an especially helpful introduction to Croce's *Guide to Aesthetics.*

33 William K. Wimsatt Jr and Cleanth Brooks, *Literary Criticism: A Short History* (1957; Chicago: University of Chicago Press, 1983), 2:499–521. See especially 500, 505, 512–14.

34 Ibid., 519.

35 Wellek, *History of Modern Criticism*, especially 6:61–6, 166; and 8:187–223. In addition, see René Wellek, *Four Critics: Croce, Valéry, Lukács, and Ingarden* (Seattle: University of Washington Press, 1981), 3–18, and the numerous references to Croce in *The Attack on Literature and Other Essays* (Chapel Hill: University of North Carolina Press, 1982).

36 John Paul Russo, 'Antihistoricism in Benedetto Croce and I.A. Richards,' in *Theoretical Issues in Literary Theory*, ed. David Perkins (Cambridge, MA: Harvard University Press, 1991), 268–99.

37 Irving Babbitt, 'Croce and the Philosophy of Flux,' originally in *Yale Review*, 1925, republished in *Spanish Character and Other Essays* (Boston: Houghton Mifflin, 1940), 66–72. The quote is from p. 66. Such charges were made repeatedly in Italy as well, perhaps most notably by Guido de Ruggiero during the 1940s. See especially his *Il ritorno alla ragione* (Bari: Laterza, 1946), 13–16. Babbitt had criticized Croce's conception of art as expression as early as 1910, but without addressing Croce's larger concerns. See Irving Babbitt, *The New Laokoon: An Essay on the Confusion of the Arts* (Boston: Houghton Mifflin, 1910), 222–8, 238. In a highly critical review essay on Spingarn's *Creative Criticism* in 1918, Babbitt condemned 'recent primitivists like Spingarn and his master, Benedetto Croce' and went on to link the Croce-Spingarn position to emotional indulgence unlimited by any standards of judgment. In fact, however, Croce was just as opposed to 'decadent aestheticism' but sought to head it off on a differ-

ent, more novel basis than Babbitt did – and in a way Babbitt failed to grasp. See Irving Babbitt, 'Genius and Taste,' from *Nation*, 7 February 1918, now in James Cloyd Bowman, ed., *Contemporary American Criticism* (New York: Holt, 1926), 95–108. See 96 and 104 for the passages quoted.

38 Babbitt, 'Croce and the Philosophy of Flux,' in *Spanish Character*, 68–70.

39 Ibid., 71–2.

40 Paul Elmer More, *The Demon of the Absolute* (*New Shelburne Essays*, in 3 vols.) (Princeton, NJ: Princeton University Press, 1928), 1:29–41.

41 Croce offered a critical review of Babbitt's *The New Laokoon* in *La critica* 23 (1925): 161–3. See also Claes G. Ryn, *Will, Imagination and Reason: Irving Babbitt and the Problem of Reality* (Chicago: Regnery, 1986), 48.

42 Spingarn, *Creative Criticism*, 194–7 (first pub. 1913–14).

43 Ryn, *Will*, especially 50–1. See also the comparative study by another recent student of Babbitt, Folke Leander, 'Irving Babbitt and Benedetto Croce,' in *Irving Babbitt in Our Time*, ed. George A. Panichas and Claes G. Ryn (Washington, DC: Catholic University of America Press, 1986), 75–102.

44 In a later article, Ryn referred to Croce as 'perhaps the greatest technical and systematic philosopher of our own century.' See Claes G. Ryn, 'Universality and History: The Concrete as Normative,' *Humanitas* 6 (Fall 1992–Winter 1993): 19. Ryn had in mind Croce's way of treating such categories as imagination, will, and reason.

45 Babbitt, 'Genius and Taste,' 108.

46 Ryn's work, including his use of Croce, has recently attracted the attention of an able Italian scholar, Germana Paraboschi. See her *Leo Strauss e la destra americana* (Rome: Riuniti, 1993), 102–23, and 'Etica ed estetica in Croce e Irving Babbitt: La sintesi di un conservatore americano,' *La cultura* 32, no. 2 (August 1994): 303–19.

47 Harcourt, Brace published Croce's *History: Its Theory and Practice*, which is Douglas Ainslie's translation of *Teoria e storia della storiografia*. James Harvey Robinson's *The New History* appeared in 1912.

48 See Ellen Nore, *Charles A. Beard: An Intellectual Biography* (Carbondale: Southern Illinois University Press, 1983), 156, 158–62, 165, on Beard's encounter with Croce's work during the 1920s. The extent of Croce's influence on Becker was the subject of controversy in the early 1970s. Hayden V. White, in 'Croce and Becker: A Note on the Evidence of Influence,' *History and Theory* 10, no. 2 (1971): 222–7, sharply criticized Chester McArthur Destler's 'The Crocean Origin of Becker's Historical Relativism,' *History and Theory* 9, no. 3 (1970): 335–42, for overstating the extent of Croce's direct influence on Becker. See also Burleigh Taylor Wilkins, *Carl*

Becker: A Biographical Study in American Intellectual History (Cambridge, MA: MIT Press, 1961), 193–4.

49 Carl Becker, 'History as the Intellectual Adventure of Mankind,' *New Republic* 30 (5 April 1922): 174–6.

50 Now in Carl L. Becker, *Everyman His Own Historian: Essays on History and Politics* (New York: Crofts, 1935), 233–55. See especially 239, 242–6.

51 Ibid., 248, 251–4.

52 Cushing Strout, *The Pragmatic Revolt in American History: Carl Becker and Charles Beard* (New Haven, CT: Yale University Press, 1958), 45–6, is particularly good on this point.

53 Charles A. Beard, 'Written History as an Act of Faith,' *American Historical Review* 39 (January 1934): 219–31, especially 220–1. Croce was also invited to attend the 1934 convention of the American Historical Association to explain his views at the plenary session on 'philosophy and history.' This time, in fact, the Carnegie Fund for International Peace seconded the invitation, but again Croce declined. However, he sent a paper, translated as 'The Study of History: Its Different Forms and Its Present Tasks,' which Crane Brinton read to the convention. The paper had been translated into English, at Croce's request, by Gian N.G. Orsini and was later published in Croce's *Il carattere della filosofia moderna* (Bari: Laterza, 1941), one of his most important works. See Henry E. Bourne's summary of both the circumstances and the paper itself in *American Historical Review* 40, no. 3 (April 1935): 427–8. See also Orsini, 'Note sul Croce e la cultura americana,' 363.

54 Nore, *Charles A. Beard*, 158–64, offers a discerning discussion of Beard's divergence from Croce, although she does not do justice to the more radical Crocean positions that troubled Beard. See note 62.

55 Wilkins, *Carl Becker*, 194–7.

56 It should also be noted that before encountering Croce, Beard had offered a famous economic interpretation of the forging of the U.S. Constitution, and he came to associate relativism with economic determinism. Although Beard understood that his own interest in economic interpretation was itself relative, and although Croce for a time had welcomed historical materialism as one canon of historical interpretation, Beard's interest in the scope for such economic interpretation was far from the spirit of Croce. See Strout, *The Pragmatic Revolt*, 50–55, for some aspects of this comparison.

57 R.L. Schuyler, 'Some Historical Idols,' *Political Science Quarterly* 47 (March 1932): 13–18. The quotation is from p. 15.

58 Nore, *Charles A. Beard*, 159.

59 (New York: Liveright, 1938). See especially 54–7, for the core of his case against Croce. Mandelbaum would remain a significant philosopher and historian of ideas until his death in 1987.
60 Now in Croce's *Nuove pagine sparse* (Bari: Laterza, 1966), 2:59–60. See also the balanced but ultimately critical review of Mandelbaum by Carl Becker in *Philosophical Review* 49 (April 1940): 361–4. Although he made the argument repeatedly, Croce offered his classic statement about relativism in 1915 in his 'Contributo alla critica di me stesso,' now in *Etica e politica* (Bari: Laterza, 1967), 350. Writing in 1971, Hans-Georg Gadamer made in much the same terms the argument that Croce had made in 1915. See Gadamer's 'Replik' in *Hermaneutik und Ideologiekritik*, ed. Karl-Otto Apel (Frankfurt: Suhrkamp, 1971), 299.
61 Strout, *The Pragmatic Revolt*, 44, 56.
62 In her solid *Charles A. Beard*, 159–61, Ellen Nore portrayed Beard as having borrowed selectively from Croce to avoid falling into the extravagance of Croce's alleged solipsism. The key for Beard was to maintain belief in a sphere of fact that exists, potentially knowable, independently of the observer. In a similar way, B.T. Wilkins played up the differences between Croce and Becker but did not do justice to Croce's understanding of the connection between historical knowing and practical life. See Wilkins, *Carl Becker*, 194–7.
63 (New York: Random House), especially 11–38, 42, 62, 81.
64 The Italian title of Antoni's book is *Dallo storicismo alla sociologia.* Hayden White, 'The Abiding Relevance of Croce's Idea of History,' *Journal of Modern History* 37 (June 1963): 109–24.
65 Hayden White, *Metahistory: The Historical Imagination in Nineteenth-Century Europe* (Baltimore: Johns Hopkins University Press, 1973), chap. 10. See especially 378–9, 397–400.
66 Ibid., 385.
67 Ibid., 394–402, 406–7, 415, 422–5.
68 Richard V. Burks, 'Benedetto Croce,' in *Some Historians of Modern Europe: Essays in Historiography*, ed. Bernadotte Schmitt (1942; Port Washington, NY: Kennikat, 1966), 66–99; A. Robert Caponigri, *History and Liberty: The Historical Writings of Benedetto Croce* (London: Routledge & Kegan Paul, 1955). Although it is based almost entirely on translations and secondary sources, Burks's essay makes good sense of Croce's understanding of the scope for generalization and philosophical clarification in a world of historical particulars.
69 Guido Calogero, 'Benedetto Croce: Philosopher and Humanist of Modern Italy,' *Atlantic* 202 (December 1958): 129–32.

70 Nore, *Charles A. Beard*, 192, notes that Charles and Mary Beard quoted Croce's anti-Marxism in arguing that Stalinism was the logical outcome of Marxism. Summing up Croce's achievement for a standard American reference work in 1947, Giuseppe Prezzolini included Croce's observations on Germany in enumerating what he found to be the unfortunately restricted handful of subjects for which Croce was known in the United States. See Giuseppe Prezzolini, 'Croce, Benedetto,' in *Columbia Dictionary of Modern European Literature*, ed. Horatio Smith (New York: Columbia University Press, 1947), 180–2. Croce's later essays on Germany were translated with an introduction by the novelist and popular essayist Vincent Sheean as *Germany and Europe: A Spiritual Dissension* (New York: Random House, 1944).

71 In his entry on Croce in the *Columbia Dictionary*, 181, Prezzolini noted the disparity between the Crocean and the American conceptions of freedom. Katharine Gilbert's 'The Vital Disequilibrium in Croce's Historicism,' in *Essays in Political Theory Presented to George H. Sabine*, ed. Milton R. Konvitz and Arthur E. Murphy (Ithaca, NY: Cornell University Press, 1948), gave some sense of Croce's position in his highly symptomatic exchange with Guido de Ruggiero during the mid-1940s over the bases of political action – and the sources of Europe's recent political disasters.

72 Chester McArthur Destler, 'Some Observations on Contemporary Historical Theory,' *American Historical Review* 55 (1950): 504, 517.

73 For a discerning account of the debates among Italian exiles in America during this period, see Dante Della Terza, 'L'immagine dell'Italia nella cultura americana, 1942–1952,' in his *Da Vienna a Baltimora*, 103–121, especially 108–12.

74 Borgese, *Goliath*, 23, 295–302. See 23, 297–8, and 299 for the passages quoted.

75 Gaetano Salvemini, *Scritti sul fascismo*, ed. Roberto Vivarelli (Milan: Feltrinelli, 1974), 3:440, 452. On Salvemini's influence during this period, see H. Stuart Hughes, *The Sea Change: The Migration of Social Thought, 1930–1965* (New York: McGraw-Hill, 1977), 82–100. See especially 87–9 on Salvemini's differences with Croce.

76 Published in 1945 as *Italian Democracy in the Making*, Salomone's book was republished in 1960 as *Italy in the Giolittian Era: Italian Democracy in the Making* (Philadelphia: University of Pennsylvania Press). See xiv, in Salvemini's introduction, for the passage quoted.

77 Giuseppe A. Borgese et al., *Benedetto Croce* (Boston: Edizioni 'Controcorrente,' 1946). Among the other contributors was Nicola Chiaromonte, who characterized Croce as 'Pangloss reborn.' See 48. Although such char-

acterizations were ill-considered, the aging Croce was ill-suited for the political role he found himself called upon to play after fascism, and some of his political choices were indeed ill-advised. See David D. Roberts, 'Benedetto Croce and the Dilemmas of Liberal Restoration,' *Review of Politics* 44, no. 2 (April 1982): 214–41.

78 N. Orsini, 'Benedetto Croce During the War Years,' *Italica* 23, no. 1 (March 1946): 1–3; Maria L. Cortone, 'Benedetto Croce,' (summarizing a lecture by Arthur Livingston of Columbia University in October 1943), *Italica* 20, no. 4 (December 1943): 214–15. *Italica* was the journal of the American Association of Teachers of Italian.

79 Thus he found as one the most dubious features of Croce's thought 'its insistence on the pervasive role of a quasi-deity called "the spirit,"' essentially derived from Hegel. See H. Stuart Hughes, *Consciousness and Society: The Reorientation of European Social Thought, 1890–1930* (New York: Random House [Vintage], 1958), 208. See also 26. Hughes was well versed in modern Italian culture, even confessing on p. 433 that he had borrowed heavily from the work of Carlo Antoni and Pietro Rossi in putting his book together. Thus it is all the more striking that in his recent memoir, *Gentleman Rebel* (New York: Ticknor & Fields, 1990), 160–1, Hughes, in recalling his personal encounters with Croce in Italy at the end of the Second World War, says that Croce left little impression on him.

80 Destler, 'Some Observations on Contemporary Historical Theory,' 504; Patrick Romanell, 'Romanticism and Croce's Conception of Science,' *Review of Metaphysics* 9 (March 1956): 505–14.

81 L.M. Palmer and H.S. Harris, eds., *Thought, Action, and Intuition: A Symposium on the Philosophy of Benedetto Croce* (Hildesheim: Georg Olms Verlag, 1975). In a telephone conversation with the author in May 1994, Professor Palmer explained the circumstances that led her to settle for this publication strategy and expressed her hope that the proceedings might yet be republished in an appropriate format.

82 In Verene's view, Croce ended up linking Vico to an 'absolute idealism' that seeks 'to comprehend being as a progressive movement of categories,' and that offers only the wisdom of the concept, as opposed to the imaginative or poetic wisdom that Vico uncovered. See Donald Phillip Verene, *Vico's Science of Imagination* (Ithaca, NY: Cornell University Press, 1981), 217; see also 23, 68–69. Although his account of Vico differed from Verene's, Mooney, too, assumed at the outset that he needed 'to run clear of the Idealist framework with its epistemological orientation, which Benedetto Croce had imposed

on Vico interpretation.' See Michael Mooney, *Vico in the Tradition of Rhetoric* (Princeton, NJ: Princeton University Press, 1985), xi; see also 26–9.

The anti-Crocean reading of Vico in the United States stemmed partly from the influence of Pietro Piovani's 'Vico Without Hegel,' in *Giambattista Vico: An International Symposium*, ed. Giorgio Tagliacozzo and Hayden V. White (Baltimore: Johns Hopkins University Press, 1969), 103–23. See also Hayden White's critique, 'What Is Living and What Is Dead in Croce's Criticism of Vico,' originally in the same volume, reprinted in Hayden White, *Tropics of Discourse: Essays in Cultural Criticism* (Baltimore: Johns Hopkins University Press, 1978), 218–29.

83 Verene, *Vico's Science*, 33. For Croce's way of making the point, see, for example, *Estetica come scienza dell'espressione e linguistica generale* (Bari: Laterza, 1958), 242–4, 254–6, 489.

84 Though relatively limited in its range, John M. Cammett's *Antonio Gramsci and the Origins of Italian Communism* (Stanford, CA: Stanford University Press, 1967), was central in bringing Gramsci to currency in the United States. Among the most prominent of those indebted to Gramsci was Eugene Genovese, a student of the American south and one of the most distinguished American historians of his generation. In conversations with the author in October 1993, Genovese stressed the importance of Cammett's work in bringing Gramsci's thought to his own attention – and to more general currency among historians in the United States.

85 See Maurice A. Finocchiaro, 'Croce as Seen in a Recent Work on Gramsci,' *Rivista di studi crociani* 21 (1984): 139–54, for a penetrating discussion of this tendency in one of the best books on Gramsci in English, Walter L. Adamson's *Hegemony and Revolution: A Study of Antonio Gramsci's Political and Cultural Theory* (Berkeley: University of California Press, 1980). Finocchiaro later contributed his own full-length study of Gramsci, *Gramsci and the History of Dialectical Thought* (Cambridge: Cambridge University Press, 1988), which offers the most extended and balanced account of Gramsci's encounter with Croce in the recent English-language literature. See also Finocchiaro's review essay on the present author's *Benedetto Croce and the Uses of Historicism* in *Theory and Society* 18 (March 1989): 282–7. For another discerning account of Gramsci's complex relationship with Croce's thought, see William Hartley, 'Notebook Ten and the Critique of Benedetto Croce,' *Italian Quarterly* 31 (Winter–Spring 1990): 21–42.

86 Paul Piccone, *Italian Marxism* (Berkeley: University of California Press, 1983), 22–3, 103.

87 *Croce and Marxism: From the Years of Revisionism to the Last Postwar Period* (Naples: Morano, 1987).

88 Edmund E. Jacobitti, *Revolutionary Humanism and Historicism in Modern Italy* (New Haven, CT: Yale University Press, 1981). See, for example, 152–4 for suggestions that Croce 'surrendered human autonomy to the inevitability of history' and left humanity 'with a lay religion that celebrated the past.' The present author reviewed Jacobitti's book in *Canadian Journal of History* 17, no. 2 (August 1982): 386–8. Jacobitti offered a comparably critical assessment of Croce's role in Italian culture in 'Hegemony Before Gramsci: The Case of Benedetto Croce,' *Journal of Modern History* 52 (March 1980): 66–84. Daniela Coli's *Croce, Laterza e la cultura europea* (Bologna: Il Mulino, 1983), offers a useful corrective, but it is not likely to be translated into English. [It is, however, available in a new edition: Daniela Coli, *Il filosofo, i libri, gli editori: Croce, Laterza e la cultura europea* (Naples: Editoriale Scientifica, 2002).]

89 M.E. Moss, *Benedetto Croce Reconsidered: Truth and Error in Theories of Art, Literature, and History* (Hanover, NH: University Press of New England, 1987); David D. Roberts, *Benedetto Croce and the Uses of Historicism* (Berkeley: University of California Press, 1987). For a discussion of these two works, along with Caserta's *Croce and Marxism*, see Raffaello Franchini, 'La filosofia di Croce nell'odierno mondo di lingua inglese,' *Criterio* 6 (Spring 1988): 1–20. Croce also figures prominently in my more recent *Nothing but History: Reconstruction and Extremity after Metaphysics* (Berkeley: University of California Press, 1995), which treats the tradition of post-metaphysical thinking from Nietzsche and Heidegger to Derrida and Rorty. [The Davies Group published a reprint edition, for which I supplied a new introduction, in 2007.]

90 See Peter Novick, *That Noble Dream: The 'Objectivity Question' and the American Historical Profession* (Cambridge: Cambridge University Press, 1988).

91 Roberts, *Nothing but History*, 107–8, 226–7, 231, 233, 234, 249–50.

92 Rorty's work has been particularly central; see, for example, his *Contingency, Irony, and Solidarity* (Cambridge: Cambridge University Press, 1989). See also David Kolb, *The Critique of Pure Modernity: Hegel, Heidegger, and After* (Chicago: University of Chicago Press, 1986); and Brook Thomas, *The New Historicism and Other Old-Fashioned Topics* (Princeton, NJ: Princeton University Press, 1991). My own recent *Nothing but History* seeks to contribute to this wider effort.

93 I focus on the United States, but I am including the leading North American expert on Gentile, H.S. Harris. Although he works in Canada, Harris published his major works on Gentile in the United States, and he explicitly placed his work in the context of American interest in Gentile.

Despite some important omissions, Ernesto G. Caserta's *Studi crociani negli stati uniti: Bibliografia critica (1964–1984)* (Naples: Loffredo, 1988), provides a useful critical assessment of much recent work on Croce. For work on Gentile prior to 1960, see H.S. Harris, 'Bibliography of Gentile Studies in English,' in his edition of Gentile's *Genesis and Structure of Society* (Urbana: University of Illinois Press, 1960), 53–63. For the subsequent period, see Giovanni Gullace, 'Gli studi gentiliani nei paesi di lingua inglese (1960–1975),' in *Il pensiero di Giovanni Gentile* (Istituto della enciclopedia italiana, 1977), 1: 459–72.

94 The American who treated both in the most sustained way was Patrick Romanell (Pasquale Romanelli), beginning with a dissertation on Gentile at Columbia University in 1937, and followed by several books and articles, some focused on Croce, some comparative. See also Merle S. Brown, *Neo-Idealist Aesthetics: Croce-Gentile-Collingwood* (Detroit: Wayne State University Press, 1966).

95 Croce's protests against the label 'Italian neo-idealism' and such identifications with Hegel were to be found in essays translated into English. See, for example, *My Philosophy and Other Essays on the Moral and Political Problems of Our Time* (London: Allen & Unwin, 1949), 19.

96 Frederic S. Simoni, 'Benedetto Croce: A Case of International Misunderstanding,' *Journal of Aesthetics and Art Criticism* 11 (September 1952): 7–14. The quoted passage is from p. 9. Simoni found especially damaging an early review of Croce's *Estetica* by George Santayana, to be discussed later. [This has of course been discussed earlier, in the Croce portion of the present essay.]

97 Ransom to Tate, 25 June 1927, in *Selected Letters of John Crowe Ransom*, ed. Thomas Daniel Young and George Core (Baton Rouge: Louisiana State University Press, 1985), 175.

98 Seeking to explain why Croce did not receive the recognition he deserved in the United States, Italo De Feo noted that Croce declined several opportunities to come to the United States, though he travelled frequently in Europe. See Italo De Feo, *Croce: l'uomo e l'opera* (Milan: Mondadori, 1975), 636–42. De Feo also noted that the Italian language was an obstacle, but though American scholars were less likely to read Italian than French or German, major early students of Croce like Joel Spingarn and Irving Babbitt did read Italian.

99 As Norberto Bobbio wrote in 1974, Gentile's philosophy not only seems dead, but literally incomprehensible. Yet not long ago it seems not only to be have been understood but eagerly embraced. See Maurizio Ferraris, 'Il Gentile di Garin,' *Aut Aut*, n.s., no. 247 (January–February 1992): 26.
100 Harris, introduction to Gentile, *Genesis*, 24.
101 Ibid., 1.
102 Van Deusen, *J.E. Spingarn*, 67–8.
103 In addition, Gentile's educational thought was the subject of a doctoral dissertation by Merritt Moore Thompson, *The Educational Philosophy of Giovanni Gentile* (Los Angeles: University of Southern California Press, 1934). Thompson compared Gentile with Dewey and other American thinkers in several subsequent articles.
104 Harris, introduction to Gentile, *Genesis*, 25.
105 Charles W. Morris, *Six Theories of Mind* (Chicago: University of Chicago Press, 1932), 88–101.
106 Roger W. Holmes, *The Idealism of Giovanni Gentile* (New York: Macmillan, 1937). See especially 225–45, Holmes's balanced concluding assessment.
107 Harris, introduction to Gentile, *Genesis*, 28–31. Holmes reviewed Italian books for the *Philosophical Review* thereafter, but did not pursue his interest in Gentile.
108 'L'essenza del fascismo' is included in Gentile's *Origini e dottrina del fascismo* [now available in an English edition prepared by A. James Gregor; see earlier, in the introduction to the present chapter]. The translation, which condenses the original, is in *Foreign Affairs* 6 (January 1928): 290–304. On American assessments of fascism, see John P. Diggins, *Mussolini and Fascism: The View from America* (Princeton, NJ: Princeton University Press, 1972), a thorough and balanced study by a respected historian of the United States. See especially 252–61, as well as the Bibliographical Note, 497–506, which discusses American cultural interaction with Italy in general, as well as the specific question of fascism.
109 H.W. Schneider, *Making the Fascist State* (New York: Oxford University Press, 1928); Howard R. Marraro, *The New Education in Italy* (New York: Vanni, 1936); Herbert L. Matthews, *The Fruits of Fascism* (New York: Harcourt, Brace, 1943). Matthews was a distinguished European correspondent for the *New York Times*. Along with Marraro, Isaac Kandel, as editor of the *Yearbook* of the International Institute at Columbia, followed the fascist educational reform with discernment.
110 George Boas, 'Gentile and the Hegelian Invasion of Italy,' *Journal of Philosophy* 23 (1 April 1926): 184–8, especially 188 on fascism.
111 Brown, *Neo-Idealist Aesthetics* (1966), cited earlier. Gullace translated

Gentile's *La filosofia dell'arte* (1931) as *The Philosophy of Art* (Ithaca, NY: Cornell University Press, 1972), with a lengthy introduction. He emphasized that Gentile's philosophy of art had attracted little attention in the United States; there had apparently been only two reviews of the original 1931 edition. Gullace's English translation fared no better.

112 Gentile, *Genesis*; H.S. Harris, *The Social Philosophy of Giovanni Gentile* (Urbana: University of Illinois Press, 1960).

113 Harris, introduction to Gentile, *Genesis*, 7n6.

114 Tracy H. Koon, *Believe, Obey, Fight: Political Socialization of Youth in Fascist Italy, 1922–1943* (Chapel Hill: University of North Carolina Press, 1985), especially 40–59.

115 *The Ideology of Fascism: The Rationale of Totalitarianism* (New York: Free Press, 1969), especially 199–240. Gentile figured less explicitly in Gregor's subsequent works, the most important of which were *The Fascist Persuasion in Radical Politics* (Princeton, NJ: Princeton University Press, 1974); *Italian Fascism and Developmental Dictatorship* (Princeton, NJ: Princeton University Press, 1979); and *Young Mussolini and the Intellectual Origins of Fascism* (Berkeley: University of California Press, 1979). In *Young Mussolini*, Gregor found Mussolini's own belief system to have been sufficiently coherent by the end of 1918 to have encompassed futurism, revolutionary syndicalism, nationalism, and neo-idealism. See especially 242.

116 Published in 2 vols. by the Istituto della enciclopedia italiana.

Chapter 5

1 Stephen Holmes has noted that the long shadow of totalitarianism continues even to inhibit criticism of liberalism. By extension, there may be a certain softness in the liberal self-understanding and something a bit facile in our present understanding of the central political categories. See Stephen Holmes, *The Anatomy of Antiliberalism* (Cambridge, MA: Harvard University Press, 1993), 154.

2 Jane Caplan, 'Postmodernism, Poststructuralism, and Deconstruction: Notes for Historians,' *Central European History* 22 (September–December 1989): 274–8. The quotation is from p. 276.

3 I have explored the interest, such as it was, in Croce and Gentile in the United States in 'La fortuna di Croce e Gentile negli Stati Uniti,' in 'Croce e Gentile un secolo dopo,' special issue, *Giornale critico della filosofia italiana* 73, nos. 2–3 (May–December 1994): 253–81. A revised and expanded version of the Croce portion was published as 'Croce in America: Influ-

ence, Misunderstanding, Neglect,' in *Humanitas* 8, no. 2 (1995): 3–34. [See essay 4 in the present collection.]

4 Writing in 1968, the noted Catholic thinker Augusto Del Noce insisted that study of Gentile's actual idealism is indispensable for understanding fascism – and that the relationship between them is far more complex than is usually understood. Renzo De Felice, in the fourth of his volumes on Mussolini, maintained that Gentile's ideas constituted 'an important and authentic component' in Mussolini's political culture. See Augusto Del Noce, *Giovanni Gentile: Per una interpretazione filosofica della storia contemporanea* (Bologna: Il Mulino, 1990), 123–94; and Renzo De Felice, *Mussolini il Duce: Gli anni del consenso, 1929–1936* (Turin: Einaudi, 1974), 35. See also Emilio Gentile, *Il mito dello stato nuovo dall'antigiolittismo al fascismo* (Rome: Laterza, 1982), 231–61; and Gabriele Turi, *Il fascismo e il consenso degli intellettuali* (Bologna: Il Mulino, 1980), 5–10.

5 Emilio Gentile, *The Sacralization of Politics in Fascist Italy* (Cambridge: Harvard University Press, 1996), 58.

6 In his comprehensive and fair-minded biography, Gabriele Turi falls into unconvincing commonplaces when confronting the ideas that Gentile brought to fascism. Thus, for example, Gentile offered 'a static and authoritarian vision of society.' Gabriele Turi, *Giovanni Gentile: Una biografia* (Florence: Giunti, 1995), 244–5.

7 Bobbio's characterization is cited, and endorsed, in Maurizio Ferraris, 'Il Gentile di Garin,' *Aut Aut*, n.s., no. 247 (January–February 1992): 26.

8 Giuseppe Calandra is typical in suggesting that fascism embraced Gentile's actualism because, in light of the varied – even contradictory – quality of fascist elements, it needed an overarching ideological principle of unification. Fascism, for Calandra, was essentially a movement of reaction on the part of erstwhile liberals like Croce and Gentile; such people were afraid of the emergence of a new mass politics from war that the old political liberalism apparently could not contain. See Giuseppe Calandra, *Gentile e il fascismo* (Rome: Laterza, 1987), especially vii, 4, 12–13, 113, 156.

9 For example, Giovanni Gentile, *Fascismo e cultura* (Milan: Fratelli Treves, 1928), 57–8.

10 Giovanni Gentile, *Saggi critici*, 2nd ser. (Florence: Vallecchi, 1927), 29.

11 Domenico Settembrini finds the ultimate inadequacy of both Croce and Gentile in their pretense of responding to the death of God on a genuinely religious level, with a doctrine of salvation that was purely earthly but still total, without shadows or uncertainties of any kind. See his *Storia dell'idea antiborghese in Italia, 1860–1989* (Rome: Laterza, 1991), 260–1.

12 Daniela Coli, *Croce, Laterza e la cultura europea* (Bologna: Il Mulino, 1983), 77–80, 85–6.

13 Benedetto Croce, *L'Italia dal 1914 al 1918: Pagine sulla guerra* (Bari: Laterza, 1965), 95, 107–12, 235–8; Benedetto Croce, 'prefazione,' 3rd ed. (1917), *Materialismo storico ed economia marxistica* (Bari: Laterza, 1968), xiii–xiv.

14 The key documents in the philosophical split of 1913 are now in Benedetto Croce, *Conversazioni critiche*, 2nd ser. (Bari: Laterza, 1950), 67–95; and Gentile, *Saggi critici*, 11–35. For the quoted phrases, see 68–9 (Croce) and 29 (Gentile). See also Calandra, *Gentile e il fascismo*, 91–105, for one of the many treatments of the split.

15 Del Noce, *Giovanni Gentile*, 123–94; H.S. Harris, *The Social Philosophy of Giovanni Gentile* (Urbana: University of Illinois Press, 1966), 4–7.

16 Giovanni Gentile, *Teoria generale dello spirito come atto puro* (Florence: Le Lettere, 1987). See especially 254–65 for Gentile's response to Croce's charge of mysticism. This work, which Gentile developed from his Pisa lectures of 1915–16, was translated into English as *The Theory of Mind as Pure Act* by the British scholar H. Wildon Carr (London: Macmillan, 1922). Carr also wrote one of the notable early works on Croce, published in 1917.

17 This theme is especially clear in Giovanni Gentile, *Sommario di pedagogia come scienza filosofica* (Florence: Sansoni, 1954–5). See also Calandra, *Gentile e il fascismo*, 176.

18 Now in Francesco De Sanctis, *Scritti critici* (Bari: Laterza, 1969), 3:1–25.

19 Gentile, *Fascismo e cultura*, 1–15 (1918).

20 Gentile's earliest work on education was *L'insegnamento della filosofia nei licei* (1900); he changed the title to *Difesa della filosofia* when publishing the second edition in 1921. See also Calandra, *Gentile e il fascismo*, 63–6, and Turi, *Giovanni Gentile*, 91, 160, 170–1, 181–2, on the import of pedagogical concerns in Gentile's intellectual development.

21 See David D. Roberts, 'Croce and Beyond: Italian Intellectuals and the First World War,' *International History Review* 3, no. 2 (April 1981): 201–35, for a fuller treatment.

22 Giovanni Gentile, 'Il carattere storico della filosofia italiana,' inaugural lecture at the University of Rome, 10 January 1918, now in *I problemi della scolastica e il pensiero italiano* (Florence: Sansoni, 1963), 235–6.

23 Turi, *Giovanni Gentile*, 217.

24 Ibid., 263–4, 267–9.

25 Gentile, 'Il carattere storico della filosofia italiana,' 235–6. See also Luigi Russo, *Vita e morale militare*, later entitled *Vita e disciplina militare* (Bari:

Laterza, 1946). This classic work by one of Gentile's younger followers, first published in a limited edition during the war, was promptly republished with a laudatory introduction by Gentile in 1919.

26 Gentile, 'Il carattere storico della filosofia italiana,' 209–18, 235–6.

27 Giovanni Gentile, *Guerra e fede* (Naples: Ricciardi, 1919), 158–9(1915).

28 Ibid., 222–3. In the third edition (Florence: Le Lettere, 1989), the relevant passage is on p. 147.

29 Gentile, *Guerra e fede,* 175. See also Giovanni Gentile, 'Il significato della vittoria' (October 1918), now in his *Dopo la vittoria* (Rome: La Voce, 1920), 3–25, especially 24–5.

30 Gentile, *Guerra e fede,* 205–6, 209–12, 217–18, 288–90. Gentile established the bases of his political theory, rethinking the relationships between liberty and authority and between the individual and the state, in his *Fondamenti della filosofia del diritto* in 1916, 3rd ed., rev. and exp. (Florence: Sansoni, 1937). See also Settembrini, *Storia dell'idea antiborghese,* 266.

31 Gentile, *Guerra e fede,* 209–12; Manlio Di Lalla, *Vita di Giovanni Gentile* (Florence: Sansoni, 1975), 259–60.

32 Giovanni Gentile, *I profeti del Risorgimento italiano* (Florence: Sansoni, 1944), 1–63; Armando Carlini, *Studi gentiliani* (Florence: Sansoni, 1958), 109–12; Raffaele Colapietra, *Benedetto Croce e la politica italiana* (Bari: Edizioni del centro librario, 1969), 1:302n78.

33 See Turi, *Giovanni Gentile,* 274–5, 278, 283–4, on Gentile's pedagogical concerns at this point. Gentile's lectures to the teachers of Trieste were published in English translation, with a laudatory introduction by Croce, as *The Reform of Education* (New York: Harcourt, Brace, 1922).

34 Eugenio Garin, *La cultura italiana tra '800 e '900* (Rome: Laterza, 1976), 183–4. 'Senza tenere conto di questa che fu, prima ancora che una meditata teorizzazione, una esperienza originaria, si rischia di non intendere la posizione di tanti giovani che al tempo della prima guerra mondiale trovarono in Croce e Gentile due maestri incomparabili, e ne composero in cuor loro differenze e dissidi. In quell'*idealismo* videro tradotta la loro fede in una necessaria convergenza del corso della storia coi loro ideali.'

35 Gentile to Mussolini, 31 May 1923, as cited in Jader Jacobelli, *Croce Gentile: Dal sodalizio al dramma* (Milan: Rizzoli, 1989), 41.

36 Herbert Marcuse, 'The Struggle against Liberalism in the Totalitarian View of the State' (1934), now in his *Negations: Essays in Critical Theory* (Boston: Beacon, 1968), 10–11.

37 Especially important was 'Il fascismo in Sicilia,' a lecture Gentile presented in Palermo on 31 March 1924, during the 1924 election campaign. It was first published in Giovanni Gentile, *Che cosa è il fascismo* (Florence: Vallec-

chi, 1925), the entirety of which is now included in Giovanni Gentile, *Politica e cultura*, vol. 1 (Florence: Le Lettere, 1990); see 38–60. See also Turi, *Giovanni Gentile*, 335–7.

38 See especially the three well-known interviews from 1923–4, now in Croce's *Pagine sparse* (Bari: Laterza, 1960), 2:475–86.

39 Gentile, *Che cosa è il fascismo*, 153–61; Gioacchino Volpe, *Guerra dopoguerra fascismo* (Venice: La Nuova Italia, 1928), 293–9. See also the whole argument of Ulisse Benedetti, *Benedetto Croce e il fascismo* (Rome: Volpe, 1967).

40 Di Lalla, *Vita di Giovanni Gentile*, 315–16; Sergio Romano, *Giovanni Gentile: La filosofia al potere* (Milan: Bompiani, 1984), 236–48, 272.

41 Considering Gentile's role in the 1930s, Emilio Gentile notes, 'Even when his cultural leadership within the régime began to decline, his mark on the fascist vision of the state remained strong and clear.' See Gentile, *Sacralization of Politics*, 58.

42 See the later testimony of Delio Cantimori, *Conversando di storia* (Bari: Laterza, 1967), 138–9. See also Delio Cantimori, *Politica e storia contemporanea: Scritti (1927–1942)*, ed. and intro. Luisa Mangoni (Turin: Einaudi, 1991).

43 The key statement of Gentile's fascism is *Origini e dottrina del fascismo* (Rome: Libreria del Littorio, 1929); see especially 35–53. [See the introduction to chapter 4 for a reference to A. James Gregor's recent English-language edition of this and other works on fascism by Gentile.] See also Gentile, *Fascismo e cultura*, 44–66 (1925). Both these works are now included in Gentile, *Politica e cultura*, vol. 1.

44 Compare Harris, *Social Philosophy*, 189n72. Harris accents the convergence of Gentile and Rocco in practice, despite differences in accent. See also Turi's negative characterizations in his *Giovanni Gentile*, 244–5.

45 Gentile, *Origini e dottrina*, 43–8, especially 46–8. See also Harris, *Social Philosophy*, 169–70.

46 Holmes, *Anatomy of Antiliberalism*, 187–256.

47 Settembrini, *Storia dell'idea antiborghese*, 270.

48 See especially Alfredo Rocco, 'Crisi dello Stato e sindacati' (1920), now in his *Scritti e discorsi politici*, vol. 2 (Milan: Giuffrè, 1938), especially 631, 639–45. See also David D. Roberts, *The Syndicalist Tradition and Italian Fascism* (Chapel Hill: University of North Carolina Press, 1979), 144–52.

49 Gentile, *Origini e dottrina*, 35–6, 52–3.

50 This point was made with particular clarity by one of Gentile's most enthusiastic admirers abroad, Aline Lion, a French woman who lived in Italy from 1913 to 1927 and who studied philosophy at Oxford. See *The Pedigree of Fascism: A Popular Essay on the Western Philosophy of Politics* (London:

Sheed & Ward, 1927), 189–210, especially 190. See also her *Idealistic Conception of Religion: Vico, Hegel, Gentile* (Oxford: Clarendon, 1932).

51 Gabriele Turi notes, for example, that Gentile allowed open debate in the periodicals he directed. See Turi, *Giovanni Gentile*, 368–70.

52 Gentile, *Origini e dottrina*, 47–8; Harris, *Social Philosophy*, 203, 241–2n34.

53 Giovanni Gentile, 'Discorsi agli italiani,' in *Politica e cultura*, 2:190–208.

54 Turi, *Giovanni Gentile*, is especially good on the dramatic and tragic final phases of Gentile's career. See especially 482–5, 488, 497–9.

55 Calandra, *Gentile e il fascismo*, 168.

56 Giovanni Gentile, *La filosofia di Marx: Studi critici*, rev. and exp. ed., ed. Vito A. Bellezza (Florence, Sansoni, 1974). This work was originally published in Pisa by Spoerri in 1899. On the centrality of Gentile's encounter with Marx, see Eugenio Garin, 'Croce e Gentile interpreti di Marx,' in *Croce e Gentile fra tradizione nazionale e filosofia europea*, ed. Michele Ciliberto (Rome: Riuniti, 1993), 3–13.

57 Gentile, *La filosofia di Marx*, 8–9.

58 Calandra, *Gentile e il fascismo*, 49–52, is good on the import – and the limits – of this thrust in Gentile's early critique of Marx.

59 Ibid., 52.

60 See Turi, *Giovanni Gentile*, 263–4, 267–9, on Gentile's influence on the young Turinese socialist intellectuals Tasca, Togliatti, and Gramsci.

61 Robert C. Tucker, ed., *The Marx-Engels Reader*, 2nd ed. (New York: Norton, 1978), 145.

62 See, for example, Benedetto Croce, *Ultimi saggi* (Bari: Laterza, 1963), 310–11.

63 Benedetto Croce, *Etica e politica* (Bari: Laterza, 1967), 147–8, 188, 190–1, 293–4; Benedetto Croce, *Cultura e vita morale* (Bari: Laterza, 1955), 301–2.

64 Benedetto Croce, *Filosofia e storiografia* (Bari: Laterza, 1969), 143–4 (1946); see also 253–5 in the same volume.

65 For examples from his later years of Croce's repeated insistence on world-historical modesty, see his *Il carattere della filosofia moderna* (1941; Bari: Laterza, 1963), 209–10; and *Discorsi di varia filosofia* (Bari: Laterza, 1959), 1:297 (1942).

66 Responding just after the Second World War 'to my friends who are seeking the "transcendent,"' Croce argued that whereas there is no heavenly searchlight, we have, each of us, a portable lantern – and these lanterns are sufficient, enabling us to go on responding ethically to the world, taking responsibility for it. See Benedetto Croce, 'Agli amici che cercano il "trascendente,"' (8 May 1945), now in *Etica e politica*, 378–84.

67 See David D. Roberts, *Benedetto Croce and the Uses of Historicism* (Berkeley: University of California Press, 1987), 223–38, for a fuller discussion.

68 See ibid., 172–3, 189–98, on the Croce-Camus contrast.

69 See Nicola Abbagnano, *Critical Existentialism* (Garden City, NY: Doubleday Anchor, 1969), 1–18, for a good example of such critical characterizations of Croce's thought. See also Antonio Santucci, *Esistenzialismo e filosofia italiana* (Bologna: Il Mulino, 1959), 17–23, 68–77, 160–227; and Roberts, *Benedetto Croce*, 187–98.

70 Croce, *Carattere*, 119.

71 Croce, 'Frammenti di etica,' in *Etica e politica*, 22–3, 25, 99–101, 123. See also Roberts, *Benedetto Croce*, 174–82.

72 Croce, 'Frammenti di etica,' 99–101, 123; Croce, *Conversazioni critiche*, 4th ser., 201–2 (1923).

73 Croce, 'Frammenti di etica,' 106; Benedetto Croce, *Filosofia della pratica: Economia ed etica* (Bari: Laterza, 1963), 173–4; Benedetto Croce, *Teoria e storia della storiografia* (Bari: Laterza, 1973), 325–7. See also Roberts, *Benedetto Croce*, 180–2, 190–8.

74 Croce, *Ultimi saggi*, 263–4 (1930).

75 As early as 1908, concluding his *Filosofia della pratica*, Croce noted that the philosopher labours knowing full well that his work will promptly be superseded, but faith in history overcomes the resulting feeling of futility. See Croce, *Filosofia della pratica*, 406.

76 Richard Rorty, *Contingency, Irony, and Solidarity* (Cambridge: Cambridge University Press, 1989), 21, 40–1.

77 Richard Rorty, *Consequences of Pragmatism (Essays: 1972–1980)* (Minneapolis: University of Minnesota Press, 1982), 87–8.

Chapter 6

1 Eugenio Garin, *Cronache di filosofia italiana 1900/1943* (Rome: Laterza, 1975), 2:621. This work was published first in 1955, then in definitive form in 1962.

2 Writing in 1937, the exiled Italian scholar Giuseppe Antonio Borgese, by now a long-time antagonist, found Croce 'the most famed Italian abroad, at least in the scholarly world, since the days perhaps of Galileo.' See his *Goliath: The March of Fascism* (New York: Viking, 1937), 295–6.

3 *La critica* ran without interruption for forty-two years, until December 1944, then appeared irregularly as *Quaderni della critica* until 1951. The Treccani *Enciclopedia italiana*, published in 1929–36, in the midst of the

fascist period, is similarly to be found in research libraries throughout the world. Gentile was editor-in-chief.

4 This was true abroad as well. In the United States, the historian Chester McArthur Destler found Croce not only the major source of a deplorable new presentism in historiography, but also the outstanding exponent of a dangerous new philosophy that stressed relativism in values, impressionism in the arts, subjective activism for the individual, violence as a mode of social action, and success as the supreme value in public affairs. Croce, according to Destler, had thereby 'helped lay the intellectual foundations of Italian fascism.' Chester McArthur Destler, 'Some Observations on Contemporary Historical Theory,' *American Historical Review* 55 (1950): 504, 517.

5 Raffaello Franchini, *Intervista su Croce*, ed. Arturo Fratta (Naples: Società Editrice Napoletana, 1978), 5.

6 Bobbio also noted that not so long before, intelligent, idealistic young Italians had found Gentile's thinking exciting and inspiring. Bobbio's characterization is cited, and endorsed, in Maurizio Ferraris, 'Il Gentile di Garin,' *Aut Aut*, n.s., no. 247 (January–February 1992): 26. Though there is much force to Bobbio's point, Gentile certainly had not disappeared altogether, thanks partly to the continuing interest of earlier followers like Ugo Spirito, who had turned from Gentilian fascism to communism, and to continuing efforts of Gentile's publishing house, G.C. Sansoni in Florence. It is striking that the cover of *Giornale critico della filosofia italiana*, one of the most distinguished journals of its kind in Europe, continued (and continues) to indicate Gentile as its founder. Gentile had started the journal in 1920.

7 One thinks of senior scholars like Girolamo Cotroneo, those in mid-career like Giuseppe Gembillo in the history of science, or those younger like Raffaele Prodomo in bioethics. It is arguable that each, on the basis of the Crocean heritage, is making a distinctive contribution that could only have come from Italy.

8 Keith Luria and Romulo Gandolfo, 'Carlo Ginzburg: An Interview,' *Radical History Review* 35 (1986): 104–6; Carlo Ginzburg, 'Microhistory: Two or Three Things I Know about It,' *Critical Inquiry* 20 (Autumn 1993): 29. Especially influential among Gianni Vattimo's many works is *The End of Modernity: Nihilism and Hermeneutics in Postmodern Culture*, trans. Jon R. Snyder (Baltimore, MD: Johns Hopkins University Press, 1988). Giovanna Borradori offers at least a start at bringing Vattimo and other contemporary Italian thinkers under an umbrella broad enough to include the earlier idealist-historicist tradition in her introduction to Giovanna Bor-

radori, ed., *Recoding Metaphysics: The New Italian Philosophy* (Evanston, IL: Northwestern University Press, 1988), 1–26.

9 Frederic S. Simoni, 'Benedetto Croce: A Case of International Misunderstanding,' *Journal of Aesthetics and Art Criticism* 11 (September 1952): 7–14. The quoted passage is from p. 9.

10 Wellek noted that in movements influential since Croce's death – from Russian formalism and structuralism to hermeneutics and deconstruction – Croce 'is not referred to or quoted, even when he discusses the same problems and gives similar solutions.' And yet Croce, for Wellek, had been perhaps the most erudite and wide-ranging figure in the history of criticism. See René Wellek, *History of Modern Criticism* (New Haven, CT: Yale University Press, 1992), 8:187, 189.

For overall assessments of Croce's fortunes in the United States, see Myra E. Moss, 'Benedetto Croce negli Stati Uniti,' in the collaborative volume *I progressi della filosofia nell'italia del novecento* (Naples: Morano, 1992), 299–394; and David D. Roberts, 'La fortuna di Croce e Gentile negli Stati Uniti,' in 'Croce e Gentile un secolo dopo,' special issue, *Giornale critico della filosofia italiana* 73, nos. 2–3 (May–December 1994): 253–81. A slightly expanded version of the Croce portion of this latter essay appeared as David D. Roberts, 'Croce in America: Influence, Misunderstanding, and Neglect,' *Humanitas*, 8, no. 2 (1995): 3–34. [See essay 4 in the present volume.]

11 Carlo Ginzburg, 'Just One Witness,' in *Probing the Limits of Representation: Nazism and the 'Final Solution,'* ed. Saul Friedländer (Cambridge, MA: Harvard University Press, 1992), 82–96. Important reflections on the controversy included Martin Jay, 'Of Plots, Witnesses, and Judgments,' in the same volume, 97–107 (see especially 101–2); and Jeremy Varon, 'Probing the Limits of the Politics of Representation,' *New German Critique* 72 (Fall 1997): 83–114, especially 91.

Though he began as a Croce partisan, White explicitly rejected Croce in his pathbreaking *Metahistory*, where Croce nonetheless plays a crucial role as the ironically sterile culmination of nineteenth-century historiographical traditions. See Hayden White, *Metahistory: The Historical Imagination in Nineteenth-Century Europe* (Baltimore: Johns Hopkins University Press, 1973), chap. 10, especially 378–9, 385, 397–400. To my knowledge, the sources and implications of White's wilful, even bizarre misreading of Croce have yet to be probed systematically in print. Ginzburg's case against White rests in part on White's brief but significant reference to Gentile on 'the historical sublime' in his influential article of 1982, 'The Politics of Historical Interpretation: Discipline and

De-Sublimation,' now in *The Content of the Form: Narrative Discourse and Historical Representation* (Baltimore: Johns Hopkins University Press, 1987), 74–5; see also 66–7, 69, 72, for the keys to the context of this reference. White's way of linking Gentile to Nietzsche got the Italian thinker almost precisely backwards.

12 Abbott Gleason, *Totalitarianism: The Inner History of the Cold War* (New York: Oxford University Press, 1995). On p. 9, Gleason notes that 'the philosopher Giovanni Gentile, operating in the highly abstract vocabulary of conservative Hegelianism, produced a brilliant and premonitory justification of the totalitarian state that seems amazingly like Hannah Arendt's and George Orwell's demonic visions of the later 1940s, only with the value signs inverted.' The basis for the link to Orwell is clearest on pp. 94–5, where totalitarianism is to be internalized and willed by all – true to Gentile as far as it goes, but why would anyone advocate *that*? We get no insight into Gentile's vision even from Arendt and Orwell. On p. 19 Gleason notes that 'Gentile deserves to be called the first philosopher of totalitarianism.'

13 Writing in 1985, the noted historian Rosario Romeo lamented the 'denationalization of culture' in postwar Italy. Openness to every current from abroad had gone hand-in-hand with a kind of cultural self-denigration; thus the cultural mediocrity of contemporary Italy. From *Corriere della Sera*, 2 November 1985; as quoted in Domenico Settembrini, *Storia dell'idea antiborghese in Italia* (Rome: Laterza, 1991), 459–60. Writing in 1993, Michele Ciliberto took it for granted that during the reign of Croce and Gentile, Italians had indeed been too quick to assume the universalism of the Italian tradition. But by now, he said, the commonplace charge of provincialism had itself become an ideological prejudice – the mirror image of the earlier provincialism. It was time for a reassessment, which Ciliberto sought to promote in his aptly titled collaborative volume *Croce e Gentile fra tradizione nazionale e filosofia europea* (Rome: Riuniti, 1993). See Ciliberto's introduction, p. x, for the point here.

14 Introducing his translation of Giovanni Gentile, *Genesis and Structure of Society* (Urbana: University of Illinois Press, 1966), H.S. Harris noted that 'the possibility of Gentile having any influence in America perished when [Josiah] Royce died at the age of sixty-one in 1916' (24). During his last years, even after most American philosophers had abandoned idealism for a radical empiricism and naturalism, Royce had sought to work from the pragmatism of C.S. Peirce to a kind of idealist historicism. So his death removed the most likely avenue for Gentile to affect philosophical thinking in the United States.

15 Said Cassirer, '[Croce's] whole doctrine, even though it proclaims logic as the basic science, in fact turns out to be an unlimited historical relativism in which change is studied so to speak for its own sake, in which no objective-logical enduring factors of any kind are discerned or set off.' Cassirer understood that Croce's was no ordinary logic; it was rather a kind of giving in to history, and he himself wanted no part of it. See Ernst Cassirer, 'Erkenntnistheorie nebst den Grenzfragen der Logik,' *Jahrbücher der Philosophie* 1 (1913): 34.

16 Benedetto Croce, *Discorsi di varia filosofia*, 2 vols. (Bari: Laterza, 1959), 2:15–17 (1945).

17 Eugenio Garin, 'Agonia e morte dell'idealismo italiano,' in *La filosofia italiana dal dopoguerra a oggi*, ed. Adriano Bausola (Rome: Laterza, 1985), 25–6.

18 Despite Garin's accents on disparity, the recent Italian effort at reassessment has included a growing recognition that for certain key questions we need to conceive Croce and Gentile as pillars within a single tradition. Among the examples are 'Croce e Gentile un secolo dopo'; Ciliberto, ed., *Croce e Gentile*; and Jader Jacobelli, *Croce Gentile: Dal Sodalizio al dramma* (Milan: Rizzoli, 1989).

19 Michele Maggi, *La filosofia di Benedetto Croce* (Naples: Bibliopolis, 1998), 315–16.

20 Ibid., 66.

21 Ibid., 111–12, 139, 149, 153.

22 Ibid., 263.

23 On p. 239n82, Maggi refers to Giuseppe Galasso, *Croce e lo spirito del suo tempo* (Milan: Arnaldo Mondadori 'Il Saggiatore,' 1990), 376–7, as an example of what he takes to be a misplaced emphasis on rupture. Whereas Galasso finds a *svolta* from conservatism to liberalism, Maggi insists that, whatever the earlier Croce might have said about immediate political matters, his later liberalism followed easily from his overall historicism.

24 Maggi, *La filosofia di Benedetto Croce*, 333. Croce's need to sharpen the categories occasionally led him to a level of abstraction that recalled his more-or-less systematic works of the first decade of the century. In connection with *La poesia* of 1936, Maggi offers some especially effective discussion of Croce's changing ideas on language, translatability, the conventions of communication, and the creativity of reliving or reception. And Maggi concludes that new preoccupations had led Croce to a problematic that was altogether different from that of his *Logica* of 1908. But Maggi still takes pains to accent continuity; Croce did not find it necessary to repudiate what he had said earlier.

25 Maggi, *La filosofia di Benedetto Croce*, 361. See also 239–40, 248, 264.
26 Ibid. 266, 269, 273, 304.
27 See ibid., 313, for Maggi's point. See also Benedetto Croce, *Il carattere della filosofia moderna*, 3rd ed. (Bari: Laterza, 1963), 119, on idyll and tragedy, a passage that Maggi quotes as part of his argument on p. 313.
28 Benedetto Croce, 'L'anticristo che è in noi,' in Benedetto Croce, *Filosofia e storiografia: Saggi*, 2nd ed. (Bari: Laterza, 1969), 313–19.
29 'Antistoricismo' was the title of one of Croce's most sustained early diagnoses, offered first as a lecture at the Seventh International Congress of Philosophy, Oxford, 3 September 1930, and now in Benedetto Croce, *Ultimi saggi*, 3rd ed. (Bari: Laterza, 1963), 251–64.
30 Against the longstanding tendency to play down the totalitarianism of fascist Italy, in comparison with Nazi Germany or the Stalinist Soviet Union, the recent work of Emilio Gentile (no relation to Giovanni Gentile) argues convincingly that totalitarianism was central to the complex dynamic of Mussolini's regime. See especially *La via italiana al totalitarismo: Il partito e lo Stato nel regime fascista* (Rome: La Nuova Italia Scientifica, 1995).
31 Gennaro Sasso, *Le due italie di Giovanni Gentile* (Bologna: Il Mulino, 1998), 588.
32 Gennaro Sasso, *Benedetto Croce: La ricerca della dialettica* (Naples: Morano, 1975). The book numbers 1172 pages.
33 Most recent is Gennaro Sasso, *Filosofia e idealismo*, vol. 4, *Paralipomeni* (Naples: Bibliopolis, 2000), 4:577.
34 Marta Herling and Mario Reale, eds., *Storia, Filosofia e letteratura: Studi in onore di Gennaro Sasso* (Naples: Bibliopolis, 1999).
35 Sasso engages Del Noce (1910–89) throughout *Le due italie*, especially in the notes. For important examples, see 199–200n22, 386–7, and 399–400n13. For Del Noce's argument, see especially Augusto Del Noce, *Giovanni Gentile: Per una interpretazione filosofia della storia contemporanea* (Bologna: Il Mulino, 1990). See also Augusto Del Noce, *Il problema del ateismo*, 2nd ed. (Bologna: Il Mulino, 1990); Augusto Del Noce, *Il suicidio della rivoluzione* (Milan: Giuffrè, 1978); and Augusto Del Noce, *L'epoca della secolarizzazione* (Milan: Giuffrè, 1970).
36 Sasso, *Le due italie*, 280, 286, 568–9.
37 Ibid., 45, 145–6.
38 Ibid., 191–2, 216–18, 241, 244–53.
39 Ibid., 266–8, 390–2, 511–13.
40 Ibid., 243, 445.
41 Ibid., 447–51, 455–6.

42 Ibid., 528–9, 556.
43 Ibid., 266–7, 274–5, 507–8.
44 Ibid., 402–3.
45 Emanuele Severino, 'Giovanni Gentile distruttore degli assoluti,' in *Giovanni Gentile: La filosofia, la politica, l'organizzazione della cultura,* ed. Maria Ida Gaeta (Venice: Marsilio, 1995), 57–9; Emanuele Severino, *Pensieri sul cristianesimo* (Milan: Rizzoli, 1995), 64–7; and Emanuele Severino, *Oltre il linguaggio* (Milan: Adelphi, 1992), 88–99.
46 Sasso, *Le due italie,* 576; see also 294–5.
47 Giovanni Gentile, *Sistema di logica come teoria del conoscere,* 3rd ed. (Florence: Sansoni, 1959), 1:33–34.
48 Sasso, *Le due italie,* 9, 548–9.
49 The import of Gentile's embrace of Bruno is especially clear in his 1912 essay '*Veritas Filia Temporis,*' now in his *Il pensiero italiano nel rinascimento,* 3rd ed. (Florence: Sansoni, 1955), 331–55; see especially 337–9. Sasso comes close to the key point in *Le due italie,* 140, but his overall accent is on Gentile's hesitations and uncertainties in dealing with Bruno and late Renaissance thought. See 133, 136–8, 140.
50 Sasso, *Le due italie,* 565.
51 Ibid., 315.
52 Severino, 'Giovanni Gentile distruttore degli assoluti,' 57–9.
53 Sasso, *Le due italie,* 59–61.
54 Ibid., 139, 446–7. Even as he usefully warned against any preoccupation with this sensitive issue, Sasso was himself prepared to confront it on occasion. Exploring Gentile's relations (or non-relations) with Heidegger, especially in the context of Heidegger's 1936 visit to Rome to lecture at the German Academy, Sasso accented the mutual indifference of the two thinkers, despite the efforts of Ernesto Grassi and Armando Carlini to establish bridges between them. Sasso found Heidegger's attitude symptomatic of German cultural arrogance in general, and anti-Italian prejudice in particular. But he also noted that Gentile showed no more interest in the possible encounter than Heidegger did. See Gennaro Sasso, *Filosofia e idealismo,* vol. 2, *Giovanni Gentile* (Naples: Bibliopolis, 1995), 383–97, especially 393–4.
55 As already cited; see note 29.
56 Some typical indications come up in Maggi's account, e.g., 328, 329, and 347.
57 Even in the wake of the split by 1925, Gentile and other fascists continued to claim that Croce was one of them, 'a fascist without the black shirt.' See especially Giovanni Gentile, *Che cosa è il fascismo: Discorsi e polemiche*

(Florence: Vallecchi, 1925), 153–61; and Gioacchino Volpe, *Guerra dopoguerra fascismo* (Venice: La Nuova Italia, 1928), 293–9. Note also the whole argument of Ulisse Benedetti, *Benedetto Croce e il fascismo* (Rome: Volpe, 1967).

58 Giovanni Gentile, *Origini e dottrina del fascismo* (Rome: Libreria del Littorio, 1929), 43–8, especially 46–8. See also 35–6, 52–3.

59 Among Italians taking that tack were such long-time allies as Guido De Ruggiero, who explicitly criticized what now seemed the dangerous emptiness of Croce's position. See his *Il ritorno alla ragione* (Bari: Laterza, 1946), especially 13–16, from an essay originally published 21 January 1945. Croce's response, entitled 'Indagine storica e risoluzione morale' and dated 30 January 1945, is now in *Nuove pagine sparse*, 2nd ed. (Bari: Laterza, 1966), 2:151–9. See also Benedetto Croce, 'Agli amici che cercano il "trascendente,"' (8 May 1945), now in his *Etica e politica* (Bari: Laterza, ed. economica, 1967), 378–84.

60 Giovanni Gentile, *Saggi critici*, 2nd ser. (Florence: Vallecchi, 1927), 29.

61 I have sought to show how Croce might be newly encompassed in contemporary cultural debate in *Benedetto Croce and the Uses of Historicism* (Berkeley: University of California Press, 1987), and *Nothing but History: Reconstruction and Extremity After Metaphysics* (Berkeley: University of California Press, 1995). I develop aspects of the Croce-Gentile contrast in 'History as Thought and Action: Croce's Historicism and the Contemporary Challenge,' in *The Legacy of Benedetto Croce: Contemporary Critical Views*, ed. Jack D'Amico, Dain A. Trafton, and Massimo Verdicchio (Toronto: University of Toronto Press, 1999); see especially 209–24.

62 Writing in 1974, E.J. Hobsbawm noted that the Italian culture from which Gramsci had emerged, around the time of the First World War, was 'both extremely sophisticated and relatively provincial.' E.J. Hobsbawm, 'The Great Gramsci,' *New York Review of Books*, 4 April 1974, 39.

Chapter 7

1 Versus the longstanding tendency to treat fascism as merely reactive, or to subsume it within 'totalitarianism,' Stanley Payne notes that for such major scholars as Ernst Nolte, George Mosse, Eugen Weber, and Roger Griffin, fascism was a revolutionary new epochal phenomenon with an ideology and a distinctive set of ambitions in its own right. See Stanley G. Payne, *A History of Fascism, 1914–1945* (Madison: University of Wisconsin Press, 1995), 494. In addition to those like Payne and Griffin, I also have in mind

the notable recent work of Emilio Gentile, such as *La via italiana al totalitarismo: Il partito e lo Stato nel regime fascista* (Rome: La Nuova Italia Scientifica, 1995); and *The Sacralization of Politics in Fascist Italy*, trans. Keith Botsford (Cambridge: Harvard University Press, 1996).

2 I will refer later to significant recent works by Jeffrey T. Schnapp, Mabel Berezin, and Barbara Spackman. Another prominent example of the genre is Simonetta Falasca-Zamponi, *Fascist Spectacle: The Aesthetics of Power in Mussolini's Italy* (Berkeley: University of California Press, 1997), which, like the others, is sophisticated and illuminating – yet still limited because of its way of engaging, or not engaging, 'fascist ideology.'

3 Zeev Sternhell, with Mario Sznajder and Maia Asheri, *The Birth of Fascist Ideology: From Cultural Rebellion to Political Revolution*, trans. David Maisel (Princeton, NJ: Princeton University Press, 1994). The most influential of Sternhell's earlier works were *La Droite Révolutionnaire: Les Origines Françaises du Fascisme* (Paris: Ed. du Seuil, 1978); and *Neither Right nor Left: Fascist Ideology in France* (Berkeley: University of California Press, 1986; original French ed. 1983). These works were controversial in France, though Sternhell's critics were sometimes self-serving. On 'the Sternhell controversy,' see António Costa Pinto, 'Fascist Ideology Revisited: Zeev Sternhell and His Critics,' *European History Quarterly* 16 (1986): 465–83; and Robert Wohl, 'French Fascism, Right and Left: Reflections on the Sternhell Controversy,' *Journal of Modern History* 63, no. 1 (March 1991): 91–8.

4 Stephen Holmes has noted that the long shadow of totalitarianism continues even to inhibit criticism of liberalism. By extension, there may be a certain softness in the liberal self-understanding and something a bit facile in our present way of conceiving the central political categories. See Stephen Holmes, *The Anatomy of Antiliberalism* (Cambridge: Harvard University Press, 1993), 154.

5 Sternhell, *Birth of Fascist Ideology*, 4–5.

6 Central to Gregor's contribution were *The Ideology of Fascism: The Rationale of Totalitarianism* (New York: Free Press, 1969); *The Fascist Persuasion in Radical Politics* (Princeton, NJ: Princeton University Press, 1974); and *Italian Fascism and Developmental Dictatorship* (Princeton, NJ: Princeton University Press, 1979).

7 In a review essay on Antonio Gramsci in 1974, E.J. Hobsbawm noted that the Italian culture from which Gramsci had emerged, around the time of the First World War, was 'both extremely sophisticated and relatively provincial.' See E.J. Hobsbawm, 'The Great Gramsci,' *New York Review of Books*, 4 April 1974, 39.

8 As Sternhell puts it in *The Birth of Fascist Ideology* (4): 'The France of integral nationalism, of the revolutionary Right, was the real birthplace of fascism. We have already demonstrated this elsewhere, so it does not have to be dealt with here. Moreover, France was the birthplace of Sorelian revolutionary syndicalism, the second elementary component of fascism. Originating in France, it was in Italy that revolutionary syndicalism developed into an intellectual, social, and political force.'
9 Ibid., 256.
10 Payne, *A History of Fascism,* 291. See 291–9 for the section on fascism in France, accenting its overall political weakness.
11 Indeed, the notion seems almost a commonplace by now, thanks to the pioneering work of such scholars as Detlev Peukert and Michael Burleigh. Two books focused explicitly on the relationship between the Enlightenment tradition and the Holocaust are Berel Lang, *Act and Idea in the Nazi Genocide* (Chicago: University of Chicago Press, 1990); and Zygmunt Bauman, *Modernity and the Holocaust* (Ithaca, NY: Cornell University Press, 1992).
12 Sternhell, *Birth of Fascist Ideology,* 192–4, 217, 223–5.
13 Ibid., 251. The late George Mosse was prominent among those who accented the scope for alternative forms of mass politics, beyond the liberal parliamentary system. For Mosse, the alternative was primarily aesthetic, to be sure, but it did not stem from fear. See especially George L. Mosse, *The Nationalization of the Masses: Political Symbolism and Mass Movements in Germany from the Napoleonic Wars to the Third Reich* (Ithaca, NY: Cornell University Press, 1991), 4.
14 Sternhell avoids sustained encounter with my own work, *The Syndicalist Tradition and Italian Fascism* (Chapel Hill: University of North Carolina Press, 1979), especially 73–9, which presented evidence of the limits of Sorelian influence on the Italian syndicalists, whose understanding even of myth, violence, and elitism defies Sternhell's reading.
15 For an example of the widespread tendency to treat myth as a way to direct and control mass movements, see Mosse, *Nationalization of the Masses,* 12.
16 See, for example, Sternhell, *Birth of Fascist Ideology,* 118.
17 Note, for example, Enrico Leone's *Anti-Bergson* (Naples: La Luce del Pensiero, 1923), the culmination of his explicit repudiation of Sorel, myth, and irrationalism. In a similar vein, Sergio Panunzio, writing in 1910, charged that F.T. Marinetti's futurist ideas could only lead to 'the most brutal and mechanical irrationalism' (quoted in Roberts, *Syndicalist Tradition,* 75).

18 Sternhell, *Birth of Fascist Ideology*, 231.

19 Although myth was indeed bound up with violence for Sorel, Sternhell is not clear on the relationship – the mechanism through which violence can nurture moral commitment. See especially ibid., 242–3.

20 Ibid., 254. See also 233. For Lanzillo on fascist violence, see Roberts, *Syndicalist Tradition*, 236–7.

21 See especially Sternhell, *Birth of Fascist Ideology*, 254.

22 Sorel accents individual initiative in discussing 'the ethics of producers,' for example. See Georges Sorel, *Reflections on Violence*, trans. T.E. Hulme and J. Roth (London: Collier-Macmillan, 1961), chap. 7. Compare Sternhell, *Birth of Fascist Ideology*, 127–8.

23 Sternhell, *Birth of Fascist Ideology*, 251.

24 Ibid., 230.

25 Ibid.

26 Paolo Ungari, *Alfredo Rocco e l'ideologia giuridica del fascismo* (Brescia: Morcelliana, 1963). For my own assessment of Rocco, see Roberts, *Syndicalist Tradition*, especially 139–52.

27 Sternhell, *Birth of Fascist Ideology*, 253.

28 Ibid., 253–4.

29 This is the thrust of the later chapters of my *Syndicalist Tradition*; see especially chapters 10 and 11 – and the evidence upon which they are based.

30 Sternhell, *Birth of Fascist Ideology*, 219.

31 Among early examples were the composition of the Commission of Fifteen (later Eighteen), charged with proposing a blueprint for institutional change, and the circumstances surrounding the drafting of the Labor Charter of 1927. See Roberts, *Syndicalist Tradition*, 281–3. Throughout his multi-volume biography of Mussolini, Renzo De Felice accents Mussolini's desire to keep his options open, to avoid being cornered – and thus his tendency to become a balancer or juggler on this level.

32 The polemic unfolded in *Rivista internazionle di filosofia del diritto*. See Roberts, *Syndicalist Tradition*, 240–4.

33 A.O. Olivetti, 'Le corporazioni come volontà e come rappresentazione,' *La stirpe* 9, no. 4 (April 1931): 145–6. See also Roberts, *Syndicalist Tradition*, 291, 293–4.

34 See, for example, Sternhell, *Birth of Fascist Ideology*, 22–3, 44–5, 90–1, 145, 157–8, 189–91. Even in discussing early syndicalism, Sternhell confuses the value of the market economy for struggle *at this stage* with permanent acceptance of the market economy. Syndicalist *liberismo* meant anti-protectionism, not defence of private property. Protection seemed to entail cozy political arrangements that impeded the desired economic development.

For the syndicalists, just as for Marx, the capitalist dynamic was the crucial prerequisite for proletarian maturation, revolution, and socialism. The anti-protectionist argument was made by all critics of the Giolittian system in Italy, perhaps most tellingly by the reform socialist Gaetano Salvemini, who would become an influential anti-fascist from exile in the United States. And the syndicalist accent on *liberismo* was not to give up the ideal of a post-capitalist economic alternative. I will return to this point.

Sternhell criticizes me in a note (283–4n5) for exaggerating the anti-political bias of early syndicalism – the result, he says, of my failure to pay sufficient attention to the 'economistic' tendencies that syndicalism derived from Marxism. In light of our many disagreements, Sternhell's decision to single out this point for criticism is curious, especially since he himself quite correctly notes the economic and anti-political thrust of syndicalism on occasion. Whether a particular accent is to be understand as political, anti-political, or economic obviously depends on the frame of reference. Although my *Syndicalist Tradition* is cited here and there in Sternhell's notes, this note is his only engagement with my work.

35 Sternhell, *Birth of Fascist Ideology*, 144–51.

36 Ibid., 152.

37 Ibid., 227–9.

38 See ibid., 129, for an example of Sternhell's way of linking market economics to his reductive understanding of corporativism.

39 Roland Sarti's *Fascism and the Industrial Leadership in Italy, 1919–1940: A Study in the Expansion of Private Power under Fascism* (Berkeley: University of California Press, 1971), remains fundamental on the limited reach of corporativism vis-à-vis big business during the 1930s.

40 For Sternhell's way of conceiving the matter, see especially *Birth of Fascist Ideology*, 183–5.

41 See Roberts, *Syndicalist Tradition*, 267–71, 324–5, for a critical analysis of the Italian syndicalist understanding of the political sphere. In important respects, that understanding recalls Charles S. Maier's theme of 'society as factory,' as outlined especially in his *In Search of Stability: Explorations in Historical Political Economy* (Cambridge: Cambridge University Press, 1987), chap. 1. But the wider framework of postwar syndicalist thinking reminds us how contested these issues were – and that the axes of debate did not correspond neatly with class. Guido de Ruggiero was one prominent liberal who criticized mightily the syndicalist-fascist accent on economic roles and technical expertise, even as he recognized that the older liberal understanding of politics was genuinely in crisis. For a discussion, and the relevant references, see David D. Roberts, 'Frustrated Liberals: De Rug-

giero, Gobetti, and the Challenge of Socialism,' *Canadian Journal of History* 17 (April 1982): 59–86. See also Roberts, *Syndicalist Tradition*, 250–1, on the polemic between De Ruggiero and Panunzio over this issue.

42 Indeed, Gentile was arguably the most distinguished European intellectual to become an out-and-out fascist. For an introduction to recent scholarship, see Gabriele Turi, 'Giovanni Gentile: Oblivion, Remembrance, and Criticism,' trans. Lydia G. Cochrane, *Journal of Modern History* 70, no. 4 (December 1998): 913–33. For an assessment of Gentile's reception in the United States, see David D. Roberts, 'La fortuna di Croce e Gentile negli Stati Uniti,' *Giornale critico della filosofia italiana* 73, nos. 2–3 (May–December 1994): 253–81. [For the material on Gentile in this article, see the appendix to chapter 4 in the present volume.]

43 See especially G.A. Fanelli, *Contra Gentiles: Mistificazioni dell'idealismo attuale nella rivoluzione fascista* (Rome: Biblioteca del Secolo Fascista, 1933). See also Alessandra Tarquini, 'Gli antigentiliani nel fascismo degli anni venti,' *Storia contemporanea* 27, no. 1 (February 1996): 5–59.

44 Sternhell, *Neither Right nor Left*, 6.

45 Sternhell, *Birth of Fascist Ideology*, 251–2.

46 Indeed, there remains much point to Norberto Bobbio's comment of 1974 that even in Italy, Gentile's philosophy seems not only dead, but literally incomprehensible. Yet Bobbio also noted that not so long before, intelligent, idealistic young Italians had found Gentile's thinking exciting and inspiring. Bobbio's characterization is cited, and endorsed, in Maurizio Ferraris, 'Il Gentile di Garin,' *Aut Aut*, n.s., no. 247 (January–February 1992): 26.

47 On the wartime divergence of Croce and Gentile, see David D. Roberts, 'Croce and Beyond: Italian Intellectuals and the First World War,' *International History Review* 3 (April 1981): 201–35.

48 Jeffrey T. Schnapp, *Staging Fascism: 18 BL and the Theater of Masses for Masses* (Stanford, CA: Stanford University Press, 1996), 5–7. The quotation is from p. 6.

49 Mabel Berezin, *Making the Fascist Self: The Political Culture of Interwar Italy* (Ithaca, NY: Cornell University Press, 1997). See especially 2–3, 16, for explicit engagement with Sternhell.

50 Ibid., 29–30. This notion leads Berezin to some astonishingly unnuanced claims about the overall Italian cultural situation. With its 'quasi-educated' middle class, she says, Italy was 'a culture that rejected text in favor of gesture or performance' (46–7). Can this be the same culture that elicited E.J. Hobsbawm's characterization (see note 7 above) a generation earlier?

51 Ibid., 56–63, 82, 110.

52 Ibid., 62.

53 Barbara Spackman, *Fascist Virilities: Rhetoric, Ideology, and Social Fantasy in Italy* (Minneapolis: University of Minnesota Press, 1996), 49–52, 178n10.

54 There remains much thinking to be done about the place of intellectual antecedents and ideational content in such phenomena as Italian fascism. But several recent scholars, while addressing the connection between earlier ideas and aspects of the ongoing problem of Nazism or totalitarianism, have contributed significantly to the necessary clarification. In his probing study of the Nietzschean legacy in Germany, Steven Aschheim well articulates what we miss insofar as we minimize the role of prior intellectual innovation. Referring to approaches to Nazism that encompass Nietzsche, Aschheim notes that 'these exercises at least attempt to confront what much of recent historiography has attempted to duck: the vexed question of Nazi motivation and intent. This view implies that in some meaningful way nazism was, at least in part, a frame of mind and that ideas (in their most general sense) were both central to its disposition as a historical project and to its subsequent comprehension.' Aschheim recognizes that such explanations, too, have shortcomings and that 'clearly, for events as complex and thick as these, there can be no question of a theoretical or methodological monopoly. Nevertheless, explanations that entirely dismiss nazism's frame of mind and render ideational motivations as mere background leave an essential dimension untapped. In this respect the more conventional modes of historical analysis soon reach their limits and leave one with a sense of frustrating incompleteness.' See Steven E. Aschheim, *The Nietzsche Legacy in Germany, 1890–1990* (Berkeley: University of California Press, 1992) 320, 329.

In a similar vein, Bernard Yack has argued that because of the present tendency to privilege certain contexts of expression, the use of shared philosophical concepts as explanatory context appears more abstract than common economic interests or shared use of language. Though they *seem* more concrete, these latter are no less constructions – abstractions from the context of acts of expression – than a shared set of concepts. The question, Yack stresses, is which context yields the greatest insight into the material at issue. And the answer is not to be determined a priori but only on the basis of historical research. See Bernard Yack, *The Longing for Total Revolution: Philosophic Sources of Social Discontent from Rousseau to Marx and Nietzsche* (Berkeley: University of California Press, 1992), xxi–xxii.

Berel Lang similarly argues for a more open-ended approach to the relevance of antecedent ideas, based on a clearer sense of how they might interface with subsequent practice: 'Historical events in which human agents figure would be unintelligible as deliberate or intentional unless certain conceptual forms could be identified in them. Obviously, such events do not occur only as ideas, but it is by way of ideas that they are almost invariably defined internally and even more obviously retrospectively; its conceptual form is to this extent a characteristic of the event or act.' Not that ideas are privileged as causal factor, but to exclude them seriously compromises our ability to imagine and understand historical events. See Lang, *Act and Idea*, 165–70, 189–206, on 'the affiliation of ideas.' The passage discussed is from 167–8.

55 Jane Caplan, 'Postmodernism, Poststructuralism, and Deconstruction: Notes for Historians,' *Central European History* 22 (September–December 1989): 274–8. The quotation is from 276.

56 This was Giuseppe Antonio Borgese writing from exile in his influential *Goliath: The March of Fascism* (New York: Viking, 1937), 295–96 . Borgese was sharply critical of Croce in this work.

57 See especially the three well-known interviews from 1923 and 1924, now in Croce's *Pagine sparse* (Bari: Laterza, 1960), 2:475–86.

58 Giovanni Gentile, *Che cosa è il fascismo: Discorsi e polemiche* (Florence: Vallecchi, 1925), 153–61; Gioacchino Volpe, *Guerra dopoguerra fascismo* (Venice: La Nuova Italia, 1928), 293–9. See also the whole argument of Ulisse Benedetti, *Benedetto Croce e il fascismo* (Rome: Volpe, 1967).

59 Croce adopted a stance of haughty superiority when he looked back on his 'relations or non-relations with Mussolini' in 1944; see his *Nuove pagine sparse* (Bari: Laterza, 1942), 1:80–95.

60 For Sternhell's critique of Croce, see *Birth of Fascist Ideology*, 195, 226–7, 251, 254, 256–7.

61 I treat Croce's political stance, and his recasting of liberalism, in David D. Roberts, *Benedetto Croce and the Uses of Historicism* (Berkeley: University of California Press, 1987), especially chap. 5. I have developed some of the points further in David D. Roberts, *Una nuova interpretazione del pensiero di Croce: Lo storicismo crociano e il pensiero contemporaneo* (Pisa: Istituti Editoriali e Poligrafici Internazionali, 1995); and David D. Roberts, 'History as Thought and Action: Croce's Historicism and the Contemporary Challenge,' in *The Legacy of Benedetto Croce*, ed. Jack D'Amico, Dain Trafton, and Massimo Verdicchio (Toronto: University of Toronto Press, 1999), 196–230.

Chapter 8

1 See, for example, Theodor W. Adorno, 'What Does Coming to Terms with the Past Mean?' (1959), in *Bitburg in Moral and Political Perspective*, ed. Geoffrey H. Hartman (Bloomington: Indiana University Press, 1986), 114–29.

2 David D. Roberts, *Benedetto Croce and the Uses of Historicism* (Berkeley: University of California Press, 1987), 281–3, 299–301.

3 See, for example, the critical treatment by David Ward in his *Antifascisms: Cultural Politics in Italy, 1943–1946* (Madison, NJ: Fairleigh Dickinson University Press, 1996), especially chap. 3. Perhaps most problematic was the role Croce claimed for the reconstituted Liberal party. Although there were significant intellectual reasons for his polemic with, for example, Guido Calogero over the respective roles of liberty and justice, Croce's characterizations of the Liberal party came to misrepresent the conservative role it was playing in fact. At the same time, a plausible concern with the wider international situation and, more specifically, with how Italy was now to be treated by the victorious democracies no doubt helped tilt his account of fascism is such a way as to minimize Italian culpability. Some suggest, in fact, that Croce's way of scapegoating the Nazis helped whitewash Italy, contributing to an Italian tendency to sidestep confrontation with the fascist past thereafter. Concern to make the best case for Italy was evident, for example, in his important speech of September 1944 at the Eliseo Theatre in Rome. Even a long-time critic of Croce's, Eugenio Garin, plausibly suggested that the immediate practical circumstances pushed Croce in this speech to accents having little to do with the thrust of his wider historicism. See Ward, *Antifascisms*, 77, for this point, and 76–85 on Croce's Eliseo speech and its effects.

4 Giovanni Gentile, *Che cosa è il fascismo* (Florence: Vallecchi, 1925), 153–61; Gioacchino Volpe, *Guerra dopoguerra fascismo* (Venice: La Nuova Italia, 1928), 293–9.

5 Such accents were central to 'Antistoricismo,' Croce's noted Oxford lecture of 1930, now in Benedetto Croce, *Ultimi saggi* (Bari: Laterza, 1963), 251–64.

6 Benedetto Croce, *Scritti e discorsi politici (1943–1947)* (Bari: Laterza, 1973), 1:7–16 (1943); 2:156–7 (1945); 174 (1945); 361 (1947); 408 (1947). See also Benedetto Croce, *Filosofia e storiografia: Saggi* (Bari: Laterza, 1969), 313–19 (1946), and 327–34 (1948).

7 Erich Fromm, *Escape from Freedom* (1941; New York: Avon, 1965); J.L. Talmon, *The Origins of Totalitarian Democracy* (1950; New York: Norton,

1970), 254–5; Karl Dietrich Bracher, *Turning Points in Modern Times: Essays on German and European History* (Cambridge, MA: Harvard University Press, 1995), 143–52.

8 Michele Maggi, *La filosofia di Benedetto Croce* (Naples: Bibliopolis, 1998), 23–4, 152, 336.

9 Ibid., 313, 315.

10 Ibid., 239–40, 248, 306–7, 361.

11 Ibid., 270, 273, 307, 313.

12 Benedetto Croce, 'L'obiezione contro le "storie dei proprî tempi,"' in *Terze pagine sparse* (Bari: Laterza, 1955), 1:108–16, especially 115–16.

13 Croce first made this argument in 1912 in an essay criticizing Leo Tolstoy and the ideal of 'universal history,' an essay that he recast for *Teoria e storia della storiografia* (Bari: Laterza, 1976), 43–54 (1917). See 47 for the passage quoted. [At first glance, this notion may seem to confirm the image of Croce as at once extravagant and blandly optimistic, even vacuous, but I argue that it suggests, in typically paradoxical form, one of Croce's central insights. I discuss the issue in chapter 10 here, in the context of Carlo Ginzburg's critique of Croce.]

14 Benedetto Croce, *La storia come pensiero e come azione* (Bari: Laterza [Edizione economica], 1966), 162–70. [In the English version, *History as the Story of Liberty*, trans. Sylvia Sprigge (New York: Norton, 1941), see 178–86, for the same discussion; see especially 179, 182, on the distinction between 'party history' and the mode of historical inquiry and understanding that Croce advocates.]

15 Croce, *Terze pagine sparse*, 1:115–16.

16 Croce, *La storia*, 49–51. [Croce, *History as the Story of Liberty*, 59–62.]

17 Croce, *La storia*, 168–70, 183–4. [Croce, *History as the Story of Liberty*, 193–5, 200–1].

18 Croce, *Terze pagine sparse*, 1:94–95, 116.

19 Benedetto Croce, 'Frammenti di etica,' in *Etica e politica* (Bari: Laterza, 1967), 167–8.

20 Croce, *La storia*, 123–6. [Croce, *History as the Story of Liberty*, 135–6.]

Chapter 9

1 Breaking the story in the English-speaking world was the British writer Timothy Garton Ash, especially in articles for *New York Review of Books* that proved remarkably prescient in articulating what was in progress, the stakes of the ideas in play. Garton Ash featured Michnik, Konrad, and

Havel. These essays are now included in his *Uses of Adversity: Essays on the Fate of Central Europe* (New York: Random House [Vintage], 1990), which, however, has by now been overshadowed by his less remarkable, though still important, *The Magic Lantern.*

2 Jeffrey C. Goldfarb, *Beyond Glasnost: the Post-Totalitarian Mind* (1989; Chicago: University of Chicago Press, 1991). In seeking to draw broader lessons for the West, Goldfarb featured the post-totalitarian accent on the complexity of language, the scope for ambiguity and paradox, defying not only official communism but the totalizing tendencies he found in the Western confidence in systematic explanation and scientific truths about the human world. See especially 113–15, 117–18, 185, 206, 214–15. For his treatment of Hannah Arendt, see especially 5, 16–17, 25–6, and 129–31. Arendt not only wrote a classic, though always-controversial, study of the origins of totalitarianism but suggested, somewhat obscurely, that totalitarianism stemmed from a specifically modern orientation toward history that posed an ongoing danger for the West. And far from warranting liberal triumphalism, the eruption of totalitarianism demanded a rethinking of the significance of the political sphere itself. Although her own rethinking of politics has been controversial, it has remained central, even since her death in 1975, to discussions of political priorities in light of the apparent continuance of at least some of the historically specific conditions of possibility for totalitarianism. For a good introduction, see Margaret Canovan, *Hannah Arendt: A Reinterpretation of Her Political Thought* (Cambridge: Cambridge University Press, 1992), especially 86–7, 102–103.

3 Thus begins Milan Kundera, *The Book of Laughter and Forgetting,* trans. Aaron Asher (New York: HarperCollins Perennial Classics, 1999), 3–4.

4 Philip Roth, *Shop Talk: A Writer and His Colleagues and Their Work* (Boston: Houghton Mifflin, 2001), 97–8 (based on conversations in London and Connecticut in 1980).

5 Kundera, *The Book of Laughter and Forgetting,* 213–62.

6 Ibid., 217, 238, 256–9.

7 Ibid. 257.

8 Ibid., 247–9.

9 For a few examples, see Milan Kundera, *The Unbearable Lightness of Being,* trans. Michael Henry Heim (New York: HarperCollins [Perennial], 1991), 141–2, 165–6, 179–84, 187–8, 212, 221–32.

10 Ibid., 112–13. As Kundera put it in an interview, 'Every evil comes from the moment when a false word is accepted. Capitulation begins there.' See Alain Finkielkraut, 'Milan Kundera Interview,' in *Critical Essays on Milan Kundera,* ed. Peter Petro (New York: Hall, 1999), 37.

11 Kundera, *The Unbearable Lightness of Being*, 223.
12 See ibid., 248, for the definition, including the explicit use of *shit*. See 248–57, 277–8, for the overall place of 'kitsch' in Kundera's sense.
13 The notion that any accent on history encompasses faith in the Grand March is implicit throughout *The Unbearable Lightness of Being;* see especially 268–9. The key passage for the Grand March is on p. 25. See, more generally, 257–69, for the 'Cambodia protest.' Kundera's withering scorn is unmistakable.
14 The contemporary anti-totalitarian kitsch was just as monochromatic as the earlier embrace of communism had been. Those opposing totalitarianism, as Kundera put it, 'can't function with queries and doubts. They too need certainties and simple truths to make the multitudes understand, to provoke collective tears.' Ibid., 254; see also 261.
15 Ibid., 254. See also 102–4.
16 Ibid., 219–20.
17 Ibid., 196–7, 313.
18 Finkielkraut, 'Milan Kundera Interview,' 44.
19 Václav Havel, *Disturbing the Peace: A Conversation with Karel Hvízdala*, trans. Paul Wilson (New York: Random House [Vintage], 1991), 10–11, 13–14, 129, 166; Václav Havel, 'The Power of the Powerless,' in Václav Havel et al., *The Power of the Powerless: Citizens against the State in Central-Eastern Europe* (Armonk, NY: Sharpe, 1985), 27, 38–9, 45.
20 Havel, *Disturbing the Peace*, 167.
21 Havel, 'The Power of the Powerless,' 38–9, 89–92.
22 Havel, *Disturbing the Peace*, 182; Havel, 'The Power of the Powerless,' 27–31, 36–7.
23 Having turned from Marxism, Kolakowski in 1976 linked Marx and Nietzsche as the sources of the ideology of unlimited human self-creation and self-perfection that, as he saw it, had justified the two most malignant tyrannies of the century. Christianity had weakened in proportion to the universalization of that Promethean faith, which, however, was now weakening in turn. Though the result would not necessarily be the renewed growth of Christianity in traditional forms, it would surely entail a renewed fertilization of the soil from which Christianity has always grown. See Leszek Kolakowski, *Modernity on Endless Trial* (Chicago: University of Chicago Press, 1990, 90–1.
24 Havel, *Disturbing the Peace*, 166.
25 Ibid., 10–12, 166–7, 182–3. Havel's sense of priorities reflected his almost instinctive sense – converging with one familiar conception – of the intellectual's role, which is constantly to disturb, to rebel. As the chief doubter

of systems of power, the intellectual is at odds with those hard and fast categories that tend to be instruments used by the victors. And of course this role was by no means confined to the intellectual within communist systems. As Havel saw it, intellectuals do not belong anywhere; they are irritants – essential irritants – wherever they find themselves.

26 Ibid., 180.

27 Havel, 'The Power of the Powerless,' 78–81, 92.

28 Ibid., 93–4; Havel *Disturbing the Peace,* 15–16, 21.

29 Havel, 'The Power of the Powerless,' 89.

30 See, for example, David Ward, *Antifascisms: Cultural Politics in Italy, 1943–1946* (Madison, NJ: Fairleigh Dickinson University Press, 1996), 66, 73, 78. Ward finds Croce's confidence in the values of secular liberalism squarely in the bourgeois tradition of large-scale master narratives, as attacked by Gianni Vattimo. Though by now anyone could and should know better, Ward's is typical of a certain stubborn criticism that imputes to Croce the easily pilloried, essentially Hegelian notion that history is rational and positive. Even before the eruption of totalitarianism, Croce sought to recast the Hegelian conception of history for a post-Hegelian world. And the advent of totalitarianism made him still more attentive to the negative, even absurd side of the human challenge. But in light of the terms of that challenge, as they appeared in the wake of totalitarianism, the key was to specify how we proceed without losing our nerve or lapsing into one of the various irrationalist or neo-transcendentalist directions that had opened. Responding just after the Second World War 'to my friends who seek the "transcendent,"' Croce argued that as opposed to some heavenly searchlight we have, each of us, only a portable lantern – but these lanterns are sufficient, enabling us to go on responding ethically to the world, taking responsibility for it. See Benedetto Croce, 'Agli amici che cercano il "trascendente,"' (8 May 1945), now in his *Etica e politica* (Bari: Laterza [Edizione economica], 1967), 378–84.

31 For Croce's theme of the immortality of the act, as reaffirmed in the post-totalitarian situation, see Benedetto Croce, *Terze pagine sparse* (Bari: Laterza, 1955), 1:13–14 (1948). This was Croce's first lecture at the *Istituto italiano per gli studi storici* that he founded in Naples, as his major postwar institutional legacy.

32 Kundera, *The Book of Laughter and Forgetting,* 120.

33 Kundera, *The Unbearable Lightness of Being,* 218.

34 Richard Rorty, *Essays on Heidegger and Others: Philosophical Papers,* vol. 2 (Cambridge: Cambridge University Press, 1991), 195.

35 Though the point cannot be developed here, it is worth questioning

Kundera's way of using Nietzsche's notoriously slippery concept of eternal recurrence to explore lightness and weight in *The Unbearable Lightness of Being*. My own reading of the category suggests that Kundera misses a key step in Nietzsche's rumination. For Nietzsche the experience of the world as merely historical yields a sense of weight, responsibility, so the question is how we might come to experience what we do as 'dance,' how we might restore 'the innocence of becoming,' in light of that framework. See David D. Roberts, *Nothing but History: Reconstruction and Extremity after Metaphysics* (Berkeley: University of California Press, 1995), especially chap. 4 on Nietzsche, but also chap. 5 for some comparisons between Nietzsche and Croce. The incompleteness of Kundera's grasp of the Nietzschean framework is symptomatic of a wider incompleteness in his sense of the cultural alternatives that have opened over the past century or so.

36 Kundera, *The Book of Laughter and Forgetting*, 4.

37 The earlier criticism of Robert Boyers is surely on the right track, but in light of the cultural currents still at work, we need a wider historical-political frame to make the point. See Robert Boyers, 'Between East and West: A Letter to Milan Kundera,' in *Atrocity and Amnesia: The Political Novel Since 1945*, ed. Robert Boyers (New York: Oxford University Press, 1985), 212–33.

38 I have sought to place Croce's historicism in the wider framework of (post-) modern thought, especially in my *Nothing but History*. See also David D. Roberts, *Benedetto Croce and the Uses of Historicism* (Berkeley: University of California Press, 1987).

Chapter 10

1 F.R. Ankersmit, 'Historiography and Postmodernism,' *History and Theory* 28, no. 2 (1989): 137–53.

2 Wellek noted that in movements influential since Croce's death – from Russian formalism and structuralism to hermeneutics and deconstruction – Croce 'is not referred to or quoted, even when he discusses the same problems and gives similar solutions.' And yet Croce, for Wellek, had been perhaps the most erudite and wide-ranging figure in the history of criticism. René Wellek, *History of Modern Criticism* (New Haven, CT: Yale University Press), 8:187, 189. See also 6:63.

3 David D. Roberts, 'La fortuna di Croce e Gentile negli Stati Uniti,' in 'Croce e Gentile un secolo dopo,' special issue, *Giornale critico della filosofia italiano* 73, nos. 2–3 (May–December 1994), 253–81. [See chapter 4 in the present volume.]

4 Massimo Mastrogregori, *Il genio dello storico: Le considerazioni sulla storia di Marc Bloch e Lucien Febvre e la tradizione metodologica francese* (Naples: Edizioni Scientifiche Italiane, 1987). I reviewed this work in *American Historical Review* (February 1990): 124–5.

5 Above all, both Ginzburg and Levi have been bitterly critical of the skepticism and relativism in certain postmodern directions. Ginzburg's antiskepticism led him to attack Hayden White, who has been central to emergence of postmodern modes in the English-speaking world; see Carlo Ginzburg, 'Just One Witness,' in *Probing the Limits of Representation: Nazism and the 'Final Solution,'* ed. Saul Friedländer (Cambridge, MA: Harvard University Press, 1992), 82–96. Ginzburg attributes White's relativistic tendencies to the influence of Giovanni Gentile. I have criticized White's treatment of Croce elsewhere, and I treat Ginzburg, White, and the Italian tradition in a separate article. [This is of course chapter 11 in this volume.]

6 Carlo Ginzburg, 'Microhistory: Two or Three Things I Know about It,' *Critical Inquiry* 20 (Autumn 1993): 23; see also 21.

7 Giovanni Levi, 'On Microhistory,' in *New Perspectives on Historical Writing*, ed. Peter Burke (University Park: Pennsylvania State University Press, 1992), 97–8. On p. 97 Levi noted that 'the unifying principle of all microhistorical research is the belief that microscopic observation will reveal factors previously unobserved.'

8 Ginzburg, 'Microhistory,' 33.

9 Levi, 'On Microhistory,' 107.

10 Hans-Georg Gadamer, *Reason in the Age of Science* (Cambridge, MA: MIT Press, 1981), 104–5. Hans-Georg Gadamer, *Philosophical Hermeneutics* (Berkeley, 1976), 203, 208, 226. I explore this dimension, and the contrast with Croce, in David D. Roberts, *Nothing but History: Reconstruction and Extremity after Metaphysics* (Berkeley: University of California Press, 1995), 172–5.

11 Keith Luria, 'The Paradoxical Carlo Ginzburg,' *Radical History Review* 35 (1986): 85.

12 Keith Luria and Romulo Gandolfo, 'Carlo Ginzburg: An Interview,' *Radical History Review* 35 (1986): 110.

13 Ibid., 104–6. Croce's essay on Hegel is now in his *Saggio sullo Hegel seguito di altri scritti di storia della filosofia* (Bari: Laterza, 1927). The English translation was first published as *What Is Living and What Is Dead of the Philosophy of Hegel* in 1912.

14 Edward Muir, 'Introduction: Observing Trifles,' in *Microhistory and the Lost Peoples of Europe*, ed. Edward Muir and Guido Ruggiero (Baltimore: Johns Hopkins University Press, 1991), xii.

15 Ibid., xx–xxi.
16 Levi, 'On Microhistory,' 100–1.
17 Carlo Ginzburg, *The Cheese and the Worms: The Cosmos of a Sixteenth-Century Miller*, trans. John and Anne Tedeschi (New York: Penguin, 1982), xxvi. The original Italian is as follows: '(Menocchio) è anche il frammento sperduto, giuntoci casualmente, di un mondo oscuro, opaco, che solo con un gesto arbitrario possiamo ricondurre alla nostra storia. Quella cultura è stata distrutta. Rispettare in essa il residuo d'indecifrabilità che resiste a ogni analisi non significa cedere al fascino idiota dell'esotico e dell'incomprensibile. Significa semplicemente prendere atto di una mutilazione storica di cui in un certo senso noi stessi siamo vittime. "Nulla di ciò che si è verificato va perduto per la storia," ricordava Walter Benjamin. Ma "solo all'umanità redenta tocca interamente il suo passato." Redenta, cioè liberata.' Carlo Ginzburg, *Il formaggio e i vermi: Il cosmo di un mugnaio del '500* (Turin: Einaudi, 1976), xxv. The passage from Benjamin is to be found in Walter Benjamin, *Illuminations* (New York: Schocken, 1969), 254, though the translation in that edition differs slightly from that in the English version of *The Cheese and the Worms.*
18 Ginzburg, 'Microhistory,' 24, 28.
19 Ibid. 28–30, on Serra. I have treated the Croce–Serra relationship in David D. Roberts, *Benedetto Croce and the Uses of Historicism* (Berkeley: University of California Press, 1987), 172–4.
20 Renato Serra to Benedetto Croce, 11 November 1912, in *Epistolario di Renato Serra*, ed. Luigi Ambrosini, Giuseppe De Robertis, and Alfredo Grilli, 2nd ed. (Florence: LeMonnier, 1953), 459–61.
21 Renato Serra, 'Partenza di un gruppo di soldati per la Libia' (1912), in *Scritti letterari, morali e politici: Saggi e articoli dal 1900 al 1915*, ed. Mario Isnenghi (Turin: Einaudi, 1974), 277–88. See especially 285–7.
22 Ibid., 286. 'C'è della gente che s'immagina in buona fede che un documento possa essere un'espressione della realtà ... Come se un documento potesse esprimere qualche cosa di diverso da se stesso ... Un documento è un fatto. La battaglia è un altro fatto (un'infinità di altri fatti) ... Fra i due non ci può essere rapporto di identità, di adequatezza.' Thus the anomaly of the 'fiducia massiccia che con tutti quei pezzi insieme si possa ricostruire la realtà!'
23 Ginzburg, 'Microhistory,' 29. For Croce's original ('noi, a ogni istante, conosciamo tutta la storia che c'importa conoscere'), see Benedetto Croce, *Teoria e storia della storiografia* (Bari: Laterza, 1976), 47.
24 Croce, *Teoria e storia della storiografia*, 43–54. See especially 45–7.
25 Ibid. 51–3.
26 Croce's emphasis on the immortality of the act and its corollary, the

premium on individual vocation, is most striking in his 'Frammenti di etica,' now in *Etica e politica* (Bari: Laterza, 1967); see especially 22–3, 25, 99–101, 123. See also Roberts, *Benedetto Croce*, 174–82.

27 Even Siegfried Kracauer, writing in the mid-1960s, noted among the impulses at work in contemporary historiography the ultimately theological notion that all facts should be assembled because 'nothing should go lost. It is as if the fact-oriented accounts breathed pity with the dead.' Siegfried Kracauer, *History: The Last Things Before the Last* (Princeton, NJ: Wiener, 1995), 136.

28 Benedetto Croce, *Ultimi saggi* (Bari: Laterza, 1963), 263–4 (1930). 'Chi apre il suo cuore al sentimento storico non è piú solo, ma unito alla vita dell'universo, fratello e figlio e compagno degli spiriti che già operarono sulla terra e vivono nell'opera che compierono, apostoli e martiri, genî creatori di bellezza e di verità, umile gente buona che sparsero balsamo di bontà e serbarono l'umana gentilezza; e ad essi tutti mentalmente s'indirizza a invocare, e da essi gli viene, sostegno nei suoi lavori e travagli, e nel loro grembo aspira a risposarsi, versando l'opera sua nell'opera loro.'

29 E.P. Thompson, *The Making of the English Working Class* (New York: Random House [Vintage], 1963), 12.

30 Ginzburg, 'Microhistory,' 30. See also Ginzburg, 'Just One Witness,' 82–96.

31 Luria and Gandolfo, 'Carlo Ginzburg: An Interview,' 106.

32 Mark Poster, *Cultural History and Postmodernity: Disciplinary Readings and Challenges* (New York: Columbia University Press, 1997), 14–37. I have treated this work in a review essay entitled 'Postmodern Continuities: Difference, Dominance, and the Question of Historiographical Renewal,' *History and Theory* 37, no. 3 (1998): 388–400.

33 Poster, *Cultural History and Postmodernity*, 29.

34 Conversely, Claes Ryn, one of the few other recent Americans to have seriously studied Croce, has shown how easy it is for those who have *not* lost sight of such earlier thinkers – with Croce prominent among them – to puncture certain excesses in what passes as the most innovative contemporary thought. See Claes G. Ryn, *Will, Imagination and Reason: Babbitt, Croce, and the Problem of Reality*, 2nd ed. (New Brunswick, NJ: Transaction Books, 1997), ix–xxx, especially xxvii–xxx.

Chapter 11

1 On Croce's fortunes in the United States, see David D. Roberts, 'Croce in America: Influence, Misunderstanding, and Neglect,' *Humanitas* 8, no. 2 (1995): 3–34. This article adapts and expands the sections on Croce in my

'La fortuna di Croce e Gentile negli Stati Uniti,' in 'Croce e Gentile un secolo dopo,' special issue, *Giornale critico della filosofia italiana* 73, nos. 2–3 (May–December 1994): 253–81. [See chapter 4 in the present volume.] Pondering the anomalies in Croce's eclipse outside Italy since his death in 1952, the noted historian of criticism René Wellek noted that in movements influential since Croce's death – from Russian formalism and structuralism to hermeneutics and deconstruction – Croce 'is not referred to or quoted, even when he discusses the same problems and gives similar solutions.' And yet Croce, for Wellek, had been perhaps the most erudite and wide-ranging figure in the history of criticism. See René Wellek, *History of Modern Criticism* (New Haven, CT: Yale University Press), 8:187, 189.

2 I have compared Croce and Gadamer in several publications. See especially David D. Roberts, *Nothing but History: Reconstruction and Extremity after Metaphysics* (Berkeley: University of California Press, 1995), 159–78, 299–300.

3 Benedetto Croce, *Teoria e storia della storiografia*, 10th ed. (Bari: Laterza, 1976), 4–7, 10–12, 16, 99–106.

4 Siegfried Kracauer, *History: The Last Things before the Last*, 62–79 (Princeton, NJ: Wiener, 1995), chap. 3; see especially 70, 72, 73–4. By this point Croce was widely linked with R.G. Collingwood; Kracauer was typical in lumping them together.

5 Keith Luria and Romulo Gandolfo, 'Carlo Ginzburg: An Interview,' *Radical History Review* 35 (1986): 104–6. Croce's essay *Ciò che è vivo e ciò che è morto della filosofia di Hegel* is now in his *Saggio sullo Hegel, seguito da altri scritti di storia della filosofia*, 3rd ed. (Bari: Laterza, 1927). Ginzburg admitted that he had read Croce especially through Antonio Gramsci; see Carlo Ginzburg, *Clues, Myths, and the Historical Method* (Baltimore: Johns Hopkins University Press, 1989), vii.

6 Carlo Ginzburg, 'Microhistory: Two or Three Things I Know about It,' *Critical Inquiry* 20 (Autumn 1993): 24, 28.

7 Ibid., 24–30, especially 28–30. Serra was killed early in the First World War. I have treated the Croce–Serra relationship in David D. Roberts, *Benedetto Croce and the Uses of Historicism* (Berkeley: University of California Press, 1987), 172–4.

8 Renato Serra to Benedetto Croce, 11 November 1912, in *Epistolario di Renato Serra*, ed. Luigi Ambrosini, Giuseppe De Robertis, and Alfredo Grilli, 2nd ed. (Florence: LeMonnier, 1953), 459–61.

9 Renato Serra, 'Partenza di un gruppo di soldati per la Libia' (1912), in *Scritti letterari, morali e politici: Saggi e articoli dal 1900 al 1915*, ed. Mario Isnenghi (Turin: Einaudi, 1974), 277–88. See especially 285–7.

10 Ibid., 286.

11 As translated in Ginzburg's 'Microhistory,' 29. The original phrasing is 'noi, a ogni istante, conosciamo tutta la storia che c'importa conoscere.' See Croce, *Teoria e storia della storiografia*, 47, and note 75 in this chapter.

12 Carlo Ginzburg, *The Cheese and the Worms: The Cosmos of a Sixteenth-Century Miller* (New York: Penguin, 1982), xxvi. The original Italian edition was published as *Il formaggio e i vermi: Il cosmo di un mugnaio del '500* (Turin: Einaudi, 1976). The passage from Benjamin is in Walter Benjamin, *Illuminations* (New York: Schocken, 1969), 254, though the translation there differs slightly from the one here.

13 The postmodernist Mark Poster, for example, valued microhistory precisely for disrupting linear narratives and thereby helping to produce a truth that de-legitimates modern sociocultural forms. See especially his *Cultural History and Postmodernity: Disciplinary Readings and Challenges* (New York: Columbia University Press, 1997). I have treated this work in a review essay, 'Postmodern Continuities: Difference, Dominance, and the Question of Historiographical Renewal,' in *History and Theory* 37, no. 3 (1998): 388–400.

14 Even as they focused on constructedness at all phases of historiography, Ginzburg contended, he and his colleagues sought ways of countering the tendency to conceive that constructedness in terms of characteristic rhetorical strategies for narrative – a tendency that they felt could only compromise the cognitive dimension in historiography. Ginzburg, 'Microhistory,' 32. Said Ginzburg in his 1986 interview, 'I am deeply against every kind of Derrida trash, that kind of cheap skeptical attitude ... It is a kind of cheap nihilism.' (Luria and Gandolfo, 'Carlo Ginzburg: An Interview,' 100). See also Carlo Ginzburg, 'Just One Witness,' in *Probing the Limits of Representation: Nazism and the 'Final Solution,'* ed. Saul Friedländer (Cambridge, MA: Harvard University Press, 1992), 94.

15 Luria and Gandolfo, 'Carlo Ginzburg: An Interview,' 101, 104.

16 Ibid., 100; Ginzburg, 'Microhistory,' 30.

17 Hayden White, 'The Abiding Relevance of Croce's Idea of History,' *Journal of Modern History* 37 (June 1963): 109–24. In 1959 White had translated *Dallo storicismo alla sociologia*, a significant work by Carlo Antoni, one of Croce's major disciples, as *From History to Sociology*.

18 White, 'The Burden of History,' now in Hayden White, *Tropics of Discourse: Essays in Cultural Criticism* (Baltimore: Johns Hopkins University Press, 1978), 41.

19 Ibid., 49.
20 Ibid., 36.
21 Ibid., 50.
22 Ibid., 40–1.
23 Ibid., 50.
24 Ibid., 39.
25 Ibid., 44.
26 Ibid., 50.
27 Hayden White, 'What Is Living and What Is Dead in Croce's Criticism of Vico,' now in his *Tropics of Discourse*, 218–29. For the beginnings of a critique of White's treatment of Croce's conception of scientific laws in the study of society, see Roberts, *Benedetto Croce*, 369–70n139.
28 Hayden White, *Metahistory: The Historical Imagination in Nineteenth-Century Europe* (Baltimore: Johns Hopkins University Press, 1973), chap. 10. See especially 378–9, 397–400.
29 Ibid., especially 36–8 for White's understanding of 'irony' in this context. For a nice summary of the point, see Lloyd S. Kramer, 'Literature, Criticism, and Historical Imagination: The Literary Challenge of Hayden White and Dominick LaCapra,' in *The New Cultural History*, ed. Lynn Hunt (Berkeley: University of California Press, 1989), 104.
30 See especially White, *Metahistory*, 397–400, for the association of Croce with passivity, foreclosing action. For a fuller critique, see Roberts, *Benedetto Croce*, 376n41.
31 White, *Metahistory*, 394–402, 406–7, 415, 422–5.
32 Ibid., 385.
33 Especially prominent were White's essays that made up his influential subsequent collections *Tropics of Discourse*, and *The Content of the Form: Narrative Discourse and Historical Representation* (Baltimore: Johns Hopkins University Press, 1987). As Ginzburg saw it, White was still using Croce as a foil, essentially taking for granted the explicit placement of Croce in *Metahistory*. In 'Just One Witness,' 89, Ginzburg deemed a passage from White's *Tropics of Discourse*, 2, to be directed against Croce's 'realism.'
34 White, *Metahistory*, ix–xii, 426–34. See also Roberts, *Benedetto Croce*, 379–80n75, on White's assumptions and aims, and Roberts, *Nothing but History*, 254–62, on the bases of his presentism.
35 White, *Metahistory*, 394–402, 406–7, 415, 422–5. See also Hayden White, '"Figuring the nature of the times deceased": Literary Theory and Historical Writing,' in *The Future of Literary Theory*, ed. Ralph Cohen (New York: Routledge, 1989), 20, 28–9, 34–5. On pp. 31–6 White summarizes, and responds to, the standard objections to his argument. White's leading dis-

ciple, Hans Kellner, similarly insisted that White emphasized narrativity and emplotment not to undermine historiography but to deepen its cultural impact. See Hans Kellner, *Language and Historical Representation: Getting the Story Crooked* (Madison: University of Wisconsin Press, 1989), x–xi, 7, 24–5, 122–3.

36 White, 'The Politics of Historical Interpretation: Discipline and De-Sublimation' (1982), in *The Content of the Form*, 66–7, 69, 72.

37 Ibid., 72.

38 White, '"Figuring the nature of the times deceased,"' 20–2, 34–5.

39 Ibid., 25–6. See also White, *Tropics of Discourse*, 98.

40 Among major examples are F.R. Ankersmit, *History and Tropology: The Rise and Fall of Metaphor* (Berkeley: University of California Press, 1994); Lionel Gossman, *Between History and Literature* (Cambridge, MA: Harvard University Press, 1990); and Stephen Bann, *The Clothing of Clio: A Study of the Representation of History in Nineteenth-Century Britain and France* (Cambridge: Cambridge University Press, 1984).

41 Hayden White, 'The Absurdist Moment in Contemporary Literary Theory,' in *Tropics of Discourse*, 261–82.

42 Hans Kellner, 'A Bedrock of Order: Hayden White's Linguistic Humanism,' *History and Theory* 19, no. 4 (Beiheft 19, 'Metahistory': Six Critiques, 1980): 20–1, 26–7, 29. The quotation is from 20.

43 Dominick LaCapra, *Rethinking Intellectual History: Texts, Contests, Language* (Ithaca, NY: Cornell University Press, 1983), 72–83, especially 77–80.

44 The symposium was held at UCLA in April 1990 and yielded a major book, *Probing the Limits of Representation*, ed. Friedländer. The core of Ginzburg's argument is his 'Just One Witness,' 92–6. The historian Omer Bartov, pondering Ginzburg's assault on White, noted that 'Holocaust denial' was only an extreme case of the wider complexity of efforts to get at the historical truth when confronting the Holocaust: 'In Auschwitz the truth, as constructed by western civilization, was shattered,' and Auschwitz remains for us a test of any theory of historical explanation. See Omer Bartov, *Murder in Our Midst: The Holocaust, Industrial Killing, and Representation* (New York: Oxford University Press, 1996), 130–6.

45 Hayden White, 'Historical Emplotment and the Problem of Truth,' in *Probing the Limits of Representation*, ed. Friedländer, 37–53; Martin Jay, 'Of Plots, Witnesses, and Judgments,' in *Probing the Limits of Representation*, ed. Friedländer, 97–9.

46 Ginzburg, 'Just One Witness,' 89, 94.

47 Ibid., 88, where Ginzburg invokes the authority of E. Colorni, 'one of [Croce's] most intelligent critics' – citing a piece from 1934. One must question Ginzburg's range of reference.

48 Gentile was arguably the most distinguished European intellectual to identify with fascism over the long term. In his *Totalitarianism: The Inner History of the Cold War* (New York: Oxford University Press, 1995), 19, the Soviet specialist Abbott Gleason found Gentile's conception of the totalitarian state 'extraordinary' and 'prophetic' and concluded that 'Gentile deserves to be called the first philosopher of totalitarianism.'

49 Ginzburg, 'Just One Witness,' 90.

50 Ibid., 94.

51 White, 'The Politics of Historical Interpretation,' 74–5.

52 Jay, 'Of Plots, Witnesses, and Judgments,' 101–2.

53 Jeremy Varon, 'Probing the Limits of the Politics of Representation,' *New German Critique* 72 (Fall 1997): 91.

54 Ginzburg, 'Just One Witness,' 95–6.

55 Jay, 'Of Plots, Witnesses, and Judgments,' 102–3.

56 Ibid., 104. See also 103. Jay had himself earlier championed Siegfried Kracauer, but the web proves too thick to seek to untangle more fully here.

57 Jay, 'Of Plots, Witnesses, and Judgments,' 105. See also 107.

58 Jay insisted that we have more than 'mere effectiveness in terms of winning agreement' 'as a criterion of truth or plausibility.' Professional practice entails the regulative ideal of an 'uncoerced consensus of opinion.' Although complicated by non-discursive factors, and though the outcome is endlessly inconclusive, 'the professional institutionalization of communicative rationality means that "effectiveness" can be more than merely a neutral description of what the majority believes is true or right.' In that sense, Jay implies that we have what Ginzburg seemed to miss – 'criteria for deciding what constitutes a rational or irrational process of achieving that agreement.' Jay, 'Of Plots, Witnesses, and Judgments,' 102–3, 105–6. I have sought elsewhere to show the value of keeping Crocean historicism as part of the mix, in tension with such Habermasian accents on unforced agreement and criteria of communicative rationality. The key is precisely how we are caught up in history and why we seek to learn. See especially Roberts, *Nothing but History*, 301–6.

59 Jeremy Varon, 'Probing the Limits,' 83–114, especially 94–5, 98–9, 105n13.

60 Though he was arguably the most accomplished modern European intellectual historian of his generation, even Jay was no expert on the Italian tradition. In light of his longstanding interest in the Frankfurt School, I surmise that he may have been influenced by Herbert Marcuse's critique of Gentile in *Reason and Revolution: Hegel and the Rise of Social Theory* (Boston: Beacon, 1960; first pub. 1941), 402–9. Marcuse was plausibly seeking to rescue the Hegelian legacy from association with fascism, but his way of understanding Gentile's 'activism,' anticipating some of Jay's

characterizations, misconstrued Gentile's thinking. This is not to suggest that Gentile was indeed Hegelian. On this level Marcuse was right; it was the step beyond Hegel that led to fascism.

61 Benedetto Croce, *Discorsi di varia filosofia*, 2nd ed. (Bari: Laterza, 1959), 2:15–17 (1945).

62 Giovanni Gentile, *La riforma della dialettica hegeliana* (Florence: Sansoni, 1975), 247–8, 256–7.

63 Benedetto Croce, *Conversazioni critiche*, 2nd ser., 2nd ed. (Bari: Laterza, 1950), 68–9; Giovanni Gentile, *Saggi critici*, 2nd ser. (Florence: Vallecchi, 1927), 29.

64 For Croce's critique of Ranke, see *La storia come pensiero e come azione* (Bari: Laterza [Edizione economica], 1966), 65–7, 73–88. See also *Teoria e storia della storiografia*, 304–5.

65 White, *Tropics of Discourse*, 54 (essay dated 1972–3).

66 See, for example, Croce, *Teoria e storia della storiografia*, 29–30.

67 White, *Tropics of Discourse*, 75.

68 Benedetto Croce, *Letture di poeti* (Bari: Laterza [Edizione economica], 1966), 232–5 (1946).

69 I refer to the influential reading of Nietzsche by Alexander Nehamas, *Nietzsche: Life as Literature* (Cambridge, MA: Harvard University Press, 1985).

70 Benedetto Croce, *Il carattere della filosofia moderna* (Bari: Laterza, 1963), 176; see also Benedetto Croce, *Filosofia della pratica: Economia ed etica* (Bari: Laterza, 1963), 43.

71 Croce recognized, for example, that an element of 'oratory,' even political polemic, will inform every historical account; see, for example, Benedetto Croce, *Indagini su Hegel e schiarimenti filosofici* (Bari: Laterza, 1967), 125 (1949).

72 See White, 'The Burden of History,' 47, for an example of his tendency to suggest that if there is not a single correct view, then anything goes.

73 Among influential contemporaneous works of diagnosis and critique were Stanislav Andrecki, *The Social Sciences as Sorcery* (New York: St Martin's, 1973); Richard J. Bernstein, *The Restructuring of Social and Political Theory* (Philadelphia: University of Pennsylvania Press, 1976); and Zygmunt Bauman, *Hermeneutics and Social Science* (New York: Columbia University Press, 1978).

74 Although he made the argument repeatedly, Croce offered his classic statement about relativism in his 'Contributo alla critica di me stesso' (1915), now in Benedetto Croce, *Etica e politica* (Bari: Laterza [Edizione economica], 1967), 350. See also Croce, *Teoria e storia della storiografia*, 43–8; and Croce, *La storia come pensiero e come azione*, 122. Compare Hans-

Georg Gadamer, 'Replik,' in *Hermaneutik und Ideologiekritik*, ed. Karl-Otto Apel et al. (Frankfurt: Suhrkamp, 1971), 299.

75 Croce first offered this critique of the idea of 'universal history' in 1912 in an essay subsequently revised for inclusion in the book that reached definitive form as *Teoria e storia della storiografia* in 1917. See 43–54, especially 45–7, 51–3.

76 Ginzburg, 'Microhistory,' 30. See also Ginzburg, 'Just One Witness,' 82–96.

77 E.P. Thompson, *The Making of the English Working Class* (New York: Random House [Vintage], 1963), 12.

78 Benedetto Croce, 'Antistoricismo,' (1930), in his *Ultimi saggi* (Bari: Laterza, 1963), 263–4.

79 Brook Thomas, *The New Historicism and Other Old-Fashioned Topics* (Princeton, NJ: Princeton University Press, 1991), 153, 166, 171, 211. On occasion, however, Thomas, too, falls into the unwarranted conflations that continue to muddy this discussion. See Roberts, *Nothing but History*, 264–9.

80 Bloom's understanding of 'misreading' was bound up with his notion of 'the anxiety of influence' and is of course much richer than my characterization here suggests. However, in connection with Rorty's use of Bloom's categories, I seek to address their uses and limits in *Nothing but History*, chap. 9, especially 241–3. See also Richard Rorty, *Consequences of Pragmatism (Essays: 1972–1980)* (Minneapolis: University of Minnesota Press, 1982), 151–4, 157–8; and Richard Rorty, *Contingency, Irony, and Solidarity* (Cambridge: Cambridge University Press, 1989), 24–5, 29–30, 40–2, 53, 61. Harold Bloom elaborated these categories in *The Anxiety of Influence: A Theory of Poetry* (New York: Oxford University Press, 1973), and *A Map of Misreading* (New York: Oxford University Press, 1975).

81 Croce, *Filosofia della pratica*, 406.

Chapter 12

1 Michael S. Roth, 'Classic Postmodernism,' *History and Theory* 43, no. 3 (2004): 378.

2 Richard J. Evans, *In Defense of History* (New York: Norton, 1999). Evans is a distinguished British historian of modern Germany.

3 Hans Kellner, *Language and Historical Representation: Getting the Story Crooked* (Madison, WI: University of Wisconsin Press, 1989).

4 Hayden White, 'The Politics of Historical Interpretation: Discipline and De-Sublimation' (1982), in his *The Content of the Form: Narrative Discourse and Historical Representation* (Baltimore, 1987), 58–82.

5 Carlo Ginzburg, 'Just One Witness,' in *Probing the Limits of Representation: Nazism and the 'Final Solution,'* ed. Saul Friedländer (Cambridge, MA: Harvard University Press, 1992), 82–96.
6 Reinhart Koselleck, *Futures Past: On the Semantics of Historical Time* (Cambridge, MA: MIT Press, 1985), 92–4.
7 Christian Meier, *From Athens to Auschwitz: The Uses of History* (Cambridge, MA: Harvard University Press, 2005), 173; see also 170.
8 Lawrence L. Langer, *Holocaust Testimonies: The Ruins of Memory* (New Haven, CT: Yale University Press, 1991), 78–9.
9 Walter Benjamin, *Illuminations* (New York: Schocken, 1969), 257–8.
10 Mark Lilla, 'Slouching Toward Athens,' *New York Review of Books,* 23 June 2005, 47.
11 Milan Kundera, *The Unbearable Lightness of Being* (New York: HarperCollins, 1991), 223.
12 Ibid., 248, for Kundera's definition. See also 248–57, 277–8.
13 Massimo Mastrogregori, 'Liberation from the Past,' *European Legacy* 6, no. 1 (2001): 43.
14 Caroline Castiglione, *Patrons and Adversaries: Nobles and Villagers in Italian Politics, 1640–1760* (Oxford: Oxford University Press, 2005), 179.
15 Thomas V. Cohen, *Love and Death in Renaissance Italy* (Chicago: University of Chicago Press, 2004). 225–7.
16 Carlo Ginzburg, *Il formaggio e i vermi: Il cosmo di un mugnaio del '500* (Turin: Einaudi, 1976), xxv: The passage from Benjamin is to be found in his *Illuminations,* 254.
17 Patrick Joyce, *Democratic Subjects: The Self and the Social in Nineteenth-Century England* (Cambridge: Cambridge University Press, 1994), 12–14; see also 5–7, 17, 19–20, 26.
18 Lloyd S. Kramer, 'Literature, Criticism, and Historical Imagination,' in *The New Cultural History,* ed. Lynn Hunt (Berkeley: University of California Press, 1989), 103; Dominick LaCapra, *Rethinking Intellectual History: Texts, Contexts, Language* (Ithaca, NY: Cornell University Press, 1983), 62–4.
19 *Nothing But History: Reconstruction and Extremity after Metaphysics* (Berkeley: University of California Press, 1995); Giuseppe Galasso, *Nient'altro che storia: Saggi di teoria e metodo della storia* (Bologna: Il Mulino, 2000).
20 Richard Rorty, 'Being That Can Be Understood Is Language,' *London Review of Books* 22, no. 6 (16 March 2000): 23. The dictum itself comes from Gadamer.
21 Mastrogregori, 'Liberation from the Past,' 43.
22 Evans, *In Defense of History,* 99.
23 Benedetto Croce, *History as the Story of Liberty* (London: Allen and Unwin,

1941), 118–26; see p. 122 for the passage quoted. For the Italian original, see Benedetto Croce, *La storia come pensiero e come azione* (Bari: Laterza, 1966), 112: 'conoscere ... quanto l'umanità è stata effettualmente capace di agire e soffrire in bene e in male, e che perciò è da pensare che ancor possa fare e patire o da chiedere ragionevolmente che faccia.'

24 Keith Luria and Romulo Gandolfo, 'Carlo Ginzburg: An Interview,' *Radical History Review* 35 (1986): 104–6.

25 Gordon S. Wood, 'Apologies to the Iroquois,' *New York Review of Books*, 6 April 2006, 50–1.

26 Mastrogregori, 'Liberation from the Past,' 44.

27 Richard Rorty, 'Nineteenth-Century Idealism and Twentieth-Century Textualism,' in *Consequences of Pragmatism (Essays: 1972–1980)* (Minneapolis: University of Minnesota Press, 1982), 139–59.

Index

www.ingramcontent.com/pod-product-compliance
Lightning Source LLC
LaVergne TN
LVHW040756070826
844660LV00025B/1163

* 9 7 8 0 8 0 2 0 9 4 9 4 0 *